arihant
SUCCESS AND NOTHING LESS

Ignite

Topicwise MCQs

*"Give Fire to **Your Prelims Prep**"*

Art & Culture

For **Civil Services** & **State PCS** Preliminary Examination

MentorsHut

ARIHANT PUBLICATION (INDIA) LIMITED

All Rights Reserved

© **Publisher**

No part of this publication may be re-produced, stored in a retrieval system or by any means, electronic mechanical, photocopying, recording, scanning, web or otherwise without the written permission of the publisher. Arihant has obtained all the information in this book from the sources believed to be reliable and true. However, Arihant or its editors or authors or illustrators don't take any responsibility for the absolute accuracy of any information published, and the damages or loss suffered thereupon.

All disputes subject to Meerut (UP) jurisdiction only.

卐 **Administrative & Production Offices**

Regd. Office

'Ramchhaya' 4577/15, Agarwal Road, Darya Ganj, New Delhi -110002
Tele: 011- 47630600, 43518550

卐 **Head Office**

Kalindi, TP Nagar, Meerut (UP) - 250002 Tel: 0121-7156203, 7156204

卐 **Sales & Support Offices**

Agra, Ahmedabad, Bengaluru, Bareilly, Chennai, Delhi, Guwahati, Hyderabad, Jaipur, Jhansi, Kolkata, Lucknow, Nagpur & Pune.

卐 **PRICE**: ₹ 275.00

卐 **PO No :** TXT-59-T062799-01-25

Published by Arihant Publications (India) Ltd.

For further information about the books published by Arihant, log on to www.arihantbooks.com or e-mail at info@arihantbooks.com

Follow us on

Preface

The *Ignite Series* is more than just a resource - it's your ultimate guide to conquering one of the toughest examinations in India. With nearly **10 lakh aspirants** filling the forms for UPSC Civil Services Preliminary Examination each year and **only around 15,000 qualifying for Mains**, the success rate stands at a staggering **1.5%**. Designed by the authors of the bestselling *Pulse Handwritten Notes for Prelims*, this series is meticulously crafted to transform your preparation and significantly enhance your chances of success.

What truly sets the *Ignite Series* apart is its ability to **bridge the gap between rote learning and deep conceptual understanding**. Packed with over **6,000+ carefully designed MCQs**, the series offers comprehensive coverage of the Prelims syllabus, ensuring no topic is left unexplored. Each question is strategically designed to challenge your knowledge and sharpen your problem-solving skills.

In an exam where every mark counts, **standing out isn't optional - it's essential**. To equip you for this challenge, the *Ignite Series* introduces a **three-tiered evaluation system**, testing your knowledge at **Factual, Conceptual and Analytical levels**. This innovative approach mirrors the demands of the UPSC, ensuring you are thoroughly prepared to tackle its dynamic and unpredictable nature. Additionally, **topic-wise Previous Years' Questions (PYQs)** included at the end of each chapter provide valuable insights into trends and patterns, helping you craft a data-driven strategy.

Understanding concepts is important, but **retaining and applying them under pressure** is the key to success. To make this process seamless, every question in this series is accompanied by **detailed explanations**, enriched with **infographics, tables and maps** that simplify complex topics.

Recognizing the importance of self-assessment, the series offers **free access to 3 All India Mock Tests**. These simulated tests replicate real exam conditions, allowing you to benchmark your performance, identify areas of improvement, and refine your preparation strategy. By offering a clear picture of where you stand, these tests ensure that you are not just prepared but **exam-ready**.

With the *Ignite Series*, you're not merely preparing for an exam - you're gearing up to outshine the competition and achieve your dreams. Let this book be the tool that empowers you to break into the top **1.5%** and take a giant step toward becoming a civil servant.

I extend my heartfelt gratitude to the incredible individuals who have been the cornerstone of my journey and success. A special thanks to **my grandfather, Suresh Singh and my entire family** for their unwavering support, endless encouragement, and belief in my dreams as they have been my greatest source of strength. To **my teacher, Amit Mangtani Sir**, for his invaluable guidance and mentorship, which have profoundly shaped my path and inspired me to strive for excellence. I am also deeply grateful for the steadfast support of my friends, **Tushar Maurya, Priyanshu Negi, Nitin Chandra, Naveen Singh, and Vishal Tyagi**, whose presence and encouragement have uplifted me through every challenge. Each of you holds a special place in my journey, and this work is a testament to your unwavering belief in me. Thank you for being my pillars of strength and inspiration.

We at MentorsHut remain committed to excellence and continuous improvement. Your feedback is invaluable to us. If you have suggestions or ideas to make this series even better, please don't hesitate to reach out to us at **info@mentorshut.com**.

Here's wishing you the very best for your preparation - may this series **ignite the spark of excellence within you** and guide you toward achieving your goals.

Vishal Singh
Academic Director, MentorsHut

Contents

1. Architecture and Sculpture **1-51**
- Cave Architecture 1-2
- Stupa Architecture 3-4
- Sculpture 5-7
- Temple Architecture 7-12
- Pillars and Inscriptions 12-14
- Indo-Islamic Architecture 15-16
- Modern Architecture 16-17

2. Religion **52-93**
- Indus Valley Civilization and Hinduism 52-54
- Buddhism 54-60
- Jainism 60-63
- Islam, Christianity and Sikhism 63-64

3. Philosophy **94-111**
- Upanishadic Philosophy 94
- Buddhist Philosophy 95
- Jaina Philosophy 95-97
- Other Ancient Philosophies 97-98
- Six System of Philosophies 98-99
- Philosophies in Medieval India 99-100

4. Bhakti and Sufi Movements **112-127**
- Bhakti Movement 112-115
- Sufi Movement 116-117

5. Paintings **128-148**
- Paintings in Ancient India 128-129
- Paintings in Medieval India 129-132
- Paintings in Modern India 132-133
- Folk Paintings 133-134

6. Literature **149-176**
- Sanskrit and Brahmanical Literature 149-154
- Prakrit and Pali Literature 154-155
- Tamil Literature 155-156
- Literature in Medieval India 156-158

7. Dance **177-198**
- Conceptual Aspect 177-178
- Classical Dance Forms 178-181
- Folk Dances 181-183

8. Drama, Theatre and Puppetry **199-213**
- Drama 199-200
- Theatre 200-202
- Puppetry 202-203

9. Music **214-231**
- Classical Music 214-217
- Folk Music 217-219

10. Foreign Travelers **232-241**

11. Science and Technology **242-252**
- Ancient India 242-244
- Medieval India 244-245

12. Education System **253-259**

13. UNESCO World Heritage Sites **260-279**
- UNESCO World Heritage Sites 260-264
- UNESCO Intangible Cultural Heritage 264-266
- UNESCO Creative Cities Network 266

Topical PYQ Trend Last 8 Years'

Section	2024	2023	2022	2021	2020	2019	2018	2017
Visual Arts: Architecture & Sculpture ; Paintings	0	2	2	3	1	3	2	2
Religion and Religious Movements	1	4	3	0	1	0	2	0
Literature	3	0	0	0	1	0	0	0
Performing Arts: Dance ; Drama, Theatre and Puppetry ; Music	0	1	0	1	0	0	2	1
Miscellaneous: Foreign Travellers + Science and Technology + Education System + UNESCO Heritage	3	1	0	3	1	1	2	3
Total	**07**	**08**	**05**	**07**	**04**	**04**	**08**	**06**

Section-wise Analysis: Indian History & Culture
Last 5 Years' Trend

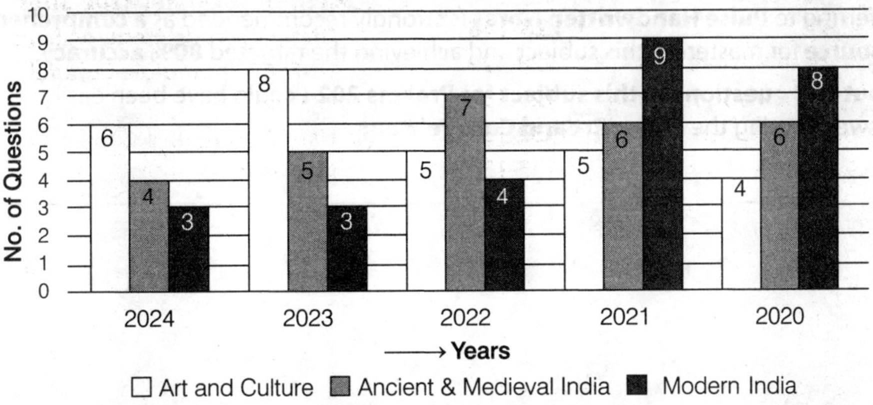

Overall PYQ Trend Last 8 Years'

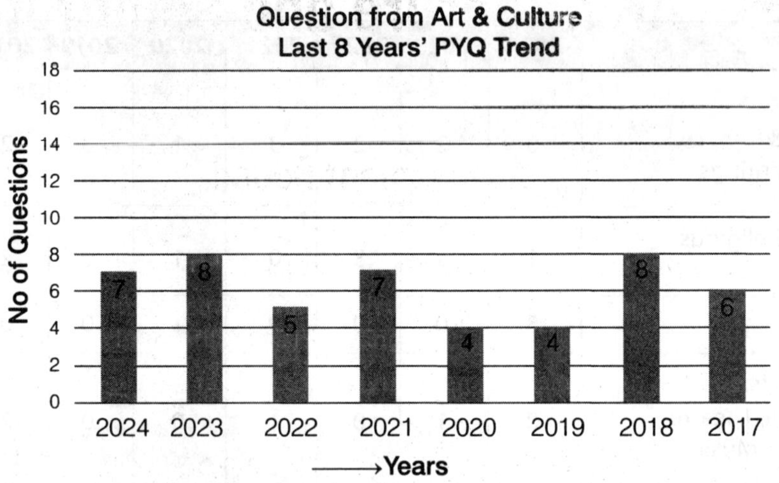

Key Learnings from the PYQs of 'Art and Culture'

1. Art and Culture consistently **contribute 5-6 questions in the Prelims**, with topics such as **architecture, religion and literature** dominating this section.
2. The questions often require **linking historical events with cultural developments**, demanding an integrated understanding.
3. Questions range from **factual to analytical**, emphasizing both a **deeper understanding of concepts** and **application-based insights**.
4. Visual aids like flowcharts and timelines, along with interlinking history and culture, and practicing **PYQs**, are essential to mastering the evolving question patterns.
5. Referring to **Pulse Handwritten Notes** is strongly recommended as a **comprehensive resource** for mastering this subject and achieving the targeted **80% accuracy**.
6. **6 out of 7 questions in this subject for Prelims 2024** could have been easily answered using the **Pulse 'Art and Culture' Book**.

CHAPTER 01

Architecture and Sculpture

Assessment Round

Topic 1 : Cave Architecture

1. Consider the following statements about 'Udayagiri and Khandagiri Caves':

1. They were located in Odisha.
2. They were built during the 1st-2nd century BCE.
3. They belong to Buddhism.

How many of the statements given above is/are correct?

(a) Only one
(b) Only two
(c) All three
(d) None

2. With reference to the Mauryan Age rock-cut caves, consider the following statements:

1. Ashoka was the first ruler to construct rock-cut caves.
2. The caves were located in Barabar Hills in Bihar.
3. Sudama cave is the oldest among them.

How many of the statements given above is/are correct?

(a) Only one
(b) Only two
(c) All three
(d) None

3. Consider the following statements about Bhaja Caves:

Statement I: Bhaja Caves are located in Pune, Maharashtra.

Statement II: They are part of the Mahayana sect of Buddhism.

Which one of the following is correct in respect of the above statements?

(a) Both Statement I and Statement II are correct and Statement II is the correct explanation for Statement I.
(b) Both Statement I and Statement II are correct, but Statement II is not the correct explanation for Statement I.
(c) Statement I is correct and Statement II is incorrect.
(d) Statement I is incorrect and Statement II is correct.

4. Consider the following caves:

1. Karna Chaupar cave
2. Lomas Rishi cave
3. Sudama cave
4. Visva Zhopri cave

How many of the above is/are part of the Barabar Hills caves constructed by Ashoka?

(a) Only one (b) Only two
(c) Only three (d) All four

5. Consider the following caves:

1. Ellora Caves
2. Elephanta Caves
3. Bagh Caves
4. Mandargiri Caves

How many of the given above caves is/are located in Maharashtra?

(a) Only one
(b) Only two
(c) Only three
(d) All four

6. Which of the following caves has the Hathigumpha inscription written in Brahmi script?
(a) Ajanta Caves
(b) Udayagiri and Khandagiri Caves
(c) Bhaja Caves
(d) Karle Caves

7. The Karle Caves are famous for having the largest Chaitya-griha among all Buddhist monuments in India. Who among the following rulers built these caves?
(a) Satavahana rulers and traders
(b) Pallava rulers
(c) Chola rulers
(d) Rashtrakuta rulers

8. Which ruler's reign saw the construction of the monolithic Kailash Temple at Ellora?
(a) Chandragupta II (b) Harsha
(c) Krishnaraja I (d) Ashoka

9. The Elephanta Caves, located on the island of Gharapuri, were named by the Portuguese due to what features?
(a) Massive image of elephant at the entrance
(b) Elephant statues inside the cave
(c) Elephant carvings on the walls
(d) Elephant-shaped entrance

10. What is the significance of Cave 16 at Ellora?
(a) It is a monolithic Kailash Temple built during the reign of Krishnaraja I.
(b) It contains Buddhist Viharas.
(c) It is dedicated to the Jain Tirthankaras.
(d) It features a mural of the Dying Princess.

11. Consider the following architectural features:
1. The sculpture of a 24-foot-long reclining Buddha.
2. The sculpture of the seated Buddha with the Bodhi tree in the background.
3. The sculpture of the Jain leader Bahubali.
4. The sculptures are associated with Tantric Buddhism.

How many of the features given above is/are found in the Ellora Caves?
(a) Only one (b) Only two
(c) Only three (d) All four

12. With reference to the Nasik Caves, consider the following statements:
1. The Nasik Caves are also known as Trirashmi Caves or Pandavleni Caves.
2. The caves were first documented by Captain James Delamine in 1723.
3. The term 'Leni' is a Marathi word for caves and these caves belong to the Hinayana sect of Buddhism.
4. An inscription mentions that Gautamiputra Satakarni's mother, Gautami Balashri, financed the third cave.

How many of the statements given above is/are correct?
(a) Only one
(b) Only two
(c) Only three
(d) All four

13. With reference to the Ajanta caves, consider the following statements:
1. They are located on the banks of the Purna River.
2. The caves from the Vakataka period are dedicated to Hinayana Buddhism.
3. It also houses a sculpture of the Mahaparinirvana of Buddha.

How many of the statements given above is/are incorrect?
(a) Only one
(b) Only two
(c) All three
(d) None

14. With reference to the Ellora caves, consider the following statements:
1. Jain caves belonging to the Shwetambara sect are found here.
2. A Buddha sculpture in Vitarka Mudra has been found in these caves.

Which of the statements given above is/are correct?
(a) 1 only
(b) 2 only
(c) Both 1 and 2
(d) Neither 1 nor 2

Topic 2 : Stupa Architecture

15. Consider the following pairs :

Built by	Location
1. Ajatashatru	Vaishali
2. Brahmins of Vetthadipa	Betiah district, Bihar
3. Mallas of Kushinagar	Pipilivana

How many of the above pairs is/are not correctly matched?
(a) Only one
(b) Only two
(c) All three
(d) None

16. Which of the following names for stupas is correctly matched with the country?

1. Caitya	Nepal
2. Dagoba	Sri Lanka
3. Pagoda	Thailand

Select the correct answer from the codes given below:
(a) Only one (b) Only two
(c) All three (d) None

17. Arrange the following parts of a Stupa by their significance in Buddhist Architecture:
1. Anda
2. Harmika
3. Chhatra
4. Pradakshina Patha

Choose the correct order from the most fundamental to the additional elements:
(a) 1-2-3-4
(b) 2-1-3-4
(c) 4-1-3-2
(d) 1-4-2-3

18. Consider the following statements about Relic Stupas:
1. They contain the bodily remains of the Buddha or his disciples.
2. Piprahwa Stupa is an example of a Relic Stupa.
3. They are the most sacred and venerated of all stupas.

How many of the above statements is/are correct?
(a) Only one (b) Only two
(c) All three (d) None

19. Consider the following statements regarding the classification of stupas:

Statement I: Symbolic Stupas are built to represent the presence of Buddha everywhere.

Statement II: Votive Stupas are built by devotees near the main stupas to earn grace.

Which one of the following is correct in respect of the above statements?
(a) Both Statement I and Statement II are correct and Statement II is the correct explanation for Statement I.
(b) Both Statement I and Statement II are correct, but Statement II is not the correct explanation for Statement I.
(c) Statement I is correct, but Statement II is incorrect.
(d) Statement I is incorrect, but Statement II is correct.

20. With reference to the Gandhara Stupa, consider the following statements:
1. It has a sculpted base, dome and hemisphere.
2. It is known for its intricate relief carvings depicting Buddhist legends.
3. It was patronised by the Kushan rulers.

Which of the given above statements are correct?
(a) 1 and 2 only
(b) 2 and 3 only
(c) 1 and 3 only
(d) 1, 2 and 3

21. The Amaravati Stupa, located on the right bank of the Krishna River, was built during which period?
(a) Mauryan Period
(b) Satavahana Period
(c) Gupta Period
(d) Early Medieval Period

22. Which stupa is considered the oldest and most sacred, built to house the bodily remains of the Buddha?
(a) Sanchi Stupa
(b) Dhamma Stupa
(c) Piprahwa Stupa
(d) Dhamek Stupa

23. Identify the stupa based on the following statements:
1. It was built in the Sarnath complex where Buddha delivered his first sermon.
2. The stupa was encased with stone-carved floral designs during the Gupta Period.
3. An Ashokan pillar edict is engraved near it.

Choose the correct answer from the codes given below:
(a) Dhamek Stupa
(b) Sanchi Stupa
(c) Amaravati Stupa
(d) Bharhut Stupa

24. Arrange the following events in the correct chronological order:
1. Discovery of the Piprahwa Stupa
2. Construction of the Sanchi Stupa
3. Destruction of the Dharmarajika Stupa
4. Renovation of the Sanchi Stupa by Agnimitra

Choose the correct order from the codes given below:
(a) 2-4-3-1
(b) 2-3-4-1
(c) 1-3-2-4
(d) 3-2-4-1

25. Consider the following statements about the Dharmarajika Stupa:
1. It is located in Taxila, Pakistan.
2. It was built by Ashoka.
3. The stupa was destroyed in 1749 to reuse its bricks for other construction.

How many of the above statements is/are correct?
(a) Only one
(b) Only two
(c) All three
(d) None

26. Consider the following statements regarding the Sanchi Stupa:

Statement I: The Sanchi Stupa was originally built by Ashoka with bricks.

Statement II: Kanishka later enlarged the stupa to twice its original size.

Which one of the following is correct in respect of the above statements?
(a) Both Statement I and Statement II are correct and Statement II is the correct explanation for Statement I.
(b) Both Statement I and Statement II are correct, but Statement II is not the correct explanation for Statement I.
(c) Statement I is correct, but Statement II is incorrect.
(d) Statement I is incorrect, but Statement II is correct.

27. Consider the following pairs:

	Depiction on Toran and Vedika	Representation
1.	Nagas and Nagis	Cult of Serpent
2.	Yaksha and Yakshini	Symbolise wealth and fertility
3.	Lotus	Birth of Buddha

How many of the above pairs is/are correctly matched?
(a) Only one (b) Only two
(c) All three (d) None

28. Consider the following depictions of the Toran and Vedika:

	Depiction	Significance
1.	Scenes from Jataka Stories	Past lives of the Buddha
2.	Fantastic animals	Imaginary animals not found in the real world
3.	Birds like Swans and Peacock	Symbolise the birth of Buddha

How many of the above pairs is/are correctly matched?
(a) Only one (b) Only two
(c) All three (d) None

Topic 3 : Sculpture

29. Consider the following statements regarding architecture and sculpture:

Statement I: Architecture is the art of designing and constructing buildings, while sculpture is the expression of human creativity.

Statement II: The material used in architecture is usually a mixture of various types of materials, whereas sculpture is usually made up of a single material.

Which one to the following is correct in respect to the above statements?

(a) Both Statement I and Statement II are correct and Statement II is the correct explanation for Statement I.
(b) Both Statement I and Statement II are correct, but Statement II is not the correct explanation for Statement I.
(c) Statement I is correct, but Statement II is incorrect.
(d) Statement I is incorrect, but Statement II is correct.

30. With reference to the Indus Valley Civilisation, consider the following statements:

1. The Bearded Priest was excavated from Mohenjodaro.
2. The Dancing Girl is a terracotta sculpture found in Lothal.
3. The technique used in making sculptures included the lost wax technique.

How many of the statements given above is/are incorrect?

(a) Only one (b) Only two
(c) All three (d) None

31. With reference to the Indus Valley Civilisation, consider the following statements:

1. Most of the sculptures were independent and not attached to larger pieces of architecture.
2. The primary materials used in sculptures were terracotta, stone and metal.
3. Seals found during excavations were made only of terracotta.

How many of the statements given above is/are correct?

(a) Only one
(b) Only two
(c) All three
(d) None

32. In the context of the Indus Valley Civilisation's economic system, which of the following artifacts indicates the existence of trade?

1. Seals made of steatite.
2. Bronze sculptures like the Dancing Girl.
3. Tools and pottery.

Select the correct answer using the codes given below:

(a) 1 and 2 only (b) 2 and 3 only
(c) 1 and 3 only (d) 1, 2 and 3

33. With reference to Mauryan age sculpture and architecture, consider the following statements:

1. The Lomas Rishi Cave was built during the Mauryan period and had an ornamented facade.
2. The capitals of Ashokan pillars feature inverted lotuses at their shafts.
3. Yaksha and Yakshini sculptures were exclusively found in the southern part of India.

Which of the statements given above are correct?

(a) 1 and 2 only
(b) 2 and 3 only
(c) 1 and 3 only
(d) 1, 2 and 3

34. Consider the following pairs:

1.	Four lions capital	Sarnath
2.	Bull and single lion	Sanchi
3.	Elephant capital	Rampurva

How many pairs given above is/are correctly matched?

(a) Only one
(b) Only two
(c) Only three
(d) None

35. Identify the period based on the following characteristics:

1. It saw the emergence of the Gandhara, Mathura and Amaravati schools of art.
2. The period witnessed significant influence from Greco-Roman art.
3. Sculptures often depicted Buddha and had a realistic representation of the human body.

Choose the correct period from the options given below :

(a) Mauryan Period
(b) Post-Mauryan Period
(c) Gupta Period
(d) Early Medieval Period

36. Identify the patron dynasty of the following art schools:

1. Gandhara School	Shakas and Kushanas
2. Mathura School	Local rulers and Kushanas
3. Amaravati School	Satavahanas and Ikshavakus

Choose the correct answer from the codes given below:

(a) 1 and 2 only (b) 2 and 3 only
(c) 1 and 3 only (d) 1, 2 and 3

37. Consider the following characteristics of the Mathura School of Art:

1. Use of locally found red sandstone.
2. Depiction of inner beauty and calmness in Buddha statues.
3. Absence of secular elements in its art.

How many of the statements given above is/are correct?

(a) Only one (b) Only two
(c) All three (d) None

38. With reference to the Nataraja sculpture, consider the following statements:

1. The sculpture represents Lord Shiva as the cosmic dancer.
2. It was made using the lost-wax technique.
3. The form depicts the destruction of the universe only.

Which of the statements given above are correct?

(a) 1 and 3 only (b) 2 and 3 only
(c) 1 and 2 only (d) 1, 2 and 3

39. With reference to the Pallavas' architectural contributions, consider the following statements:

1. The relief carvings at Mahabalipuram are among the world's largest and oldest sculptural panels.
2. The carvings depict the descent of the river Ganga from heaven.
3. The Pallava period is known for its extensive use of metal in sculpture.

Which of the statements given above are correct?

(a) 1 and 2 only (b) 2 and 3 only
(c) 1 and 3 only (d) 1, 2 and 3

40. Consider the following statements about the Chola period:

1. The Chola bronze sculptures reached their zenith during this period.
2. The most famous Chola sculpture is the Nataraja.
3. The Chola sculptures were primarily religious in nature.

How many of the statements given above is/are correct?

(a) Only one (b) Only two
(c) All three (d) None

41. In the context of the Gupta period's economy, which of the following materials were used extensively in art?

1. Cream-coloured sandstone
2. Metal for sculptures
3. Black stone

Select the correct answer using the codes given below :

(a) 1 and 2 only (b) 2 and 3 only
(c) 1 and 3 only (d) 1, 2 and 3

42. Consider the following transactions during the Gupta period:

1. Use of gold coins in trade.
2. Patronage of Buddhist monasteries by Gupta rulers.
3. Export of Gupta art to Southeast Asia.

How many of the above transactions would be correct in respect to the Gupta's Economy?

(a) Only one (b) Only two
(c) All three (d) None

43. What is the difference between independent sculptures and relief sculptures as seen in the Early Medieval Phase?

(a) Independent sculptures were 3-dimensional and free-standing, while relief sculptures were part of a larger architectural structure.
(b) Independent sculptures were religious, while relief sculptures were secular.
(c) Independent sculptures were made of metal, while relief sculptures were made of stone.
(d) There is no material difference between the two.

44. Consider the following statements about the Gomateshwara statue:

Statement I: It is located at Shravanabelagola in Karnataka.

Statement II: It is the world's tallest monolithic free-standing structure.

Which one of the following is correct in respect of the above statements?

(a) Both Statement I and Statement II are correct and Statement II is the correct explanation for Statement I.
(b) Both Statement I and Statement II are correct, but Statement II is not the correct explanation for Statement I.
(c) Statement I is correct, but Statement II is incorrect.
(d) Statement I is incorrect, but Statement II is correct.

Topic 4 : Temple Architecture

45. Consider the following pairs related to temple architecture terminologies:

1. Mandap	Assembly hall for devotees
2. Shikhar	Stone disc-like structure at the top of the temple
3. Kalasha	Topmost point of the temple above Amalaka

How many of the above pairs is/are correctly matched?

(a) Only one
(b) Only two
(c) All three
(d) None

46. Consider the following pairs related to temple architecture styles:

1. Rekha Deul	Curvilinear shape of the Shikhar
2. Pitha Deul	Pyramidal structure of the Shikhar
3. Vimana	Garbhagriha + Pyramidical structure + Shikhar

How many of the above pairs is/are correctly matched?

(a) Only one
(b) Only two
(c) All three
(d) None

47. Which one of the following statements is correct regarding temple architecture?

(a) The Mandap is always situated above the Garbhagriha.
(b) The Shikhar is the structure above the Mandap.
(c) The Kalasha is placed below the Amalaka in the Shikhar.
(d) The Garbhagriha is always located under the tallest tower of the temple.

48. Consider the following features:

1. Panchayatana Style
2. Curvilinear Shikhar
3. Vesara Style

Which of the above are associated with the Nagara style of temple architecture?

(a) 1 and 2 only (b) 2 and 3 only
(c) 1 and 3 only (d) 1, 2 and 3

49. In the context of temple architecture, which of the following features are associated with the Nagara style?

1. Water tanks are mostly absent
2. The Garbhagriha is always located under the tallest tower
3. Elaborate boundary walls or gateways are common

Select the correct answer using the codes given below:

(a) 1 and 2 only (b) 2 and 3 only
(c) 1 and 3 only (d) 1, 2 and 3

50. Identify the architectural style based on the following statements:

1. It is a mixture of Nagara and Dravida styles.
2. It was patronised by the Hoysala and Kalyani Chalukya dynasties.

Which architectural style is being described?

(a) Nagara Style (b) Dravida Style
(c) Vesara Style (d) Solanki Style

51. Consider the following pairs related to Nagara-style temple examples:

1. Konark Sun Temple	Odisha
2. Lingaraja Temple	Gujarat
3. Jagannath Temple	Odisha

How many of the above pairs is/are correctly matched?

(a) Only one (b) Only two
(c) All three (d) None

52. Consider the following pairs regarding elements of Nagara temple architecture:

1. Gavaksha	A motif representing a bull's or cow's eye.
2. Kalasha	The spire or pinnacle of a temple.
3. Amlaka	A stone disc at the base of the Shikhar.

How many of the above pairs is/are correctly matched?

(a) Only one (b) Only two
(c) All three (d) None

53. With reference to the features of Dravidian temple architecture, consider the following statements:

1. The main temple tower is known as Shikhar in Dravidian architecture.
2. Dravidian temples are known for their curved and intricate Shikhar structures similar to the Nagara style.
3. The Vimana in Dravidian architecture rises geometrically rather than curving like in Nagara temples.

Which of the statements given above is/are correct?

(a) 1 and 2 only (b) 2 and 3 only
(c) 3 only (d) 1, 2 and 3

54. In the context of Indian temple architecture, which of the following elements are characteristic of the Dravidian style?

1. Vimana 2. Gopuram 3. Mandapa

Select the correct answer using the codes given below :

(a) 1 and 2 only (b) 2 and 3 only
(c) 1, 2 and 3 (d) 1 and 3 only

55. Consider the following Dravidian temples and their respective dynasties:

1. Ratha Temple	Cholas
2. Shore Temple	Pallavas
3. Brihadeshwar	Cholas

Which of the pairs given above is/are incorrectly matched?

(a) 1 and 3 only
(b) 1 only
(c) 2 and 3 only
(d) 1, 2 and 3

56. With reference to Vesara-style temple architecture, consider the following statements:

1. Vesara style is a hybrid of Nagara and Dravidian styles.
2. The temples are typically built on a high platform with a stellate plan.
3. The temples were predominantly built under the Hoysala dynasty.

Which of the statements given above are correct?

(a) 1 and 2 only (b) 2 and 3 only
(c) 1 and 3 only (d) 1, 2 and 3

57. In the context of Vesara temple architecture, which of the following are key features?

1. Multi Garbhagriha format
2. Influence of Dravida style in intricate carvings
3. Stellate plan

Select the correct answer using the codes given below:

(a) 1 and 2 only
(b) 2 and 3 only
(c) 1 and 3 only
(d) 1, 2 and 3

58. With reference to the Nagara-style temple architecture, consider the following statements:

1. Nagara-style temples typically do not have boundary walls or gateways.
2. The Garbhagriha is always under the tallest tower known as the Shikhar.
3. Panchayatana style, where the main shrine is surrounded by four subsidiary shrines, is a common feature.

Which of the statements given above are correct?

(a) 1 and 2 only
(b) 2 and 3 only
(c) 1 and 3 only
(d) 1, 2 and 3

59. In the context of Nagara-style temple architecture, which of the following features are characteristic?

1. Curvilinear Shikhar
2. Panchayatana style
3. Use of stellate plan

Select the correct answer using the codes given below :

(a) 1 and 2 only (b) 2 and 3 only
(c) 1, 2 and 3 (d) 1 and 3 only

60. Which of the following statements correctly describes the Rekha Deul?

(a) A tall building with a sugar loaf shape, resembling a Shikhar.
(b) A rectangular building with a truncated pyramid-shaped roof.
(c) A square building with a pyramidal-shaped roof, like Vimana.
(d) A rectangular building with a barrel-vaulted roof.

61. Consider the following pairs regarding types of Deul (temple towers) in Odisha:

1. Rekha Deul	A building with a barrel-vaulted roof.
2. Pidha Deul	Square building with a pyramidal-shaped roof.
3. Khakhara Deul	Rectangular building with a truncated pyramid-shaped roof.

How many of the above pairs is/are not correctly matched?

(a) Only one (b) Only two
(c) All three (d) None

62. With reference to the Solanki/Maru-Gurjara school of temple architecture, consider the following statements:

1. Garbhagriha is connected to the Mandapa both internally and externally.
2. The Solanki school is known for its decorative arched gateways called Toranas.
3. The walls of the central shrine are typically devoid of carvings.

Which of the statements given above are correct?

(a) 1 and 2 only
(b) 2 and 3 only
(c) 1 and 3 only
(d) 1, 2 and 3

63. With reference to the Ahom style of temple architecture, consider the following statements:

1. Ahom style emerged in the 17th century with the migration of the Tais from Burma.
2. It features the worship of idols in temples.
3. Kamakhya Temple, dedicated to Goddess Kamakhya, is an example of this style.

Which of the statements given above are incorrect?

(a) 1 and 2 only
(b) 2 and 3 only
(c) 1 and 3 only
(d) 1, 2 and 3

64. In the context of temple architecture, which of the following features are associated with the Pala/Sena style?

1. Use of black to grey basalt and chlorite stone.
2. Curving or sloping side of the roof known as the Bangla roof.
3. Decorative arched gateways (Toranas).

Select the correct answer using the codes given below:

(a) 1 and 2 only
(b) 2 and 3 only
(c) 1, 2 and 3
(d) 1 and 3 only

65. Identify the temple architectural style based on the following statements:

1. It was dominated by the Pala rulers in Southern Bihar and Bengal.
2. The temples feature a local vernacular tradition expressed through the Bangla roof.
3. Buddhist temples under this style are known to express the local Vanga style.

Choose the correct architectural style from the codes given below:

(a) Dravida Style (b) Nagara Style
(c) Pala/Sena Style (d) Ahom Style

66. With reference to the Khajuraho school of temple architecture, consider the following statements:

1. It was built mainly under the Chandela rulers.
2. The temples follow the Panchayatana style, where the main shrine is surrounded by four subsidiary shrines.
3. The sculptures are generally erotic and heavily influenced by Vatsyayana's Kamasutra.

Which of the statements given above are correct?

(a) 1 and 2 only (b) 2 and 3 only
(c) 1 and 3 only (d) 1, 2 and 3

67. With reference to the Pala/Sena style of temple architecture, consider the following statements:

1. This style was patronised between the 9th and 13th centuries in Southern Bihar and Bengal.
2. The style is known for its use of black-to-grey basalt stone and the distinct Bangla roof.
3. The temples in this style are often located in North-Western India.

Which of the statements given above are correct?

(a) 1 and 2 only (b) 2 and 3 only
(c) 1 and 3 only (d) 1, 2 and 3

68. Consider the following features:

1. High boundary walls
2. Large gopurams
3. Water tank inside the temple complex

Which of the above features are associated with Chola architecture?

(a) 1 and 2 only (b) 2 and 3 only
(c) 1 and 3 only (d) 1, 2 and 3

69. In the context of Indian temple architecture, which of the following elements are characteristic of Chola architecture?

1. Vimana with an octagonal dome
2. Dvarapalas at the entrance
3. Panchayatana style

Select the correct answer using the codes given below:

(a) 1 and 2 only (b) 2 and 3 only
(c) 1 and 3 only (d) 1, 2 and 3

70. With reference to Brihadeshwara Temple at Thanjavur, consider the following statements:

1. It is topped with a 90-tonne monolithic mandapa.
2. The temple is known for its large gopurams.
3. It was built by Rajendra Chola.

Which of the statements given above is/are incorrect?

(a) 1 and 2 only (b) 2 only
(c) 3 only (d) 1 and 3 only

71. With reference to Pallava architecture, consider the following statements:

1. The architecture started from cave temples and evolved into structural temples.
2. The Mahendra group is known for building rock-cut cave temples.
3. The Shore Temple at Mahabalipuram belongs to the Nandivarman group.

Which of the statements given above are correct?

(a) 1 and 2 only (b) 2 and 3 only
(c) 1 and 3 only (d) 1, 2 and 3

72. Consider the following architectural features associated with Pallava temples:

1. Mandapa built into separate rathas.
2. Sculptures of Dvarapalas.
3. Trimurti temple dedicated to Brahma, Shiva and Vishnu.

Which of the above features are associated with the Narasimha group?

(a) 1 and 2 only (b) 2 and 3 only
(c) 1 and 3 only (d) 1, 2 and 3

73. Identify the Pallava king based on the following statements:

1. He was responsible for constructing rock-cut rathas at Mahabalipuram.
2. He is credited with the construction of the Shore Temple.
3. He expanded the Pallava Empire and contributed to architectural advancements.

Choose the correct answer from the options given below:

(a) Mahendravarman I (b) Narasimhavarman I
(c) Rajaraja Chola (d) Rajendra Chola

74. With reference to the Chola architecture, consider the following statements:

1. Chola temples are characterized by high boundary walls.
2. The Brihadeshwara Temple is known for its tallest Vimana.
3. The temples generally followed the Panchayatana style.

Which of the statements given above are correct?

(a) 1 and 2 only
(b) 2 and 3 only
(c) 1 and 3 only
(d) 1, 2 and 3

75. Consider the following pairs related to Chola architecture:

1. Brihadeshwara Temple, Thanjavur	Rajendra Chola I
2. Airatesvara Temple, Thanjavur	Rajaraja II
3. Brihadeshwara Temple, Gangaikondacholapuram	Rajaraja Chola I

Which of the pairs given above is/are correctly matched?

(a) 1 and 3 only
(b) 3 only
(c) 2 only
(d) 1 and 3 only

76. With reference to the Vijayanagara architecture, consider the following statements:

1. Vijayanagara temples are known for their large gopurams and chariot mandaps.
2. The temple complex features highly decorated pillars and small shrines.
3. The Virupaksha Temple was built by Krishnadevaraya.

Which of the statements given above are correct?

(a) 1 and 2 only
(b) 2 and 3 only
(c) 1 and 3 only
(d) 1, 2 and 3

77. Consider the following features associated with Nayaka architecture:

1. Elaborate 100 and 1000 pillar mandap.
2. Intricate carvings on the temple walls.
3. Large gopurams with a pillared portico.

Which of the above features are associated with the Nayaka dynasty?

(a) 1 and 2 only (b) 2 and 3 only
(c) 1 and 3 only (d) 1, 2 and 3

78. With reference to the Pandya architecture, consider the following statements:

1. Pandya temples often feature rock-cut sculptures and a 1000-pillar mandap.
2. The Meenakshi Temple in Madurai is an example of Pandya architecture.
3. The temples have a garbhagriha, ardhamandap and a larger mahamandap.

Which of the statements given above are correct?

(a) 1 and 2 only (b) 2 and 3 only
(c) 1 and 3 only (d) 1, 2 and 3

79. With reference to the Rashtrakuta architecture, consider the following statements:

1. The Kailashnath Temple at Ellora is a monolithic rock-cut temple in Nagara style.
2. The Rashtrakuta temples are mainly located in Maharashtra.

Which of the statements given above is/are correct?

(a) 1 only
(b) 2 only
(c) Both 1 and 2
(d) Neither 1 nor 2

80. Identify the dynasty based on the following features:

1. It ruled over Karnataka during the 10th to 12th centuries.
2. It is known for its contribution to the Vesara style of temple architecture.
3. It built temples like Virupaksha Temple at Pattadakal.

Choose the correct answer from the options given below:
(a) Chalukyas of Kalyani
(b) Hoysalas
(c) Chalukyas of Badami
(d) Rashtrakutas

81. With reference to the architectural and construction aspects of the Ayodhya Ram Temple, consider the following statements:

1. The temple is built in the Dravidian style and features five mandaps named Nritya, Ranga, Sabha, Prarthana and Kirtan.
2. The temple's main entrance, Singh Dwar, is located on the eastern side, featuring 32 ascending stairs.
3. The temple avoids the use of iron and steel, showcasing the application of ancient technology.

Which of the statements given above are correct?
(a) 1 and 2 only (b) 2 and 3 only
(c) 1 and 3 only (d) 1, 2 and 3

Topic 5 : Pillars and Inscriptions

82. Consider the following pairs regarding inscriptions and their locations :

1. Bhattiprolu Relic Casket Inscription	Andhra Pradesh
2. Sohgaura Copper Plate Inscription	Gorakhpur, Uttar Pradesh
3. Bairat Pillar Inscription	Rajasthan

How many of the above pairs is/are correctly matched?
(a) Only one (b) Only two
(c) All three (d) None

83. With reference to the pillar architecture in India, consider the following statements:

1. Pillars were first used during the Mauryan Age as part of Buddhist structures.
2. Pillars in the pre-Mauryan Age were primarily used in forts and served as structural supports.

Which of the statements given above is/are correct?
(a) 1 only (b) 2 only
(c) Both 1 and 2 (d) Neither 1 nor 2

84. With reference to the pillar architecture of the Mauryan Age, consider the following statements:

1. The use of stone pillars was prominent during Ashoka's reign.
2. Ashokan edicts were first deciphered by James Prinsep in 1837.
3. The Kandahar Rock Inscription is the only bilingual inscription of Ashoka.

Which of the statements given above are correct?
(a) 1 and 2 only
(b) 2 and 3 only
(c) 1 and 3 only
(d) 1, 2 and 3

85. Consider the following features:

1. Stone pillars used by Ashoka.
2. Excavations at Kumrahar and Bulandibagh.
3. Megasthenes mention of wooden pillar palaces.

Which of the above features are associated with the Mauryan Age?
(a) 1 and 2 only (b) 2 and 3 only
(c) 1 and 3 only (d) 1, 2 and 3

86. Consider the following sites associated with Ashoka's Minor Rock Edicts:

1. Bahapur in New Delhi
2. Bairat in Rajasthan
3. Rupnath in Madhya Pradesh

How many of the above sites contain Ashoka's Minor Rock Edicts?
(a) Only one (b) Only two
(c) All three (d) None

87. With reference to the Major Rock Edicts of Ashoka, consider the following statements:
1. The Major Rock Edicts were found at 10 major locations across India.
2. Inscriptions refer to Ashoka as Devanampiya Piyadasi.
3. The Kandahar inscription is written in Prakrit and Brahmi.

Which of the statements given above are correct?
(a) 1 and 2 only
(b) 2 and 3 only
(c) 1 and 3 only
(d) 1, 2 and 3

88. Consider the following about major rock edicts of Ashoka:
1. **Edict I** : Prohibits animal slaughter and killing of animals.
2. **Edict VI** : Stresses the importance of religious tolerance.
3. **Edict XIII** : Describes Ashoka's remorse over the Kalinga War.

How many of the above edicts is/are incorrectly matched with their descriptions?
(a) Only one
(b) Only two
(c) All three
(d) None

89. Consider the following features associated with the Ashokan Pillars:
1. The pillars were typically made of a single piece of polished sandstone.
2. They were topped with capitals depicting animal figures, often lions.
3. The pillars were inscribed with edicts in Brahmi script.

Which of the statements given above are correct?
(a) 1 and 2 only
(b) 2 and 3 only
(c) 1 and 3 only
(d) 1, 2 and 3

90. Consider the following components of an Ashokan Pillar:
1. Shaft 2. Capital 3. Abacus

Which of the following components are correct regarding same?
(a) 1 and 2 only (b) 2 and 3 only
(c) 1 and 3 only (d) 1, 2 and 3

91. Consider the following statements regarding the Lion Capital of Sarnath:
1. It was made from Chunar sandstone.
2. It depicts four lions, which represent the Four Noble Truths of Buddhism.
3. The capital has been adopted as the National Emblem of India.

Which of the statements given above are correct?
(a) 1 and 2 only (b) 2 and 3 only
(c) 1 and 3 only (d) 1, 2 and 3

92. With reference to the Ashokan pillars, consider the following pairs:

1. Shaft	Monolithic structure made of a single piece of stone
2. Inverted Lotus	The portion placed over the shaft
3. Lion Capital	Represents the Dharmachakra

Which of the pairs given above are correctly matched?
(a) 1 and 2 only
(b) 2 and 3 only
(c) 1 and 3 only
(d) 1, 2 and 3

93. Consider the following inscriptions found on the major Pillar Edicts of Ashoka:
1. Prohibits animal slaughter and killing of animals.
2. Emphasises religious tolerance and welfare measures.
3. Describes Ashoka's remorse over the Kalinga War.

How many of the above inscriptions is/are correctly associated with the Pillar Edicts of Ashoka?
(a) Only one
(b) Only two
(c) All three
(d) None

94. With reference to the structure of Ashokan pillars, consider the following pairs:

1. Inverted Lotus	Placed below the abacus
2. Abacus	Platform on which the capital rests
3. Capital	Topmost component with animal figures

How many of the above pairs is/are correctly matched?
(a) Only one (b) Only two
(c) All three (d) None

95. With reference to the Lion Capital of Sarnath, consider the following statements:
1. It was built to commemorate the first sermon of Buddha.
2. The capital depicts four lions facing in different directions.
3. The capital is adopted as the National Emblem of India.

Which of the statements given above are correct?
(a) 1 and 2 only (b) 2 and 3 only
(c) 1 and 3 only (d) 1, 2 and 3

96. With reference to the Minor Pillar Edicts of Ashoka, consider the following statements:
1. The Schism Edicts were found at Sarnath and Sanchi.
2. The Prayagraj Pillar talks about charitable deeds of Ashoka's queen, Karuvaki.
3. The Rummindei pillar commemorates Ashoka's visit to Lumbini.

How many of the statements given above is/are incorrect?
(a) Only one (b) Only two
(c) All three (d) None

97. With reference to the analysis of Ashokan and Persian pillars, consider the following statements:
1. Ashokan pillars are monolithic, while Persian pillars are composite, consisting of pieces joined together.
2. The use of animal capitals was unique to Ashokan pillars and was not found in Persian pillars.
3. Persian pillars were mainly used for supporting forts and palaces, while Ashokan pillars were primarily used for inscriptions.

Which of the statements given above are correct?
(a) 1 and 3 only (b) 2 and 3 only
(c) 1 and 2 only (d) 1, 2 and 3

98. Which one of the following inscriptions is located at the Udayagiri-Khandagiri caves?
(a) Besnagar Pillar Inscription
(b) Hathigumpha Inscription
(c) Junagadh Rock Inscription
(d) Ayodhya Inscription

99. Consider the following pairs:

Inscription	Location
1. Prayag Prashasti	Allahabad
2. Mehrauli Inscription	Delhi
3. Mandasor Pillar Inscription	Rajasthan

Which of the pairs given above are correctly matched?
(a) 1 and 2 only
(b) 2 and 3 only
(c) 1 and 3 only
(d) 1, 2 and 3

100. Consider the following pairs:

Pillar Inscription	Dynasty
1. Prayag Prashasti	Gupta
2. Bhitari Pillar Inscription	Skandagupta
3. Aihole Inscription	Satavahanas

How many pairs given above is/are correctly matched?
(a) Only one pair
(b) Only two pairs
(c) All three pairs
(d) None

101. Which one of the following inscriptions is correctly associated with the Satavahanas?
(a) Aihole Inscription
(b) Hathigumpha Inscription
(c) Naneghat Inscription
(d) Junagadh Rock Inscription

Topic 6 : Indo-Islamic Architecture

102. **Assertion** (A) : The Qutb Minar was constructed to commemorate the victory of Qutb-ud-din Aibak over the Rajput rulers.

Reason (R) : The construction of the Qutb Minar was completed by Iltutmish.

Which one of the following is correct in respect of the above statements?

(a) Both A and R are true and R is the correct explanation of A.

(b) Both A and R are true, but R is not the correct explanation of A.

(c) A is true, but R is false.

(d) A is false, but R is true.

103. Match the following monuments with their locations:

Monuments	Locations
A. Taj Mahal	1. Agra
B. Qutb Minar	2. Delhi
C. Gol Gumbaz	3. Bijapur
D. Madarsa of Mahmud Gawan	4. Bidar

Choose the correct from the codes given below.

(a) A-1, B-2, C-3, D-4
(b) A-4, B-3, C-2, D-1
(c) A-3, B-4, C-1, D-2
(d) A-2, B-1, C-4, D-3

104. Consider the following statements regarding the Charbagh style:

1. The Charbagh style of gardens was introduced by Humayun in India.
2. The Charbagh refers to a garden layout with a square plot divided into four equal parts.

Which of the statements given above is/are correct?

(a) 1 only (b) 2 only
(c) Both 1 and 2 (d) Neither 1 nor 2

105. Arrange the following structures in chronological order of their construction:

1. Qutb Minar
2. Red Fort
3. Tughlaqabad Fort
4. Gol Gumbaz

Select the correct sequence using the codes given below:

(a) 1-3-2-4 (b) 3-1-2-4
(c) 4-3-2-1 (d) 1-2-3-4

106. With reference to Indo-Islamic architecture, consider the following statements:

1. The use of coloured sandstone was first introduced during the Mughal period.
2. Pietra Dura was a form of inlay work that became prominent under Shah Jahan.
3. The Charbagh style of garden layout was introduced in India by Babur.

How many of the above statements is/are correct?

(a) Only one (b) Only two
(c) All three (d) None

107. With reference to the features of Indo-Islamic architecture, consider the following statements:

1. The use of marble as a primary material began with the construction of the Qutb Minar.
2. Geometric designs and calligraphy were common decorative elements.
3. The Mughal architecture prominently featured red sandstone in its structures.

How many of the above statements is/are correct?

(a) Only one (b) Only two
(c) All three (d) None

108. **Assertion** (A): The use of Pietra Dura became highly popular under Shah Jahan's reign.

Reason (R): Pietra Dura involves embedding semi-precious stones into white marble for ornamental purposes.

Which one of the following is correct in respect of the above statements?

(a) Both A and R are true and R is the correct explanation of A.

(b) Both A and R are true, but R is not the correct explanation of A.

(c) A is true, but R is false.

(d) A is false, but R is true.

109. With reference to the two methods for building architecture, consider the following statements:

1. The Trabeate style is based on arches and keystones.
2. The Arcuate style became predominant after the advent of Islam in India.
3. Both styles blend into Indo-Islamic architecture.

How many of the above statements is/are incorrect?

(a) Only one
(b) Only two
(c) All three
(d) None

110. Consider the following pairs:

	Monument	Description
1.	Qutb Minar	Built by Alauddin Khalji
2.	Feroz Shah Kotla	Designed by Malik Ghazi
3.	Sher Shah Suri Tomb	Octagonal building

How many of the pairs given above is/are correctly matched?

(a) Only one pair (b) Only two pairs
(c) All three pairs (d) None of the pairs

111. Which of the following statements is correct regarding the construction of the Agra Fort?

(a) It was built by Humayun and Sher Shah Suri.
(b) It is located on the banks of the Ganges river.
(c) It was the main residence of the Mughal rulers uill 1585.
(d) It served as the Mughal capital from 1526 to 1658.

112. With reference to Fatehpur Sikri, consider the following statements:

1. It was built by Akbar as a new Mughal capital.
2. The first structure built in Fatehpur Sikri was the Rang Mahal.
3. It is recognised as a UNESCO World Heritage site.

Which of the statements given above are correct?

(a) 1 and 2 only (b) 2 and 3 only
(c) 1 and 3 only (d) 1, 2 and 3

113. Consider the following pairs :

1.	Ibrahim Rauza	Mausoleum of Ibrahim Adil Shah II
2.	Gol Gumbaz	Mausoleum of Mohammad Adil Shah
3.	Madarsa of Mahmud Gawan	a center of non-Islamic Secular learning

How many of the pairs given above is/are correctly matched?

(a) Only one pair (b) Only two pairs
(c) All three pairs (d) None of the pairs

114. Consider the following statements regarding Mughal Architecture in India:

1. The tomb of Salim Chishti, constructed during Akbar's reign, is renowned for its exquisite Jaali work in white marble.
2. During Jahangir's reign, white marble replaced red sandstone as the primary building material.
3. Mughal architecture reached its pinnacle under the reign of Aurangzeb.

How many of the statements given above is/are correct?

(a) Only one (b) Only two
(c) All three (d) None

Topic 7 : Modern Architecture

115. Assertion (A) : Gothic architecture is known for its tall pointed arches and large windows.

Reason (R) : The Gothic style emphasised verticality and light, which was achieved through the use of pointed arches and large windows.

Which one of the following is correct in respect of the above statements?

(a) Both A and R are true and R is the correct explanation of A.
(b) Both A and R are true, but R is not the correct explanation of A.
(c) A is true, but R is false.
(d) A is false, but R is true.

116. **Assertion** (A): Neo-Classical architecture in Indo-Saracenic style was characterised by large structures and the use of domes.

Reason (R): Neo-classical architecture was heavily influenced by classical Roman architecture.

Which one of the following is correct in respect of the above statements?

(a) Both A and R are true and R is the correct explanation of A.

(b) Both A and R are true, but R is not the correct explanation of A.

(c) A is true, but R is false.

(d) A is false, but R is true.

117. **Assertion** (A): The Gateway of India was designed by George Wittet and is often called the 'Taj Mahal of Mumbai'.

Reason (R): It was built to commemorate the visit of King George V and Queen Mary to India.

Which one of the following is correct in respect of the above statements?

(a) Both A and R are true and R is the correct explanation of A.

(b) Both A and R are true, but R is not the correct explanation of A.

(c) A is true, but R is false.

(d) A is false, but R is true.

118. **Assertion (A)** : The India Gate in New Delhi was inspired by the Arc de Triomphe in Paris.

Reason (R) : The India Gate was designed by Edwin Lutyens and commemorates the soldiers of British India who died in World War II and the Third Anglo-Afghan War.

Which one of the following is correct in respect of the above statements?

(a) Both A and R are true and R is the correct explanation of A.

(b) Both A and R are true, but R is not the correct explanation of A.

(c) A is true, but R is false.

(d) A is false, but R is true.

119. Consider the following statements regarding Rashtrapati Bhawan:

1. It is located on top of Raisina Hill in New Delhi.
2. Originally, it was called Viceroy's House.
3. The building was designed by Edwin Lutyens and Herbert Baker.
4. It is the world's largest Presidential palace.

Which of the statements given above are correct?

(a) 1, 2 and 3 only

(b) 1 and 3 only

(c) 2, 3 and 4 only

(d) 1, 2, 3 and 4

120. With reference to Connaught Place, consider the following statements:

1. Connaught Place is located in Mumbai.
2. It was designed by Robert Tor Russell.
3. The construction of Connaught Place began in 1929 and was completed in 1933.
4. Connaught Place is named after the Duke of Connaught.

Which of the statements given above are correct?

(a) 1 and 2 only (b) 2, 3 and 4 only

(c) 2 and 4 only (d) 1, 2, 3 and 4

OMR SHEET

Assessment Round

1	a b c d	31	a b c d	61	a b c d	91	a b c d
2	a b c d	32	a b c d	62	a b c d	92	a b c d
3	a b c d	33	a b c d	63	a b c d	93	a b c d
4	a b c d	34	a b c d	64	a b c d	94	a b c d
5	a b c d	35	a b c d	65	a b c d	95	a b c d
6	a b c d	36	a b c d	66	a b c d	96	a b c d
7	a b c d	37	a b c d	67	a b c d	97	a b c d
8	a b c d	38	a b c d	68	a b c d	98	a b c d
9	a b c d	39	a b c d	69	a b c d	99	a b c d
10	a b c d	40	a b c d	70	a b c d	100	a b c d
11	a b c d	41	a b c d	71	a b c d	101	a b c d
12	a b c d	42	a b c d	72	a b c d	102	a b c d
13	a b c d	43	a b c d	73	a b c d	103	a b c d
14	a b c d	44	a b c d	74	a b c d	104	a b c d
15	a b c d	45	a b c d	75	a b c d	105	a b c d
16	a b c d	46	a b c d	76	a b c d	106	a b c d
17	a b c d	47	a b c d	77	a b c d	107	a b c d
18	a b c d	48	a b c d	78	a b c d	108	a b c d
19	a b c d	49	a b c d	79	a b c d	109	a b c d
20	a b c d	50	a b c d	80	a b c d	110	a b c d
21	a b c d	51	a b c d	81	a b c d	111	a b c d
22	a b c d	52	a b c d	82	a b c d	112	a b c d
23	a b c d	53	a b c d	83	a b c d	113	a b c d
24	a b c d	54	a b c d	84	a b c d	114	a b c d
25	a b c d	55	a b c d	85	a b c d	115	a b c d
26	a b c d	56	a b c d	86	a b c d	116	a b c d
27	a b c d	57	a b c d	87	a b c d	117	a b c d
28	a b c d	58	a b c d	88	a b c d	118	a b c d
29	a b c d	59	a b c d	89	a b c d	119	a b c d
30	a b c d	60	a b c d	90	a b c d	120	a b c d

Calculate Your Score

Correct (✓)	
Incorrect (✓)	
Unattempted	
Total Score	
Accuracy (%)	

Reasons for Incorrect Answers?

1. Lack of Knowledge/Existing Source Insufficient	
2. Lack of Multiple Revision	
3. Common Sense Mistakes	

Note :

1. Calculate total score as correct answers carry 2 marks each 1/3rd marks will deducted for **Incorrect** Answers.
2. Calculate Accuracy (%) by dividing the number of correct answers to the total number of attempted questions.

Past Learning

1. With reference to ancient India, consider the following statements : **(2023)**

1. The concept of Stupa is Buddhist in origin.
2. Stupa was generally a repository of relics.
3. Stupa was a votive and commemorative structure in Buddhist tradition.

How many of the statements given above is/are correct?

(a) Only one (b) Only two
(c) All three (d) None

2. Consider the following pairs: **(2023)**

	Site	Well known for
1.	Besnagar	Shaivite cave shrine
2.	Bhaja	Buddhist cave shrine
3.	Sittanawasal	Jain cave shrine

How many of the above pairs is/are correctly matched?

(a) Only one (b) Only two
(c) All three (d) None

3. Consider the following pairs: **(2022)**

	Site of Ashoka's major rock edicts	Location in the State of
1.	Dhauli	Odisha
2.	Erragudi	Andhra Pradesh
3.	Jaugada	Madhya Pradesh
4.	Kalsi	Karnataka

How many pairs given above is/are correctly matched?

(a) Only one pair (b) Only two pairs
(c) Only three pairs (d) All four pairs

4. The Prime Minister recently inaugurated the new Circuit House near Somnath Temple Veraval. Which of the following statements are correct regarding Somnath Temple? **(2022)**

1. Somnath Temple is one of the Jyotirlinga shrines.
2. A description of Somnath Temple was given by Al-Biruni.
3. Pran Pratishtha of Somnath Temple (installation of the present day temple) was done by President S. Radhakrishnan.

Select the correct answer using the codes given below :

(a) 1 and 2 only (b) 2 and 3 only
(c) 1 and 3 only (d) 1, 2 and 3

5. Consider the following pairs : **(2021)**

	Historical place	Well-known for
1.	Burzahom	Rock-cut shrines
2.	Chandraketugarh	Terracotta art
3.	Ganeshwar	Copper artefacts

Which of the pairs given above is/are correctly matched?

(a) 1 only (b) 1 and 2
(c) 3 only (d) 2 and 3

6. Which one of the following statements is correct? **(2021)**

(a) Ajanta Caves lie in the gorge of Waghora River.
(b) Sanchi Stupa lies in the gorge of Chambal River.
(c) Pandu-lena Cave shrines lie in the gorge of Narmada River.
(d) Amaravati Stupa lies in the gorge of Godavari River.

7. With reference to Chausath Yogini Temple situated near Morena, consider the following statements: **(2021)**

1. It is a circular temple built during the reign of Kachchhapaghata Dynasty.
2. It is the only circular temple built in India.
3. It was meant to promote the Vaishnava cult in the region.
4. Its design has given rise to a popular belief that it was the inspiration behind the Indian Parliament building.

Which of the statements given above are correct?

(a) 1 and 2 only (b) 2 and 3 only
(c) 1 and 4 only (d) 2, 3 and 4 only

8. With reference to the history of India, consider the following pairs. **(2020)**

Famous Places	Present States
1. Bhilsa	Madhya Pradesh
2. Dwarasamudra	Maharashtra
3. Girinagar	Gujarat
4. Sthanesvara	Uttar Pradesh

Which of the pairs given above are correctly matched?

(a) 1 and 3 (b) 1 and 4
(c) 2 and 3 (d) 2 and 4

9. Building 'Kalyaana Mandapas' was a notable feature in the temple construction in the kingdom of **(2019)**

(a) Chalukya
(b) Chandela
(c) Rashtrakuta
(d) Vijayanagara

10. In which of the following relief sculpture inscriptions is 'Ranyo Ashoka' (King Ashoka) mentioned along with the stone portrait of Ashoka? **(2019)**

(a) Kanganahalli (b) Sanchi
(c) Shahbazgarhi (d) Sohgaura

11. With reference to the cultural history of India, consider the following statements

1. White marble was used in making Buland Darwaza and Khankah at Fatehpur Sikri.
2. Red sandstone and marble were used in making Bara Imambara and Rumi Darwaza at Lucknow.

Which of the statements given above is/are correct? **(2018)**

(a) 1 only
(b) 2 only
(c) Both 1 and 2
(d) Neither 1 nor 2

12. Which of the following is/are famous for Sun temples? **(2017)**

1. Arasavalli
2. Amarakantak
3. Omkareshwar

Select the correct answer using the codes given below :

(a) 1 only (b) 2 and 3 only
(c) 1 and 3 only (d) 1, 2 and 3

13. Consider following pairs: **(2016)**

Famous place	Region
1. Bodhgaya	Baghelkhand
2. Khajuraho	Bundelkhand
3. Shirdi	Vidarbha
4. Nasik (Nashik)	Malwa
5. Tirupati	Rayalaseema

Which of the pairs given above are correctly matched?

(a) 1, 2 and 4 (b) 2, 3, 4 and 5
(c) 2 and 5 only (d) 1, 3, 4 and 5

14. What is/are common to the two historical places known as Ajanta and Mahabalipuram? **(2016)**

1. Both were built in the same period.
2. Both belong to the same religious denomination.
3. Both have rock-cut monuments.

Select the correct answer using the codes given below.

(a) 1 and 2 only
(b) 3 only
(c) 1 and 3 only
(d) None of the statements given above is correct

15. With reference to the art and archaeological history of India, which one among the following was made earliest? **(2015)**

(a) Lingaraja Temple at Bhubaneswar
(b) Rock-cut Elephant at Dhauli
(c) Rock-cut Monuments at Mahabalipuram
(d) Varaha Image at Udayagiri

16. With reference to the cultural history of India, the term 'Panchayatan' refers to **(2014)**

(a) an assembly of village elders
(b) a religious sect
(c) a style of temple construction
(d) an administrative functionary

17. With reference to the Indian history of art and culture, consider the following pairs: **(2014)**

	Famous work of sculpture	Site
1.	A grand image of Buddha's Mahaparinivana with numerous celestial musicians above and the sorrowful figures of his followers below	Ajanta
2.	A huge image of Varaha Avatar (boar incarnation) of Lord Vishnu, as he rescues Goddess Earth from the deep and chaotic waters, sculptured on rock	Mount Abu
3.	"Arjuna's penance:/ Descent of Ganga" sculpted on the surface of huge boulders	Mamallapuram

Which of the pairs given above is/are correctly matched?

(a) 1 and 2 only (b) 3 only
(c) 1 and 3 only (d) 1, 2 and 3

18. With reference to the history of Indian rock-cut architecture, consider the following statements: **(2013)**

1. The caves at Badami are the oldest surviving rock-cut caves in India.
2. The Barabar rock-cut caves were originally made for Ajivikas by Emperor Chandragupta Maurya.
3. At Ellora, caves were made for different faiths.

Which of the statements given above is/are correct?

(a) 1 only (b) 2 and 3 only
(c) 3 only (d) 1, 2 and 3

19. Some Buddhist rock-cut caves are called Chaityas, while the others are called Viharas. What is the difference between the two? **(2013)**

(a) Vihara is a place of worship, while Chaitya is the dwelling place of the monks.
(b) Chaitya is a place of worship, while Vihara is the dwelling place of the monks.
(c) Chaitya is the stupa at the far end of the cave, while Vihara is the hall axial to it.
(d) There is no material difference between the two.

20. The Nagara, the Dravida, the Vesara are **(1995, 2012)**

(a) the three main racial group of the Indian Subcontinent
(b) the three main linguistic divisions into which the languages of India can be classified
(c) the three main styles of Indian temple architecture
(d) the three main musical gharanas prevalent in India.

21. In which state is the Buddhist site Tabo Monastery located? **(2009)**

(a) Arunachal Pradesh (b) Himachal Pradesh
(c) Sikkim (d) Uttarakhand

22. Match List I with List II and select the correct answer using the codes given below the lists. **(2009)**

List I (Famous Temples)	List II (States)
A. Vidyashankara temple	1. Andhra Pradesh
B. Rajarani temple	2. Karnataka
C. Kandariya Mahadev temple	3. Madhya Pradesh
D. Bhimeswara temple	4. Odisha

Codes

	A	B	C	D
(a)	2	4	3	1
(b)	2	3	4	1
(c)	1	4	3	2
(d)	1	3	4	2

23. Where is the famous Virupaksha temple located? **(2009)**

(a) Bhadrachalam (b) Chidambaram
(c) Hampi (d) Srikalahasti

24. Near which one of the following cities are Palitana temples located? **(2008)**

(a) Bhavnagar (b) Mount Abu
(c) Nasik (d) Ujjain

25. Where is the famous Vijaya Vittala Temple, having its 56 carved pillars emitting musical notes located? **(2007)**

(a) Belur (b) Bhadrachalam
(c) Hampi (d) Srirangam

26. Which one of the following pairs is correctly matched? **(2006)**

(a) Vikramshila Monastery	Uttar Pradesh
(b) Hemkund Gurudwara	Himachal Pradesh
(c) Udayagiri Caves	Maharashtra
(d) Amaravati Buddhist Stupa	Andhra Pradesh

27. The initial design and construction of which massive temple took place during the reign of Suryavarman II? **(2006)**

(a) Sri Mariamman temple
(b) Angkor Vat temple
(c) Batu Caves temple
(d) Kamakhya temple

28. Which one of the following pairs is not correctly matched? **(2006)**

	Monasteries	States
(a)	Dhankar Monastery	Himachal Pradesh
(b)	Rumtek Monastery	Sikkim
(c)	Tabo Monastery	Himachal Pradesh
(d)	Kye Monastery	Arunachal Pradesh

29. The Allahabad Pillar Inscription is associated with which one of the following? **(2006)**

(a) Mahapadma Nanda
(b) Chandragupta Maurya
(c) Ashoka
(d) Samudragupta

30. The Archaeological Survey of India is an attached office of the Department/Ministry of **(2004)**

(a) Culture
(b) Tourism
(c) Science and Technology
(d) Human Resource Development

31. Which one of the following statements is not correct? **(2002)**

(a) The statue of Gomateshwara at Sravana-belagola represents the last Tirthankara of Jains.
(b) India's largest Buddhist monastery is in Arunachal Pradesh.
(c) The Khajuraho temples were built under Chandela kings.
(d) The Hoysaleswara temple is dedicated to Shiva.

32. Match List I (Ancient sites) with List II (Archaeological findings) and select the correct answer using the codes given below the lists. **(2002)**

List I (Ancient sites)	List II (Archaeological findings)
A. Lothal	1. Ploughed field
B. Kalibangan	2. Dockyard
C. Dholavira	3. Treplica of a plough
D. Banawali	4. An inscription comprising ten large sized signs of the Harappan script

Codes

	A	B	C	D		A	B	C	D
(a)	1	2	3	4	(b)	2	1	4	3
(c)	1	2	4	3	(d)	2	1	3	4

33. Which one of the following pairs is correctly matched? **(2001)**

(a) Harappan Civilisation	Painted Grey Ware
(b) The Kushans	Gandhara School of Art
(c) The Mughals	Ajanta Paintings
(d) The Marathas	Pahari School of Painting

34. Which one of the following animals was not represented out seals arid terracotta art of Harappan culture? **(2001)**

(a) Cow (b) Elephant
(c) Rhinoceros (d) Tiger

35. In which one of the following cities is the Lingaraja temple located? **(2001)**

(a) Bhubaneswar (b) Bijapur
(c) Kolkata (d) Shravanambelagola

36. Hoysala monuments are found in **(2001)**

(a) Hampi and Hosper
(b) Halebid and Belur
(c) Mysore and Bangalore
(d) Sringeri and Dharwar

37. Consider the following. **(1998)**

1. Tughlaqabad fort 2. Lodi Garden
3. Qutub Minar 4. Fatehpur Sikri

The correct chronological order in which they were built is

(a) 3, 1, 4, 2 (b) 3, 1, 2, 4
(c) 1, 3, 2, 4 (d) 1, 3, 4, 2

Detailed Solutions

Assessment Round

1. *(b)* Only two

- **Statement 1 is correct**: The Udayagiri and Khandagiri Caves are situated near **Bhubaneswar, the capital city of Odisha.** The caves are located on two hills, **Udayagiri** (meaning **'Sunrise Hill'**) and **Khandagiri** (meaning **'Broken Hill') which are described as Kumari Parvata in Hathigumpha inscription.**
- **Statement 2 is correct:** These caves were excavated during the **reign of King Kharavela of the Mahameghavahana dynasty.** These caves were likely built as residential quarters for Jain monks during the **1st-2nd century** BCE and inscriptions were written here in Brahmi script.
- **Statement 3 is incorrect:** Udayagiri and Khandagiri Caves are famous for their Jain iconography, including **carvings and inscriptions** related to Jain **Tirthankaras** and other religious figures. The caves served as both **monastic retreats** and places for **religious** congregations for the Jain community.

Thus, option (b) is the correct answer.

2. *(c)* All three

- **Statement 1 is correct**: Ashoka, the Mauryan emperor, is recognized as the **first ruler to commission rock-cut caves.** These caves were primarily intended to serve as sanctuaries for the Ajivika sect **(founded by Makkhali Gosala)**, a religious group that thrived during his reign.
- **Statement 2 is correct**: The rock-cut caves commissioned by Ashoka are located **in the** Barabar Hills in Bihar. These hills are **home** to some of the oldest surviving rock-cut caves in India, which include the famous **Barabar** and **Nagarjuna caves.**
- **Statement 3 is correct**: Sudama cave, located in the **Barabar Hills, is indeed the oldest** among the rock-cut caves constructed **during** the Mauryan period. Sudama cave is particularly notable for its **semicircular (horse-shoe) arch** and **highly polished surface**, which exemplifies the advanced stone-cutting techniques of the Mauryan artisans.

Thus, option (c) is the correct answer.

3. *(c)* Statement I is correct but Statement II is incorrect.

- **Statement I is correct:** Bhaja Caves are a group of 22 **rock-cut caves located near Lonavala**, in the **Pune district of Maharashtra**. Bhaja Caves are particularly known for their chaitya (prayer hall) and viharas (monasteries).
- **Statement II is incorrect:** The Bhaja Caves are associated with the **Hinayana (Theravada) sect of Buddhism, which predates the Mahayana** sect. The Hinayana tradition focused on the original teachings of Buddha and did not involve the worship of Bodhisattvas, which became prominent in the Mahayana tradition.

Thus, option (c) is the correct answer.

4. *(d)* All four

- **Barabar Hills in Bihar** are home to some of the oldest surviving rock-cut caves in India, dating back to the 3rd century BCE during the reign of Emperor Ashoka of the Maurya Empire. These caves were dedicated to the Ajivika sect, an ancient Indian religion that existed alongside Jainism and Buddhism.
- **Lomas Rishi Cave** is famous in the Barabar group and is known for its highly polished interior walls and ornate entrance, which resembles the wooden architecture of that period.
- **Sudama Cave** is also part of the Barabar group, the Sudama Cave is renowned for its simple, hemispherical hall, which was also dedicated to the Ajivika sect.
- **Visva Zhopri Cave**, too, belongs to the Barabar group and like the other caves, it was used by the Ajivika sect.

- **Karna Chaupar Cave** is also part of the Barabar Hills. A single rectangular room with polished walls and dimensions of 10.2x4.27m, located on the northern side of the hill.

Thus, option (d) is the correct answer.

5. *(b)* Only two

- **Ellora Caves** are located in Maharashtra, these caves are a UNESCO World Heritage site and one of the largest **rock-cut monastery-temple cave** complexes in the world. They feature monuments from **Buddhism, Hinduism and Jainism,** reflecting the religious harmony of the period.
- **Elephanta Cave** also located in **Maharashtra,** the Elephanta Caves are a collection of cave temples primarily **dedicated to the Hindu god Shiva**. These caves are also a UNESCO World Heritage site and are known for their stunning rock-cut sculptures, including the famous **three-headed Shiva,** known as **Trimurti.**
- **Bagh Caves** are located in the **Dhar district of Madhya Pradesh,** not Maharashtra. They are known for their **Buddhist murals,** which are among the earliest examples of Indian painting. Bagh Caves are a Buddhist rock-cut architecture tradition.
- **Mandargiri Caves are located in Bihar,** these caves are not situated in Maharashtra. They are pilgrimage site for Jains.

Thus, option (b) is the correct answer.

6. *(b)* Udayagiri and Khandagiri Caves

- The Hathigumpha inscription, carved in Brahmi script, is a vital historical record found in the **Udayagiri and Khandagiri Caves.** These caves, located in Odisha, were constructed under the patronage of **King Kharavela of the Kalinga dynasty** in the 1st-2nd century BCE.
- The inscription details **Kharavela's military victories, religious donations** and public works, offering significant insights into the socio-political landscape of ancient Odisha.

Thus, option (b) is the correct answer.

7. *(a)* Satavahana rulers and traders

- **Karle Caves,** situated in **Lonavala, Pune,** are renowned for having the largest Chaitya-griha among all Buddhist monuments in India. These caves were built by the **Satavahana rulers and local traders** who played a significant role in the maritime trade of that era.
- **Grand Chaitya at Karle** is notable for its **horse-shoe-shaped windows** that illuminate the interiors with natural light, creating an ethereal atmosphere. Additionally, the **two 15-metre high pillars** outside the Chaitya, **adorned with four lions at the top,** are emblematic of the grandeur of the Satavahana architectural style.

Thus, option (a) is the correct answer.

8. *(c)* Krishnaraja I

- The monolithic Kailash Temple at Ellora, Cave 16, was constructed during the reign of the **Rashtrakuta King Krishnaraja I in the 8th century** CE. This temple is considered one of the most remarkable achievements of ancient Indian rock-cut architecture, representing **Mount Kailasha, the abode of Lord Shiva.**
- The entire structure was carved out of a single rock, involving the **removal of over 200,000 tons of rock,** a feat of engineering and artistic ingenuity. The **Kailash Temple's elaborate carvings and grand scale make it a UNESCO World Heritage site.**

Thus, option (c) is the correct answer.

9. *(a)* Massive image of elephant at the entrance

- The Elephanta Caves, located on the island of **Gharapuri near Mumbai,** were named by the Portuguese in the 16th century due to the massive stone image of **an elephant that stood at the entrance of the caves.** These caves contain significant **Shaivism and Vaishnavism** and Buddhist sculptures, with the main cave dedicated to **Lord Shiva.**
- The most famous sculpture within the Elephanta Caves is the **Trimurti,** a three-headed depiction of Shiva, representing his roles as the **Creator, Preserver and Destroyer.**

Thus, option (a) is the correct answer.

10. *(a)* It is a monolithic Kailash Temple built during the reign of Krishnaraja I.

- **Cave 16 at Ellora, known as the Kailash Temple**, is a remarkable monolithic structure carved out of a single rock during the reign of Rashtrakuta King **Krishnaraja I in the 8th century CE**. The temple is an architectural marvel, representing Mount Kailasha, the mythological abode of Lord Shiva.
- The Kailash Temple at Ellora is considered one of the largest rock-cut temples in the world, symbolising the zenith of rock-cut architecture and the **religious tolerance** that characterised the period, as the Ellora complex also houses **Buddhist and Jain caves.**

Thus, option (a) is the correct answer.

11. *(c)* Only three

- **Statement 1 is incorrect:** The 24 feet long reclining Buddha sculpture is not found in the Ellora Caves but in the Ajanta Caves, specifically in Cave No. 26. This sculpture depicts the Mahaparinirvana (the death of the Buddha), a significant iconographic representation in Buddhism. The Ajanta Caves, dating from the 2nd century BCE to the 6th century CE, are renowned for their paintings and sculptures, including this massive reclining Buddha.
- **Statement 2 is correct:** In Ellora's Cave No. 10, also known as the Vishwakarma Cave, a seated Buddha is depicted with a Bodhi tree in the background. This cave is a Buddhist Chaitya hall and is one of the most important examples of rock-cut architecture. The seated Buddha represents the teaching posture, often associated with significant events in the Buddha's life.
- **Statement 3 is correct:** The sculpture of Bahubali, a Jain leader, can be found in Cave No. 32 at Ellora. Bahubali, also known as Gomateshwara, is depicted in a meditative pose with vines growing around his limbs, symbolising his deep penance. The Jain caves at Ellora are known for their intricate carvings and represent the ascetic traditions of Jainism.
- **Statement 4 is correct:** The Ellora Caves, particularly Cave No. 12, feature sculptures associated with Tantric Buddhism. This cave, known as the Tin Thal, is a significant representation of Vajrayana or Tantric Buddhism, where various deities and ritualistic symbols associated with this form of Buddhism are depicted.

Thus, option (c) is the correct answer.

12. *(c)* Only three

- **Statement 1 is correct:** Nasik Caves, also known as **Trirashmi Caves or Pandavleni Caves**, are a group of **24 caves** located near Nasik, Maharashtra. The term 'Trirashmi' refers to the three hills on which these caves are situated. The name 'Pandavleni' is derived from a local legend **associating the caves with the Pandavas** from the Mahabharata.
- **Statement 2 is incorrect:** Nasik Caves were first documented by **Captain James Delamine in 1823** not in **1723**. The caves served as monasteries for Buddhist monks and were places for meditation and worship.
- **Statement 3 is correct:** 'Leni' is a Marathi word that translates to 'caves' in English. Nasik Caves are significant for their association with the **Hinayana (Theravada) sect of Buddhism.** Hinayana Buddhism emphasises the strict adherence to the original teachings of the Buddha and focuses on the individual's path to enlightenment.
- **Statement 4 is correct:** An inscription found in the **Nasik Caves** mentions that the third cave was financed by **Gautami Balashri**, the **mother of Gautamiputra Satakarni**, a prominent ruler of the Satavahana dynasty. This inscription not only highlights the involvement of royalty in the construction and maintenance of these religious sites but also underscores the role of women in ancient Indian society as patrons of religious and cultural institutions.

Thus, option (c) is the correct answer.

13. *(b)* Only two

- **Statement 1 is incorrect:** The Ajanta Caves are located on the banks of the **Waghora River**, not the Purna River. The Waghora River is a small stream that meanders through the rugged Sahyadri hills, near Aurangabad in Maharashtra.

- **Statement 2 is incorrect:** The Ajanta Caves were constructed in **two distinct phases.** The **early phase,** which is associated with Hinayana Buddhism, features caves that were primarily used as viharas (monasteries) and chaityas (prayer halls). However, during the **Vakataka period,** the caves were primarily dedicated to **Mahayana Buddhism.**
- **Statement 3 is correct:** The Ajanta Caves do indeed house a sculpture of the Mahaparinirvana of Buddha. This 24-foot-long and nine-foot-tall sculpture is located in **Cave No. 26** and depicts the Buddha in his final resting position before his death, signifying his attainment of Nirvana.

Thus, option (b) is the correct answer.

14. *(b)* 2 only

- **Statement 1 is incorrect:** The Jain caves at Ellora belong to the **Digambara sect,** not the Shwetambara sect. The Jain caves are located towards the Northern end of the Ellora complex, specifically Cave Nos. 30-34 and are known for their detailed carvings and the representation of Jain Tirthankaras.
- **Statement 2 is correct:** The Ellora Caves feature a **Buddha sculpture in Vitarka Mudra.** This mudra, or hand gesture, signifies the teaching and intellectual discussion posture of the Buddha, found in the **Vishvakarma Cave (Cave No. 10), which is also known as the 'Carpenter's Cave'.**

Thus, option (b) is the correct answer.

15. *(b)* Only two

- **Pair 1 is incorrect:** Ajatashatru built the stupa at **Rajgir (Rajgriha), not Vaishali.** Rajgir was a power center during the **Haryanka Dynasty** and Ajatashatru's contributions there marked the early development of stupa architecture.
- **Pair 2 is correct:** The **Brahmins of Vetthadipa** built the stupa in the **Betiah district, Bihar.** This reflects the importance of **local communities** in the spread of Buddhism through stupa construction.
- **Pair 3 is incorrect:** The **Mallas of Kushinagar** built the **stupa at Kushinagar,** which is historically significant as the site of **Buddha's Parinirvana.** Pipilivana, however, is **associated with the Moriyas.**

Thus, option (b) is the correct answer.

16. *(b)* Only two

- **Pair 1 is correct: Caitya** is correctly matched with **Nepal,** where it is a common term for stupas, reflecting the country's rich **Buddhist heritage. Boudhanath** (Boudha Stupa) is one of the famous stupas located in Kathmandu, Nepal, it contains the relics and remains of Buddha.
- **Pair 2 is correct:** Dagoba is correctly matched with **Sri Lanka,** where this term is used for stupas, indicating the deep-rooted presence of **Theravada Buddhism** in the island nation.
- **Pair 3 is incorrect: Pagoda** is not correctly matched with **Thailand.** it is associated with **Japan and Vietnam.** In Thailand, stupas are typically referred to as 'chedi'.

Thus, option (b) is the correct answer.

17. *(d)* 1-4-2-3

- **Anda is the core structure** of the stupa, representing the dome or hemisphere, which symbolises the universe and the burial mound over the **Buddha's relics.**
- **Pradakshina Patha** is constructed around the Anda, providing a space for devotees to walk around the stupa in a ritualistic manner, symbolising **reverence** and **meditation.**
- **Harmika** is the small platform at the **top of Anda,** representing the **abode of the gods** and the connection between the divine and the earthly realms.
- **Chhatra** is an umbrella-like structure at the **top of Harmika,** symbolising protection and honour. It is often seen as a symbol of **sovereignty and respect.**

Thus, option (d) is the correct answer.

18. *(c)* All three

- **Statement 1 is correct: Relic Stupas** are built specifically to enshrine the **bodily remains of the Buddha or his disciples,** making them the most revered type of stupa. Stupa provides a focal point for devotion and pilgrimage.

- **Statement 2 is correct: Piprahwa Stupa** is a prime example of a **Relic Stupa**, where relics of the Buddha were discovered.
- **Statement 3 is correct:** These stupas are highly venerated because they house the remains of the Buddha, making them sites of immense spiritual importance for Buddhists around the world. The presence of relics elevates these stupas to the highest level of sanctity within the Buddhist faith.

Thus, option (c) is the correct answer.

19. *(b)* Both Statement I and Statement II are correct and Statement II is not the correct explanation for Statement I.

- **Statement I is correct: Symbolic Stupas** are constructed to symbolise the **omnipresence of Buddha**, serving as reminders of his teachings and spiritual presence throughout the world. These stupas are erected in places where the Buddha is believed to have visited or meditated, making them significant for both their symbolic and historical value.
- **Statement II is correct:** Votive Stupas are smaller stupas built by devotees at pilgrimage sites or near larger stupas. They are constructed as offerings to earn spiritual merit or grace and they often commemorate personal vows or significant life events.
- However, Statement II does not explain Statement I, as they address different purposes and meanings within Buddhist practices.

Thus, option (b) is the correct answer.

20. *(d)* 1, 2 and 3

- **Statement 1 is correct:** Gandhara Stupa features a sculpted **base, dome and hemisphere,** typical of the **Gandhara art style**, which combines **Greco-Roman** and Indian **artistic traditions.**
- **Statement 2 is correct:** Stupa is particularly noted for its intricate relief carvings that depict various scenes from the life of the **Buddha** and **Jataka tales.**
- **Statement 3 is correct:** Stupa was indeed patronised by the Kushan rulers, who played a crucial role in the development and spread of Buddhism across Central and South Asia. Under their patronage, the Gandhara region became a major center of Buddhist art and culture.

Thus, option (d) is the correct answer.

21. *(b)* Satavahana Period

- **Amaravati Stupa**, situated on the right bank of the **Krishna River** in **Andhra Pradesh**, was constructed during the **Satavahana period**, between the 3rd century BCE and the 2nd century CE.
- The stupa is known for its large circular altar and the depiction of the Buddha in human form, which is a hallmark of the mature phase of Buddhist art. Amaravati Stupa was rediscovered in **1797 by Colin Mackenzie and** it remains one of the most important Buddhist monuments in India, illustrating the grandeur and architectural innovation of the Satavahana period.

Thus, option (b) is the correct answer.

22. *(c)* Piprahwa Stupa

- **Piprahwa Stupa**, located in **Uttar Pradesh** near the Indo-Nepal border, India, is considered one of the oldest and most sacred stupas, believed to have been built to house the bodily remains of the Buddha. It was discovered in **1897 by William Claxton Peppe** during an excavation, where he unearthed a large stone coffer containing relics believed to be those of the Buddha, including bone fragments.
- Its sacred status is attributed to its direct association with the physical remains of the Buddha, making it a focal point for devotion and veneration.

Thus, option (c) is the correct answer.

23. *(a)* Dhamek Stupa

- The Dhamek Stupa is a **Buddhist monument** located in **Sarnath, Uttar Pradesh,** which marks the site where the **Buddha delivered his first sermon** to his five disciples, an event known as the '**Dhamma Chakka-Pavattana Sutta**' or '**Setting in Motion of the Wheel of Dharma**'.
- Stupa was originally built during the **Mauryan period by Emperor Ashoka**, but it was later encased with **intricate stone-carved** floral designs during the Gupta Period, a time when Buddhist art and architecture flourished in India.

- An Ashokan pillar with an edict engraved on it is located **near the Dhamek Stupa** inscribed with Ashoka's messages promoting **Dharma and non-violence.**

Thus, option (a) **is the correct answer.**

24. *(b)* 2-3-4-1

- **Sanchi Stupa** was originally constructed by Ashoka in the **3rd century BCE**, making it the earliest event.
- **Dharmarajika Stupa** was destroyed in 1794 by Jagat Singh for bricks, following the Sanchi Stupa's construction.
- **Sanchi Stupa** was later renovated and enlarged by Agnimitra, the son of Pushyamitra Sunga, after its partial destruction by Pushyamitra Sunga.
- **Piprahwa Stupa** was discovered much later in 1897 by William Claxton Peppé, placing it as the most recent event in this sequence.

Thus, option (b) is the correct answer.

25. *(c)* All three

- **Statement 1 is correct**: The **Dharmarajika Stupa** is indeed located in **Taxila, Pakistan,** which was an important center of Buddhist learning and culture during the **time of Ashoka.**
- **Statement 2 is correct**: It was built by **Ashoka**, the Mauryan emperor who is known for his widespread promotion of **Buddhism** and the construction of stupas across his empire.
- **Statement 3 is correct**: The stupa was destroyed in **1749 by Jagat Singh**, who used the bricks from the stupa for other construction purposes. The remains of the stupa, including a box containing relics, were discovered later and are now preserved at the Indian Museum in Kolkata.

Thus, option (c) is the correct answer.

26. *(c)* Statement I is correct, but Statement II is incorrect.

- **Statement I is correct: Sanchi Stupa** was originally built by Emperor **Ashoka** with bricks in the 3rd century BCE. This stupa is one of the oldest and most significant examples of **Buddhist architecture,** symbolising the spread of **Buddhism under Ashoka's patronage.**
- **Statement II is incorrect**: Sanchi Stupa was enlarged and renovated by the rulers of the Sunga dynasty, particularly by **Pushyamitra Sunga** and his successors. The enlargement included the addition of the **stone railing**, the **toranas (gateway)** and the stone casing around the original brick stupa.

Thus, option (c) is the correct answer.

27. *(b)* Only two

- **Pair 1 is correct**: Nagas and Nagis are indeed depicted on Toran and Vedika, representing the cult of the serpent, which was a significant part of ancient Indian religious symbolism.
- **Pair 2 is correct**: Yaksha and Yakshini are associated with wealth and fertility and are commonly represented in folk traditions, which were later incorporated into Hinduism and Jainism.
- **Pair 3 is incorrect**: The lotus symbolises purity, spiritual awakening and the birth of the Buddha. However, while it is related to the birth of Buddha, its primary representation is purity and spiritual awakening.

Thus, option (b) is the correct answer.

28. *(b)* Only two

- **Pair 1 is correct**: Scenes from Jataka stories are depicted in Toran and Vedika, representing the **past lives of the Buddha,** which are significant in Buddhist teachings.
- **Pair 2 is correct**: Fantastic animals are imaginary creatures not found in the real world and their depiction often adds a **mythical or symbolic dimension** to the narratives.
- **Pair 3 is incorrect**: While birds like swans and peacocks are depicted, they do not specifically symbolise the **birth of Buddha**; rather, they are part of the broader symbolic and decorative motifs that represent different aspects of life and **spirituality** in **Buddhist art.**

Thus, option (b) is the correct answer.

29. *(b)* Both Statement I and Statement II are correct and Statement II is not the correct explanation for Statement I.

- **Statement I is correct:** Architecture involves the complex **art and science of designing and constructing buildings** and other structures. Construction of memorials like the Humayun's **Tomb** serves as a **tribute to loved ones** while also being a remarkable piece of architectural design. Sculpture, on the other hand, is fundamentally **an expression of human creativity,** often without the utilitarian purpose that architecture carries. It aims to **evoke emotions,** tell stories, or represent abstract ideas through form, **texture and material.**
- **Statement II is correct:** In architecture, the use of diverse materials like stone, glass, metal and even sand ensures durability, strength and beauty. Sculptures, contrastingly, rely on a single material, such as stone, metal, or clay, **to convey the artist's vision.** The **singularity of material in sculpture emphasises purity of form and directness in artistic expression.**
- **However, Statement II does not directly explain Statement I:** The choice of materials in both architecture and sculpture relates to their specific functional and artistic needs rather than serving as an explanation of their fundamental nature.

Thus, option (b) is the correct answer.

30. *(a)* Only one

- **Statement 1 is correct: Bearded Priest** is one of the most iconic stone sculptures from the Indus Valley Civilisation, discovered in the **ruins of Mohenjodaro.** This sculpture, **made of steatite,** depicts a male figure with a contemplative expression, **adorned with a fillet** around his head, a **trefoil-patterned robe and** a trimmed beard.
- **Statement 2 is incorrect: Dancing Girl,** another famous artifact from the Indus Valley Civilisation, is not made of terracotta but of bronze and it was found in **Mohenjodaro, not Lothal.** This small yet evocative sculpture represents a young girl in a confident stance, **her right hand on her hip and** her left arm covered with **bangles.**
- **Statement 3 is correct: Lost-wax technique (Cire Perdu)** was used in the Indus Valley for creating metal sculptures like the **Dancing Girl.** This method involved making a wax model, covering it with clay to make a mold, then melting and removing the wax, then pouring molten metal into the mold. After the metal cooled, the clay was broken away to reveal the sculpture.

Thus, option (a) is the correct answer.

31. *(b)* Only two

- **Statement 1 is correct:** Sculptures from the Indus Valley Civilisation, such as the Bearded Priest and the Dancing Girl, **were indeed independent artifacts,** not part of larger architectural structures. This independence suggests that these sculptures were likely used for **religious, ritualistic, or decorative purposes, separate from their architectural surroundings.**
- **Statement 2 is correct:** In Indus Valley sculptures were made of **terracotta, stone and metal. Terracotta was widely used for making small figurines, toys and decorative objects,** such as the numerous female figurines representing fertility goddesses. Stone was another material, as seen in the Bearded Priest and other carved figures, which required precise workmanship. **Metal,** particularly bronze, was used for more refined and complex sculptures like the **Dancing Girl,** showcasing the advanced metallurgical techniques of the civilisation.
- **Statement 3 is incorrect:** Seals of the Indus Valley Civilisation were predominantly made from steatite, a soft stone that could be easily carved and then hardened by firing. While terracotta was also used for some seals, it was not the exclusive material.

Thus, option (b) is the correct answer.

32. *(d)* 1, 2 and 3

- Presence of **seals,** especially those **made of steatite,** is one of the strongest indicators of a complex trade network. These seals often featured animal motifs, scripts and symbols and were likely used to mark ownership or goods, akin to a form of branding or authentication.

- **Bronze sculptures like the Dancing Girl (found in Mohenjodaro)** highlight the sophisticated metallurgical skills that were likely in demand **both within and beyond the Indus Valley**. The complexity of the lost-wax technique required to create such sculptures indicates a **high degree of specialisation** and possibly a trade network that facilitated the exchange of **raw materials like copper and tin**, which are not locally abundant in the region.
- **Tools and pottery** are further evidence of trade. The standardised sizes and shapes of **Harappan pottery** suggest mass production, possibly for trade purposes.

All three artifacts indicate the existence of trade in the Indus Valley Civilisation.

Thus, option (d) is the correct answer.

33. *(a)* 1 and 2 only

- **Statement 1 is correct: Lomas Rishi Cave**, one of the earliest examples of rock-cut architecture in India, dates back to **Mauryan period**. It features an **elaborate facade** carved to **resemble wooden architecture**, complete with a semi-circular chaitya arch at the entrance. This cave was intended for use by the **Ajivikas**, an ascetic sect that predated **Buddhism and Jainism.**
- **Statement 2 is correct: Ashokan pillars,** particularly the one at Sarnath have inverted lotus symbolising spiritual awakening, while the animal motifs-such as lions, elephants and bulls-symbolise different virtues.
- **Statement 3 is incorrect**: Yaksha and Yakshini sculptures were not limited to the Southern part of India; rather, they were widespread across the subcontinent, particularly in northern and central India. The **Didarganj Yakshi, a well-known example from Bihar**, is a testament to the exquisite stone-carving skills of the period.

Thus, option (a) is the correct answer.

34. *(a)* Only one

- **Pair 1 is correct**: Four Lions capital at Sarnath has been adopted as the national emblem of India, featuring **four lions standing back to back**, symbolising **power, courage, pride and confidence.** Beneath the lions is a **circular abacus** adorned with a Dharma Chakra (wheel of law).
- **Pair 2 is incorrect: Bull and single lion** capital is associated with **Rampurva, not Sanchi.** This pillar features a beautifully carved bull, interpreted as symbolising **strength** and **perseverance,** qualities associated with the emperor's rule and the Buddhist path.
- **Pair 3 is incorrect**: Elephant capital from **Sankisa not from Rampurva** is another significant Ashokan artifact. The elephant symbolises **Buddha's conception**, where it is said that **Queen Maya** dreamt of a white elephant entering her womb, heralding the birth of Siddhartha Gautama (Buddha).

Thus, option (a) is the correct answer.

35. *(b)* Mauryan Period

- **Post-Mauryan period**, particularly from the 2nd century BCE to the 3rd century CE, was marked by the development of three distinct schools of art: **Gandhara, Mathura and Amaravati.** Gandhara school, influenced by **Greco-Roman art**, was known for its **realistic depictions of Buddha** in human form. **Mathura school,** was more indigenous, focusing on **robust and earthy representations** of Buddha. **Amaravati school,** flourishing in southern India, was known for its elaborate narrative reliefs depicting the life and teachings of the Buddha.
- **Influence of Greco-Roman art** on Indian sculpture. This **influence** is evident in **naturalistic treatment** of human body, use of **draped garments** similar to those seen in **Greek and Roman sculptures** and the **realistic portrayal** of figures.

Thus, option (b) is the correct answer.

36. *(d)* 1, 2 and 3

- **Pair 1 is correct**: Gandhara School of Art flourished under the patronage of the Shakas and Kushanas, who ruled over the North-Western regions of **India and parts of Central Asia.** Kushana king, Kanishka, extended his support of Buddhism and the arts, leading to the creation of exquisite examples of Gandharan sculpture.

- **Pair 2 is correct: Mathura School**, located in heart of **northern India**, was patronized by local rulers and the Kushanas. Kushanas, under rulers like Kanishka and Huvishka, contributed to development of this school. Mathura artists favoured use **of red sandstone and** their work is distinguished by its **spiritual expressiveness** and a more indigenous Indian style, focusing on the depiction of divine and royal figures with **symbolic gestures (Mudras)** and **serene expressions.**
- **Pair 3 is correct: Amaravati School**, which flourished in South-Eastern region of India, particularly in Andhra Pradesh area, was supported by the **Satavahana and Ikshvaku dynasties.** These rulers, who were strong patrons of Buddhism, oversaw creation of elaborate stupa complexes and narrative reliefs that depicted the **Jataka tales** (stories of the Buddha's previous lives).

Thus, option (d) is the correct answer.

37. *(b)* Only two

- **Statement 1 is correct**: Mathura School of Art is known for its extensive **use of locally sourced red sandstone. Reddish hue** of stone became a **hallmark of the Mathura School,** contributing to the distinct visual style that set it apart from the Gandhara and Amaravati schools.
- **Statement 2 is correct**: One of defining features of the **Mathura School of Art** was its focus on **depicting the inner beauty and calmness of its subjects**, particularly in representations of Buddha. This approach reflected the Indian aesthetic values of portraying divine figures with a sense of inner **peace and tranquility**, which was believed to inspire similar feelings in the viewer.
- **Statement 3 is incorrect**: While the Mathura School is renowned for its religious art, particularly the creation of Buddha images, it also included secular elements in its sculptures. It produced numerous images of Hindu deities, **Yakshas** (nature spirits) and **royal figures**, reflecting the diverse religious and cultural landscape of the region.

Thus, option (b) is the correct answer.

38. *(c)* 1 and 2 only

- **Statement 1 is correct: Nataraja sculpture** is one of most iconic representations of Lord Shiva, depicting him as the **cosmic dancer** performing **Ananda Tandava**, the **dance of bliss.** This dance represents the dynamic and cyclical nature of universe, where creation and destruction are in constant interplay.
- **Statement 2 is correct: Nataraja sculpture,** like many other Chola bronzes, was crafted using the lost-wax technique, also known as **Cire Perdue**. In this form, Shiva is shown with four arms, each holding symbolic objects or making specific gestures (Mudras) that convey deeper philosophical meanings.
- **Statement 3 is incorrect**: Dance of Shiva as Nataraja symbolises both creation and destruction, essential aspects of the cosmic cycle. Nataraja's sculpture captures this duality through various elements: **fire in one of Shiva's hands** represents power of destruction, while drum on another hand symbolises beat of creation. A figure of **Apasmara**, the dwarf demon crushed under **Shiva's foot**, represents ignorance, which is conquered by the divine dance.

Thus, option (c) is the correct answer.

39. *(a)* 1 and 2 only

- **Statement 1 is correct**: The relief carvings at Mahabalipuram, particularly the famous panel known as '**Arjuna's Penance**' or '**The Descent of the Ganges**', are indeed among the largest and most ancient sculptural panels in the world. This massive open-air rock relief, carved on two monolithic rocks, measures approximately **29 metres long and 13 metres high.**
- **Statement 2 is correct**: The relief at Mahabalipuram is traditionally interpreted as depicting the **descent of the river Ganga from the heavens to the Earth**, a story from Hindu mythology. According to the legend, **King Bhagiratha** performed intense penance to bring the **Ganga down** from the heavens to purify the ashes of his ancestors. The descent was so powerful that Lord Shiva had to break the fall of the river by catching it in his matted hair.

- **Statement 3 is incorrect:** While the Pallava period is celebrated for its remarkable contributions to architecture and sculpture, particularly in stone, it is **not known for** its extensive use of **metal in sculpture.** Pallavas primarily focused on rock-cut temples, such as the Shore Temple and the Pancha Rathas and on large-scale reliefs like those at Mahabalipuram.

Thus, option (a) is the correct answer.

40. *(c)* All three

- **Statement 1 is correct:** Chola period marked a high point in the production of **bronze sculptures,** particularly during the reigns of kings **like Rajaraja Chola I and his son Rajendra Chola I.** The Cholas patronised the arts extensively, commissioning large numbers of bronze sculptures for temples, which were meant to be carried in processions during religious festivals. T
- **Statement 2 is correct:** Among the many exquisite Chola bronzes, the Nataraja (Lord Shiva as the cosmic dancer) is undoubtedly the most iconic and widely recognised. The Nataraja sculpture represents the synthesis of Shiva's roles as creator, preserver and destroyer of the universe and conveys the cyclical nature of time.
- **Statement 3 is correct:** The majority of Chola sculptures were indeed religious in nature. These bronzes were created primarily for temple worship and professional purposes and they depict various Hindu deities such as Shiva, Vishnu, Parvati and others. Cholas also produced sculptures of **saints and devotees.**

This option (c) is the correct answer.

41. *(d)* 1, 2 and 3

- **Cream-coloured sandstone** softness made it ideal for intricate carvings, allowing artisans to produce finely **detailed images of deities,** especially in temples like those at Sarnath. **Seated Buddha statues** made from this sandstone are noted for their **serene expressions.**
- **Metal for sculptures:** The Gupta period witnessed use of metal, especially bronze, for making religious sculptures. Famous standing **Buddha from Sultanganj,** made of copper, is a prime example of the Gupta metallurgical skills.
- **Black stone** was another material commonly used during the Gupta period, particularly **for creation of Hindu deities.** The use of black stone provided a stark contrast to the cream-coloured sandstone and allowed for the depiction of intricate details, especially in relief work.

Thus, option (d) is the correct answer.

42. *(b)* Only two

- **Statement 1 is correct:** Gupta period is often referred to as Golden Age of India, partly due to the extensive use of **gold coins in trade.** These coins, known as Dinars, were issued by Gupta rulers and featured **intricate designs,** including images of the **kings and various deities.**
- **Statement 2 is correct:** Gupta rulers were known for their patronage of Buddhism, even though they were primarily Hindu. Kings like **Chandragupta II and Kumaragupta I** provided endowments to Buddhist institutions, which helped maintain the religious and cultural diversity of the empire. Emperor Kumaragupta I founded **Nalanda University.**
- **Statement 3 is incorrect:** Gupta art had a profound influence on South-East Asia, but the direct export of Gupta art i.e., the physical movement of artworks **was not as prevalent.** Instead, diffusion of cultural elements was facilitated by the movement of monks, traders and scholars, who carried with them the aesthetic and religious traditions of the Gupta Empire, leading to the development of distinct regional art forms in places like Cambodia, Thailand and Indonesia.

Thus, option (b) is the correct answer.

43. *(a)* Independent sculptures were 3-dimensional and free-standing, while relief sculptures were part of a larger architectural structure.

- **Independent sculptures** during the Early Medieval Phase were 3-dimensional images and designed to be viewed from multiple angles like the iconic bronze statue of Buddha from Gandhara, are fully 3-dimensional and can be viewed from any side.

- **Relief sculptures were integral parts of larger architectural structures** such as temple walls, pillars and gateways. These sculptures were not free-standing but were carved directly onto the surfaces of buildings. Relief sculptures could be either high relief, where the figures stand out significantly from the background, or low relief, where the carving is more shallow. me.

Thus, option (a) is the correct answer.

44. *(b)* Both Statement I and Statement II are correct and Statement II is the correct explanation for Statement I.

- **Statement 1 is correct: Gomateshwara statue**, also known as Bahubali, is indeed located at **Shravanabelagola in Karnataka.** It is one of the most important pilgrimage sites for Jains and is revered as a **symbol of renunciation, self-control** and the fight against woridly desires.
- **Statement 2 is correct:** It is recognised as one of the tallest monolithic (carved from a single piece of stone) free-standing statues in the world. Standing at about **57 feet (17 meters) tall.** The statue was carved out of a single block of granite and remains remarkably well-preserved, a testament to the skill of the artisans who created it.

However, Statement II is not the correct explanation for Statement I.

Thus, option (b) is the correct answer.

45. *(b)* Only two

- **Pair 1 is correct:** The **Mandap** is an assembly hall where **devotees gather for religious ceremonies, prayers and rituals.** The Mandap is often situated in front of the Garbhagriha (sanctum sanctorum) and may have different types depending on its function, such as the Rang Mandap for dance and music performances or the Utsav Mandap for festivals.
- **Pair 2 is incorrect: Shikhar** refers to the rising tower or spire above the Garbhagriha **symbolising the connection between the temple and the heavens,** serving as a visual representation of the spiritual ascent from the earthly to the divine. The stone disc-like structure mentioned in the question refers to the Amalaka, which is placed at the top of the Shikhar and represents the fruit of immortality or a lotus, symbolising the divine essence.
- **Pair 3 is correct:** The **Kalasha is the topmost point** of the temple structure, placed above the Amalaka on the Shikhar. It is often a pot-shaped structure **filled with water, grains, or other offerings**, symbolising **fertility, prosperity and the essence of life.** It represents the cosmic waters from which creation emerged and serves as a receptacle of divine blessings.

Thus, option (b) is the correct answer.

46. *(c)* All three

- **Pair 1 is correctly matched: Rekha Deul** is a term used in the Kalinga style of temple architecture, particularly in Odisha, to describe the **curvilinear shape of the Shikhar.** The Rekha Deul is characterised by its vertical ridges that taper towards the top, creating a smooth, curvilinear profile.
- **Pair 2 is correctly matched: Pitha Deul** refers to the **pyramidal structure of the Shikhar,** another significant feature of the Kalinga style. This structure is designed with stepped, tiered levels that give the Shikhar a pyramidal appearance. The pyramidal structure adds stability and grandeur to the temple, emphasising the **temple's sacred nature** and **its role as a spiritual axis.**
- **Pair 3 is correctly matched: Vimana** is a term used primarily in **Dravidian (South Indian)** temple architecture to refer to the tructure that includes the **Garbhagriha (sanctum sanctorum)**, the pyramidical superstructure above it and the Shikhar. The design of the Vimana is intended to represent **Mount Meru,** the cosmic mountain in **Hindu, Buddhist and Jain cosmology, symbolising** the axis of the universe and the connection between heaven and earth.

Thus, option (c) is the correct answer.

47. *(d)* The Garbhagriha is always located under the tallest tower of the temple.

- **Statement 1 is incorrect:** The Mandap is not situated above the Garbhagriha but rather in front of it. The Mandap serves as a space for congregational worship and other religious activities. It is typically an open, pillared hall that provides a transition from the outer parts of the temple to the innermost sanctum.

- **Statement 2 is incorrect**: The Shikhar is the **rising tower or spire above the Garbhagriha**, not above the Mandap. It serves as a symbolic connection between the earthly realm and the divine, guiding devotees towards the sanctum where the deity resides.
- **Statement 3 is incorrect**: The **Kalasha is placed at the very top of the Shikhar, above the Amalaka**, not below it. It represents the pot of nectar that emerged during the churning of the ocean (Samudra Manthan) in Hindu mythology, symbolising immortality, abundance and divine grace.
- **Statement 4 is correct**: The **Garbhagriha is the innermost sanctum** of the temple, where the main deity is enshrined. It is **always located under the tallest tower of the temple**, known as the Shikhar in the Nagara style or the Vimana in the Dravidian style. This architectural arrangement emphasises the central importance of the deity within the temple complex and symbolises the sacred axis that connects the earthly plane with the divine.

Thus, option (d) is the correct answer.

48. *(a)* 1 and 2 only

- **Option 1 is correct**: The **Panchayatana style** is a specific temple layout in which a **central shrine is surrounded by four subsidiary shrines at the four corners** of the temple complex, forming a quincunx. The Panchayatana layout allows for the simultaneous worship of multiple deities and reflects the syncretic nature of Hinduism.
- **Option 2 is correct**: The **curvilinear Shikhar, also known as Rekha Deul**, is characterised by its smooth, convex shape that tapers upward, creating a towering spire that rises above the Garbhagriha. The Shikhar is often decorated with vertical ridges or bands that emphasise its height and curvature, symbolising the upward spiritual journey from the earthly realm to the heavens.
- **Option 3 is incorrect**: The **Vesara style is a hybrid architectural style**, not specific to the Nagara style alone. The Vesara style emerged in the Deccan region during the rule of the Western Chalukyas and the Hoysalas and is characterised by a combination of the curvilinear Shikhar from Nagara and the stepped pyramidal Vimana from Dravida.

Thus, option (a) is the correct answer.

49. *(a)* 1 and 2 only

- **Statement 1 is correct**: The Nagara style of temple architecture typically does not include large water tanks or temple tanks (like the **Pushkarini in Dravidian temples**) in contrast to the Dravidian style of South India, where temple tanks are an integral part of the temple complex, used for ritualistic purposes. The **absence of water tanks in the Nagara style** can be attributed to the different climatic and cultural contexts in which this style developed.
- **Statement 2 is correct**: In the **Nagara style, the Garbhagriha**, which is the innermost sanctum of the temple where the main deity resides, is always located under the tallest tower, known as **the Shikhar**. The Shikhar serves as a visual focal point, **guiding devotees'** attention towards the sanctum and the divine presence within.
- **Statement 3 is incorrect**: Elaborate boundary walls and **grand gateway towers (Gopurams)** are more characteristic of Dravidian temple architecture in South India, rather than the Nagara style. Nagara temples typically have simpler enclosures and do not emphasise **grand entrances**. The focus in Nagara temples is primarily on the Shikhar and the overall verticality of the structure, rather than on elaborate peripheral elements.

Thus, option (a) is the correct answer.

50. *(c)* Vesara Style

- **Vesara Style**: The Vesara style is a distinct architectural style that emerged as a blend of the Nagara style of Northern India and the Dravida style of Southern India. This hybrid style is **particularly associated with the Deccan region** and was patronised by dynasties such as the Western Chalukyas and the Hoysalas.

- The Vesara style incorporates elements from both traditions: the **curvilinear Shikhar** from Nagara and the **pyramidal, tiered Vimana** from Dravida. The result is a unique architectural synthesis that combines the vertical emphasis of Nagara with the elaborate superstructure of Dravida.
- Temples built in the Vesara style often feature **intricate carvings**, complex layouts and a harmonious blend of Northern and Southern design elements. Prominent examples of Vesara architecture include the temples at **Badami, Aihole and Pattadakal.**

Thus, option (c) is the correct answer.

51. *(b)* Only two

- **Pair 1 is correctly matched:** The Konark Sun Temple, located in Odisha, built in the 13th **century by King Narasimhadeva I of the Eastern Ganga dynasty**, is designed as a massive chariot with 12 pairs of intricately carved stone wheels, pulled by seven horses. It is **dedicated to the Sun God, Surya.**
- **Pair 2 is incorrectly matched:** The Lingaraja Temple is located in Bhubaneswar, Odisha, not Gujarat built in the **Kalinga style of architecture**. The temple is dedicated to Lord Shiva and is noted for its majestic Shikhar, which rises to a **height of over 180 feet**, making it one of the tallest structures in Bhubaneswar.
- **Pair 3 is correctly matched:** The Jagannath Temple in Puri, Odisha, built in the Kalinga style of Nagara architecture is **dedicated to Lord Jagannath, a form of Vishnu and** is famous for its annual Rath Yatra (chariot festival), where the deities Jagannath, Balabhadra and Subhadra are paraded through the streets of Puri.

Thus, option (b) is the correct answer.

52. *(b)* Only two

- **Pair 1 is correctly matched:** Gavaksha is a distinctive architectural feature often found in **Nagara-style** temples. It is also known as the **'bull's eye' or 'cow's eye' and serves as a window or opening through which the deity within the temple is believed to gaze out into the world.**
- **Pair 2 is incorrectly matched:** The Kalasha is not the spire or pinnacle of a temple, but rather the **pot-like structure placed at the very top of the Shikhar, above the Amalaka.** It represents cosmic waters and the essence of life. It is often filled with sacred substances during the consecration of the temple and is a common feature in both Nagara and Dravidian temples.
- **Pair 3 is correctly matched:** The Amlaka is a large, **circular stone disc** that sits at the Kalasha's base, at the Shikhar's top. It is typically **ribbed or fluted**, resembling the cross-section of **a fruit (Amalaka or Amla, Indian gooseberry)** and symbolises the fruit of immortality.

Thus, option (b) is the correct answer.

53. *(c)* 3 only

- **Dravidian Temple Architecture** is a distinctive style that developed in the southern part of India, primarily under the **Pallavas, Cholas and Vijayanagara** empires. Unlike the Nagara style of North India, which features curvilinear towers known as Shikhars, the Dravidian style has a different terminology and structure.
- **Statement 1 is incorrect:** The **main temple tower** in Dravidian architecture is called a **Vimana**, not a Shikhar. The term Shikhar is specific to the Nagara style of North India, where it refers to the curving, tower-like structure above the sanctum.
- **Statement 2 is incorrect:** Dravidian temples **do not feature the curved Shikhar.** Instead, the Vimana in Dravidian architecture is generally **more geometric, often resembling a stepped pyramid.** These structures are adorned with intricate carvings and rise vertically in a stepped fashion, unlike the curvilinear forms in Nagara temples.
- **Statement 3 is correct:** The Vimana in Dravidian architecture rises geometrically, reflecting the influence of the indigenous architecture of the southern regions. The stepped nature of the Vimana symbolises the **transition from the earthly to the divine,** with each tier representing a different level of spiritual ascent.

Thus, option (c) is the correct answer.

54. *(c)* 1, 2 and 3

- **Option 1 is correct:** The Vimana is the most prominent feature of Dravidian temples, serving as the **tower or spire above the Garbhagriha** (sanctum sanctorum). It is typically **pyramidal** and is adorned with detailed sculptures that depict various deities, mythological stories and other symbolic motifs.
- **Option 2 is correct:** The Gopuram is the **monumental entrance tower** that leads into the temple complex. These towers are **often taller than the Vimana** itself and are richly decorated with intricate carvings and statues. The presence of multiple Gopurams in a single temple complex is common, each marking a different entrance.
- **Option 3 is correct:** The Mandapa is the **pillared hall or pavilion that serves as a space for worship**, rituals and gatherings. In Dravidian temples, the Mandapa can range from a simple structure to a large, elaborate hall with intricately carved pillars. It often precedes the Garbhagriha and provides an area where devotees can gather before approaching the sanctum.

Thus, option (c) is the correct answer.

55. *(b)* 1 only

- **Pair 1 is incorrectly matched:** Located in **Mahabalipuram**, the Ratha temples are **monolithic rock-cut structures** resembling chariots (Rathas) constructed during the reign of **Narasimhavarman I (Mamalla)** of the **Pallava dynasty in the 7th century**. Each Ratha is dedicated to a different deity and is an early example of the Dravidian style of architecture.
- **Pair 2 is correctly matched:** Shore temple is indeed associated with the **Pallavas.** Also located in Mahabalipuram, the Shore Temple is a structural temple built by Narasimhavarman II (**Rajasimha**) **in the 8th century**. It is one of the earliest stone-built temples in Southern India and is notable for its **twin shrines dedicated to Shiva and Vishnu**, showcasing the early transition from rock-cut to structural temple architecture in the Dravidian style.
- **Pair 3 is correctly matched:** Brihadeshwar magnificent temple was built by **Raja Raja Chola I in the early 11th century in Tanjore (Thanjavur)**. Its massive Vimana rises to a height of 216 feet (66 meters). The temple complex includes extensive mural paintings, intricate sculptures and a colossal statue of Nandi (the bull, mount of Shiva), reflecting the grandeur of **Chola temple architecture**.

Thus, option (b) is the correct answer.

56. *(d)* 1, 2 and 3

- **Statement 1 is correct:** Vesara Style is indeed a **hybrid** that combines elements of both the Nagara (North Indian) and Dravidian (South Indian) architectural styles. It **emerged in the Deccan region** during the rule of the Chalukyas of Badami and later flourished under the Hoysala dynasty.
- **Statement 2 is correct:** Vesara temples are often **built on elevated platforms**, which adds to their grandeur and visibility. The **stellate (star-shaped)** plan is a distinctive feature, particularly in Hoysala temples. This plan creates multiple projections and recesses in the temple structure, enhancing its visual complexity and allowing for more elaborate carvings on the exterior walls.
- **Statement 3 is correct:** The Hoysala dynasty is known for its significant contributions to Vesara architecture. Temples like the **Hoysaleswara Temple at Halebidu** and the **Chennakesava Temple at Belur** are renowned for their intricate sculptures, detailed friezes and complex stellate plans.

Thus, option (d) is the correct answer.

57. *(d)* 1, 2 and 3

- **Option 1 is correct:** In Vesara temples, it is not uncommon to find **multiple Garbhagrihas** (sanctums) within a single temple complex. Each Garbhagriha typically houses a different deity, reflecting the pluralistic and inclusive nature of worship in the Deccan region during this period.
- **Option 2 is correct:** The intricate carvings and detailed sculptures seen in Vesara temples are heavily influenced by the Dravidian style. The exterior walls, pillars and doorways of these temples are **adorned with elaborate**

depictions of gods, goddesses, mythological scenes and floral motifs. The influence of Dravidian style is evident in the use of tiered and elaborately carved Vimanas.

- **Option 3 is correct:** The **star-shaped (stellate) plan** is a hallmark of Vesara architecture, especially in Hoysala temples. This plan creates a dynamic and complex exterior, with numerous projections and recesses that enhance the overall aesthetic appeal of the temple.

Thus, option (d) is the correct answer.

58. *(d)* 1, 2 and 3

- **Statement 1 is correct:** The **Nagara style** of temple architecture, prevalent in northern India, is characterised by its focus on the **main shrine and its tower (Shikhar).** Unlike the Dravidian style, which often features extensive boundary walls and **elaborate gateways (Gopurams)**, Nagara temples typically do not have such external enclosures.
- **Statement 2 is correct:** In the Nagara style, the **Garbhagriha** (sanctum sanctorum) is always located under the tallest tower, known as the Shikhar. The **Shikhar** serves as the visual and spiritual focal point of the temple, symbolising the **axis mundi (cosmic axis)** that connects the earthly realm with the divine.
- **Statement 3 is correct:** The **Panchayatana style** is a common feature in Nagara temples, where the main shrine is surrounded by **four subsidiary shrines**, usually placed at the four corners of the temple complex. This arrangement **symbolises the cosmic order**, with the central deity representing the axis of the universe and the subsidiary shrines representing the four cardinal directions.

Thus, option (d) is the correct answer.

59. *(a)* 1 and 2 only

- **Option 1 is correct:** The most distinctive feature of Nagara-style temples is the **Curvilinear Shikhar**, which is a towering spire that rises above the Garbhagriha. The Shikhar is usually adorned with intricate carvings and is often topped with a Kalasha (finial) and an Amalaka (circular disc), symbolising the connection between the earthly and celestial realms.
- **Option 2 is correct: Panchayatana style** is a layout in which the main shrine is surrounded by four subsidiary shrines. This layout is prevalent in Nagara temples and reflects the architectural emphasis on symmetry and cosmic symbolism.
- **Option 3 is incorrect:** The **Stellate plan** (star-shaped ground plan) is not characteristic of the Nagara style. It is more commonly associated with the Vesara style, particularly in Hoysala temples, where the star-shaped plan allows for complex and intricate carvings on the temple walls. Therefore, statement 3 does not apply to Nagara architecture.

Thus, option (a) is the correct answer.

60. *(a)* A tall building with a sugar loaf shape, resembling a Shikhar.

- **Rekha Deul** is a type of temple tower (Deul) found in the Kalinga style of architecture, which is predominant in Odisha. The term 'Rekha' means 'straight line' in Odia and it refers to the verticality and linearity of the Deul, which rises straight up in a **sugar loaf shape.** This curvilinear form closely resembles the Shikhar of Nagara temples, though it is distinct in its simplicity and emphasis on vertical height.
- Rekha Deul temples are often associated with the main sanctum and their towering presence is designed to draw the **devotee's gaze upward,** symbolising the ascent towards the divine. These structures are typically adorned with **intricate carvings** that depict various deities, mythological scenes and floral patterns, reflecting the rich artistic traditions of the region.

Thus, option (a) is the correct answer.

61. *(a)* Only one

- **Pair 1 is incorrectly matched:** As explained earlier, a Rekha Deul is a tall, curvilinear structure resembling a Shikhar, not a building with a barrel-vaulted roof. This type of Deul is characterised by its straight, vertical lines and the sugar loaf shape that gives it a unique and striking appearance.
- **Pair 2 is correctly matched:** This type of Deul features a **pyramidal-shaped roof** and is often square in plan. It is typically used for

assembly halls or other subsidiary structures in Odisha temples. The Pidha Deul is designed to complement the **towering Rekha Deul**, creating a harmonious architectural ensemble.

- **Pair 3 is correctly matched**: The Khakhara Deul is a **rectangular building with a truncated pyramid-shaped roof**, often used for temples dedicated to female deities. The roof shape is similar to the Gopuram found in Dravidian temples, though it is adapted to the regional style of Odisha.

Thus, option (a) is the correct answer.

62. *(d)* 1, 2 and 3

- **Statement 1 is correct**: In the Solanki or **Maru-Gurjara school** of temple architecture, which flourished in Gujarat and Rajasthan, the **Garbhagriha** (sanctum) is intricately connected to the Mandapa (pillared hall) both internally and externally. This connection allows for a smooth transition between the inner sanctum and the outer halls, facilitating the flow of devotees and the performance of rituals.
- **Statement 2 is correct**: The **Toranas** are decorative arched gateways that are a hallmark of Maru-Gurjara architecture. The Toranas serve both as an ornamental feature and as a symbolic threshold, marking the transition from the secular world to the sacred space of the temple.
- **Statement 3 is correct**: The **walls of the central shrine** (Garbhagriha) in Solanki temples are typically **devoid of carvings**, emphasising the sanctity and simplicity of the inner sanctum. The absence of carvings in the Garbhagriha contrasts with the richly decorated outer walls and pillars, highlighting the central shrine's purity and spiritual significance.

Thus, option (d) is the correct answer.

63. *(a)* 1 and 2 only

- **Statement 1 is incorrect**: The Ahom style of temple architecture was influenced by the arrival of the **Tais from Burma in the early 13th century**, not the 17th century as mentioned. The Ahoms established their kingdom in Assam and the 17th century marked a significant period of temple construction, especially with the rebuilding of important temples like the Kamakhya Temple.
- **Statement 2 is incorrect**: Ahom temples do indeed feature idol worship. The Ahoms, originally **followers of animism** and ancestor worship, gradually adopted Hinduism, particularly Shaktism and began building temples dedicated to Hindu deities.
- **Statement 3 is correct**: The **Kamakhya Temple** in Guwahati is a prominent example of the Ahom style of architecture. This temple, dedicated to **Goddess Kamakhya**, is one of the oldest and most revered Shakti Peethas in India. It does not house a conventional idol but instead venerates the yoni (vagina) of the goddess, symbolised by a rock formation. Constructed by the Ahom king Nara Narayan in the 17th century, showcasing a fusion of local, Pala and Ahom architectural styles.

Thus, option (a) is the correct answer.

64. *(a)* 1 and 2 only

- **Option 1 is correct**: The **Pala/Sena style** of temple architecture, which flourished in Bengal and Bihar from the 8th to the 13th century, is known for its use of **black-to-grey basalt and chlorite stone**. These materials were favoured for their durability and the fine detailing they allowed in sculptural work.
- **Option 2 is correct**: The **Bangla roof** is another characteristic feature of the Pala/Sena style. This roof style is inspired by the traditional thatched huts of Bengal, with a curving or sloping side that resembles the shape of a bamboo roof.
- **Option 3 is incorrect: Toranas**, or decorative arched gateways, are not a prominent feature of the Pala/Sena style. They are more commonly associated with the **Solanki/ Maru-Gurjara school** of architecture, where they serve as ornate entranceways to the temple complex.

Thus, option (a) is the correct answer.

65. *(c)* Pala/Sena Style

- **Pala dynasty** ruled over Bihar and Bengal from the 8th to the 12th centuries and their reign was marked by the flourishing of **Buddhist architecture**, particularly the Mahaviharas (great monasteries) like Nalanda and Vikramshila.

- The **Vanga style** refers to the regional architectural and artistic traditions of Bengal. **Bangla roof** is a distinctive feature of Pala/Sena architecture, inspired by the **traditional rural huts of Bengal.** The roof is characterised by its sloping sides, which mimic the bamboo and thatch construction of the region.These temples often served as important centers for the **propagation of Mahayana Buddhism.**

Thus, option (c) is the correct answer.

66. *(d)* 1, 2 and 3

- **Statement 1 is correct:** The **Khajuraho temples** were built primarily under the patronage of the Chandela dynasty between the 10th and 12th centuries. The temples are located in Madhya Pradesh and are renowned for their architectural beauty and intricate sculpture work. The Chandelas were devout followers of Hinduism and Jainism and their temples reflect the religious and cultural diversity of the region.
- **Statement 2 is correct:** The **Panchayatana style** is a distinctive feature of Khajuraho temples. In this style, the main shrine (Garbhagriha) is surrounded by four subsidiary shrines, often placed at the four corners of the temple platform. This layout symbolises the centrality of the main deity and the cosmic order represented by the subsidiary deities.
- **Statement 3 is correct:** The **Khajuraho temples** are famous for their **erotic sculptures**, which depict various **forms of human sexuality and sensuality.** These sculptures are believed to be heavily influenced by **Vatsyayana's Kamasutra**, an ancient Indian text on love, sex and relationships. The erotic art of Khajuraho is integrated into the temple's exterior walls, interspersed with **depictions of gods, goddesses, celestial beings and everyday life.** The sculptures are not just about sensuality but also represent the cycle of life, the **union of male and female principles** and the spiritual journey.

Thus, option (d) is the correct answer.

67. *(a)* 1 and 2 only

- **Statement 1 is correct: Pala/Sena style** of temple architecture was indeed patronised between the 9th and 13th centuries in the regions of **Southern Bihar and Bengal.** They were a great supporter of Buddhism and under their reign, many significant Buddhist monuments were constructed.
- **Statement 2 is correct:** Pala/Sena style is noted for its use of black-to-grey basalt stone and chlorite stone, which were locally available in the region. These materials were used to create finely detailed sculptures and temple structures.
- **Statement 3 is incorrect:** The geographical focus of the Pala/Sena style is in the eastern part of India, specifically in the regions that now constitute the states of **West Bengal, Bihar and parts of Bangladesh** not in North-Western India.

Thus, option (a) is the correct answer.

68. *(d)* 1, 2 and 3

- **Option 1 is correct:** Chola temples were often enclosed by high walls, which served both **protective and symbolic purposes.** These walls demarcated the sacred space of the temple, separating it from the **mundane world outside.** The presence of such walls was a common feature in large Chola temples, such as the **Brihadeshwara Temple in Thanjavur.**
- **Option 2 is correct:** The entrance to Chola temples was marked by **towering gateways known as gopurams.** These gopurams were **intricately decorated** with carvings and served as an imposing entry point to the temple complex. The grandeur of these structures reflected the power and devotion of the Chola rulers.
- **Option 3 is correct:** The Khajuraho temples are renowned for their erotic sculptures, inspired by **Vatsyayana's Kamasutra** (an ancient Indian text on love, sex and relationships). Carved with **depictions of deities and everyday life** on the outer walls of the temple, these Khajuraho arts **symbolize not just sensuality** but also the cycle of life, the union of male and female and the spiritual journey.

Thus, option (d) is the correct answer.

69. *(a)* 1 and 2 only

- **Option 1 is correct:** The vimana is the tower above the sanctum sanctorum (Garbhagriha). In Chola architecture, the Vimana often **features an octagonal dome**, a distinctive element that sets it apart from other styles. This octagonal shape not only adds to the aesthetic appeal but also showcases the advanced architectural knowledge of the **Chola builders.**
- **Option 2 is correct:** Dvarapalas are guardian figures that are placed at the entrance of the temple. These figures, often depicted in **a fierce and protective stance**, symbolise the guardianship of the temple, **warding off evil forces.** This feature is commonly seen in Chola temples and adds to the grandeur of the temple entrance.
- **Option 3 is incorrect:** The Panchayatana style, where the main shrine is surrounded by four **subsidiary shrines**, is more associated with the Nagara style of temple architecture, particularly in Northern India. It is not a characteristic **feature of Chola architecture**, which primarily focuses on the **central sanctum** and its surrounding structures.

Thus, option (a) **is the correct answer.**

70. *(d)* 1 and 3 only

- **Statement 1 is incorrect:** The Brihadeshwara Temple in Thanjavur is known for its colossal Vimana, which is one of the **tallest in the world**. The 90-tonne monolithic Shikhara not Mandapa of this temple is octagonal, which is a hallmark of Chola architecture.
- **Statement 2 is correct:** The entrance of the Brihadeshwara Temple is adorned with large gopurams, which are gateway towers typical of Dravidian architecture.
- **Statement 3 is incorrect:** The temple was built by Raja Raja Chola I, not Rajendra Chola, who was his son. While Rajendra Chola also built significant temples, the Brihadeshwara Temple at Thanjavur is specifically attributed to Raja Raja Chola I.

Thus, option (d) is the correct answer.

71. *(a)* 1 and 2 only

- **Statement 1 is correct:** Pallava architecture began with rock-cut cave temples, as seen in the Mahendra group under King **Mahendravarman I.** These temples were simple in design but marked the beginning of structural innovation in South India.
- **Statement 2 is correct:** The Pallava king Narasimhavarman I, also known as Mamalla, is credited with constructing the **rock-cut rathas at Mahabalipuram.** These rathas, named after the Pandavas, are monolithic structures carved out of single rocks and represent an early form of structural temples.
- **Statement 3 is incorrect:** The **Shore Temple at Mahabalipuram, a UNESCO World Heritage site,** was built during the reign of **Narasimhavarman II, also known as Rajasimha.** The Shore Temple is one of the earliest structural temples in South India, marking a transition from rock-cut to freestanding architecture.

Thus, option (a) **is the correct answer.**

72. *(d)* 1, 2 and 3

- **Option 1 is correct:** The **Narasimha group at Mahabalipuram** is known for its Mandapas, which are separate from the main temple structure and are shaped like chariots (rathas). Each ratha represents a different deity and is named after a member of the Pandava brothers. This innovation allowed for greater architectural experimentation and variety in temple design.
- **Option 2 is correct: Dvarapalas are guardian figures** that are commonly found at the entrance of temples from this period. These figures are depicted as fierce protectors and are intricately carved, showcasing the Pallavas' skill in stone sculpture.
- **Option 3 is correct:** The cave temple of **Mandagapattu**, which is a part of this architectural tradition, is **dedicated to the Trimurti - Brahma, Vishnu and Shiva.** This temple is an excellent example of early Pallava rock-cut architecture and reflects the religious syncretism of the time.

Thus, option (d) **is the correct answer.**

73. *(b)* Narasimhavarman I

Narasimhavarman I, also known as Mamalla, was a Pallava king who made significant contributions to the development of South Indian temple architecture:

- **Construction of Rathas at Mahabalipuram:** Narasimhavarman I is credited with the creation of the monolithic rathas at Mahabalipuram. These rathas, carved out of single pieces of rock, represent a significant advancement in the transition from rock-cut caves to structural temples. Each ratha is intricately carved and reflects the Pallava's architectural innovation.
- **Shore Temple:** Narasimhavarman I also initiated the construction of the Shore Temple at Mahabalipuram, although it was completed by his successors. This temple, which stands on the seashore, is one of the earliest examples of structural temples in South India.

Thus, option (b) is the correct answer.

74. *(a)* 1 and 2 only

- **Statement 1 is correct:** High boundary walls served both protective and ritualistic purposes, separating the sacred space of the temple from the outside world. The high boundary walls are a distinctive feature of Chola architecture and are evident in many of their grand temples.
- **Statement 2 is correct:** The **Vimana is the towering structure above the sanctum** and it is often crowned with an **octagonal dome**. Chola temples also feature large gopurams, which are intricately decorated gateway towers that lead into the temple complex.
- **Statement 3 is incorrect:** The Chola temples did not generally follow the Panchayatana style (a style where the main shrine is surrounded by four subsidiary shrines). The Panchayatana style is more common in Nagara temples, whereas the Chola temples usually followed the Dravida style.

Thus, option (a) is the correct answer.

75. *(c)* 2 only

- **Pair 1 is incorrectly matched:** Brihadeshwara Temple, Thanjavur was built by Raja Raja Chola I in 1010 CE. It is notable for its towering Vimana (temple tower) and the massive stone Shikhara (topmost part of the Vimana), which weighs approximately 80 tonnes.
- **Pair 2 is correctly matched: Airatesvara Temple, Thanjavur** was indeed built by **Rajaraja II** and it is smaller compared to the Brihadeshwara Temple. The temple's sanctum is without a circumambulatory path, which is a unique feature among Chola temples.
- **Pair 3 is incorrectly matched:** Brihadeshwara Temple, Gangaikondacholapuram was built by **Rajendra Chola I**, not by Rajaraja Chola I. It was constructed to commemorate Rajendra Chola's victories in the northern regions and served as the capital of the Chola Empire.

Thus, option (c) is the correct answer.

76. *(a)* 1 and 2 only

- **Statement 1 is correct:** Vijayanagara temples are renowned for their large, towering gopurams (gateway towers) and elaborately designed **chariot mandaps (pillared halls).** These features are particularly prominent in temples such as the **Virupaksha Temple** and the **Vittala Temple.**
- **Statement 2 is correct:** The temples of Vijayanagara are also known for their **intricately carved pillars and chariot mandapas.**, many of which depict scenes from Hindu mythology, animals and floral motifs.
- **Statement 3 is incorrect:** While the **Virupaksha Temple** is one of the most important and famous temples in **Hampi**, it was originally built by **Lakkan Dandesha**, a Nayaka **under the ruler Deva Raya II**, in the 7th century and later expanded by the Vijayanagara rulers.

Thus, option (a) is the correct answer.

77. *(d)* 1, 2 and 3

- **Statement 1 is correct:** One of the most distinctive features of **Nayaka architecture** is the construction of large mandaps with numerous pillars, often numbering in the hundreds or thousands. The **1000-pillar mandap** in the **Meenakshi Temple** at **Madurai** is a famous example.

- **Statement 2 is correct**: Nayaka temples are known for their detailed and intricate carvings on the temple walls, depicting scenes from Hindu mythology, daily life and nature. These carvings are often highly stylized and elaborate, showcasing the artisans' skill and creativity.
- **Statement 3 is correct**: The Nayakas were also responsible for the construction of **massive gopurams (temple towers)** that served as grand entrances to the temple complex. These gopurams often featured a **pillared portico**, adding to the architectural splendor of the temple.

Thus, option (d) is the correct answer.

78. *(b)* 2 and 3 only

- **Statement 1 is incorrect**: While Pandya architecture includes rock-cut sculptures, the mention of a **1000-pillar mandap is more closely associated with the later Nayaka period**, particularly in the Meenakshi Temple at Madurai. Thus, the first statement is partially correct but misleading.
- **Statement 2 is correct**: The **Meenakshi Temple** is one of the most significant examples of **Pandya architecture**. The temple complex is famous for its large gopurams, extensive mandaps and intricate sculptures, making it a masterpiece of South Indian temple architecture.
- **Statement 3 is correct**: The typical layout of Pandya temples includes a garbhagriha (sanctum sanctorum), an ardhamandap (anteroom or vestibule) and a larger mahamandap (hall).

Thus, option (b) is the correct answer.

79. *(b)* 2 only

- **Statement 1 is incorrect**: **Kailashnath Temple at Ellora** is an outstanding example of **Dravidian architecture**, despite being located in the Deccan region, traditionally associated with the Nagara style. The temple was carved out of a single rock and is dedicated to Lord Shiva.
- **Statement 2 is correct**: Most Rashtrakuta temples, including the Kailashnath Temple, are located in Maharashtra, particularly in the region around Ellora and Ajanta. The Rashtrakutas were known for their patronage of rock-cut architecture, which has left a lasting legacy in this area.

Thus, option (b) is the correct answer.

80. *(a)* Chalukyas of Kalyani

- The **Chalukyas of Kalyani**, also known as the **Western Chalukyas**, ruled over Karnataka during the 10th to 12th centuries. They are known for their contributions to the Vesara style of temple architecture:
- **Ruling Period**: The Chalukyas of Kalyani were a powerful dynasty in the Deccan region, with their capital at Kalyani (modern-day Basavakalyan in Karnataka).
- **Vesara Style of Temple Architecture**: The Chalukyas of Kalyani played a crucial role in developing the Vesara style, which is a hybrid of the Nagara and Dravidian styles.
- **Virupaksha Temple at Pattadakal**: The Virupaksha Temple, a UNESCO World Heritage site, was built by the Chalukyas of Kalyani and is one of the finest examples of Vesara architecture.

Thus, option (a) is the correct answer.

81. *(b)* 2 and 3 only

- **Statement 1 is incorrect**: Ayodhya Ram Temple was built in the **Nagara style** of temple architecture, not the Dravidian style. It is characterised by a curvilinear tower (shikhara) over the sanctum sanctorum. The temple features **five mandaps named Nritya, Ranga, Sabha, Prarthana and Kirtan**, which are typical elements of a Nagara-style temple.
- **Statement 2 is correct**: The temple's main entrance, known as **Singh Dwar**, is located on the eastern side. This entrance is notable for its **32 ascending stairs**, which add to the grandeur and symbolic significance of the temple. The eastern entrance aligns with **traditional Vastu principles**, emphasising the importance of the eastern direction in Hindu temple architecture.
- **Statement 3 is correct**: The construction of the **Ayodhya Ram Temple** avoids the use of iron and steel, instead relying on traditional methods and materials. This approach showcases the application of **ancient technology**, **wherein the temple's**

construction emphasises the use of materials like stone and wood, which have been used in Indian temple architecture for centuries.

Thus, option (b) is the correct answer.

82. *(c)* All three

- **Pair 1 is correctly matched: Bhattiprolu Relic Casket Inscription** is located in present-day **Andhra Pradesh**, Bhattiprolu is an ancient Buddhist site where **relics were found** inside a casket. The inscription is written in Bhattiprolu script, which is a precursor to the Telugu script and a variant of the early Brahmi script.
- **Pair 2 is correctly matched: Sohgaura Copper Plate Inscription**, found in Gorakhpur, Uttar Pradesh, is one of the earliest known examples of an Indian **copper plate inscription**, dating back to the 3rd century BCE. Written in **Prakrit language and Brahmi script** it records measures taken to mitigate a famine, including the establishment of grain depots (Kosthagaras) by local authorities.
- **Pair 3 is correctly matched: Bairat Pillar Inscription** located in **Bairat, Rajasthan** is one of the earliest Jain inscriptions, believed to be written by Emperor Ashoka. It is inscribed on a stone pillar and is written in Brahmi script. It emphasises the importance of **non-violence (Ahimsa) and ethical living.**

Thus, option (c) is the correct answer.

83. *(b)* 2 only

- **Statement 1 is incorrect**: While the Mauryan Age, particularly **under Emperor Ashoka**, is famous for its use of stone pillars **inscribed with edicts**, the use of pillars in India predates the Mauryan period. Simple brick pillars have been discovered in the Indus Valley Civilisation, particularly in structures like the **Pillared Hall at Mohenjodaro.**
- **Statement 2 is correct**: During the Pre-Mauryan Age, pillars were **primarily used in forts** and other architectural structures for support. These pillars were likely made of wood and brick, as stone pillars became more common later, particularly during the Mauryan period.

Thus, option (b) is the correct answer.

84. *(d)* 1, 2 and 3

- **Statement 1 is correct.** The Mauryan Age, especially under **Emperor Ashoka**, is renowned for its stone pillars, typically made of a single **piece of polished sandstone** and often topped with animal capitals. These pillars were not just architectural elements but also carried inscriptions known as Ashokan edicts.
- **Statement 2 is correct. James Prinsep**, a British scholar and antiquary, is credited with deciphering the **Brahmi script in 1837**, used in many of Ashoka's inscriptions. Prinsep's work marked a significant advancement in Indian epigraphy and ancient history.
- **Statement 3 is correct.** The **Kandahar Rock Inscription**, located in modern-day Afghanistan, is unique among Ashoka's inscriptions as it is **bilingual and written in both Greek and Aramaic.** This inscription reflects Ashoka's efforts to communicate his Buddhist policies to the **Hellenistic** world following Alexander the Great's conquests.

Thus, option (d) is the correct answer.

85. *(d)* 1, 2 and 3

- **Statement 1 is correct.** Stone pillars used by Ashoka are one of the most iconic symbols of the Mauryan Age. The pillars are masterpieces of Mauryan architecture, characterised by their polished surfaces and intricate capitals, such as the **Lion Capital at Sarnath.**
- **Statement 2 is correct.** Excavations at sites like **Kumrahar and Bulandibagh** in Patna (ancient Pataliputra) have unearthed remains of the Mauryan period, including evidence of Ashoka's pillars and other architectural structures.
- **Statement 3 is correct. Megasthenes, the Greek ambassador** to the Mauryan court, mentioned a magnificent **wooden pillar palace in Pataliputra**, constructed during the reign of Chandragupta Maurya, Ashoka's grandfather.

Thus, option (d) is the correct answer.

86. *(c)* All three

- **Option 1 is correct**: This site contains one of the lesser-known Minor Rock Edicts of Ashoka. The inscription at Bahapur is significant as it marks the **northernmost extent of Ashoka's empire.** The edict emphasises Ashoka's moral precepts and his efforts to propagate Buddhism.

- **Option 2 is correct**: The **Bairat Minor Rock Edict** is another crucial site where Ashoka's messages are preserved. This inscription is particularly important as it reveals Ashoka's instructions to his local administrators and the Buddhist monks, emphasising non-violence and ethical conduct.
- **Option 3 is correct**: Located in the **Rewa district of Madhya Pradesh, the Rupnath Minor Rock Edict** is another example of Ashoka's extensive communication network. The inscription reiterates the themes of Dharma and Ashoka's dedication to the well-being of his subjects.

Thus, option (c) is the correct answer.

87. *(a)* 1 and 2 only

- **Statement 1 is correct**: The Major Rock Edicts of Ashoka have been discovered at **10 major locations across India, such as Dhauli, Girnar, Kalsi** and others. These edicts, inscribed on large rock surfaces, were intended to communicate Ashoka's policies of Dharma (righteousness) and his governance principles.
- **Statement 2 is correct**: The inscriptions in Ashoka's Major Rock Edicts refer to him as **'Devanampiya Piyadasi'**, which translates to **'Beloved of the Gods, He who looks on with Affection'**. This title reflects Ashoka's transformation into a benevolent ruler and helped him establish his authority and the moral legitimacy of his rule across his empire.
- **Statement 3 is incorrect**: The **Kandahar inscription, found in modern-day Afghanistan**, is unique among Ashoka's inscriptions because it is written in **Greek and Aramaic**, not in Prakrit and Brahmi. This bilingual inscription reflects the cultural and linguistic diversity of Ashoka's empire.

Thus, option (a) is the correct answer.

88. *(d)* None

- **Pair 1 is correctly matched**. This edict reflects **Ashoka's commitment to non-violence**, particularly in the treatment of animals. This edict also led to the **establishment of animal hospitals** and the prohibition of certain forms of hunting and animal sacrifice.
- **Pair 2 is correctly matched**. This edict emphasises **religious tolerance and respect for all sects**. Ashoka recognised the diversity of religious practices within his empire and advocated for mutual respect and understanding among different communities.
- **Pair 3 is correctly matched**. The thirteenth edict describes **Ashoka's deep remorse** over the massive loss of life in the Kalinga War and his subsequent embrace of Buddhism. Ashoka's experience in Kalinga marked a turning point in his life and reign, leading him to renounce violence and promote Dharma as a guiding principle of his administration.

Thus, option (d) is the correct answer.

89. *(d)* 1, 2 and 3

- **Statement 1 is correct**. The Ashokan pillars are renowned for their **craftsmanship**, particularly the use of a **single piece of polished sandstone**, which was quarried from specific regions like **Chunar in Uttar Pradesh.**
- **Statement 2 is correct**. The capitals of the Ashokan pillars often depicted animal figures such as lions, bulls and elephants. The most famous of these is the **Lion Capital at Sarnath**, which features four lions sitting back to back. This capital was later adopted as the national emblem of India.
- **Statement 3 is correct**. The pillars were inscribed with Ashoka's edicts, which were written in the Brahmi script. These inscriptions conveyed messages of **Dharma and guided ethical living, religious tolerance and social welfare.**

Thus, option (d) is the correct answer.

90. *(d)* 1, 2 and 3

- **Option 1 is correct**: The shaft of an Ashokan pillar was typically monolithic. The shafts were polished to a **high sheen and tapered slightly towards the top**. The uniformity and precision of the shafts are remarkable, showcasing the high level of craftsmanship achieved by Mauryan artisans.

- **Option 2 is correct:** The capital sat atop the shaft and was the most decorative part of the pillar. It typically featured **animal sculptures such as lions, bulls, or elephants.** The **Lion Capital at Sarnath** is the most famous example, depicting four lions standing back to back.
- **Option 3 is correct:** The abacus was the **platform on which the animal figures of the capital were placed.** Usually circular or rectangular, it served both a decorative and functional purpose, acting as a base for the capital and adding to the overall stability of the structure.

Thus, option (d) is the correct answer.

91. *(c)* 1 and 3 only

- **Statement 1 is correct:** The Lion Capital of Sarnath, like many other Ashokan pillars, was made from **Chunar sandstone.** This particular type of sandstone was favoured for its durability and fine grain, which allowed for intricate carving and polishing.
- **Statement 2 is incorrect:** While the four lions in the Lion Capital are often associated with the spread of Buddhism, they **do not specifically represent the Four Noble Truths.** Instead, they are symbolic of Ashoka's rule and the **spread of his Dharma across the four cardinal directions.**
- **Statement 3 is correct:** The Lion Capital was adopted as the National Emblem of India on **26th January, 1950.** The emblem represents the **power, courage and confidence** of the nation. It also serves as a reminder of India's rich cultural heritage and the values of justice, liberty and equality.

Thus, option (c) is the correct answer.

92. *(a)* 1 and 2 only

- **Pair 1 is correct:** The shafts of Ashokan pillars were indeed monolithic, meaning they were carved out of a single block of stone, typically **polished sandstone.** These shafts were renowned for their smooth finish and elegant tapering.
- **Pair 2 is correct:** The **inverted lotus, also known as the bell-shaped base,** was indeed placed over the shaft. It served as a **transitional element between the shaft and the abacus** or capital.
- **Pair 3 is incorrect:** Lion Capital of Sarnath does not directly represent the Dharmachakra. Instead, the **Dharmachakra is depicted below the lions on the abacus,** symbolising the spread of Dharma in all directions.

Thus, option (a) is the correct answer.

93. *(c)* All three

- **Statement 1 is correct: In Edict I,** Ashoka **prohibits animal slaughter and killing of animals,** which is associated with his broader policies of non-violence (Ahimsa) following his conversion to Buddhism.
- **Statement 2 is correct: Edict VII** emphasises **religious tolerance and welfare measures.** Ashoka promoted **respect for all religious sects** and encouraged his subjects to live in harmony, irrespective of their religious beliefs.
- **Statement 3 is correct: Edict XIII** describes Ashoka's **remorse over the Kalinga War,** which is one of the most famous aspects of his legacy. After witnessing the widespread **destruction and loss of life during the war,** Ashoka experienced deep regret and vowed to renounce violence.

Thus, option (c) is the correct answer.

94. *(c)* All three

- **Pair 1 is correct: The inverted lotus,** or **bell-shaped base,** was indeed placed below the abacus on Ashokan pillars. It served as a **decorative and structural element,** providing a smooth transition from the shaft to the abacus.
- **Pair 2 is correct:** The **abacus was the platform on which the capital rested.** It was often elaborately carved with floral patterns or animal motifs. The abacus played a crucial role in balancing the capital on the shaft and added to the aesthetic appeal of the pillar.
- **Pair 3 is correct:** The **capital was the crowning feature** of the Ashokan pillars, typically **adorned with finely executed animal figures, such as lions, bulls, or elephants.** The most famous example is the **Lion Capital of Sarnath,** which features four lions sitting back to back.

Thus, option (c) is the correct answer.

95. *(d)* 1, 2 and 3

- **Statement 1 is correct**: The Lion Capital of Sarnath was built to commemorate the Buddha's first sermon at Sarnath, known as the **Dhammachakrapravartana (Turning of the Wheel of Law)**, marking the beginning of the Buddha's teaching career and the dissemination of his teachings to the world.
- **Statement 2 is correct**: The capital depicts four lions facing in four different directions, symbolising the spread of Dharma to the four corners of the world. The lions are seated back to back on a circular abacus, which is decorated with the Dharmachakra (Wheel of Law) and other animal figures like the bull, elephant and horse, representing various stages of the Buddha's life.
- **Statement 3 is correct**: The Lion Capital was adopted as the **National Emblem of India on 26th January, 1950.** It symbolises **power, courage, pride and confidence**, while also reflecting India's deep-rooted cultural and spiritual heritage.

Thus, option (d) is the correct answer.

96. *(d)* None

- **Statement 1 is correct**: The Schism Edicts are significant inscriptions issued by Emperor Ashoka, found at **both Sarnath (Uttar Pradesh) and Sanchi (Madhya Pradesh).** These edicts are directives aimed at the Buddhist Sangha, warning them against creating divisions within the monastic order.
- **Statement 2 is correct**: The **Prayagraj (formerly Allahabad) Pillar Inscription** is unique as it discusses the **charitable deeds of Queen Karuvaki, the wife of Ashoka.** This inscription highlights her contributions to the welfare of the people, showcasing the role of royal women in the promotion of Dharma (moral law) and public welfare.
- **Statement 3 is correct**: The **Rummindei (Lumbini) pillar** is a commemorative inscription that marks Emperor **Ashoka's pilgrimage to Lumbini, the birthplace of Buddha.** This pillar not only confirms Ashoka's deep reverence for Buddhism but also records the **exemption of Lumbini from taxes**, demonstrating the special status of religious sites during his rule.

Thus, option (d) is the correct answer.

97. *(d)* 1, 2 and 3

- **Statement 1 is correct**: Ashokan pillars are known for their **monolithic nature**, meaning they were carved out of a single piece of stone. In contrast, **Persian pillars were composite**, made from multiple pieces of stone joined together.
- **Statement 2 is correct**: The **Ashokan pillars are famous for their animal capitals**, featuring animals like lions, elephants and bulls, symbolising power, strength and the teachings of Buddhism. While **Persian pillars** also had capitals, they **often included human figures and animal motifs combined**, reflecting the syncretic cultural influences in the Persian Empire.
- **Statement 3 is correct: Persian pillars** primarily served as **structural supports** in palaces and fortifications, reflecting their role in the architectural grandeur of the Achaemenid Empire. In contrast, **Ashokan pillars were freestanding monuments** used primarily for inscribing edicts.

Thus, option (d) is the correct answer.

98. *(b)* Hathigumpha Inscription

- The **Hathigumpha Inscription** is one of the most important historical records from ancient India, located at the **Udayagiri-Khandagiri caves near Bhubaneswar, Odisha.** It was inscribed by **King Kharavela**, a ruler of Kalinga, around the 1st century BCE.
- The inscription provides a **detailed account of Kharavela's reign**, including his military victories, public works and religious patronage. It is written in Prakrit, using the Brahmi script and is considered a critical source for understanding the early history of Jainism and the political landscape of ancient Odisha.

Thus, option (b) is the correct answer.

99. *(a)* 1 and 2 only

- **Pair 1 is correctly matched**: The **Prayag Prashasti**, also known as the **Allahabad Pillar Inscription**, is a key historical document from the **reign of Samudragupta. Composed by Harisena,** this inscription gives details of the conquests and achievements of Samudragupta.

- **Pair 2 is correctly matched**: The **Mehrauli Inscription**, also known as the Iron Pillar Inscription, is located within the **Qutb Minar complex in Delhi**. This inscription was established by Chandragupta II of the Gupta dynasty and is dedicated to Lord Vishnu. It stands as a testament to the advanced metallurgical skills of ancient India.
- **Pair 3 is incorrectly matched**: The **Mandasor Pillar Inscription** is not located in Rajasthan but in **Madhya Pradesh**. It was inscribed by the **Gupta ruler Yashodharman** to commemorate his victory over the Huns. It provides details about the expansion of Gupta's influence and the challenges posed by foreign invasions.

Thus, option (a) is the correct answer.

100. *(b)* Only two pairs

- **Pair 1 is correctly matched**: The **Prayag Prashasti**, also known as the **Allahabad Pillar Inscription**, is associated with the **Gupta dynasty**. It is composed by the **court poet Harisena**, it extols the military exploits and virtues of **Samudragupta, often referred to as the 'Napoleon of India'**.
- **Pair 2 is correctly matched**: The **Bhitari Pillar Inscription** was commissioned by **Skandagupta**, one of the later Gupta rulers, around the mid-5th century CE. It is located in **Uttar Pradesh** and documents Skandagupta's efforts to restore the Sudarshana Lake and his victories over the Huns.
- **Pair 3 is incorrectly matched**: The **Aihole Inscription** is incorrectly matched with the Satavahanas. It is associated with the **Chalukyas of Badami**, specifically King **Pulakesin II.** The inscription, written in Kannada script and Sanskrit language, commemorates Pulakesin's victories over Harshavardhana and his consolidation of power in the Deccan.

Thus, option (b) is the correct answer.

101. *(c)* Naneghat Inscription

- The **Naneghat Inscription** is correctly associated with the **Satavahanas**. This inscription is found in the **Naneghat caves in Maharashtra** and dates back to the **1st century BCE**. It was inscribed by **Naganika, the wife of Satakarni**, a prominent ruler of the Satavahana dynasty. The inscription is written in Brahmi script and provides valuable information about the Satavahana dynasty, including details about their lineage, religious practices and administrative structure.
- The Naneghat Inscription is an essential source for understanding the early history of the Deccan region, offering insights into the socio-political and religious life during the Satavahana period.

Thus, option (c) is the correct answer.

102. *(b)* Both A and R are true, but R is not the correct explanation of A.

- **Assertion (A) is correct**: The Qutb Minar was indeed **initiated by Qutb-ud-din Aibak**, the founder of the Mamluk dynasty in Delhi, to commemorate his victory over the Rajput rulers, particularly the defeat of Prithviraj Chauhan. The tower was intended as a minaret to the adjacent Quwwat-ul-Islam Mosque, signifying the establishment of Muslim rule in India.
- **Reason (R) is correct**: Although Aibak laid the foundation of the Qutb Minar, he only managed to complete the first story. The remaining three stories were added by his successor and son-in-law, Iltutmish, who ensured the monument's completion. However, the reason **explains the completion but not the purpose behind its construction.**

Thus, option (b) is the correct answer.

103. *(a)* A-1, B-2, C-3, D-4

- **Taj Mahal** is located in **Agra** and it was built by Mughal Emperor **Shah Jahan** as a mausoleum for his beloved wife Mumtaz Mahal and is recognised worldwide as an architectural masterpiece of Mughal architecture, primarily using white marble with intricate inlay work.
- **Qutb Minar** is located in **Delhi**. It stands as one of the **tallest brick minarets** in the world and is a significant example of early Indo-Islamic architecture. The Qutb Minar is part of the Qutb complex, which also includes the Quwwat-ul-Islam Mosque and other historically important structures.

- **Gol Gumbaz** is located in **Bijapur**. This mausoleum was built by **Muhammad Adil** Shah, the Sultan of Bijapur and is famous for its massive dome, which is the second-largest in the world and its whispering gallery, where even the faintest sound is echoed multiple times.
- **Madarsa of Mahmud Gawan** is located in **Bidar.** It was built-in the 15th century during the reign of the **Bahmani Sultanate**, this institution served as a center of learning, akin to a university and is known for its impressive Islamic architecture, including lofty minarets and elaborate tile work.

Thus, option (a) is the correct answer.

104. *(b)* 2 only

- **Statement 1 is incorrect**: The Charbagh style of garden layout was introduced in India by **Babur**, not Humayun, the founder of the Mughal Empire. Babur brought with him the Persian influence of garden design, which **symbolised the Islamic concept of paradise**, a garden with flowing water.
- **Statement 2 is correct**: The Charbagh refers to a **quadrilateral garden layout** where the plot is divided into four parts by walkways or water channels, representing the **four rivers of paradise** mentioned in the Quran. Each quadrant could be planted with flowers, fruits, or trees, creating a symmetrical and harmonious design.

Thus, option (b) is the correct answer.

105. *(a)* 1-3-2-4

- **Qutb Minar** was started by **Qutb-ud-din Aibak in 1193 AD** and **completed by Iltutmish in 1220 AD.** It was constructed as a minaret attached to the Quwwat-ul-Islam Mosque, signaling the arrival of Muslim rule in India. The minar's design was influenced by Afghan architecture, with elements of Persian and local styles.
- **Tughlaqabad Fort** was constructed by **Ghiyasuddin Tughlaq**, the founder of the Tughlaq dynasty, in **1321 AD**. This massive fort was built to protect the newly founded city of Tughlaqabad and is noted for its grand scale, strategic design and massive stone walls, reflecting the defensive needs of the period.
- **Red Fort** was built by **Shah Jahan in Delhi between 1638-1648 AD.** It served as the main residence of the Mughal emperors and symbolised the zenith of Mughal architecture, with its extensive use of red sandstone, intricate decorations and the incorporation of Persian, Timurid and Indian architectural elements.
- **Gol Gumbaz** was constructed in **Bijapur** in **1656 AD** by **Muhammad Adil Shah** of the Adil Shahi dynasty and is famous for its **massive dome, which is one of the largest in the world and** its whispering gallery, an acoustic marvel where even a whisper can be heard clearly across the room.

Thus, option (a) is the correct answer.

106. *(b)* Only two

- **Statement 1 is incorrect:** The use of coloured sandstone predates the Mughal period and was prevalent in earlier Indo-Islamic architecture. The Qutb Minar and other structures in the Qutb complex are examples of buildings constructed using red and buff-coloured sandstone.
- **Statement 2 is correct: Pietra Dura, an inlay technique using precious and semi-precious stones** to create intricate floral and geometric designs, became highly prominent under Shah Jahan. This technique **reached its zenith in the Taj Mahal.**
- **Statement 3 is correct:** The **Charbagh garden layout was introduced by Babur,** reflecting his Persian heritage. It symbolised the paradise garden, with four rivers flowing through it, as described in Islamic tradition.

Thus, option (b) is the correct answer.

107. *(b)* Only two

- **Statement 1 is incorrect:** The use of marble as a primary material did not begin with the construction of the Qutb Minar. The Qutb Minar, built during the early 13th century, primarily utilised red sandstone and some marble in later additions. **The widespread use of marble in Indo-Islamic architecture is more closely associated with the later Mughal period**, particularly under Shah Jahan, who used white marble extensively in the construction of the Taj Mahal and other buildings.

- **Statement 2 is correct:** Geometric designs and calligraphy are hallmark features of Indo-Islamic architecture serving both decorative and symbolic purposes, with geometric patterns often representing the infinite nature of creation and calligraphy (usually Quranic verses) emphasising the spiritual aspects of the architecture.
- **Statement 3 is correct:** Mughal architecture is renowned for its use of **red sandstone,** particularly during the reigns of Akbar and Shah Jahan due to its durability and aesthetic appeal. E.g. Fatehpur Sikri, the Red Fort and many others.

Thus, option (b) is the correct answer.

108. *(a)* Both A and R are true and R is the correct explanation of A.

- **Assertion (A) is true:** Pietra Dura, an **intricate inlay technique using coloured semi-precious stones,** became especially **popular during the reign of Shah Jahan.** This technique was extensively used in the decoration of the Taj Mahal and other monuments built during his era.
- **Reason (R) is true:** Pietra Dura involves the precise embedding of semi-precious stones into a marble surface to create detailed floral, geometric and figurative designs. This process requires **significant skill and artistry, which was abundant during Shah Jahan's reign, leading to its popularity.**

Thus, option (a) is the correct answer.

109. *(a)* Only one

- **Statement 1 is incorrect:** The **Trabeate style,** also known as the **corbelled style,** is based on the use of **horizontal beams or lintels** supported by columns or walls. It does not use arches and keystones; instead, it relies on the stacking of stones to create openings.
- **Statement 2 is correct:** The **Arcuate style,** which involves the **use of arches** constructed with keystones, became more prevalent in India after the advent of Islam. This style allowed for the creation of larger, more open spaces and became a defining feature of Islamic architecture in India.
- **Statement 3 is correct:** In Indo-Islamic architecture, both the Trabeate and Arcuate styles were blended, creating a unique architectural tradition.

Thus, option (a) is the correct answer.

110. *(b)* Only two pairs

- **Pair 1 is incorrectly matched:** The **Qutb Minar** was initiated by **Qutb-ud-din Aibak** and not by Alauddin Khalji, who was responsible for building the **Alai Minar in the Qutub complex.** Therefore, the first pair is incorrectly matched.
- **Pair 2 is correctly matched: Feroz Shah Kotla was designed by Malik Ghazi and Abdul Haqq** during the reign of **Feroz Shah Tughlaq,** making the second pair correctly matched. Feroz Shah Kotla is significant for its Ashokan pillar, which Feroz Shah brought from Ambala.
- **Pair 3 is correctly matched:** The **Sher Shah Suri Tomb in Sasaram, Bihar,** is an architectural marvel of the **Pathan style,** characterised by **its octagonal shape.** It was built in memory of Sher Shah Suri, the founder of the Suri Empire and is known for its large dome and intricate design.

Thus, option (b) is the correct answer.

111. *(c)* It was the main residence of the Mughal rulers till 1585.

- The **Agra Fort, also known as the Red Fort of Agra,** was built by the **Mughal Emperor Akbar** between 1565 and 1573. It served as the main residence of the Mughal emperors until 1585, after which the capital was shifted to Delhi by Shah Jahan.
- The fort is situated on the **right bank of the Yamuna River** and was originally designed as a military structure but was later transformed into a royal residence by subsequent emperors.
- It is a **UNESCO World Heritage site** and houses many notable buildings such as the **Jahangir Mahal, Khas Mahal, Diwan-i-Khas, Diwan-i-Aam and the Pearl Mosque.**

Thus, option (c) is the correct answer.

112. *(c)* 1 and 3 only

- **Statement 1 is correct:** Fatehpur Sikri(city of victory), located near Agra, was built by Emperor Akbar in the late 16th century as a new capital of the Mughal Empire. It served as the political capital of the Mughal Empire from 1571 to 1585 before being abandoned due to water scarcity.

- **Statement 2 is incorrect**: The **first structure built** in Fatehpur Sikri was not the Rang Mahal but the **Jama Masjid**, which was followed by other significant buildings like the Buland Darwaza, Panch Mahal and the tomb of Sheikh Salim Chishti.
- **Statement 3 is correct**: It is now recognised as a **UNESCO World Heritage site** since 1986.

Thus, option (c) is the correct answer.

113. *(b)* Only two pairs

- **Pair 1 is correctly matched**: Located in **Bijapur, Karnataka, Ibrahim Rauza is a stunning mausoleum built in the early 17th century by Ibrahim Adil Shah II**, the Sultan of Bijapur. It is renowned for its symmetry and the elegance of its architecture, often drawing comparisons to the Taj Mahal.
- **Pair 2 is correctly matched**: Also situated in **Bijapur**, the **Gol Gumbaz is the mausoleum of Muhammad Adil Shah,** the seventh Sultan of the Adil Shahi dynasty. Completed in 1656, Gol Gumbaz is famed for its **massive dome, which is one of the largest in the world** with a diameter of 44 meters. The structure's most remarkable feature is the whispering gallery.
- **Pair 3 is incorrectly matched**: The **Madarsa of Mahmud Gawan** is located in **Bidar, Karnataka.** Built-in 1460s under the Bahmani Sultanate, this educational institution was a **prominent center of Islamic learning during its time.** It is part of the UNESCO tentative list of world heritage sites under the Monuments and Forts of the Deccan Sultanate.

Thus, option (b) is the correct answer.

114. *(b)* Only two

- **Statement 1 is correct**. The tomb of Salim Chishti, **constructed in 1581 AD**, is celebrated for its stunning Jaali work in white marble. The tomb also features intricate arabesque patterns adorned with inscriptions of Quranic verses on its walls.
- **Statement 2 is correct**. During Jahangir's reign, under the influence of his wife Noor Jahan, significant construction projects were undertaken, such as the tomb of **Itmad-ud-Daulah**. This period marked the transition where white marble became the dominant building material, replacing the earlier use of red sandstone.
- **Statement 3 is incorrect**. Mughal architecture saw a **decline during Aurangzeb's reign**. Aurangzeb, known for his **puritanical approach**, did not emphasise the pursuit of art and architecture. It was under Shah Jahan that Mughal architecture truly reached its zenith.

Thus, option (b) is the correct answer.

115. *(a)* Both A and R are true and R is the correct explanation of A.

- **Assertion (A) is correct**: Gothic architecture, a style that flourished in Europe during the High and Late Middle Ages, is renowned for its distinctive features, including tall pointed arches, which contribute to the verticality of the structures and large windows that allow ample light to penetrate the interiors
- **Reason (R) is correct**: The emphasis on verticality and light in Gothic architecture was a deliberate attempt to create a sense of reaching toward the heavens, reflecting the spiritual aspirations of the period. The pointed arches and large windows were key elements in achieving this effect, allowing the structures to soar upwards while also illuminating the vast interior spaces.

Thus, option (a) is the correct answer.

116. *(a)* Both A and R are true and R is the correct explanation of A.

- **Assertion (A) is correct: Neo-Classical architecture**, which became prominent in the 18th and early 19th centuries, is characterised by its grand scale, use of domes and incorporation of classical elements such as columns and porticos.
- **Reason (R) is correct:** The Neo-Classical style was indeed heavily influenced by classical Roman architecture, which emphasised symmetry, proportion and the use of grandiose forms such as domes and columns.

Thus, option (a) is the correct answer.

117. *(b)* Both A and R are true, but R is not the correct explanation of A.

- **Assertion (A) is correct**: The Gateway of India, one of Mumbai's most iconic landmarks, was designed by the **British architect George Wittet**. The structure, completed in 1924, is a magnificent blend of Hindu and Muslim architectural styles, which has led to it being affectionately dubbed the **'Taj Mahal of Mumbai'**.

- **Reason (R) is correct but not correct explanation of A**: The Gateway of India was indeed constructed to commemorate the visit of **King George V and Queen Mary to India in 1911**. The foundation stone was laid in 1913 and the structure was completed in **1924**, serving as a ceremonial entrance to India for important colonial figures.

Thus, option (b) is the correct answer.

118. *(c)* A is true, but R is false.

- **Assertion (A) is True**: India Gate, a prominent war memorial located in the heart of New Delhi, was designed by **Sir Edwin Lutyens** and is inspired by the **Arc de Triomphe in Paris**, which is evident in its triumphal arch design. The India Gate stands as a symbol of honour and sacrifice, commemorating the soldiers of British India who died in World War I and the Third Anglo-Afghan War.
- **Reason (R) is False**: The India Gate was indeed designed by Edwin Lutyens and serves as a memorial to the soldiers of British India who lost their lives during **World War I (not World War II) and the Third Anglo-Afghan War.** The names of over 13,000 soldiers are inscribed on the walls of the monument, making it a significant site of remembrance.

Thus, option (c) is the correct answer.

119. *(a)* 1, 2 and 3 only

- **Statement 1 is correct**: Rashtrapati Bhawan, the official residence of the President of India, is indeed located on Raisina Hill in New Delhi.
- **Statement 2 is correct:** Originally known as the **Viceroy's House**, this grand building served as the residence of the British Viceroy during the colonial period. The **name was changed to Rashtrapati Bhawan after India gained independence in 1947**, reflecting the transition from British colonial rule to the establishment of the Republic of India.
- **Statement 3 is correct:** The design of Rashtrapati Bhawan was a collaborative effort between **Sir Edwin Lutyens and Herbert Baker**, two of the most prominent architects of their time.
- **Statement 4 is incorrect:** While Rashtrapati Bhawan is one of the largest and most impressive Presidential residences in the world, it is not the largest.

Thus, option (a) is the correct answer.

120. *(b)* 2, 3 and 4 only

- **Statement 1 is incorrect**: Connaught Place, often referred to as CP is located in the heart of New Delhi. It is one of the largest financial, commercial and business centers in the capital and is known for its iconic circular layout.
- **Statement 2 is correct**: Connaught Place was designed by **Robert Tor Russell**, who was a British architect working in India during the early 20th century. Russell was **part of the team led by Sir Edwin Lutyens and Herbert Baker**, who were responsible for designing much of New Delhi.
- **Statement 3 is correct**: The construction of Connaught Place **began in 1929** and was completed in 1933.
- **Statement 4 is correct**: Connaught Place was named after the **Duke of Connaught**, a member of the British royal family. The Duke of Connaught, **Prince Arthur**, was the third son of Queen Victoria and held various military and administrative positions in the British Empire.

Thus, option (b) is the correct answer.

Past Learning (Answers)

1 (b)	2 (b)	3 (b)	4 (a)	5 (d)	6 (a)	7 (c)	8 (c)	9 (d)	10 (a)
11 (a)	12 (a)	13 (c)	14 (b)	15 (b)	16 (c)	17 (c)	18 (c)	19 (b)	20 (c)
21 (b)	22 (a)	23 (c)	24 (a)	25 (c)	26 (d)	27 (b)	28 (d)	29 (d)	30 (a)
31 (a)	32 (b)	33 (b)	34 (a)	35 (a)	36 (b)	37 (b)			

CHAPTER 02 Religion

Assessment Round

Topic 1 : Indus Valley Civilisation and Hinduism

1. With reference to the Indus Valley Civilisation, consider the following statements :

1. The discovery of female figurines and terracotta images indicates the presence of a Mother Goddess cult.
2. Seals and sealings of Pashupati/Mahadev found at Mohenjodaro suggest the existence of a proto-Shiva figure.
3. The presence of fire altars at sites like Banawali and Kalibangan indicates the practice of a fire cult.

How many of the statements given above is/are correct?

(a) Only one
(b) Only two
(c) All three
(d) None

2. Consider the following aspects of the Indus Valley Civilisation :

1. Presence of fire altars.
2. Discovery of female figurines.
3. Seals of Pashupati/Mahadev.
4. Great Bath at Mohenjodaro.

How many of the above aspects indicate religious or ritualistic practices?

(a) Only one
(b) Only two
(c) Only three
(d) All four

3. In the context of the Vedic Age, which of the following practices were significant during the later Vedic period?

1. Offering of Soma juice during rituals.
2. Use of fire in sacrifices.
3. Practice of metaphysical concepts like Samsara and Karma.

Select the correct answer using the codes given below:

(a) 1 and 2 only
(b) 2 only
(c) 1, 2 and 3
(d) 3 only

4. Which of the following describes correctly about the 'Vedic gods'?

(a) Agni was primarily associated with atmospheric phenomena.
(b) Varuna was considered the upholder of cosmic order.
(c) Soma was a plant used only for medicinal purposes.
(d) All Vedic gods were worshipped equally during the early Vedic period.

5. Identify the Vedic deity based on the following statements:

1. Associated with thunder and lightning.
2. Revered as the supreme deity during the early Vedic period.
3. Known as the god of rain and war.

Choose the correct answer from the codes given below:

(a) Agni (b) Varuna
(c) Indra (d) Soma

6. Consider the following pairs:

	Veda	Main Focus
1.	Rigveda	Chants and hymns
2.	Samaveda	Sacrificial formulae
3.	Yajurveda	Melodies and music

How many of the above pairs is/are correctly matched?
(a) Only one pair (b) Only two pairs
(c) All three pairs (d) None

7. Consider the following pairs related to the sects of Hinduism:

	Sect	Founding Figure
1.	Varkari Panth	Jnaneshwar
2.	Brahma Sampradaya	Madhavacharya
3.	Nimbarka Sampradaya	Vallabhacharya

How many of the above pairs is/are correctly matched?
(a) Only one pair (b) Only two pairs
(c) All three pairs (d) None

8. Consider the following pairs:

	Sect	Main Deity
1.	Varkari Panth	Vitthoba
2.	Brahma Sampradaya	Para Brahma
3.	Pushtimarg	Radha

How many of the above pairs is/are correctly matched?
(a) Only one pair
(b) Only two pairs
(c) All three pairs
(d) None

9. With reference to the sects of Vaishnavism, consider the following statements:
1. Varkari Panth is centered around the worship of Vitthoba.
2. Ramanandi Sampradaya follows the teachings of Lord Krishna.
3. Pushtimarg believes in the ultimate truth of Brahma.

Which of the statements given above is/are correct?
(a) 1 and 2 only
(b) 1 and 3 only
(c) 2 and 3 only
(d) 1 only

10. In the context of Shaivism, which of the following sects practiced extreme rituals?
1. Kalamukhas
2. Kapalikas
3. Nathpanthis

Select the correct answer using the codes given below:
(a) 1 and 2 only (b) 2 only
(c) 1, 2 and 3 (d) 3 only

11. With reference to Shaivism, consider the following statements:
1. The Aghoris perform extreme Tantrik rituals.
2. The Nathpanthis are associated with the doctrine of Hatha Yoga.
3. The Kapalikas reject all forms of idol worship.

Which of the statements given above are correct?
(a) 1 and 2 only
(b) 2 and 3 only
(c) 1 and 3 only
(d) 1, 2 and 3

12. With reference to the sects of Shaivism, consider the following statements:
1. Saiva Siddhanta is popular in Tamil Nadu and Northern Sri Lanka.
2. Kalamukhas were primarily found in the Karnataka region.
3. Pashupatas were an offshoot of the Vaishnava sect.

Which of the statements given above are correct?
(a) 1 and 2 only
(b) 2 and 3 only
(c) 1 and 3 only
(d) 1, 2 and 3

13. With reference to Kashmir Shaivism, consider the following statements:
1. Vasugupta is considered the founder of this sect.
2. This sect strictly rejected the authority of the Vedas.
3. Pratyabhijna sect emerged out of Kashmir Shaivism.

Which of the statements given above are correct?
(a) 1 and 3 only (b) 2 and 3 only
(c) 1 and 2 only (d) 1, 2 and 3

14. Consider the following pairs related to the Shakti Cult:

Goddess	Attribute
1. Kali	Fierce
2. Durga	Peaceful
3. Saraswati	Pacific

How many of the above pairs is/are correctly matched?
(a) Only one pair (b) Only two pairs
(c) All three pairs (d) None

15. Consider the following pairs:

Goddess	Aspect
1. Kali	Saviour
2. Durga	Motherhood
3. Chandi	Fierce Warrior

How many of the above pairs is/are correctly matched?
(a) Only one pair (b) Only two pairs
(c) All three pairs (d) None

Topic 2 : Buddhism

16. With reference to the origins of Buddhism, consider the following statements:
1. Buddhism emerged as a response to the expensive and complicated Vedic rituals.
2. The teachings of the Upanishads played a crucial role in shaping early Buddhist thought.
3. The rigid caste system was one of the societal issues that led to the rise of Buddhism.

How many of the statements given above is/are correct?
(a) Only one
(b) Only two
(c) All three
(d) None

17. Consider the following types of Buddhas:
1. Samyak Sambuddha
2. Pratyeka Buddha
3. Dhyani Buddha
4. Adi Buddha

How many of the above is/are included in the forms of Buddha as per Buddhist teachings?
(a) Only one
(b) Only two
(c) Only three
(d) All four

18. With reference to the life of Buddha, consider the following statements:
1. Siddhartha Gautama was born in Lumbini, Nepal.
2. He attained enlightenment at the age of 35.
3. Buddha's first sermon is known as Dharmachakra Pravartana.

Which of the statements given above are correct?
(a) 1 and 2 only
(b) 2 and 3 only
(c) 1, 2 and 3
(d) 1 and 3 only

19. Buddhism emphasises several key concepts and philosophies. In this context, which of the following are part of the Four Noble Truths?
1. Life is full of suffering.
2. The cause of suffering is desire.
3. Suffering can be ended by following the Eightfold Path.
4. Rebirth is the ultimate form of suffering.

Select the correct answer using the codes given below:
(a) 1 and 3 only
(b) 1, 2 and 3 only
(c) 2 and 4 only
(d) 1, 3 and 4 only

20. Consider the following symbols of major events in the life of Gautama Buddha:

	Symbols	Events
1.	Bodhi tree	Enlightenment
2.	Wheel	First sermon
3.	Stupa	Death
4.	Elephant	Renunciation

How many of the above pairs is/are correctly matched?

(a) Only one (b) Only two
(c) Only three (d) All four

21. In the context of the teachings of Buddhism, which of the following concepts refer to the ultimate goal of liberation?

1. Nirvana
2. Samsara
3. Bodhi
4. Pratitya Samutpada

Select the correct answer using the codes given below:

(a) 1 only
(b) 1 and 3 only
(c) 2 and 4 only
(d) 1, 3 and 4 only

22. Which of the following correctly describes the concept of Anicca in Buddhism?

(a) The universe is permanent and unchanging.
(b) The universe is in a state of constant flux.
(c) The universe is full of suffering and sorrow.
(d) The universe is governed by the law of karma.

23. Identify the Buddhist concept based on the following statements:

1. It emphasises the interconnectedness of all phenomena.
2. It describes the process of cause and effect that leads to suffering.
3. It is also known as dependent origination.

Choose the correct answer from the codes given below:

(a) Samsara
(b) Anatta
(c) Pratitya Samutpada
(d) Karma

24. Consider the following pairs:

	Buddhist Council	Presiding King
1.	First Buddhist Council	Ajatashatru
2.	Second Buddhist Council	Kalasoka
3.	Third Buddhist Council	Ashoka

How many of the above pairs is/are correctly matched?

(a) Only one pair (b) Only two pairs
(c) All three pairs (d) None

25. Which one of the following statements is correct?

(a) The Pali Canon is the scriptural foundation of Mahayana Buddhism.
(b) The Vinaya Pitaka contains the rules for monastic discipline in Buddhism.
(c) The Mahavamsa is a Tibetan Buddhist text.
(d) The Madhyamika School is part of the Theravada tradition.

26. With reference to the Buddhist Sangha, consider the following statements:

1. The Sangha was established on democratic lines.
2. Monastic rules were codified in the Vinaya Pitaka.
3. Entry into the Sangha was allowed only after the Upasampada ceremony.

Which of the statements given above are correct?

(a) 1 and 2 only
(b) 2 and 3 only
(c) 1 and 3 only
(d) 1, 2 and 3

27. With reference to the early Buddhist Councils, consider the following statements:

1. The First Buddhist Council was held at Rajagriha.
2. The Second Buddhist Council led to the first major schism in Buddhism.
3. The Fourth Buddhist Council was convened by Emperor Kanishka.

How many of the statements given above is/are correct?

(a) Only one (b) Only two
(c) All three (d) None

28. Consider the following doctrines:

1. Sunyata
2. Yogachara
3. Trikaya
4. Shunyavada

How many of the above is/are associated with the Mahayana School of Buddhism?

(a) Only one (b) Only two
(c) Only three (d) All four

29. With reference to the Theravada School, consider the following statements:

1. It is more conservative and adheres closely to the original teachings of Buddha.
2. The primary language of its scriptures is Pali.
3. It emphasises the concept of Bodhisattvas.

Which of the statements given above are correct?

(a) 1 and 2 only (b) 2 and 3 only
(c) 1, 2 and 3 (d) 1 and 3 only

30. Which of the following correctly describes the concept of Anatta in Buddhism?

(a) The belief in a permanent soul.
(b) The denial of a permanent self or soul.
(c) The belief in the transmigration of souls.
(d) The worship of Bodhisattvas.

31. Identify the Bodhisattva based on the following descriptions:

1. Known as the Bodhisattva of compassion.
2. Often depicted holding a lotus.
3. Revered in both Theravada and Mahayana traditions.

Choose the correct answer from the codes given below:

(a) Manjushri (b) Avalokiteshvara
(c) Vajrapani (d) Samantabhadra

32. Consider the following pairs related to Buddhist practices:

Practice	Description
1. Dana	Generosity or giving
2. Sila	Meditation or mental development
3. Bhavana	Virtue or morality

How many of the above pairs is/are correctly matched?

(a) Only one pair (b) Only two pairs
(c) All three pairs (d) None

33. Consider the following pairs:

Buddhist Term	Meaning
1. Paramitas	Perfections or transcendent virtues
2. Trikaya	Three bodies of Buddha
3. Anicca	Impermanence

How many of the above pairs is/are correctly matched?

(a) Only one pair (b) Only two pairs
(c) All three pairs (d) None

34. Which one of the following statements is correct?

(a) Vajrayana Buddhism emphasises the worship of Bodhisattvas.
(b) The Madhyamaka School of Mahayana Buddhism was founded by Asanga.
(c) The Yogachara School emphasises the study of consciousness and mind.
(d) Theravada Buddhism primarily uses the Sanskrit language for its scriptures.

35. With reference to Buddhist literature, consider the following statements:

1. The Sutta Pitaka contains the main teachings of the Buddha.
2. The Vinaya Pitaka deals with the rules of conduct for monks and nuns.
3. The Abhidhamma Pitaka provides a philosophical analysis of the Buddha's teachings.

Which of the statements given above are correct?

(a) 1 and 2 only (b) 2 and 3 only
(c) 1 and 3 only (d) 1, 2 and 3

36. With reference to the spread of Buddhism, consider the following statements:

1. Buddhism spread to Sri Lanka during the reign of Emperor Ashoka.
2. The Mahayana School of Buddhism was more liberal and open to new ideas compared to Theravada.
3. The Vajrayana School incorporated elements of Tantric practices.

How many of the statements given above is/are correct?

(a) Only one (b) Only two
(c) All three (d) None

37. Consider the following schools of Buddhism:

1. Theravada 2. Vajrayana 3. Yogachara

How many of the above is/are considered the major schools of Mahayana Buddhism?

(a) Only one (b) Only two
(c) Only three (d) None

38. With reference to the Mahayana School of Buddhism, consider the following statements:

1. It developed the concept of Bodhisattvas as enlightened beings who delay their own Nirvana to help others.
2. It uses Sanskrit as its primary language for scriptures.
3. It emphasises the importance of meditation as the only path to enlightenment.

Which of the statements given above are correct?

(a) 1 and 2 only (b) 2 and 3 only
(c) 1, 2 and 3 (d) 1 and 3 only

39. In the context of Zen Buddhism, which of the following are key practices?

1. Zazen meditation
2. Use of Koans
3. Study of Sutras
4. Devotion to Bodhisattvas

Select the correct answer using the codes given below:

(a) 1 and 2 only
(b) 1, 2 and 3 only
(c) 2, 3 and 4 only
(d) 1, 2, 3 and 4

40. In the context of Buddhist art and architecture, which of the following forms were commonly used to depict the teachings of Buddhism?

1. Stupas 2. Chaityas
3. Viharas 4. Paintings

Select the correct answer using the codes given below:

(a) 1 and 2 only
(b) 2 and 3 only
(c) 1, 2 and 3 only
(d) 1, 2, 3 and 4

41. Which of the following correctly describes the concept of Sunyata in Buddhism?

(a) The belief in a permanent self.
(b) The idea that all phenomena are empty of inherent existence.
(c) The concept of transmigration of souls.
(d) The emphasis on the practice of asceticism.

42. Identify the place associated with the following description:

1. It is the site where the Buddha attained enlightenment.
2. It is considered one of the holiest places in Buddhism.
3. It is marked by the Mahabodhi Temple.

Choose the correct answer from the codes given below:

(a) Lumbini (b) Sarnath
(c) Bodh Gaya (d) Kushinagar

43. Consider the following pairs related to Buddhist councils:

Buddhist Council	Significance
1. First Council	Compilation of Sutta and Vinaya Pitaka
2. Third Council	Spread of Buddhism to Sri Lanka
3. Fourth Council	Division of Buddhism into Hinayana and Mahayana

How many of the above pairs is/are correctly matched?

(a) Only one pair (b) Only two pairs
(c) All three pairs (d) None

44. Consider the following pairs:

Buddhist Text	Content
1. Digha Nikaya	Long discourses of Buddha
2. Anguttara Nikaya	Numerical teachings of Buddha
3. Vinaya Pitaka	Philosophical Analysis of Buddhism

How many of the above pairs is/are correctly matched?

(a) Only one pair (b) Only two pairs
(c) All three pairs (d) None

45. Which one of the following statements is correct?

(a) The Abhidhamma Pitaka is primarily concerned with the rules of monastic discipline.

(b) The Khuddaka Nikaya contains minor discourses and is part of the Sutta Pitaka.

(c) The Milind Panha is a Mahayana text describing the teachings of Bodhisattva Amitabha.

(d) The Mahavamsa is an important text of the Zen tradition in Japan.

46. With reference to the places visited by Buddha, consider the following statements:

1. Lumbini is the birthplace of Buddha.
2. Sarnath is where Buddha gave his first sermon.
3. Buddha attained Mahaparinirvana in the Malla Republic.

Which of the statements given above are correct?

(a) 1 and 2 only
(b) 2 and 3 only
(c) 1 and 3 only
(d) 1, 2 and 3

47. Consider the following pairs regarding Mudras (symbolic gestures) associated with the Buddha:

	Mudra (Gesture)	Description
1.	Uttarabodhi Mudra	Represents offering, welcome, charity, giving, compassion and sincerity.
2.	Vitarka Mudra	Signifies teaching, discussion and intellectual argument.
3.	Vajra Mudra	Denotes a fiery thunderbolt symbolising air, water, fire, earth and metal.
4.	Abhaymudra	A hand gesture that symbolises peace, friendship and protection

How many of the above pairs is/are correctly matched?

(a) All four (b) Only two
(c) Only three (d) Only one

48. Consider the following personalities:

1. Purana Kassapa 2. Makkhali Gosala
3. Ajita Kesakambalin 4. Bindusara
5. Parshvanatha

How many of the individuals listed above were contemporaries of Vardhamana Mahavira?

(a) Only two (b) Only three
(c) Only four (d) All five

49. Identify the Buddhist disciple based on the following descriptions:

1. He was one of Buddha's initial disciples and was given the status of the second Buddha in Theravada Buddhism.
2. He was considered the right hand of Buddha and played a significant role in the early Sangha.

Choose the correct disciple from the codes given below:

(a) Ananda (b) Sariputta
(c) Mahakassapa (d) Upali

50. Which of the following correctly describes the significance of Ananda in Buddhism?

(a) He was the Buddha's cousin and attained enlightenment after the Buddha's death.

(b) He was known as the 'Treasurer of Dhamma' for his exceptional memory of Buddha's teachings.

(c) He was responsible for the compilation of the Vinaya Pitaka.

(d) He was the first to introduce meditation practices in Buddhism.

51. Buddhism saw the emergence of several key disciples who played significant roles in the spread and preservation of the Buddha's teachings. In this context, which of the following individuals were among the first disciples of the Buddha?

1. Kondanja 2. Gautami
3. Mahanama 4. Khema
5. Assaji

Select the correct answer using the codes given below:

(a) 1, 3 and 5 only (b) 2, 3 and 4 only
(c) 1, 2 and 4 only (d) 3, 4 and 5 only

52. Which of the following correctly describes the distinction between canonical and non-canonical Buddhist texts?
(a) Canonical texts are directly linked to the sayings of Gautama Buddha.
(b) Non-canonical texts include the three Pitakas.
(c) Canonical texts are the later commentaries on the Buddha's teachings.
(d) Non-canonical texts are not based on Buddha's teachings.

53. Consider the following Buddhist texts with their contents:

1. Milindapanho	Dialogue between Indo-Greek King Menander and monk Nagasena.
2. Visuddhimagga	The Path to Purity, focusing on the development of enlightenment.
3. Nettipakarana	A book offering a connected account of the Buddha's teachings.
4. Mahavamsa	The story of the Buddha's arrival in Sri Lanka.

Which of the pairs is/are correctly matched?
(a) 1 and 2 only (b) 1, 3, and 4 only
(c) 1, 2, 3 and 4 (d) 2, 3, and 4 only

54. Which of the following books is not part of the Sutta-pitaka or Vinaya-pitaka?
(a) Digha-nikaya
(b) Majjhima-nikaya
(c) Mahavibhanga
(d) Anguttara-nikaya

55. Consider the following statement:
"The Buddha delivered his first sermon on deliverance from suffering to his five former companions in Sarnath, which is referred to as Dhammachakka-Pavattana".
Which of the following is correct?
(a) It was delivered at Lumbini.
(b) It is known as Parinirvana.
(c) It is called the 'Turning the Wheel of Dharma'.
(d) The sermon was delivered to the Mallas.

56. Which of the following symbols correctly represent different phases in Buddha's life?
(a) Horse - Birth
(b) Bodhi Tree - Renunciation
(c) Lotus and Bull - Birth
(d) Footprints - Enlightenment

57. Match the following Buddhist terms with their meanings:

1. Samma-sankappa	Right Thought
2. Samma-Vaca	Right Speech
3. Samma-Kammanta	Right Action

Choose the correct option from the codes given below:
(a) 1, 2 and 3 (b) 1 only
(c) 1 and 3 only (d) None

58. Match the following terms from the Eightfold Path with their meaning:

1. Samma-Ajiva	Right Livelihood
2. Samma-Vayama	Right Effort
3. Samma-Sati	Right Mindfulness
4. Samma-Samadhi	Right Concentration

Choose the correct option from the options given below:
(a) None (b) 1 and 2 only
(c) 3 and 4 only (d) 1, 2, 3 and 4

59. Consider the following statements:
Assertion (A): Gautama Buddha was born in 563 BCE to Suddhodana, the chief of the Sakya clan, who ruled from Kapilavastu.
Reason (R): His mother was Gautami, who gave birth to him and died seven days after his birth, after which his stepmother, Mahamaya, raised him.
Choose the correct answer from the options given below:
(a) Both A and R are correct and R is the correct explanation of A.
(b) Both A and R are correct, but R is not the correct explanation of A.
(c) A is correct, but R is incorrect.
(d) A is incorrect, and R is incorrect.

60. Identify the Bodhisattva based on the following description:

"This Bodhisattva is depicted with deep blue skin, often seated on a lotus, and holding a wheel of jewels. He is known to purify obstructions and wrong-doings faced by people on the path to enlightenment."

Who is this Bodhisattva?

(a) Avalokiteshvara
(b) Sarvanivaranavishkambhin
(c) Maitreya
(d) Manjushri

61. Identify the Bodhisattva based on the following description:

"This Bodhisattva is depicted as blue, wielding a Vajra (thunderbolt) in his right hand and surrounded by flames. He is a fierce protector, symbolizing power and forceful energy".

Who is this Bodhisattva?

(a) Avalokiteshvara (b) Vajrapani
(c) Manjushri (d) Kshitigarbha

62. Match the following schools of thought with their characteristics:

1. Sarvastivadin	Believes that everything exists in the three phases of time (past, present, and future).
2. Sautrantika	Accepts only the Sutras and Vinaya-Pitaka as valid teachings of the Buddha.
3. Sammitiya	An early Buddhist school of thought.

Which of the above pairs are correctly matched:

(a) 1 and 2 only (b) 2 and 3 only
(c) 1, 2 and 3 (d) None

63. Match the following Buddhist terms with their meanings:

1. Bhikkhuni Sangha	Sangha of nuns
2. Theragatha	Verses of elder monks
3. Therigatha	Verses of elder nuns
4. Shramana/ Samana	One who strives to realise the truth

Which of the above pairs are correctly matched :

(a) 1, 2, 3 and 4 (b) 1, 2 and 3 only
(c) 2, 3 and 4 only (d) 1, 3 and 4 only

Topic 3 : Jainism

64. With reference to Jainism, consider the following statements:

1. Jainism teaches that the Jina has conquered temporal and material existence.
2. The concept of Tirthankaras is central to Jain philosophy.
3. Siddhas are souls that have attained ultimate liberation.

How many of the statements given above is/are correct?

(a) Only one (b) Only two
(c) All three (d) None

65. Consider the following stages of progression in Jainism:

1. Jina 2. Tirthankara 3. Siddha

How many of the above is/are recognised stages in the progression of a soul in Jainism?

(a) Only one (b) Only two
(c) All three (d) None

66. Identify the Tirthankara based on the following description:

1. He was the 24th and last Tirthankara in Jainism.
2. He attained Kaivalya under a sal tree at Jimbhikagrama.
3. He preached for 30 years before attaining Nirvana.

Choose the correct answer from the codes given below:

(a) Rishabhadeva (b) Neminatha
(c) Parshvanatha (d) Mahavira

67. In the context of Jain practices, which of the following are classified as Anuvratas?

1. Dik Vrata
2. Bhoga Upbhoga Vrata
3. Atithi Samvibhaga Vrata

Select the correct answer using the codes given below:

(a) 1 and 2 only (b) 2 and 3 only
(c) 1, 2 and 3 (d) None of these

68. Identify the Tirthankara based on the following attributes:

1. His symbol is the snake.
2. He is the 23rd Tirthankara.
3. He is associated with the Yaksha Dharanendra.

Choose the correct answer from the codes given below:

(a) Rishabhadeva
(b) Neminatha
(c) Parshvanatha
(d) Mahavira

69. Consider the following pairs:

	Tirthankara	Sign
1.	Rishabhadeva	Bull
2.	Neminatha	Conch shell
3.	Mahavira	Snake

How many of the above pairs is/are correctly matched?

(a) Only one (b) Only two
(c) All three (d) None

70. Consider the following pairs:

	Doctrine	Explanation
1.	Anekantavada	Doctrine of non-absolutism
2.	Syadvada	Doctrine of Conditional Judgement
3.	Saptabhangi	Sevenfold judgment

How many of the above pairs is/are correctly matched?

(a) Only one (b) Only two
(c) All three (d) None

71. Consider the following pairs:

	Doctrine	Belief
1.	Karma	Transmigration of the soul
2.	Ahimsa	Non-violence
3.	Varna	Caste system

How many of the above pairs is/are correctly matched?

(a) Only one
(b) Only two
(c) All three
(d) None

72. With reference to the philosophy of Jainism, consider the following statements:

1. Jainism rejects the authority of the Vedas.
2. Jainism emphasises extreme non-violence as a path to liberation.
3. Jainism accepts the concept of a caste system.

Which of the statements given above are correct?

(a) 1 and 2 only (b) 2 and 3 only
(c) 1, 2 and 3 (d) None

73. In the context of Jain art and architecture, which of the following forms were commonly used to depict Jain teachings?

1. Rock-cut caves
2. Structural temples
3. Sculptures
4. Paintings

Select the correct answer using the codes given below:

(a) 1 and 2 only (b) 2 and 3 only
(c) 1, 2 and 3 only (d) 1, 2, 3 and 4

74. With reference to the Jain councils, consider the following statements:

1. The First Jain Council was held at Pataliputra in the 3rd century BCE.
2. The Second Jain Council held at Avanti led to the division of Jainism into the Digambara and Svetambara sects.
3. Both councils were convened to preserve Jain teachings and scriptures.

Which of the statements given above are correct?

(a) 1 and 2 only
(b) 2 and 3 only
(c) 1, 2 and 3
(d) 1 and 3 only

75. With reference to the Jain Tirthankaras, consider the following statements:

1. There are 24 Tirthankaras in Jainism.
2. Rishabhadeva is the first Tirthankara.
3. Mahavira is the only female Tirthankara.

Which of the statements given above are correct?

(a) 1 and 2 only (b) 2 and 3 only
(c) 1, 2 and 3 (d) 1 and 3 only

76. Consider the following pairs:

Jain Terminology	Meaning
1. Sallekhana	Ritual of voluntary fasting to death
2. Pratikramana	Ritual of repentance and introspection
3. Manastambha	Free-standing pillar erected in honour of Tirthankaras

How many of the above pairs is/are correctly matched?
(a) Only one (b) Only two
(c) All three (d) None

77. Consider the following pairs:

Jain Sect	Characteristics
1. Digambara	Sky-clad, follow more rigid monastic rules
2. Svetambara	White-clad, believe in the equality of men and women in attaining liberation
3. Yapaniya	Extinct sect, worships nude images of Tirthankaras

How many of the above pairs is/are correctly matched?
(a) Only one (b) Only two
(c) All three (d) None

78. With reference to the places associated with Jainism, consider the following statements:
1. Mount Abu is known for the Dilwara Temples, a prominent Jain pilgrimage site.
2. Shravanabelagola is famous for the Gommateshwara statue, a monolithic statue of Bahubali.
3. Ranakpur is home to the largest Jain temple in India, dedicated to the first Tirthankara, Rishabhadeva.

Which of the statements given above are correct?
(a) 1 and 2 only (b) 2 and 3 only
(c) 1 and 3 only (d) 1, 2 and 3

79. Which of the following correctly describes the concept of Gunasthanas in Jainism?
(a) It refers to the progressive stages of the soul's purification.
(b) It is the collection of vows taken by Jain monks.
(c) It is the path that leads to the attainment of Siddhahood.
(d) It is the sacred text that guides ethical conduct.

80. Which of the following principles are shared by both Jainism and Buddhism?
1. Belief in the existence of a God.
2. The practice of non-violence (Ahimsa).
3. The belief that penance and extreme austerity are the only paths to salvation.

Select the correct answer using the codes given below:
(a) 1 and 2 only (b) 2 only
(c) 2 and 3 only (d) All of these

81. Consider the following statements regarding the beliefs of the Digambara sect in Jainism:
1. Digambaras holds that women must be reborn as men before they can achieve liberation.
2. Digambara monks practice complete renunciation, which includes not owning any personal possessions, not even a begging bowl.

Which of the above statements is/are correct?
(a) 1 only (b) 2 only
(c) Both 1 and 2 (d) Neither 1 nor 2

82. Which of the following Tirthankaras is the only female Tirthankara according to the Shvetambara tradition?
(a) Mallinath (b) Parshvanath
(c) Mahavira (d) Rishabhadeva

83. With reference to the Bisapantha tradition, consider the following statements:
1. They worship the idols of Tirthankaras along with other deities such as Kshetrapala and Padmavati.
2. The followers of Bisapantha practice the waving of lights (Arati) in their temples, including at night.
3. They strictly adhere to the non-idol worshipping tradition.

How many of the statements given above is/are correct?
(a) Only one (b) Only two
(c) All three (d) None

84. With reference to the Terapantha tradition, consider the following statements:

1. Terapanthis do not worship the idols of Kshetrapala and Padmavati.
2. During worship, Terapanthis offer sacred rice and do not use flowers or fruits.

Which of the statements given above are correct?

(a) 1 only (b) 2 only
(c) Both 1 and 2 (d) Neither 1 nor 2

85. Regarding the Gumanapantha sub-sect, which of the following correctly identifies their practice?

(a) They light lamps and offer flowers during temple visits.
(b) They strictly prohibit the lighting of lamps or offerings in temples.
(c) They follow a strict vegetarian diet that includes green vegetables.
(d) They are concentrated primarily in South India.

86. Match the following Jain philosophical terms with their meanings:

1.	Chaitanya	Consciousness
2.	Virya	Energy
3.	Mohaniya	Delusion-causing karma
4.	Asarva	Flow

Choose the correct option from the codes given below:

(a) 1 and 3 only (b) 2, 3 and 4 only
(c) 1, 2, 3 and 4 (d) 1, 3 and 4 only

Topic 4 : Islam, Christianity and Sikhism

87. With reference to the origin of Islam, consider the following statements:

1. Islam is a monotheistic religion that originated in the Arabian Peninsula in the 7th century CE.
2. Prophet Muhammad is considered the last prophet in Islam.
3. The migration of Prophet Muhammad from Mecca to Medina is known as Hajj.

How many of the statements given above is/are correct?

(a) Only one (b) Only two
(c) All three (d) None

88. Consider the following elements of Islamic teachings:

1. Hadith 2. Zakat
3. Sharia

How many of the above is/are considered essential practices or teachings in Islam?

(a) Only one (b) Only two
(c) All three (d) None

89. Identify the event based on the following descriptions:

1. It marks the migration of Prophet Muhammad from Mecca to Medina.
2. It is considered a significant turning point in Islamic history.
3. It led to the establishment of the first Islamic state.

Choose the correct event from the codes given below:

(a) Hijra (b) Hajj
(c) Eid (d) Ramadan

90. In the context of Christian teachings, which of the following concepts are central to Christianity?

1. The Holy Trinity
2. Resurrection
3. Salvation through Jesus Christ

Select the correct answer using the code given below:

(a) 1 and 2 only (b) 1, 2 and 3
(c) 2 and 3 only (d) 1 and 3 only

91. Which of the following correctly describes the significance of the Bible in Christianity?

(a) It is a collection of sacred scriptures that include both the Old Testament and the New Testament.
(b) It only includes the teachings of Jesus Christ.
(c) It is a historical account of the life of Jesus written by his apostles.
(d) It was compiled by the Council of Nicaea in 325 CE.

92. Identify the branch of Christianity based on the following characteristics:

1. It emerged during the 16th century CE as a movement to reform the Catholic Church.
2. It rejects the authority of the Pope.
3. It emphasises the importance of scripture and faith alone.

Choose the correct branch from the codes given below:

(a) Catholicism (b) Protestantism
(c) Orthodoxy (d) Anglicanism

93. Consider the following pairs:

Sikh Terminology	Meaning
1. Ek Onkar	Belief in one God
2. Simran	Practice of meditation
3. Adi Granth	Sacred scripture of Sikhism

How many of the above pairs is/are correctly matched?

(a) Only one (b) Only two
(c) All three (d) None

94. Consider the following pairs:

Sikh Ritual	Description
1. Amrit Ceremony	Initiation into the Khalsa
2. Anand Karaj's	Marriage ceremony
3. Langar	Recitation of sacred hymns

How many of the above pairs is/are correctly matched?

(a) Only one (b) Only two
(c) All three (d) None

95. With reference to Sikhism, consider the following statements:

1. The Sikh faith was founded by Guru Nanak in the 15th century CE.
2. Sikhs believe in the equality of men and women before God.
3. Sikhism does not have priests and worship is led by the community.

Which of the statements given above are correct?

(a) 1 and 2 only (b) 2 and 3 only
(c) 1 and 3 only (d) 1, 2 and 3

96. Consider the following contributions of Sikh Gurus:

1. Guru Nanak Dev Ji	Founded Sikhism and initiated the practice of Langar.
2. Guru Amar Das Sahib Ji	Introduced the Anand Karaj marriage ceremony and abolished Sati among Sikhs.
3. Guru Arjan Dev Ji	Compiled the Adi Granth and completed the construction of the Golden Temple.

How many of the above contributions is/are correctly matched with the respective Sikh Gurus?

(a) Only one
(b) Only two
(c) All three
(d) None

97. Identify the Sikh Guru based on the following descriptions:

1. He was known as the 'Soldier Saint' and established the principles of Miri and Piri.
2. He constructed the Akal Takht and emphasised both spiritual and temporal power.

Choose the correct Sikh Guru from the codes given below:

(a) Guru Nanak Dev Ji
(b) Guru Har Rai Sahib Ji
(c) Guru Hargobind Sahib Ji
(d) Guru Gobind Singh Ji

98. With reference to Sikh Gurus, consider the following statements:

1. Guru Gobind Singh Ji founded the Khalsa in 1699.
2. Guru Arjan Dev Ji was executed by Mughal Emperor Jahangir.
3. Guru Har Krishan Sahib Ji was the youngest Sikh Guru.

Which of the statements given above are correct?

(a) 1 and 2 only (b) 2 and 3 only
(c) 1 and 3 only (d) 1, 2 and 3

OMR SHEET

Assessment Round

1	a	b	c	d	31	a	b	c	d	61	a	b	c	d	91	a	b	c	d
2	a	b	c	d	32	a	b	c	d	62	a	b	c	d	92	a	b	c	d
3	a	b	c	d	33	a	b	c	d	63	a	b	c	d	93	a	b	c	d
4	a	b	c	d	34	a	b	c	d	64	a	b	c	d	94	a	b	c	d
5	a	b	c	d	35	a	b	c	d	65	a	b	c	d	95	a	b	c	d
6	a	b	c	d	36	a	b	c	d	66	a	b	c	d	96	a	b	c	d
7	a	b	c	d	37	a	b	c	d	67	a	b	c	d	97	a	b	c	d
8	a	b	c	d	38	a	b	c	d	68	a	b	c	d	98	a	b	c	d
9	a	b	c	d	39	a	b	c	d	69	a	b	c	d	99	a	b	c	d
10	a	b	c	d	40	a	b	c	d	70	a	b	c	d	100	a	b	c	d
11	a	b	c	d	41	a	b	c	d	71	a	b	c	d	101	a	b	c	d
12	a	b	c	d	42	a	b	c	d	72	a	b	c	d	102	a	b	c	d
13	a	b	c	d	43	a	b	c	d	73	a	b	c	d	103	a	b	c	d
14	a	b	c	d	44	a	b	c	d	74	a	b	c	d	104	a	b	c	d
15	a	b	c	d	45	a	b	c	d	75	a	b	c	d	105	a	b	c	d
16	a	b	c	d	46	a	b	c	d	76	a	b	c	d	106	a	b	c	d
17	a	b	c	d	47	a	b	c	d	77	a	b	c	d	107	a	b	c	d
18	a	b	c	d	48	a	b	c	d	78	a	b	c	d	108	a	b	c	d
19	a	b	c	d	49	a	b	c	d	79	a	b	c	d	109	a	b	c	d
20	a	b	c	d	50	a	b	c	d	80	a	b	c	d	110	a	b	c	d
21	a	b	c	d	51	a	b	c	d	81	a	b	c	d	111	a	b	c	d
22	a	b	c	d	52	a	b	c	d	82	a	b	c	d	112	a	b	c	d
23	a	b	c	d	53	a	b	c	d	83	a	b	c	d	113	a	b	c	d
24	a	b	c	d	54	a	b	c	d	84	a	b	c	d	114	a	b	c	d
25	a	b	c	d	55	a	b	c	d	85	a	b	c	d	115	a	b	c	d
26	a	b	c	d	56	a	b	c	d	86	a	b	c	d	116	a	b	c	d
27	a	b	c	d	57	a	b	c	d	87	a	b	c	d	117	a	b	c	d
28	a	b	c	d	58	a	b	c	d	88	a	b	c	d	118	a	b	c	d
29	a	b	c	d	59	a	b	c	d	89	a	b	c	d	119	a	b	c	d
30	a	b	c	d	60	a	b	c	d	90	a	b	c	d	120	a	b	c	d

Calculate Your Score

Correct (✓)	
Incorrect (✓)	
Unattempted	
Total Score	
Accuracy (%)	

Reasons for Incorrect Answers?

1. Lack of Knowledge/Existing Source Insufficient	
2. Lack of Multiple Revision	
3. Common Sense Mistakes	

Note :

1. Calculate total score as correct answers carry 2 marks each 1/3rd marks will deducted for **Incorrect** Answers.
2. Calculate Accuracy (%) by dividing the number of correct answers to the total number of attempted questions.

Past Learning

1. In which one of the following regions was Dhanyakataka, which flourished as a prominent Buddhist centre under the Mahasanghikas, located? **(2023)**

(a) Andhra (b) Gandhara
(c) Kalinga (d) Magadha

2. With reference to ancient India, consider the following statements : **(2023)**

1. The concept of Stupa is Buddhist in origin.
2. Stupa was generally a repository of relics.
3. Stupa was a votive and commemorative structure in Buddhist tradition.

How many of the statements given above is/are correct?

(a) Only one (b) Only two
(c) All three (d) None

3. 'Souls are not only the property of animal and plant life, but also of rocks, running water and many other natural objects not looked on as living by other religious sects'. The above statement reflects one of the core beliefs of which one of the following religious sects of ancient India? **(2023)**

(a) Buddhism (b) Jainism
(c) Shaivism (d) None

4. The world's second tallest statue in sitting pose of Ramanuja was inaugurated by the Prime Minister of India at Hyderabad recently. Which one of the following statements correctly represents the teachings of Ramanuja? **(2022)**

(a) The best means of salvation was devotion.
(b) Vedas are eternal, self-existent and wholly authoritative.
(c) Logical arguments were essential means for the highest bliss.
(d) Salvation was to be obtained through meditation.

5. With reference to Indian history, consider the following texts: **(2022)**

1. Nettipakarana
2. Parishishtaparvan
3. Avadanashataka
4. Trishashtilakshana Mahapurana

Which of the above are Jaina texts?

(a) 1, 2 and (b) 2 and 4 only
(c) 1, 3 and 4 (d) 2, 3 and 4

6. With reference to Indian history, consider the following pairs: **(2022)**

	Historical person	Known as
1.	Aryadeva	Jaina scholar
2.	Dignaga	Buddhist scholar
3.	Nathamuni	Vaishnava scholar

How many pairs given above is/are correctly matched?

(a) None of the pairs (b) Only one pair
(c) Only two pairs (d) All three pairs

7. With reference to the religious history of India, consider the following statements: **(2020)**

1. Sthaviravadins belong to Mahayana Buddhism.
2. Lokottaravadin sect was an offshoot of Mahasanghika sect of Buddhism.
3. The deification of Buddha by Mahasanghikas fostered Mahayana Buddhism.

Which of the statements given above is/are correct?

(a) 1 and 2 only
(b) 2 and 3 only
(c) 3 only
(d) 1, 2 and 3

8. With reference to the cultural history of India, which one of the following is the correct description of the term 'paramitas'? **(2020)**

(a) The earliest Dharmashastra texts written in aphoristic (sutra) style.
(b) Philosophical schools that did not accept the authority of Vedas.
(c) Perfections whose attainment led to the Bodhisattva path.
(d) Powerful merchant guilds of early medieval South India.

9. Consider the following: **(2019)**
1. Deification of the Buddha
2. Treading the path of Bodhisattvas
3. Image worship and rituals

Which of the above is/are the feature/ features of Mahayana Buddhism?
(a) 1 only (b) 1 and 2 only
(c) 2 and 3 only (d) 1, 2 and 3

10. With reference to the Indian History, who among the following is a future Buddha, yet to come to save the world? **(2018)**
(a) Avalokiteshvara (b) Lokesvara
(c) Maitreya (d) Padmapani

11. With reference to the religious practices in India, the 'Sthanakvasi' sect belongs to **(2018)**
(a) Buddhism (b) Jainism
(c) Vaishnavism (d) Shaivism

12. With reference to the religious history of India, consider the following statements:
1. Sautrantika and Sammitiya were the sects of Jainism. **(2017)**
2. Sarvastivadin held that the constituents of phenomena were not wholly momentary, but existed forever in a latent form.

Which of the statements given above is/are correct?
(a) 1 only (b) 2 only
(c) Both 1 and 2 (d) Neither 1 nor 2

13. With reference to the cultural history of India, the memorising of chronicles, dynastic histories and epic tales was the profession of who of the following? **(2016)**
(a) Shramana (b) Parivrajaka
(c) Agrahaarika (d) Magadha

14. With reference to the cultural history of medieval India, consider the following statements: **(2016)**
1. Siddhas (Sittars) of Tamil region were monotheistic and condemned idolatry.
2. Lingayats of Kannada region questioned the theory of rebirth and rejected the caste hierarchy.

Which of the statements given above is/are correct?
(a) 1 only (b) 2 only
(c) Both 1 and 2 (d) Neither 1 nor 2

15. With reference to the religious history of India, consider the following statements: **(2016)**
1. The concept of Bodhisattva is central to Hinayana sect of Buddhism.
2. Bodhisattva is a compassionate one on his way to enlightenment.
3. Bodhisattva delays achieving his own salvation to help all sentient beings on their path to it.

Which of the statements given above is/are correct?
(a) 1 only (b) 2 and 3 only
(c) 2 only (d) 1, 2 and 3

16. Which of the following kingdoms were associated with the life of the Buddha? **(2015)**
1. Avanti 2. Gandhara 3. Kosala 4. Magadha

Select the correct answer using the codes given below.
(a) 1, 2 and 3 only (b) 2 and 3 only
(c) 1, 3 and 4 (d) 3 and 4 only

17. Which of the following statements is/are applicable to Jain doctrine? **(2013)**
1. The surest way of annihilating Karma is to practice penance
2. Every object, even the smallest particle has a soul
3. Karma is the bane of the soul and must be ended

Select the correct answer using the codes given below:
(a) 1 only (b) 2 and 3 only
(c) 1 and 3 only (d) 1, 2 and 3

18. In ancient Indian Buddhist monasteries, a ceremony called Pavarana used to be held. It was the: **(2002)**
(a) occasion to elect the Sanghparinayaka and two speakers one on Dhamma and the other Vinaya
(b) confession by monks of their offences committed during their stay in the monasteries during the rainy season
(c) ceremony of initiation of new person into the Buddhist Sangha is when the head shaved and when yellow robes are offered
(d) gathering of Buddhist monks on the day to the full Moon day of Ashadha when they take up a fixed abode for the next months of rainy season

Detailed Solutions

Assessment Round

1. *(c)* All three

- **Statement 1 is correct**: The discovery of numerous female figurines and terracotta images from the Indus Valley sites, especially at **Mohenjodaro and Harappa**, has led scholars to believe that the civilisation practiced the **worship of a Mother Goddess**, symbolising fertility.
- **Statement 2 is correct**: Seals and sealings of Pashupati/Mahadev, particularly the famous seal showing a figure surrounded by animals in a yogic posture, indicate early representations of a proto-Shiva figure.
- **Statement 3 is correct**: The presence of fire altars at archaeological sites like Banawali, Lothal and Kalibangan points to the practice of fire worship, which was a significant part of religious rituals. These fire altars are believed to have been used in various ceremonial rites, possibly related to the cult of fire.

Thus, option (c) is the correct answer.

2. *(d)* All four

- **Statement 1 is correct**: Fire altars found at sites such as **Kalibangan and Lothal** indicate ritualistic practices centered around fire worship, a practice that continued into later Vedic traditions.
- **Statement 2 is correct**: The discovery of female figurines across multiple Indus Valley sites points to a widespread **belief in a fertility cult, likely centered around a Mother Goddess**, emphasising the importance of fertility and agriculture in the civilisation.
- **Statement 3 is correct**: Seals depicting **Pashupati/Mahadev, often associated with Shiva**, suggest the presence of religious or spiritual beliefs connected to proto-Shiva worship. This further underscores the civilisation's complex religious structure.
- **Statement 4 is correct**: The **Great Bath at Mohenjodaro** is believed to have been used for ritualistic or ceremonial purposes, possibly for **purificatory rites**, indicating an early form of ritual bathing that was significant in the religious practices of the time.

Thus, option (d) is the correct answer.

3. *(c)* 1, 2 and 3

- **Statement 1 is correct**: The offering of Soma juice was a central element of Vedic rituals, particularly during the early and later Vedic periods. **Soma was considered a divine nectar, consumed during sacrifices to appease the gods.** It was believed to grant immortality to the gods and provide vigor to those who consumed it.
- **Statement 2 is correct**: Fire played a crucial role in Vedic rituals, serving as the medium through which offerings were made to the gods. The **Agni, or fire god**, was seen as the messenger who carried the offerings to the divine realm. This practice of fire sacrifices, known as 'yajna', was central to the religious life of the Vedic people and was performed with meticulous precision.
- **Statement 3 is correct**: Concepts like **Samsara (the cycle of rebirth) and Karma (the moral law of cause and effect)** emerged during the later Vedic period, reflecting a shift from ritualistic practices to more philosophical and ethical considerations.

Thus, option (c) is the correct answer.

4. *(b)* Varuna was considered the upholder of cosmic order.

- **Statement (a) is incorrect: Agni**, another important Vedic deity, was primarily associated with **terrestrial fires**, including the sacred fire used in rituals. Agni served as the intermediary between the gods and humans, conveying offerings made during sacrifices to the divine realm.
- **Statement (b) is correct**: Varuna was one of the most revered deities in the Vedic pantheon, often associated with the **cosmic order or 'Rita'**. He was considered the **guardian of truth and the enforcer of divine**

law, ensuring the universe's balance. As the lord of the cosmic waters, Varuna was also invoked for protection and the maintenance of social and moral order.

- **Statement (c) is incorrect: Soma, a plant whose juice** was extracted and used in rituals, was not only a sacrificial offering but was also believed to have **intoxicating** and possibly hallucinogenic properties. Soma was considered a divine elixir that invigorated the gods and played a crucial role in Vedic sacrifices, symbolising vitality and immortality.

Thus, option (b) is the correct answer.

5. *(c)* Indra

- Indra, the most prominent deity of the early Vedic period, was revered as the **God of thunder, lightning and rain.** He was also the king of the gods and the chief warrior deity, often invoked for success in battles. His thunderbolt, known as **'Vajra'**, was a powerful weapon used to defeat enemies and demons.
- Indra's prominence is reflected in the large number of hymns dedicated to him in the Rigveda. He was seen as the **protector of the Aryan tribes,** ensuring their victory in conflicts and granting them prosperity by controlling the elements.
- Indra's association with rain made him a **crucial deity for agricultural societies,** as his blessings were believed to bring about bountiful harvests. His **victory over the demon Vritra,** who had imprisoned the waters, symbolised the release of life-giving waters and the restoration of order.

Thus, option (c) is the correct answer.

6. *(a)* Only one pair

- **Pair 1 is correct:** The Rigveda, the oldest of the Vedas, is primarily a **collection of hymns** (suktas) dedicated to various deities. These hymns were **chanted during sacrifices and other rituals** to invoke the blessings of the gods. The Rigveda is thus rightly associated with invocations and hymns.
- **Pair 2 is incorrect:** The **Yajurveda** is associated with the **sacrificial formulae used in rituals.** It provides instructions on the performance of rituals and the proper recitation of prayers during the sacrifices. It is not focused on melodies or music but on the correct execution of rituals.
- **Pair 3 is incorrect:** The **Samaveda, known as the Veda of melodies and chants,** is indeed associated with music. The hymns of the Samaveda are meant to be sung in a specific manner during the rituals and they form the basis of the ancient Indian musical tradition.

Thus option (a) is the correct answer.

7. *(b)* Only two pairs

- **Pair 1 correct:** The **Varkari Panth,** a Bhakti movement sect, is associated with the worship of Vitthoba, a **manifestation of Lord Vishnu.** This sect, prominent in Maharashtra, was influenced by saints like **Jnaneshwar and Tukaram,** who emphasised devotion to Vitthoba.
- **Pair 2 is correct:** Brahma Sampradaya, founded by **Madhavacharya in the 13th century,** is a **Dvaita (dualism)** school of Vedanta. It focuses on the worship of Vishnu as Para Brahma, the Supreme Being. This sect is particularly noted for its emphasis on the duality between the individual soul (Jiva) and the Supreme Soul (Brahman).
- **Pair 3 is incorrect: Nimbarka Sampradaya** however, was not founded by Vallabhacharya. It was founded by Nimbarka, who propagated the philosophy of Dvaitadvaita (dualism and non-dualism). **Vallabhacharya founded the Pushtimarg sect,** centered around the worship of Krishna.

Thus, option (b) is the correct answer.

8. *(c)* All three pairs

- **Pair 1 is correct:** The **Varkari Panth** venerates Vitthoba, also known as **Vithoba or Panduranga,** a deity worshipped primarily in Maharashtra. Vitthoba is seen as a **form of Lord Vishnu or Krishna** and the sect's teachings revolve around devotion to him.
- **Pair 2 is correct: Brahma Sampradaya, founded by Madhavacharya, worships Para Brahma,** the Supreme Being, as different from the material world and individual souls. This school of thought advocates a **strict dualism,** where God (Vishnu) and soul are distinct.

- **Pair 3 is correct: Pushtimarg, founded by Vallabhacharya,** is centered around the worship of Radha and Krishna. It emphasises **spontaneous devotion (Pushti Bhakti) to Krishna,** considering him as the Supreme God who graces his devotees without any cause.

Thus, option (c) is the correct answer.

9. *(d)* 1 only

- **Statement 1 is correct:** The **Varkari Panth** is a prominent devotional movement within Vaishnavism, particularly in the Indian state of **Maharashtra.** It is centered around the **worship of Vitthoba** (also known as Vithoba or Panduranga), a **manifestation of Lord Vishnu or Krishna.** The followers of this sect are known for their devotion (bhakti) and pilgrimage (vari) to the **Vitthoba temple at Pandharpur.**
- **Statement 2 is incorrect:** The Ramanandi Sampradaya is a sect of Vaishnavism that primarily **follows the teachings of Lord Rama,** not Krishna. The Ramanandis regard Lord Rama as the Supreme God and advocate for devotion to Rama as the path to salvation. This sect traces its **origins to Ramananda, a 14th-century saint** and is especially prominent in North India.
- **Statement 3 is incorrect: Pushtimarg, founded by Vallabhacharya around the 16th century,** is a sect of Vaishnavism that is dedicated to the **worship of Lord Krishna,** particularly in his **form as Shrinathji.** The sect **does not focus on the concept of Brahma** as the ultimate truth in the sense that other Vedantic schools might. Instead, it **emphasises Krishna as the Supreme Being,** whose grace (pushti) is the means to attain spiritual liberation.

Thus, option (d) is the correct answer.

10. *(c)* 1, 2 and 3

- **Option 1 is correct:** The **Kalamukhas were a Shaivite sect** that emerged in the **11th century CE** in the **Karnataka region.** They were known for their extreme rituals, which included practices such as carrying skulls and performing rituals that were considered unorthodox by mainstream Shaivism.
- **Option 2 is correct:** The **Kapalikas** were another **Shaivite sect** known for their tantric practices, which included ritualistic use of human skulls, hence their name (**'Kapala' meaning skull**). They engaged in extreme forms of devotion, including rituals that involved the use of wine, meat and sexual rites, all **aimed at attaining siddhis (spiritual powers).**
- **Option 3 is correct: Nathpanthis,** although not as extreme as the Kalamukhas or Kapalikas were also associated with the **use of Hatha Yoga** to achieve spiritual awakening. Founded by **Matsyendranath** and popularised **by Gorakhnath,** the Nathpanthis focused on the union of the individual self with the supreme reality through rigorous physical and spiritual practices.

Thus, option (c) is the correct answer.

11. *(a)* 1 and 2 only

- **Statement 1 is correct:** The **Aghoris** are a sect of **ascetic Shaivites** known for their extreme and often misunderstood practices. They are associated with rituals that involve the use of cremation ashes, human skulls and living in cremation grounds. Their practices are **aimed at transcending societal norms and achieving moksha (liberation)** through the acceptance of all aspects of life, including death and decay.
- **Statement 2 is correct:** The **Nathpanthis** are closely associated with the doctrine of Hatha Yoga, which emphasises **physical postures (asanas), breath control (pranayama) and meditation** as means to attain spiritual liberation.
- **Statement 3 is incorrect:** The **Kapalikas,** despite their extreme practices, did not reject idol worship entirely. They had their own set of deities and rituals, often focusing on Bhairava, a fierce form of Shiva. Their rituals were distinct from mainstream Shaivism but still involved the worship of idols and symbols of power.

Thus, option (a) is the correct answer.

12. *(a)* 1 and 2 only

- **Statement 1 is correct: Saiva Siddhanta** is one of the major schools of Shaivism, particularly prominent in **Tamil Nadu and**

Northern Sri Lanka. It is a dualistic school that recognises **Shiva as the supreme deity** and emphasises the relationship between the soul and God. The teachings of this sect are **based on the Agamas**, which are scriptures dedicated to Shaivism.

- **Statement 2 is correct:** The **Kalamukhas** were primarily located in the **Karnataka region** and were known for their distinctive religious practices, which included rituals that were considered extreme or unorthodox.
- **Statement 3 is incorrect:** The **Pashupatas were an ancient Shaivite sect** that emerged as one of the earliest forms of Shaivism. They were **not an offshoot of Vaishnavism** but rather one of the earliest organised sects within Shaivism, known for their ascetic practices and philosophical teachings. They focused on **devotion to Pashupati, a form of Shiva** and believed in attaining liberation through a combination of asceticism and devotion.

Thus option (a) is the correct answer.

13. *(a)* 1 and 3 only

- **Statement 1 is correct: Vasugupta**, an influential philosopher and sage, is traditionally credited as the **founder of Kashmir Shaivism.** He is believed to have received the foundational teachings of this sect directly from Lord Shiva, which he then transmitted to his disciples. These **teachings were compiled in the Shiva Sutras**, which form the basis of the Trika school of Kashmir Shaivism.
- **Statement 2 is incorrect: Kashmir Shaivism** does not accept the authority of the Vedas in the same way as orthodox Hindu traditions **do not reject it completely.** Instead, it emphasises the **teachings found in the Tantras, which are esoteric texts that focus on the worship of Shiva and the divine feminine (Shakti).** The philosophy of Kashmir Shaivism is considered more non-dualistic, focusing on the oneness of the individual soul with the universal consciousness.
- **Statement 3 is correct:** The **Pratyabhijna (Recognition) school** is an important philosophical system within Kashmir Shaivism that emerged as an offshoot of the main tradition. It was **developed by thinkers like Utpaladeva and Abhinavagupta**, who emphasised that the 'individual soul realizes its inherent unity with Shiva'.

Thus, option (a) is the correct answer.

14. *(b)* Only two pairs

- **Pair 1 is correct:** Kali, one of the most **revered goddesses in the Shakti tradition**, is indeed fierce. She is often depicted in a terrifying form, symbolising the **destruction of evil forces.** Kali is associated with **death, time and change and her fierce aspect** is worshipped for protection and liberation.
- **Pair 2 is incorrect:** Durga, also fierce, is worshipped as Mahisasuramardini, the **slayer of the buffalo demon Mahisasura.** She embodies the warrior aspect of the divine feminine, protecting the universe from demonic forces. Although Durga has a peaceful aspect as well, her fierce form is the most prominent in the Shakti cult.
- **Pair 3 is correct:** Saraswati is indeed associated with **pacific or peaceful attributes.** She is the goddess of knowledge, music, art and wisdom and is often depicted as serene and calm, representing the gentle and peaceful aspect of the divine feminine.

Thus, option (b) is the correct answer.

15. *(c)* All three pairs

- **Pair 1 is correct: Kali is invoked as a saviour,** particularly in her fierce aspect where she **destroys evil forces and protects her devotees.** She is revered as the ultimate protector who grants liberation by removing obstacles, both external and internal, that stand in the way of spiritual progress.
- **Pair 2 is correct:** Durga, in her many forms, is venerated as the **mother goddess who nurtures and protects her devotees.** She is the **embodiment of Shakti** (divine energy) and is worshipped as the great mother who grants strength, courage and protection.
- **Pair 3 is correct:** Chandi is a **fierce warrior goddess**, often identified with Durga. The **Chandi Path, a text dedicated to her,** describes her exploits in battle against the forces of evil. She is worshipped for her power to overcome obstacles and enemies, symbolising the **triumph of good over evil.**

Thus, option (c) is the correct answer.

16. *(c)* All three

- **Statement 1 is correct:** Buddhism arose as a **response to the growing discontent** with the Vedic rituals, which had become highly elaborate, costly and often inaccessible to the lower classes. These rituals required the involvement of Brahmins, who monopolised religious knowledge and practice, making it difficult for common people to engage in spiritual practices without the mediation of priests.
- **Statement 2 is correct:** The **Upanishads, which are part of the later Vedic texts**, introduced complex philosophical ideas such as the **concepts of Brahman (universal soul) and Atman (individual soul)**. While these ideas influenced early Buddhist thought, Buddha's teachings diverged significantly, particularly by rejecting the notion of a **permanent self (Atman) and emphasising impermanence (Anicca) and non-self (Anatta)**.
- **Statement 3 is correct:** The **caste system**, deeply entrenched in Vedic society, was rigid and hierarchical, leading to widespread social inequality. **Buddhism's rejection of the caste system** and its emphasis on the spiritual equality of all individuals, regardless of birth, resonated with many people across different strata of society, contributing to its spread.

Thus, option (c) is the correct answer.

17. *(d)* All four

- **Statement 1 is correct: Samyak Sambuddha-** These are **fully enlightened Buddhas** who attain supreme knowledge on their own and then decide to teach the path of enlightenment to others. **Gautama Buddha is considered the 28th Samyak Sambuddha.** He preached the Dharma (law) and established the Sangha (community) to guide others to Nirvana.
- **Statement 2 is correct: Pratyeka Buddha-** These Buddhas attain enlightenment by themselves during times when the Dharma is not being taught. Unlike Samyak Sambuddhas, they do not preach or establish a following. They **are solitary practitioners** who realise the truth but do not share their knowledge with others.
- **Statement 3 is correct: Dhyani Buddha-** Also known as **celestial Buddhas, these are five transcendental Buddhas** in Mahayana and Vajrayana Buddhism, representing different aspects of the enlightened mind. Each Dhyani Buddha is associated with a specific direction, colour and symbol and they are often meditated upon for spiritual purification and protection.
- **Statement 4 is correct: Adi Buddha-** In Vajrayana Buddhism, Adi Buddha is considered the **primordial Buddha, representing the original and eternal state of enlightenment.** Vajrayana texts describe Adi Buddha as the source from which all other Buddhas emanate and he is often identified with the Dharmakaya (truth body) or the ultimate reality itself.

Thus, option (d) is the correct answer.

18. *(c)* 1, 2 and 3

- **Statement 1 is correct: Siddhartha Gautama** was born in **Lumbini**, which is now part of modern-day Nepal, around 563 BCE. His birth site is marked by the **Lumbini pillar, erected by Emperor Ashoka** and is a UNESCO World Heritage Site. Siddhartha was born into the **Shakya clan**, a warrior class and was destined to be either a great king or a spiritual leader.
- **Statement 2 is correct: Enlightenment-** At the **age of 29, Siddhartha renounced his princely life** and embarked on a quest for spiritual knowledge. After years of ascetic practices and meditation, he **attained enlightenment at the age of 35** while meditating **under the Bodhi tree in Bodh Gaya**. Enlightenment, or Nirvana, marked the realisation of the **Four Noble Truths** and the path to liberation from the cycle of birth and rebirth (Samsara).
- **Statement 3 is correct: Dharmachakra Pravartana-** After attaining enlightenment, Buddha delivered his **first sermon at Sarnath, near Varanasi**. This sermon is known as the **'Dharmachakra Pravartana' or 'Turning of the Wheel of Dharma'**. In this sermon, Buddha introduced the core principles of his teachings, including the **Four Noble Truths and the Eightfold Path**, to his first five disciples, setting the foundation for the spread of Buddhism.

Thus, option (c) is the correct answer.

19. *(b)* 1, 2 and 3 only

- **Statement 1 is correct**: The **Four Noble Truths** are the essence of Buddha's teachings, revealing the nature of suffering and the path to its cessation. The first truth, **Dukkha**, acknowledges that **life is inherently filled with suffering** due to birth, aging, illness and death. It is a fundamental aspect of existence that cannot be avoided.
- **Statement 2 is correct**: The second truth, **Samudaya**, identifies the **cause of suffering as craving or desire**. This desire leads to attachment, which binds individuals to the cycle of Samsara. Overcoming this desire is essential for ending suffering.
- **Statement 3 is correct**: The third truth, **Nirodha**, asserts that **suffering can be ended.** This cessation of suffering, also known as Nirvana, is achieved by **extinguishing desire and attachment**, leading to liberation from Samsara.
- **Statement 4 is incorrect**: The fourth truth, **Magga**, outlines the **Eightfold Path** as the means to end suffering. This path includes **right understanding, intention, speech, action, livelihood, effort, mindfulness and concentration** and serves as a practical guide to living a life that leads to enlightenment.

Thus, option (b) is the correct answer.

20. *(c)* Only three

- **Pair 1 is correct**: Bodhi Tree- The Bodhi tree **at Bodh Gaya is where Siddhartha Gautama attained enlightenment** and became the Buddha. The tree symbolises the place of awakening and is revered by Buddhists worldwide. **It represents wisdom, spiritual knowledge and the attainment of Nirvana.**
- **Pair 2 is correct: Wheel (Dharmachakra)is a symbol of Buddha's teachings and the turning of the Dharma.** It is associated with his first sermon at Sarnath, where he set the wheel of Dharma in motion. The **eight spokes of the wheel represent the Eightfold Path**, the core of Buddhist practice.
- **Pair 3 is correct**: Stupa- Stupas are **monumental structures that often contain relics of the Buddha** or other significant Buddhist figures. They **symbolise the Buddha's death and Parinirvana.** Stupas are places of meditation and pilgrimage, reminding practitioners of the impermanence of life and the possibility of enlightenment.
- **Pair 4 is incorrect: Elephant**- The elephant is associated with **Buddha's conception, not renunciation.** According to legend, **Queen Maya, Buddha's mother, dreamt of a white elephant entering her womb**, signifying the birth of a great being. The elephant is a symbol of strength, wisdom and auspiciousness.

Thus, option (c) is the correct answer.

21. *(a)* 1 only

- **Option 1 is correct: Nirvana** is the ultimate goal of Buddhism, representing the cessation of suffering and the cycle of rebirth. It is achieved by extinguishing **desire, hatred and ignorance, the root causes of suffering.** Nirvana is a state of liberation and freedom from Samsara, the cycle of birth, death and rebirth.
- **Option 2 is incorrect: Samsara** refers to the **cycle of birth, death and rebirth** that all beings are subject to. It is characterised by suffering and is the very cycle that Buddhists seek to escape through the attainment of Nirvana.
- **Option 3 is incorrect**: Bodhi refers to the enlightenment that Siddhartha Gautama attained, but it is not the same as Nirvana. Bodhi is the realisation of the truth of existence, while Nirvana is the state achieved by overcoming all desires and attachments.
- **Option 4 is incorrect**: Pratitya Samutpada (dependent origination) is a doctrine that **explains the interconnectedness of all phenomena** and how they arise due to specific causes and conditions. While it is a central teaching in Buddhism, it is not the ultimate goal like Nirvana.

Thus, option (a) is the correct answer.

22. *(b)* The universe is in a state of constant flux.

- **Anicca** (impermanence) is **one of the Three Marks of Existence in Buddhism, alongside Dukkha (suffering) and Anatta (non-self).** It teaches that all conditioned things, whether physical or mental, are in a **constant state of Flux.** This **change is inevitable** and leads to suffering when one becomes attached to things as if they were permanent.

- Everything, from our **bodies to our thoughts,** is subject to **decay and transformation.** Understanding Anicca helps in cultivating **detachment from worldly pleasures** and **material possessions,** which are temporary and subject to change. By realising the transient nature of all **things,** a practitioner can move closer to the realisation of **Anatta (non-self) and Nirvana.**

Thus, option (b) is the correct answer.

23. *(c)* Pratitya Samutpada

- **Pratitya Samutpada** (dependent origination) is a fundamental Buddhist concept explaining the **interconnectedness and causality of all phenomena.** It posits that nothing exists independently; everything is conditioned by something else. This principle is often depicted through the **Twelve Links of Dependent Origination,** which illustrate how ignorance leads to mental formations, consciousness, name and form, the six senses, contact, feeling, craving, clinging, becoming, birth and finally, aging and death.
- The concept is critical in understanding the Buddhist view of Samsara (the cycle of birth and death) and how beings are trapped in this cycle due to ignorance and desire. Recognising the interdependent nature of reality is essential for breaking the cycle and attaining Nirvana.
- **Pratitya Samutpada** also **underscores the impermanence of all phenomena.** Since everything arises dependent on conditions, it is also subject to change and eventual cessation.

Thus, option (c) is the correct answer.

24. *(c)* All three pairs

- **Pair 1 is correct:** The **First Buddhist Council was held at Rajagriha** shortly after Buddha's death. It was presided over by **King Ajatashatru** and aimed to compile the Buddha's teachings into the **Sutta Pitaka (discourses) and Vinaya Pitaka (monastic rules).**
- **Pair 2 is correct:** The **Second Council** was held at **Vaishali and presided over by King Kalasoka.** It led to the first significant schism in the Buddhist community due to disagreements over monastic practices, **dividing the community into the Sthavira (Elders) and Mahasanghika (Great Community).**
- **Pair 3 is correct:** The **Third Council** was convened by **Emperor Ashoka at Pataliputra** (modern-day Patna). It aimed to purify the Sangha by expelling corrupt monks and solidifying the teachings. The **Abhidhamma Pitaka (philosophical teachings)** was also compiled during this council.

Thus, option (c) is the correct answer.

25. *(b)* The Vinaya Pitaka contains the rules for monastic discipline in Buddhism.

- **Statement 1 is incorrect:** The **Pali Canon** is the scriptural foundation of **Theravada Buddhism,** not Mahayana Buddhism. The Mahayana tradition developed its texts, including the **Prajnaparamita Sutras** and the **Lotus Sutra,** which are written in Sanskrit and reflect the Mahayana emphasis on the Bodhisattva ideal.
- **Statement 2 is correct:** The **Vinaya Pitaka** is the section of the **Tripitaka** that deals with the **monastic rules for monks and nuns.** It includes guidelines for ethical behaviour, daily routines and procedures for resolving disputes within the Sangha. It is foundational to the monastic tradition in Buddhism.
- **Statement 3 is incorrect:** The **Mahavamsa** is a historical chronicle **from Sri Lanka,** detailing the history of Buddhism in the region, particularly during the **reign of Emperor Ashoka** and the establishment of the **Theravada tradition.** It is not a Tibetan Buddhist text and its focus is more on historical events than religious doctrine.
- **Statement 4 is incorrect:** The **Madhyamika School,** founded by Nagarjuna, is a central philosophical school within **Mahayana Buddhism.** It is known for its doctrine of **Sunyata (emptiness),** which argues that all phenomena are empty of inherent existence.

Thus, option (b) is the correct answer.

26. *(d)* 1, 2 and 3

- **Statement 1 is correct:** The Buddhist Sangha was indeed **established on democratic lines**, where decisions were made collectively during assemblies known as **Sangha Councils**. These councils followed a democratic procedure, with monks **voting on issues** and decisions being made by consensus or majority.
- **Statement 2 is correct:** The **Vinaya Pitaka** is one of the three baskets of the Tripitaka and contains the **monastic rules governing the behaviour of monks and nuns**. These rules cover various aspects of monastic life, including ethical conduct, disciplinary actions and the procedures for ordaining new monks and nuns.
- **Statement 3 is correct:** The **Upasampada** is the **higher ordination ceremony** required for full entry into the Sangha. It marks the **transition from a novice monk (Samanera) to a fully ordained monk (Bhikkhu)**. This ceremony is essential for becoming a member of the Sangha.

Thus, option (d) is the correct answer.

27. *(c)* All three

- **Statement 1 is correct:** The **First Buddhist Council** was held at **Rajagriha**, under the **patronage of King Ajatashatru**, shortly after the Buddha's death. The council was **presided over by Mahakassapa** and was aimed at preserving the Buddha's teachings. The teachings were recited orally by Ananda and Upali and later compiled into the Sutta Pitaka and Vinaya Pitaka.
- **Statement 2 is correct:** The **Second Council** held at Vaishali about 100 years after the Buddha's death, was significant because it led to the first major schism in Buddhism. The schism arose due to disagreements over monastic discipline, leading to the **formation of two groups: the Sthaviras (conservative elders) and the Mahasanghikas (more liberal group)**.
- **Statement 3 is correct:** The **Fourth Buddhist Council** was convened by **Emperor Kanishka in Kashmir**. This council is notable for the division of Buddhism into the **Hinayana and Mahayana** schools, marking a significant development in the history of Buddhism. The council also led to the compilation of a substantial amount of Buddhist literature.

Thus, option (c) is the correct answer.

28. *(d)* All four

- **Option 1 is correct: Sunyata, or emptiness**, is a fundamental doctrine of Mahayana Buddhism, particularly in the **Madhyamaka school founded by Nagarjuna**. It teaches that all phenomena are empty of inherent existence and that understanding this is crucial for achieving liberation.
- **Option 2 is correct:** The **Yogachara school, also known as Vijnanavada**, is another major school within Mahayana Buddhism. It **emphasises the role of consciousness in the creation of reality**, asserting that what we perceive as the external world is a projection of the mind.
- **Option 3 is correct:** The Trikaya doctrine in Mahayana Buddhism describes the three bodies of the Buddha: **Dharmakaya (truth body), Sambhogakaya (enjoyment body) and Nirmanakaya (manifestation body)**. This concept explains how the Buddha can manifest in different forms to help sentient beings.
- **Option 4 is correct:** Shunyavada is essentially synonymous with Sunyata and refers to the **doctrine of emptiness**. It is particularly associated with the Madhyamaka school of Mahayana Buddhism. Although closely related, 'Shunyavada' is not listed separately from Sunyata.

Thus, option (d) is the correct answer.

29. *(a)* 1 and 2 only

- **Statement 1 is correct:** Theravada, meaning '**Teaching of the Elders**', is considered the oldest and most conservative branch of Buddhism. It adheres closely to the original teachings of the Buddha as **preserved in the Pali Canon**. The school emphasises individual attainment of Nirvana through strict observance of monastic discipline and meditation.
- **Statement 2 is correct:** The Pali Canon, also known as the **Tipitaka**, is the scriptural

foundation of Theravada Buddhism. It is written in Pali and consists of **three 'baskets': the Sutta Pitaka** (discourses of the Buddha), the **Vinaya Pitaka** (monastic rules) and the **Abhidhamma Pitaka (philosophical treatises)**.

- **Statement 3 is incorrect**: The concept of Bodhisattvas, enlightened beings who delay their own Nirvana to help others, is more **central to Mahayana Buddhism than Theravada.** Theravada primarily focuses on the path of the **Arhat, an individual who attains enlightenment for themselves.**

Thus, option (a) is the correct answer.

30. *(b)* The denial of a permanent self or soul.

- **Anatta (Non-Self)**: The concept of Anatta is one of the most profound and defining teachings of Buddhism, forming one of the Three Marks of Existence along with **Anicca (impermanence) and Dukkha (suffering)**. Anatta teaches that there is **no permanent, unchanging self or soul within living beings.**
- Instead, what we consider the 'self' is a temporary aggregation of **five aggregates** (skandhas): form (physical body), sensation (feelings), perception (recognition), mental formations (thoughts, emotions, volitions) and **consciousness**. These aggregates are constantly changing and clinging to the idea of a permanent self leads to suffering (Dukkha).

Thus, option (b) is the correct answer.

31. *(b)* Avalokiteshvara

- **Avalokiteshvara:** It is one of the most important Bodhisattvas in Mahayana Buddhism, known as the the **Bodhisattvas (embodiment) of compassion.** His name means **'The Lord Who Looks Down with Compassion'.** He is often depicted with multiple arms and heads, symbolising his ability to assist all beings in their quest for enlightenment.
- **Lotus Symbolism**: In Buddhist iconography, Avalokiteshvara is frequently **shown holding a lotus flower, which symbolises purity, enlightenment and spiritual awakening.** The lotus grows in muddy water but remains unstained, representing the Bodhisattva's purity and ability to transcend the material world.
- **Reverence Across Traditions:** Avalokiteshvara is **revered across both Theravada and Mahayana traditions.** In Tibetan Buddhism, he is associated with the Dalai Lama, who is considered an incarnation of Avalokiteshvara. His compassionate vow to assist all beings is central to the Mahayana ideal of the Bodhisattva.

Thus, option (b) is the correct answer.

32. *(a)* Only one pair

- **Pair 1 is correct**: In Buddhism, **Dana** refers to the practice of generosity or giving. It is considered one of the foundational virtues and is crucial for cultivating a spirit of selflessness and detachment.
- **Pair 2 is incorrect**: Sila refers to ethical conduct or morality. It involves adhering to precepts that govern speech, action and livelihood, forming the moral foundation for spiritual practice.
- **Pair 3 is incorrect: Bhavana** means mental development or meditation. It encompasses practices that cultivate mindfulness, concentration and insight, leading to the realisation of the true nature of reality.

Thus, option (a) is the correct answer.

33. *(c)* All three pairs

- **Pair 1 is correct**: The **Paramitas** are the ten perfections or virtues practiced by Bodhisattvas on their path to enlightenment in Mahayana Buddhism. They **include generosity, morality, patience, energy, meditation and wisdom.**
- **Pair 2 is correct**: The **Trikaya** doctrine describes the three bodies of the Buddha: **Dharmakaya** (truth body), **Sambhogakaya** (enjoyment body) and **Nirmanakaya** (manifestation body). This concept explains how the Buddha can manifest in different forms to guide beings.
- **Pair 3 is correct: Anicca** refers to the concept of **impermanence,** one of the Three Marks of Existence in Buddhism. It teaches that all conditioned phenomena are in a constant state of flux and are subject to change.

Thus, option (c) is the correct answer.

34. *(c)* The Yogachara School emphasizes the study of consciousness and mind.

- **Statement (a) is incorrect: Vajrayana Buddhism** incorporates **esoteric practices, including mantras, mudras and mandalas,** rather than focusing primarily on the worship of Bodhisattvas. While devotion to Bodhisattvas exists, the emphasis in Vajrayana is on the rapid path to enlightenment through tantric practices.
- **Statement (b) is incorrect:** The **Madhyamaka School** was **founded by Nagarjuna**, not Asanga. Madhyamaka, also a Mahayana school, is known for its doctrine of **Sunyata** (emptiness), which teaches that all phenomena are devoid of intrinsic existence.
- **Statement (c) is correct:** The **Yogachara** or **Vijnanavada** school is one of the major philosophical schools within Mahayana Buddhism, **established by Asanga and his brother Vasubandhu** in the 4th century CE. Yogachara argues that consciousness **is the fundamental basis** of all experiences and that understanding the workings of the mind is essential to overcoming ignorance and attaining enlightenment. It emphasises **Yogic practices** as a means to purify the mind and gain direct insight into the **nature of reality.**
- **Statement (d) is incorrect: Theravada Buddhism** primarily uses the Pali Canon and **its scriptures are in Pali, not Sanskrit.** Sanskrit is more commonly used in Mahayana and Vajrayana traditions.

Thus, option (c) is the correct answer.

35. *(d)* 1, 2 and 3

- **Statement 1 is correct:** The **Sutta Pitaka** contains the **discourses (Suttas) of the Buddha**, covering a wide range of topics including ethics, meditation and philosophy. They form the **core teachings of Buddhism.** It is divided into five Nikayas: Digha, Majjhima, Samyutta, Anguttara and Khuddaka.
- **Statement 2 is correct:** The **Vinaya Pitaka** deals with **monastic discipline and the rules of conduct for monks and nuns.** It is crucial for maintaining the integrity and discipline of the monastic order and it reflects the Buddha's emphasis on ethical living as the foundation for spiritual practice.
- **Statement 3 is correct:** The **Abhidhamma Pitaka** offers a **systematic and philosophical analysis of the Buddha's teachings.** Abhidhamma provides a detailed examination of the nature of mind and matter, the processes of perception and the factors leading to enlightenment.

Thus option (d) is the correct answer.

36. *(c)* All three

- **Statement 1 is correct:** Buddhism was introduced to Sri Lanka during the reign of Emperor Ashoka, who played a crucial role in the spread of Buddhism across Asia. He sent his son **Mahinda** and daughter **Sanghamitra** to Sri Lanka as missionaries.
- **Statement 2 is correct:** The Mahayana School of Buddhism, which emerged around the **1st century CE**, is often described as more liberal and inclusive compared to Theravada. Mahayana introduced new philosophical concepts, such as the **Bodhisattva ideal** and also introduced new scriptures, such as the **Prajnaparamita Sutras** and the **Lotus Sutra.**
- **Statement 3 is correct: Vajrayana,** or **Tantric Buddhism,** is a branch of Mahayana that incorporates esoteric practices aimed at achieving enlightenment swiftly. Vajrayana developed in India and later spread to Tibet, Bhutan and Mongolia is characterised by the use of **mantras, mandalas, mudras and deity yoga.**

Thus, option (c) is the correct answer.

37. *(b)* Only two

- **Option 1 is incorrect:** Theravada, meaning **'Teaching of the Elders'**, is the oldest and most **conservative branch of Buddhism.** It adheres closely to the original teachings of the Buddha as preserved in the Pali Canon. Theravada is primarily practiced in South and South-East Asia, particularly in countries like Sri Lanka, Thailand, Myanmar, Laos and Cambodia.
- **Option 2 is correct:** Vajrayana, also known as **Tantric or Esoteric Buddhism**, is a major school within Mahayana Buddhism. It incorporates **tantric practices** aimed at

achieving enlightenment swiftly, often within a **single lifetime.** Vajrayana Buddhism is most prominent in Tibet, Bhutan and Mongolia.

- **Option 3 is correct:** While **Yogachara** (also known as **Vijnanavada**) is an important philosophical school within Mahayana Buddhism, focusing on the nature of consciousness. It is a school of thought within **Mahayana, alongside the Madhyamaka school.**

Thus, option (b) is the correct answer.

38. *(a)* 1 and 2 only

- **Statement 1 is correct:** The Mahayana School of Buddhism introduced and developed the concept of the **Bodhisattva**, an enlightened being who, out of compassion, chooses to delay their entry into Nirvana to help others achieve enlightenment. Famous Bodhisattvas in Mahayana include **Avalokiteshvara** (the Bodhisattva of Compassion), **Manjushri** (the Bodhisattva of Wisdom) and **Ksitigarbha** (the Bodhisattva of Well-beings).
- **Statement 2 is correct:** Mahayana scriptures were **predominantly written in Sanskrit**, as opposed to the Pali language used in Theravada Buddhism. Important Mahayana texts include the **Prajnaparamita Sutras**, the **Lotus Sutra** and the **Avatamsaka Sutra**
- **Statement 3 is incorrect:** While meditation is an important practice in Mahayana Buddhism, it is not **considered the only path to enlightenment.** Mahayana emphasises the cultivation of **Bodhisattva,** the practice of the **Six Paramitas** (perfections), ethical conduct and the study of Mahayana sutras.

Thus, option (a) is the correct answer.

39. *(b)* 1, 2 and 3 only

- **Statement 1 is correct: Zazen** is the core practice of Zen Buddhism, which means '**seated meditation**'. It is a form of meditation where practitioners sit in a specific posture, typically in the lotus or half-lotus position, with a straight back and focused breathing. The purpose of **Zazen is to quiet the mind and attain a state of awareness and insight,** leading to the realisation of one's true nature or enlightenment (satori).
- **Statement 2 is correct: Koans** are paradoxical statements, questions, or stories used in Zen practice to provoke deep thought and insight. A Koan is designed to push the mind beyond ordinary perception to achieve a direct experience of reality. The resolution of a Koan through meditation is believed to **lead to sudden enlightenment (kensho or satori).**
- **Statement 3 is correct:** Although, Zen Buddhism emphasises direct experience over intellectual study, the **study of Sutras** is still an important practice. Zen practitioners study Mahayana sutras such as the **Heart Sutra** and the **Diamond Sutra**, which encapsulate the essence of Buddhist wisdom.
- **Statement 4 is incorrect:** Zen Buddhism tends to focus more on direct experience and meditation rather than devotional practices. Zen does acknowledge Bodhisattvas like **Avalokiteshvara**, but the emphasis is **more on personal practice and realisation** rather than on rituals or devotion.

Thus, option (b) is the correct answer.

40. *(d)* 1, 2, 3 and 4

- **Option 1 is correct: Stupas** are monumental structures that were originally **built to house the relics of the Buddha** or other significant figures. They symbolise the Buddha's death and **Parinirvana (final Nirvana).** Stupas also serve as **places of meditation and pilgrimage.** The **Great Stupa at Sanchi** is one of the most famous examples of early Buddhist stupas.
- **Option 2 is correct: Chaityas** are **prayer halls or shrines** that often house a stupa at one end. They were originally rock-cut caves used by Buddhist monks for meditation and worship. The **Karle Chaitya** in India is one of the largest and most well-preserved examples of a rock-cut Chaitya hall. Chaityas typically **have a barrel-vaulted roof and are flanked by columns**, creating an impressive interior space for communal worship.
- **Option 3 is correct: Viharas** are monasteries **where Buddhist monks live and practice.** They typically consist of a central courtyard surrounded by cells for individual monks. Viharas served as important **centers of learning and spiritual practice** and were often attached to stupas and chaityas.

- **Option 4 is correct:** Buddhist art includes **murals** and **miniature paintings** that depict scenes from the life of the Buddha, Jataka tales (stories of the Buddha's past lives) and other important events in Buddhist history. These paintings are found in monasteries, caves and temples, serving both decorative and educational purposes. eg- **Ajanta Caves.**

Thus, option (d) is the correct answer.

41. *(b)* The idea that all phenomena are empty of inherent existence.

- **Sunyata**, translated as 'emptiness', is a central concept in **Mahayana Buddhism.** It refers to the idea that all phenomena, including the **self, are devoid of inherent existence** or **independent self-nature.** According to this doctrine, everything is **interdependent and arises due to causes and conditions;** nothing exists in isolation or possesses a permanent, unchanging essence.
- Sunyata is not to be confused with **nihilism or the idea that nothing exists at all.** It is a cornerstone of Buddhist philosophy that helps practitioners develop wisdom, compassion and a deep understanding of the nature of existence.

Thus, option (b) is the correct answer.

42. *(c)* Bodh Gaya

- **Bodh Gaya** is the site where **Siddhartha Gautama attained enlightenment** under the Bodhi tree, becoming the Buddha. Bodh Gaya is **one of the four main pilgrimage sites** for Buddhists, along with **Lumbini** (the Buddha's birthplace), **Sarnath** (where he gave his first sermon) and Kushinagar (where he attained Parinirvana).
- **Mahabodhi Temple** Complex at Bodh Gaya is a **UNESCO World Heritage Site** and one of the most revered places in Buddhism. The temple was **originally built by Emperor Ashoka** in the **3rd century** BCE and has been rebuilt and restored multiple times over the centuries.

Thus option (c) is the correct answer.

43. *(c)* All three pairs

- **Pair 1 is correct: First Buddhist Council** was held at **Rajagriha** shortly after the Buddha's death, around 486 BCE. It was presided over by **Mahakassapa** and was sponsored by **King Ajatashatru.** The council was convened to compile and preserve the Buddha's teachings, which were orally recited by Ananda and Upali. These teachings were organised into the **Sutta Pitaka** (discourses) and **Vinaya Pitaka** (monastic rules), forming the foundation of the Pali Canon.
- **Pair 2 is correct:** The Third Buddhist Council was convened by Emperor **Ashoka** around 250 BCE at Pataliputra to purify the Sangha by expelling corrupt monks and heretics who **had infiltrated the monastic order.** Ashoka sent missionaries, including his son **Mahendra, to various regions, including Sri Lanka,** where they successfully established Buddhism.
- **Pair 3 is correct:** Fourth Buddhist Council was held in **Kashmir** under the patronage of Emperor **Kanishka** around 78 CE. This council is particularly significant for its role in the formal division of Buddhism into **Hinayana** (Lesser Vehicle) and Mahayana (Greater Vehicle) schools. The council was presided over by **Vasumitra** and **Ashvaghosha.**

Thus, option (c) is the correct answer.

44. *(b)* Only two pairs

- **Pair 1 is correct:** The **Digha Nikaya** is part of the **Sutta Pitaka** in the Pali Canon and contains the long discourses of the Buddha. These discourses cover a wide range of topics, including ethics, meditation and cosmology. The Digha Nikaya is known for its detailed and comprehensive teachings, making it one of the most important collections of the Buddha's sermons.
- **Pair 2 is correct:** The **Anguttara Nikaya** is also part of the Sutta Pitaka and is known as the **numerical discourse** of the Buddha. The teachings in this collection are organised according to numbers, making it easier for practitioners to remember key concepts.
- **Pair 3 is incorrect:** The **Vinaya Pitaka** is not a philosophical analysis of Buddhism but rather a collection of **monastic rules and regulations** that govern the behaviour of monks and nuns. It is one of the three baskets (Tripitaka) of the Pali Canon and is essential for maintaining discipline within the monastic community.

Thus, option (b) is the correct answer.

45. *(b)* The Khuddaka Nikaya contains minor discourses and is part of the Sutta Pitaka.

- **Option 1 is incorrect:** The **Abhidhamma Pitaka** is primarily concerned with the detailed and systematic analysis of the Buddha's teachings, focusing on the nature of mind, matter and the processes of perception. It is not focused on monastic discipline, which is the domain of the Vinaya Pitaka.
- **Option 2 is correct:** The **Khuddaka Nikaya** is one of the five Nikayas that make up the **Sutta Pitaka** of the Pali Canon. It is a collection of minor discourses and texts that include various genres of literature, such as short suttas, poetry, stories and parables. Some of the well-known texts within the Khuddaka Nikaya include the Dhammapada, Jataka Tales, Udana and Sutta Nipata.
- **Option 3 is incorrect:** The **Milind Panha** (Questions of King Milinda) is a Buddhist text that records a dialogue between the Greek King Menander (Milinda) and the Buddhist monk Nagasena. It is a significant text in the Theravada tradition and is not associated with Mahayana Buddhism or the Bodhisattva Amitabha.
- **Option 4 is incorrect:** The **Mahavamsa** is a historical chronicle of Sri Lanka, detailing the history of Buddhism on the island, particularly the establishment of the Theravada tradition. It is not related to the Zen tradition in Japan, which is a school of Mahayana Buddhism that developed much later.

Thus, option (b) is the correct answer.

46. *(d)* 1, 2 and 3

- **Statement 1 is correct: Lumbini**, in **Nepal**, is recognised as the **birthplace of Siddhartha Gautama,** who later became the Buddha. According to Buddhist tradition, Queen Maya gave birth to Siddhartha in the Lumbini garden, **under a Sal tree**. The site is marked by the **Maya Devi Temple** and the **Ashoka Pillar**, erected by Emperor Ashoka to commemorate the Buddha's birth. Lumbini is one of the four main pilgrimage sites in Buddhism and is considered a UNESCO World Heritage Site.
- **Statement 2 is correct:** Sarnath, near Varanasi in India, is where Buddha delivered his first sermon, the **Dharmachakra Pravartana** (Turning of the Wheel of Dharma), marking the start of his teachings and the formation of the **Sangha** (Monks community). In this sermon, Buddha taught the **Four Noble Truths** and **the Eightfold Path**, forming the core of Buddhist doctrine. The **Dhamek Stupa** at Sarnath commemorates this key event.
- **Statement 3 is correct: Kushinagar**, located in the Indian state of Uttar Pradesh, was the capital of the Malla Republic and is the site where the Buddha attained **Mahaparinirvana** (final Nirvana) after his death. According to tradition, the Buddha passed away lying between **two sal trees** in Kushinagar and his body was cremated at the **Mahaparinirvana Stupa**

Thus, option (d) is the correct answer.

47. *(c)* Only three

- **Pair 1 is incorrect: Uttarabodhi Mudra** symbolises the **supreme enlightenment** and not the attributes like offering, welcome, charity, giving, compassion and sincerity. It is performed by joining both hands and interlocking the fingers, with the index fingers extended upwards, symbolising the ultimate victory of knowledge over ignorance.
- **Pair 2 is correct: Vitarka Mudra** is a **gesture of discussion and transmission of the teachings.** The thumb and index finger touch each other, forming a circle, while the other fingers remain extended. This Mudra symbolizes the flow of energy and information and is often seen in depictions of the Buddha giving sermons or teachings.
- **Pair 3 is correct: Vajra Mudra** does denote a fiery **thunderbolt**, which in Buddhist symbolism, represents a powerful, indestructible force. The Vajra Mudra **symbolises the union of the five elements** (air, water, **fire, earth and metal**) and the power of enlightenment. Therefore, this description is correctly matched.

- **Pair 4 is correct: Abhaymudra** is indeed a **gesture of fearlessness, protection and reassurance.** The right hand is raised to shoulder height with the palm facing outward and the fingers are extended upward.

Thus, option (c) is the correct answer.

48. *(b)* Only three

- **Purana Kassapa was a contemporary of Mahavira** and a well-known ascetic who founded his philosophical school, which denied the concepts of virtue and vice.
- **Makkhali Gosala was also a contemporary of Mahavira** and the founder of the Ajivika sect, a major philosophical school in ancient India that emphasized determinism and the influence of fate.
- **Ajita Kesakambalin was a contemporary of Mahavira.** He was a materialist philosopher who denied the existence of an afterlife and promoted a philosophy of materialism.
- Bindusara was the second Mauryan emperor and the father of Ashoka. He lived much later, **long after Mahavira's time**, so he was not a contemporary of Mahavira.
- **Parshvanatha** was the 23rd Tirthankara in Jainism and **lived about 250 years before Mahavira,** so he was not a contemporary of Mahavira either.

Thus, option (b) is the correct answer.

49. *(b)* Sariputta

- **Sariputta** was one of the most significant disciples of Gautama Buddha. He was originally born as **Upatissa** and was known for his profound wisdom and deep understanding of the Dhamma. After encountering the Buddha, Sariputta, along with his close friend Mahamoggallana, became a devoted follower of the Buddha's teachings.
- His intellectual prowess and his ability to grasp complex philosophical concepts quickly earned him the title of the **second Buddha** within the Theravada tradition, acknowledging his status just below the Buddha himself in terms of spiritual authority.

Thus, option (b) is the correct answer.

50. *(b)* He was known as the 'Treasurer of Dhamma' for his exceptional memory of Buddha's teachings.

- **Ananda** was one of the most beloved disciples of Gautama Buddha, known primarily for his exceptional memory and devotion. He served as the **personal attendant to the Buddha for 25 years,** during which he memorised numerous discourses delivered by the Buddha. This earned him the title **'Treasurer of Dhamma'**, as he was able to recite the teachings verbatim.
- Ananda's role was crucial in the preservation of the Buddha's teachings after the Buddha's Parinirvana (passing away). He was instrumental in the first Buddhist council, where he recited the Suttas (discourses) that he had memorised, forming the basis of the Sutta Pitaka, one of the three baskets of the Pali Canon. He was a key figure in advocating for the ordination of women into the Sangha, leading to the establishment of the Bhikkhuni Sangha (community of Buddhist nuns).

Thus, option (b) is the correct answer.

51. *(a)* 1, 3 and 5 only

- **Option 1, 3 and 5 are correct:** The first five disciples of Buddha, as noted in the image, were **Kondanja, Mahanama, Baddiya, Assaji** and **Vappa**. These disciples were Brahmans who initially accompanied Siddhartha Gautama during his ascetic practices before he attained enlightenment. **Kondanja was the first to comprehend the Buddha's teaching,** which marked the beginning of the Sangha, or the Buddhist monastic community. These early disciples played crucial roles in the early days of Buddhism, helping to spread the teachings of the Buddha across regions.
- **Option 2 and 4 are incorrect:** On the other hand, **Gautami** and **Khema** were among the **prominent women disciples of the Buddha**, with **Gautami being recognised as the first female disciple**. Their inclusion in the monastic order signified a major step in the Buddhist community's evolution, acknowledging the role of women in the spiritual pursuit of enlightenment.

Thus, option (a) is the correct answer.

52. *(a)* Canonical texts are directly linked to the sayings of Gautama Buddha

- **Canonical Texts:** These are the original, foundational scriptures that are directly attributed to the teachings of Gautama Buddha. They are written in Pali and Sanskrit and include the **Tipitaka (Tripitaka)**, which consists of three baskets or collections: the **Vinaya-pitaka** (rules for monks and nuns), the **Sutta-pitaka** (Buddha's discourses) and the **Abhidhamma-pitaka** (philosophical and doctrinal interpretations).
- **Non-Canonical Texts:** These include later additions, commentaries and historical writings that elaborate on, interpret, or offer reflections on the canonical texts. Examples- **Milindapanho** (dialogues between King Menander and the monk Nagasena) and **Visuddhimagga** (a commentary on the path to purity).

Thus, option (a) is the correct answer.

53. *(b)* 1, 3 and 4 only

- **Pair 1 is correctly matched:** Milindapanho is a text containing the famous dialogues between King Menander (Milinda) and the monk **Nagasena**. It blends Greek and Buddhist thought, addressing deep philosophical issues, including the nature of self and rebirth.
- **Pair 2 is incorrectly matched:** Visuddhimagga is attributed to **Buddhaghosa** and focuses on purifying the mind through ethical conduct, concentration and wisdom. It is not directly linked to Buddha's teachings but serves as a commentary.
- **Pair 3 is correctly matched:** Nettipakarana is an important text that systematically interprets the Buddha's teachings and is linked to the **Sutta-pitaka**.
- **Pair 4 is correctly matched:** Mahavamsa is a historical chronicle, written in Pali, that provides a detailed account of Buddha's arrival in Sri Lanka, his teachings and the spread of Buddhism in the region. It is an important text for understanding Buddhist history and its expansion beyond India.

Thus, option (b) is the correct answer.

54. *(c)* Mahavibhanga

- **Sutta-Pitaka:** This is one of the three baskets in the **Tipitaka** and contains the Buddha's discourses. Some key collections within this basket include the **Digha-nikaya** (long discourses), **Majjhima-nikaya** (middle-length discourses) and **Anguttara-nikaya** (numerical discourses). Each of these collections categorizes the Buddha's teachings in a structured manner.
- **Vinaya-Pitaka:** This contains the rules and regulations for the Sangha (monastic community). It is divided into various books, such as the **Mahavibhanga**, which outlines the disciplinary codes for monks and nuns.

Thus, option (c) is the correct answer.

55. *(c)* It is called the 'Turning the Wheel of Dharma'.

- **Statement 1 is incorrect: Lumbini** was the place where **Gautama Buddha** was **born** in 563 BCE. The first sermon, also called the **Dhammachakka-Pavattana Sutta**, was delivered in **Sarnath**, not in Lumbini.
- **Statement 2 is incorrect:** The term **Parinirvana** refers to the final passing away of the Buddha at the age of 80 in **Kusinara** (present-day **Kushinagar**). It signifies the Buddha's complete release from the cycle of **birth, death and rebirth** (samsara).
- **Statement 3 is correct:** The **Dhammachakka-Pavattana** is known as the **'Turning the Wheel of Dharma'** or **'Setting the Wheel of Dharma in Motion'**. This sermon is considered the first and most significant teaching of the Buddha. The wheel symbol represents the eternal nature of the teachings of the Buddha and the path to end suffering.
- **Statement 4 is incorrect:** The sermon was delivered to **five former companions** of the Buddha, known as the **Pancavaggiya monks.** These five ascetics were Buddha's companions during his early years of asceticism.

Thus, option (c) is the correct answer.

56. *(c)* Lotus and Bull - Birth

- **Lotus and Bull:** In Buddhist iconography, the **Lotus** represents purity, spiritual birth and enlightenment. It is a symbol often associated with the Buddha's birth, symbolizing purity amidst the worldly mud. The **Bull** also symbolises strength and prosperity, particularly at the time of Gautama Buddha's birth.
- **Horse (Renunciation):** The horse, particularly **Kanthaka**, is associated with the **Great Renunciation** when Siddhartha Gautama left his palace and royal life to seek enlightenment.
- **Bodhi Tree (Enlightenment):** The Bodhi Tree at **Bodh Gaya** is where Siddhartha attained enlightenment, making it a symbol of his spiritual awakening.
- **Footprints (Nirvana):** The Buddha's footprints represent **Nirvana**—the final liberation from the cycle of birth and rebirth, symbolizing his path to enlightenment and the spiritual legacy he left behind.

Thus, option (c) is the correct answer.

57. *(a)* 1, 2 and 3

- **Pair 1 is correctly matched: Samma-Sankappa (Right Thought)** refers to cultivating the right intentions or thoughts of renunciation, goodwill and non-harming. It is the mental discipline required to prevent negative thoughts and to foster positive ones.
- **Pair 2 is correctly matched: Samma-Vaca (Right Speech)** refers to using speech that is truthful, harmonious, kind and beneficial. It encourages abstaining from lying, gossip, harsh words and idle chatter.
- **Pair 3 is correctly matched: Samma-Kammanta (Right Action)** refers to behaving in ways that do not harm others. This includes refraining from killing, stealing and engaging in sexual misconduct.

Thus, option (a) is the correct answer.

58. *(d)* 1, 2, 3 and 4

- **Pair 1 is correctly matched: Samma-Ajiva (Right Livelihood)** encourages earning a living in a way that does not cause harm to others. This includes refraining from professions that involve violence, deceit, or exploitation.
- **Pair 2 is correctly matched: Samma-Vayama (Right Effort)** involves putting effort into preventing unwholesome states from arising and developing wholesome states of mind. It signifies the effort required to cultivate positive habits while letting go of negative ones.
- **Pair 3 is correctly matched: Samma-Sati (Right Mindfulness)** refers to the practice of being aware and mindful of the body, feelings, mind and mental phenomena. It is central to Buddhist meditation practices.
- **Pair 4 is correctly matched: Samma-Samadhi (Right Concentration)** refers to developing deep concentration through meditation. It represents achieving mental clarity and focus that leads to states of higher meditative absorption and ultimately enlightenment.

Thus, option (d) is the correct answer.

59. *(c)* A is correct, but R is incorrect.

- **Assertion (A) is correct:** Buddha was born in **563 BCE** and his father was **Suddhodana**, the chief of the **Sakya** clan, who ruled over the small republican kingdom of **Kapilavastu** (modern-day Nepal).
- **Reason (R) is incorrect: Mahamaya** was Buddha's biological mother. She gave birth to him at Lumbini and died seven days later. **Gautami** (also known as Prajapati Gautami) was his stepmother who raised him after Mahamaya's death.

Thus, option (c) is the correct answer.

60. *(b)* Sarvanivaranavishkambhin

Sarvanivaranavishkambhin is a **Bodhisattva** who symbolises the **purification of obstructions** and wrong-doings that hinder a person's spiritual progress. He is often depicted with **deep blue skin**, a color associated with royalty and wisdom in Buddhist art. Sarvanivaranavishkambhin is frequently portrayed **seated on a lotus**, a symbol of purity and enlightenment and holding a **wheel of jewels**, which represents the turning of the Dharma (Buddha's teachings) and the removal of obstacles.

Thus, option (b) is the correct answer.

61. *(b)* Vajrapani

- **Vajrapani** is one of the most important **Bodhisattvas** in Mahayana Buddhism, often depicted as blue and holding a **Vajra** (thunderbolt) in his right hand. The Vajra symbolizes **indestructible power** and the force of the truth. Vajrapani is also surrounded by **flames**, which represent his power to burn away ignorance and illusion.
- Vajrapani is known as a protector of the **Buddha** and his teachings (Dharma). His fierce and muscular form embodies the energy and strength required to overcome obstacles on the path to enlightenment.

Thus, option (b) is the correct answer.

62. *(c)* 1, 2 and 3

- **Pair 1 is correctly matched: Sarvastivadin** is a major early school of Buddhism that taught the doctrine that **everything exists** in the past, present and future. This belief led to the name 'Sarvastivadin' (from the Sanskrit 'sarva' meaning 'all' and 'asti' meaning 'exists').
- **Pair 2 is correctly matched: Sautrantika** is an early Buddhist school that emphasised the validity of the Sutras (the teachings directly attributed to the Buddha) and the **Vinaya-Pitaka** (the monastic discipline) as the only valid scriptures.
- **Pair 3 is correctly matched: Sammitiya** was one of the early **Hinayana** Buddhist schools. It flourished during the early centuries of Buddhism and held significant influence in South Asia.

Thus, option (c) is the correct answer.

63. *(a)* 1, 2, 3 and 4

- **Pair 1 is correctly matched: Bhikkhuni Sangha** refers to the **community of nuns** in Buddhism. It was established by the Buddha as the female counterpart to the Bhikkhu Sangha (the community of monks).
- **Pair 2 is correctly matched: Theragatha** is a collection of **verses attributed to elder monks** (Theras) and it provides valuable insights into the thoughts and spiritual experiences of these monks.
- **Pair 3 is correctly matched: Therigatha**, on the other hand, contains **verses attributed to elder nuns** (Theris), representing the spiritual journeys and enlightenment of women who followed the Buddha's teachings.
- **Pair 4 is correctly matched: Shramana/Samana** refers to one who renounces worldly life to pursue the **realisation of the truth**. In the context of early Buddhism, a Shramana is a seeker who follows a path of austerity, discipline and meditation to attain spiritual liberation (Nirvana).

Thus, option (a) is the correct answer.

64. *(c)* All three

- **Statement 1 is correct**: In Jainism, **a Jina** (literally meaning "**conqueror**") is one who has conquered inner passions such as anger, pride, deceit and greed. The term is used to denote a person who has overcome the cycle of birth and death and has achieved spiritual victory. The **Jina has transcended temporal (worldly) and material existence through strict self-discipline** and meditation, ultimately attaining a state of eternal bliss, known as **Moksha.**
- **Statement 2 is correct:** The concept of **Tirthankaras** is indeed central to Jain philosophy. A Tirthankara is a **spiritual teacher who has attained enlightenment** and serves as a guide for others on the path to liberation. There have been 24 Tirthankaras in the current cycle of time, with **Rishabhadeva** being the first and **Mahavira** being the last.
- **Statement 3 is correct: Siddhas** are souls that have attained **ultimate liberation** (Moksha) in Jainism. These souls have completely eradicated all karmic matter, which binds the soul to the cycle of birth and death. Upon achieving liberation, Siddhas exist in a state of eternal bliss at the top of the universe (Siddhashila), where they are free from all suffering and the material world. Siddhas do not take rebirth and are no longer subject to the laws of karma.

Thus, option (c) is the correct answer.

65. *(c)* All three

- **Option 1 is correct:** In Jainism, a **Jina** represents the stage of a soul that has conquered all worldly attachments and desires. The Jina is a spiritual victor who has successfully overcome the internal enemies of passion and ignorance. The term 'Jina' is often used interchangeably with Tirthankara, but technically, every Tirthankara is a Jina, though not all Jinas are Tirthankaras.
- **Option 2 is correct:** A **Tirthankara** is a specific type of Jina who has not only attained liberation but also established a path for others to follow. The word Tirthankara means "**Ford Maker**", one who builds a ford across the river of human suffering, enabling others to cross over to the shore of liberation.
- **Option 3 is correct:** The stage of **Siddha** represents the final state of the soul in Jainism, where it has attained Moksha or liberation. A Siddha is a perfected soul that has transcended the **cycle of birth and death** (**Samsara**) and exists in a state of eternal bliss. Siddhas reside in Siddhashila, a region at the top of the universe, where they remain forever free from the influences of karma and material existence.

Thus, option (c) is the correct answer.

66. *(d)* Mahavira

- **Mahavira** is one of the most prominent figures in Jainism and is regarded as the 24th and last Tirthankara. Born in **540 BCE in Kundagrama** (modern-day Bihar, India), Mahavira renounced worldly life at the age of 30 to become an ascetic. After 12 years of rigorous penance and meditation, he attained **Kaivalya** (omniscience or perfect knowledge) under a sal tree at Jimbhikagrama. Following his enlightenment, Mahavira preached the principles of Jainism for 30 years, focusing on **non-violence (Ahimsa), truth (Satya), non-stealing (Asteya), chastity (Brahmacharya) and non-possession (Aparigraha).**
- Mahavira's teachings emphasised the importance of self-discipline, austerity and the rejection of the caste system. He established the fourfold Sangha, consisting of monks, nuns, laymen and laywomen, which spread his teachings throughout India. Mahavira attained **Nirvana** at the age of 72 in Pavapuri (Bihar), where he is believed to have left his physical body and become a Siddha.

Thus, option (d) is the correct answer.

67. *(c)* 1, 2 and 3

- **Anuvratas** are the lesser vows or ethical principles that are followed by laypersons (householders) in Jainism. These vows are less stringent than the Mahavratas (great vows) followed by monks and nuns.
- **Option 1 is correct: Dik Vrata** vow involves the limitation of one's movement or area of activity. It is a vow to **restrict oneself to a limited area** to avoid causing harm to living beings in other areas. This vow reflects the principle of Ahimsa (non-violence) by minimising the potential for harm caused by one's actions.
- **Option 2 is correct: Bhoga Upbhoga Vrata** vow pertains to the **limited use of consumable and non-consumable items.** Bhoga refers to items that are consumed once (such as food), while Upbhoga refers to items that can be used multiple times (such as clothing or tools).
- **Option 3 is correct: Atithi Samvibhaga Vrata** vow involves the **practice of charity** and hospitality towards ascetics and others. It encourages sharing one's resources with those in need, especially Jain monks and nuns, who rely on the laity for their sustenance.

Thus, option (c) is the correct answer.

68. *(c)* Parshvanatha

- **Parshvanatha** is the **23rd Tirthankara** in Jainism and is one of the most revered figures in the tradition. He is often depicted with the symbol of a **snake** (serpent), which is his emblem. This symbol is a representation of the protection he received from the **Yaksha Dharanendra.** According to Jain texts, when Parshvanatha was meditating, an evil demon tried to disturb him by creating a storm. At this moment, Dharanendra, a serpent deity, emerged from the ground and spread his many hoods over Parshvanatha to shield him from the storm.

- Parshvanatha's teachings emphasised the **fourfold path: non-violence (Ahimsa), truthfulness (Satya), non-stealing (Asteya) and non-possession (Aparigraha).** His doctrines laid the foundation for Mahavira's teachings, making him a significant figure in Jain history.

Thus, option (c) is the correct answer.

69. *(b)* Only two

- **Pair 1 is correct : Rishabhadeva** is the **first Tirthankara** of Jainism and his symbol is the **bull**. The bull represents strength and stability, qualities associated with Rishabhadeva, who is considered the founder of the Jain community and the first to teach ascetic practices.
- **Pair 2 is correct: Neminatha** is the **22nd Tirthankara and** his symbol is the conch shell. The conch shell symbolises purity and the call to spiritual awakening. Neminatha is associated with the teachings of non-violence and compassion, particularly towards animals.
- **Pair 3 is incorrect:** The symbol of **Mahavira**, the **24th Tirthankara**, is the lion, not the snake. The lion symbolizes leadership and courage, qualities that Mahavira exemplified throughout his life. The **snake is the symbol of Parshvanatha, the 23rd Tirthankara**, as mentioned in the previous question.

Thus, option (b) is the correct answer.

70. *(c)* All three

- **Pair 1 is correct: Anekantavada** is one of the central tenets of Jain philosophy, emphasising that reality is complex and can be viewed from multiple perspectives. According to this doctrine, no **single point of view is the complete truth**; instead, reality encompasses a variety of viewpoints. This concept promotes tolerance and understanding of differing perspectives, acknowledging non-absolutism.
- **Pair 2 is correct: Syadvada** is closely related to Anekantavada and refers to the principle that statements about **reality are always conditional, depending on the perspective** from which they are made. The word 'Syat' means 'perhaps' or 'in some respects' and it is used to convey that any assertion is only partially true.
- **Pair 3 is correct: Saptabhangi** is a logical framework in Jain philosophy that provides seven possible judgements about any proposition. These **seven judgements (or standpoints) allow** for a comprehensive understanding of truth by considering various aspects of a statement. The **Saptabhangi framework** is used to explore the complexity of reality and avoid dogmatic assertions. The seven judgements are: 'syad-asti' (in some ways it is), 'syad-nasti' (in some ways it is not), 'syad-asti-nasti' (in some ways it is and it is not) and so forth.

Thus, option (c) is the correct answer.

71. *(b)* Only two

- **Pair 1 is correct:** In Jainism, **Karma** refers to the subtle particles that attach to the soul as a result of one's actions, thoughts and words. These karmic particles influence the soul's future lives and experiences. The doctrine of karma is closely tied to the concept of **transmigration of the soul,** which is the cycle of birth, death and rebirth. The accumulation of karma determines the conditions of the soul's future existence and liberation (Moksha) is achieved when the soul is freed from all karmic matter.
- **Pair 2 is correct: Ahimsa** is the principle of non-violence and is the most important ethical tenet in Jainism. It dictates that one must avoid causing harm to any living being, whether through actions, words, or thoughts.
- **Pair 3 is incorrect:** Jainism explicitly rejects the **caste system** (Varna) and the social hierarchy that it imposes. Jain teachings emphasise equality and the belief that spiritual progress is based on individual effort, ethical conduct and adherence to Jain principles, rather than one's birth or social status. Mahavira, the 24th Tirthankara, condemned the caste system

Thus, option (b) is the correct answer.

72. *(a)* 1 and 2 only

- **Statement 1 is correct:** Jainism distinctly **stands apart from the Vedic tradition and does not consider the Vedas as authoritative texts.** The Vedic scriptures are central to Hinduism, emphasising rituals, sacrifices and the caste system, which Jainism opposes. Instead, Jainism relies on its scriptures, such as the Agamas for the Svetambara sect and the Siddhantas for the Digambara sect.

- **Statement 2 is correct**: Jainism takes the **principle of non-violence to its most rigorous conclusion,** advocating for the protection of all forms of life, no matter how small. This principle influences every aspect of a Jain's life, from dietary choices (tilt towards vegetarianism) to daily activities that might inadvertently cause harm to living organisms
- **Statement 3 is incorrect**: Jainism rejects the notion of a caste system, which is prevalent in the Vedic tradition. **Mahavira, the 24th Tirthankara, explicitly denounced the caste system** and preached equality among all beings. Jainism teaches that spiritual progress and liberation are attainable by anyone, regardless of their birth or social status, through the right conduct, faith and knowledge.

Thus, option (a) is the correct answer.

73. *(d)* 1, 2, 3 and 4

- **Option 1 is correct**: Jainism has a rich tradition of **rock-cut caves**, which were used as places of worship and meditation. These caves often contain intricate carvings and statues of Tirthankaras. Examples include the **Udayagiri and Khandagiri caves in Odisha** and the **Sittanavasal caves in Tamil Nadu.**
- **Option 2 is correct**: Jain structural temples are architectural marvels, often characterised by elaborate carvings, intricate sculptures and ornate designs. The **Dilwara Temples in Mount Abu, Rajasthan and the Ranakpur Temple in Rajasthan** are famous examples. They house images of Tirthankaras and other deities, which are worshipped by the followers.
- **Option 3 is correct**: Jain sculptures are an essential part of Jain art, often depicting Tirthankaras in meditative poses, such as in Kayotsarga (standing) or Padmasana (seated) postures. The **Gommateshwara statue in Shravanabelagola, Karnataka**, is one of the most famous Jain sculptures, representing Bahubali, the son of the first Tirthankara, Rishabhadeva.
- **Option 4 is correct**: Jain paintings, particularly miniatures, are known for their intricate details and vibrant colours. They often depict scenes from the lives of Tirthankaras, Jain cosmology and other religious themes. These paintings are **found in manuscripts, temple walls and other religious texts.** The **Kalpa Sutra**, an important Jain text, contains many such illustrations.

Thus, option (d) is the correct answer.

74. *(d)* 1 and 3 only

- **Statement 1 is correct**: The **First Jain Council** was indeed held at **Pataliputra** (modern-day Patna) in the **3rd century** BCE. It was convened under the leadership of **Bhadrabahu** and was primarily concerned with preserving the Jain teachings and scriptures. During this council, the Jain scriptures were compiled and the canon was established.
- **Statement 2 is incorrect**: The **Second Jain Council** was held at **Vallabhi (not Avanti)** in the **5th century** CE, not Pataliputra. It was during this council that the Jain scriptures were written down for the first time. The division of Jainism into **Digambara** and **Svetambara** sects, however, was not a direct result of this council but rather due to earlier differences in interpretations and practices that gradually led to the schism.
- **Statement 3 is correct**: Both the First and Second Jain Councils were convened with the primary **objective of preserving and codifying Jain teachings and scriptures**. The councils were crucial in maintaining doctrinal purity and ensuring that the teachings of Mahavira were passed down accurately through generations.

Thus, option (d) is the correct answer.

75. *(a)* 1 and 2 only

- **Statement 1 is correct**: Jainism recognises **24 Tirthankaras**, who are revered spiritual teachers who have attained enlightenment and guided others on the path to liberation (Moksha). These Tirthankaras are the central figures in Jain religious worship and are believed to have established the fourfold Sangha (monastic community).

- **Statement 2 is correct: Rishabhadeva** is acknowledged as the **first Tirthankara** in Jainism. He is credited with founding the Jain community and is often depicted with a bull, which is his emblem. Rishabhadeva is considered the first being in the current time cycle to attain liberation.
- **Statement 3 is incorrect:. Mahavira** is the **24th and last Tirthankara**, but he was not female. He was born as Vardhamana in 540 BCE and attained enlightenment after 12 years of ascetic practices. The only female Tirthankara in Jain tradition is **Mallinatha, the 19th Tirthankara**, who is sometimes depicted as a woman, though there are variations in the stories.

Thus, option (a) is the correct answer.

76. *(c)* All three

- **Pair 1 is correct: Sallekhana** is a **voluntary ritual of fasting to death** that is practiced by Jains as a way to purify the soul and reduce karmic bondage. It is undertaken by a person who feels they have fulfilled their duties and wishes to renounce worldly life. It is considered an ethical and non-violent way of ending life, distinct from suicide, as it is performed with a sense of spiritual purpose and discipline.
- **Pair 2 is correct: Pratikramana** is an important Jain ritual that involves **repentance for past wrongdoings, introspection and the renewal of vows.** It is performed daily, semi-monthly, or annually by Jains, depending on the individual's level of commitment. The ritual includes reflecting on one's actions, confessing sins and resolving to avoid harmful behaviours in the future.
- **Pair 3 is correct: Manastambha** is a **free-standing pillar** that is typically erected in front of Jain temples or large Jain institutions. The term 'Manastambha' literally means 'pillar of pride' and is intended to remind devotees to overcome pride and ego by humbling themselves before the teachings of the Tirthankaras.

Thus, option (c) is the correct answer.

77. *(c)* All three

- **Pair 1 is correct: Digambara** is one of the two main sects of Jainism, the other being Svetambara. The name "**Digambara**" **means "sky-clad"** referring to the practice of monks who do not wear any clothes as a symbol of their renunciation of worldly possessions and desires. Digambara monks follow very strict and rigid monastic rules, emphasising austerity, self-discipline and the denial of physical comforts.
- **Pair 2 is correct: Svetambara** is the other major sect of Jainism, characterised by monks and nuns who wear white robes (hence the name '**white-clad**'). Unlike the Digambaras, the Svetambaras believe that **both men and women can attain liberation in their current form.** Svetambara monks and nuns follow **less** rigid monastic rules compared to their Digambara counterparts and they allow the use of simple possessions like a bowl and a cloth.
- **Pair 3 is correct:** The **Yapaniya** sect was an ancient Jain sect that is now extinct. It is believed to have originated from the Digambara tradition but adopted some practices similar to the Svetambara sect. Yapaniya monks **worshipped nude images of Tirthankaras**, similar to the Digambaras and were known for their inclusive practices.

Thus, option (c) is the correct answer.

78. *(d)* 1, 2 and 3

- **Statement 1 is correct: Mount Abu** in Rajasthan is home to the **Dilwara Temples**, renowned for their intricate marble carvings and stunning architecture. Built between the 11th and 13th centuries, these temples are dedicated to various Tirthankaras, with the most famous being the Vimal Vasahi and Luna Vasahi temples.
- **Statement 2 is correct: Shravanabelagola**, located in Karnataka, is famous for the **Gommateshwara** statue, a **57-foot monolithic statue of Bahubali**, commissioned by the Ganga dynasty minister and **commander Chamundaraya in 981 AD**. The site is a major pilgrimage center, especially during the **Mahamastakabhisheka festival**, which occurs once every 12 years and involves the anointing of the statue with various substances.

- **Statement 3 is correct: Ranakpur**, also in Rajasthan, is known for the **Ranakpur Temple**, dedicated to the first Tirthankara, **Rishabhadeva** (also known as Adinatha), the temple is famous for its exquisite architecture, including 1,444 marble pillars, each intricately carved and unique in design.

Thus, option (d) is the correct answer.

79. *(a)* It refers to the progressive stages of the soul's purification.

- Gunasthanas in Jainism refers to the **14 progressive stages of spiritual development** that a soul undergoes on its journey towards liberation (Moksha). Each stage represents a level of purification of the soul, determined by the reduction of karmic particles attached to it. As the soul ascends through these stages, it becomes increasingly free from the influence of karma, leading to a state of perfect knowledge, perception and conduct. Some of **Gunasthanas** are the following:
- **Ignorance and Delusion**: The soul begins at the lowest level, characterised by ignorance and spiritual delusion. Here, the soul is deeply entangled in worldly desires and attachments, which create and reinforce karmic bonds.
- **Gradual Purification**: The soul undergoes purification by following ethical conduct, practicing self-discipline and engaging in spiritual practices such as meditation. This process gradually diminishes the intensity and quantity of karma attached to the soul.
- **Spiritual Realisation**: The higher stages involve the realisation of **true knowledge (Samyak Jnana), right faith (Samyak Darshana) and right conduct (Samyak Charitra)**. In these stages, the soul transcends attachment to material things and attains higher spiritual awareness.
- **Attainment of Siddhahood**: The final stage, known as the **14th Gunasthana**, is Siddhahood, where the soul becomes completely free from all karmic particles. In this state, the soul achieves liberation, experiencing infinite knowledge, perception, bliss and power. The soul resides in the Siddhashila, a realm at the top of the universe, beyond rebirth and suffering.

Thus, option (a) is the correct answer.

80. *(b)* 2 only

- **Statement 1 is incorrect**: Jainism and Buddhism do not accept the concept of a creator God. Both religions focus on self-effort and personal spiritual development rather than devotion to a supreme deity.
- **Statement 2 is correct**: Both Jainism and Buddhism strongly emphasise Ahimsa, or non-violence, as a core ethical principle. In Jainism, Ahimsa is the highest moral duty and in Buddhism, it is integral to the practice of compassion and right action.
- **Statement 3 is incorrect**: While Jainism emphasizes severe austerity and penance as a means to purify the soul and attain liberation, Buddhism advocates for the Middle Path, which avoids extreme asceticism and indulgence.

Thus, option (b) is the correct answer.

81. *(c)* Both 1 and 2

- **Statement 1 is correct**: The **Digambara sect** of Jainism indeed believes that women cannot attain liberation (Moksha) in their current form and must be reborn as men to achieve it. This belief contrasts with the Svetambara sect, which holds that women can attain liberation directly.
- **Statement 2 is correct**: Digambara monks take the practice of renunciation to the extreme, adhering to the principle of complete non-possession. They do not own any personal items, including begging bowls and rely entirely on the charity of others for food, which they receive directly in their hands.

Thus, option (c) is the correct answer.

82. *(a)* Mallinath

- **Mallinath**, the **19th Tirthankara** in the Jain tradition, is revered as the only **female Tirthankara** according to the **Shvetambara sect** of Jainism. In the Shvetambara tradition, **Mallinath** is depicted as a woman who achieved spiritual victory and became a Tirthankara, leading countless souls toward liberation.
- However, the **Digambara sect** of Jainism does not accept Mallinath as a female Tirthankara, instead considering Mallinath to have been a male.

Thus, option (a) is the correct answer.

83. *(b)* Only two

- **Statement 1 is correct:** The **Bisapantha tradition** is a sect within **Digambara Jainism**, where the followers worship **Tirthankara idols** along with other **deities** like **Kshetrapala** and **Padmavati.** These deities are considered protective figures in Jainism.
- **Statement 2 is correct:** In the **Bisapantha tradition**, followers also engage in the practice of **Arati**, which is the **waving of lights** in front of idols during worship. This practice is not restricted by time and can occur even at **night**, as part of their temple rituals.
- **Statement 3 is incorrect:** The **Bisapantha sect** emphasizes the **worship of idols** and incorporates a variety of rituals, including the **offering of flowers, fruits** and other items. The tradition of non-idol worship is more closely associated with sects like **Sthanakvasi** and **Terapantha.**

Thus, option (b) is the correct answer.

84. *(c)* Both 1 and 2

- **Statement 1 is correct:** The **Terapantha sect**, a major sub-sect of Digambara Jainism, emphasises **non-idolatry** and therefore **does not worship idols of Kshetrapala, Padmavati, or any other deities.**
- **Statement 2 is correct:** During their worship, Terapanthis follow strict rituals, including offering **sacred rice** (Akshata) rather than **flowers, fruits, or sweets** commonly used in other sects. The use of items like **green vegetables** (known as **sagittal things**) is prohibited, as they are considered living entities that involve harm when plucked.

Thus, option (c) is the correct answer.

85. *(b)* They strictly prohibit the lighting of lamps or offerings in temples.

- The **Gumanapantha** sub-sect is a minor sect of **Digambara Jainism** that emphasizes strict adherence to non-violence (Ahimsa) and purity of conduct.
- Gumanapantha followers believe that lighting **lamps** or performing any kind of offering in Jain temples violates the core principle of **non-violence.** Lighting lamps involve harm to tiny living organisms in the air and in the oil used for the flame. Therefore, they strictly prohibit such practices in their temples, considering them contrary to the teachings of **Jain Dharma.**

Thus, option (b) is the correct answer.

86. *(c)* 1, 2, 3 and 4

- **Pair 1 is correctly matched:** Chaitanya refers to the consciousness or awareness that is the essential quality of the soul. In Jainism, consciousness is a distinguishing feature of all living beings and the degree of awareness varies depending on the karma attached to the soul.
- **Pair 2 is correctly matched:** Virya denotes energy or vigor, particularly the spiritual energy required to progress on the path to liberation. It represents the strength of will needed to overcome internal passions and karmic attachments.
- **Pair 3 is correctly matched:** Mohaniya is the type of karma that causes delusion and leads the soul into attachments and desires. It is one of the most powerful forms of karma that binds the soul to the cycle of birth and rebirth (Samsara), making it difficult to attain liberation.
- **Pair 4 is correctly matched:** Asarva refers to the flow of karmic matter into the soul, causing the soul to become impure. The concept of Asarva highlights the process by which karmic particles enter the soul, affecting its purity and hindering its spiritual progress.

Thus, option (c) is the correct answer.

87. *(b)* Only two

- **Statement 1 is correct:** Islam is indeed a **monotheistic religion** that originated in the **Arabian Peninsula** in the **7th century** CE. It is part of the Abrahamic tradition, which includes Judaism and Christianity. Islam emphasises the worship of one God, Allah and considers the Quran as its holy book.
- **Statement 2 is correct: Prophet Muhammad** is considered the **last prophet** in Islam, known as the **Seal of the Prophets.** Muslims believe that Muhammad was the final messenger sent by Allah to guide humanity and his teachings form the foundation of the Islamic faith.

- **Statement 3 is incorrect**: The migration of Prophet Muhammad from Mecca to Medina is known as the Hijra, not Hajj. The **Hajj** is a pilgrimage to Mecca that every Muslim is expected to undertake at least once in their lifetime if they are physically and financially able. The Hijra marks the beginning of the Islamic calendar and was a significant turning point in Islamic history.

Thus, option (b) is the correct answer.

88. *(c)* All three

- **Option 1 is correct**: The **Hadith** refers to the **sayings, actions and approvals of Prophet Muhammad,** which provide important guidance for Muslims in understanding the Quran and living according to Islamic principles. The Hadiths are second only to the Quran in terms of religious authority and are considered essential in shaping Islamic law and practices.
- **Option 2 is correct: Zakat** is one of the **Five Pillars of Islam** and refers to the mandatory act of giving a portion of one's wealth to charity, specifically to help the needy and support the welfare of the Muslim community. It is considered an essential practice in Islam as it **embodies the principles of social justice and compassion.**
- **Option 3 is correct: Sharia** is the **body of Islamic law derived from the Quran, Hadith and other Islamic texts.** It covers all aspects of a Muslim's life, including religious rituals, family life, finance and morality. Sharia is central to Islamic teachings and provides a comprehensive guide for Muslims to live a life that is pleasing to Allah.

Thus, option (c) is the correct answer.

89. *(a)* Hijra

- The **Hijra** refers to the migration of Prophet Muhammad and his followers from **Mecca to Medina** in 622 CE. This event is of immense significance in Islamic history because it **marked the beginning of the Islamic calendar and the establishment of the first Islamic state in Medina.**
- The Hijra allowed Muslims to practice their faith freely and marked the transition of the Muslim community from a persecuted minority in Mecca to a powerful religious and political entity. The unity and brotherhood established in Medina set the foundation for the spread of Islam across the Arabian Peninsula and beyond. The other options, **Hajj, Eid** and **Ramadan**, are important aspects of the Islamic faith, but they correspond to the event described.

Thus, option (a) is the correct answer.

90. *(b)* 1, 2 and 3

- **Option 1 is correct: The Holy Trinity** is a central doctrine in Christianity, referring to the belief in one God in three persons: the **Father, the Son (Jesus Christ) and the Holy Spirit.** This doctrine emphasises the unity and co-equality of the three persons, which is fundamental to the Christian understanding of God.
- **Option 2 is correct: Resurrection** refers to the belief that Jesus Christ was raised from the dead on the third day after his crucifixion. The Resurrection is a cornerstone of the Christian faith, symbolising victory over sin and death and offering the promise of eternal life to believers.
- **Option 3 is correct: Salvation through Jesus Christ** is the belief that humanity can be saved from sin and its consequences through the sacrificial death and resurrection of Jesus Christ. This concept is central to Christian teachings, emphasising that faith in Jesus and acceptance of his sacrifice are necessary for salvation.

Thus, option (b) is the correct answer.

91. *(a)* It is a collection of sacred scriptures that include both the Old Testament and the New Testament.

- The **Bible** is the holy scripture of Christianity, consisting of two main parts: the Old Testament and the **New Testament**. The Old Testament, which is also sacred in Judaism, contains the Hebrew Bible, including the Law (Torah), Prophets (Nevi'im) and Writings (Ketuvim). It was **written between 1200 BCE and 165 BCE** and includes religious laws, historical narratives, poetry and prophecies.

- The New Testament, written between 50 CE and 100 CE, contains the Gospels (the life and teachings of Jesus), the Acts of the Apostles, the Epistles (letters) and the Book of Revelation. Together, the Old and New Testaments provide a comprehensive account of God's relationship with humanity and the teachings of Jesus Christ, forming the theological foundation of Christianity.
- **The other options are incorrect**: Because the Bible is not limited to the teachings of Jesus, nor is it solely a historical account or a product of the Council of Nicaea.

Thus, option (a) is the correct answer.

92. *(b)* Protestantism

- **Protestantism** emerged in the **16th century CE** during the **Protestant Reformation**, which was a movement aimed at reforming the practices and beliefs of the **Roman Catholic Church**. Led by figures such as Martin Luther, John Calvin and others, the Reformation sought to address issues such as the sale of indulgences, the authority of the Pope and the perceived corruption within the Church.
- Protestants rejected the Pope's authority, emphasising that salvation is achieved through faith alone (sola fide) and that the Bible is the sole source of religious authority (sola scriptura).

Thus, option (b) is the correct answer.

93. *(c)* All three

- **Pair 1 is correct: Ek Onkar** is a foundational concept in Sikhism that symbolises the **oneness of God**. It is the opening line of the Mool Mantar in the Guru Granth Sahib and underscores the belief that there is only one Supreme Being who is the creator, protector and destroyer.
- **Pair 2 is correct**: Simran refers to the **practice of meditation and remembrance of God's name** in Sikhism. It is a central spiritual practice aimed at fostering a constant awareness of the divine and achieving spiritual growth. Simran involves the repetition of God's name and is considered essential for attaining a higher spiritual state.
- **Pair 3 is correct**: The **Adi Granth**, also known as the **Guru Granth Sahib**, is the **sacred scripture of Sikhism**. Compiled by Guru Arjan Dev Ji, the fifth Sikh Guru, it contains the hymns and writings of the Sikh Gurus as well as contributions from various other saints and poets. The Adi Granth is revered as the eternal Guru by Sikhs and serves as the central religious text guiding their faith and practice.

Thus, option (c) is the correct answer.

94. *(b)* Only two

- **Pair 1 is correct**: This ceremony, also known as **Amrit Sanchar** or Amrit **Pahul**, was established by Guru Gobind Singh Ji, the tenth Sikh Guru, in 1699. During this ceremony, Sikhs who wish to become part of the Khalsa are baptized by drinking Amrit (a mixture of sugar and water stirred with a double-edged sword) and taking vows to live by the principles of Sikhism, including the five Ks and the avoidance of certain prohibitions.
- **Pair 2 is correct**: The term '**Anand Karaj**' means '**blissful union**' and refers to the joyous and spiritual nature of the marriage. The ceremony involves the couple taking four rounds (Laavaan) around the Guru Granth Sahib, symbolising their commitment to each other and their devotion to God.
- **Pair 3 is incorrect**: Langar refers to the **community kitchen found in Sikh Gurdwaras**, where free meals are served to all visitors, regardless of their religion, caste, gender, or social status. The concept of Langar is rooted in the principles of equality, humility and selfless service and it plays a vital role in promoting communal harmony.

Thus, option (b) is the correct answer.

95. *(d)* 1, 2 and 3

- **Statement 1 is correct: Guru Nanak Dev Ji** is recognised as the **founder of Sikhism** and he established the faith in the **15th century CE.** Born in **1469 in Punjab**, Guru Nanak's teachings emphasised devotion to one God, social equality, and the rejection of caste distinctions.

- **Statement 2 is correct:** Sikhism strongly advocates for the **equality of all people**, regardless of gender, caste, or social status. Sikhs believe that men and women are equal before God and this belief is reflected in the practices and teachings of Sikhism, such as the inclusion of women.
- **Statement 3 is correct:** Sikhism does not have an ordained priesthood. Instead, **worship is led by the community**, often by a Granthi, who is a caretaker of the Guru Granth Sahib but not a priest in the traditional sense. Sikh worship, including the reading of the Guru Granth Sahib, prayers and singing of hymns (Kirtan), can be performed by any member of the community, emphasising the importance of collective worship and the absence of hierarchical clergy.

Thus, option (d) is the correct answer.

96. *(c)* All three

- **Option 1 is correct:** Langar, or the community kitchen, was started by Guru Nanak as a means to promote equality and social justice, breaking down the barriers of caste and ensuring that all people, regardless of background, could eat together as equals.
- **Option 2 is correct: Guru Amar Das Sahib Ji** introduced several significant reforms, including the **Anand Karaj**, which is the Sikh **marriage ceremony**. He also played a crucial role in promoting gender equality, one of his notable actions being the **abolishment of Sati** among Sikhs
- **Option 3 is correct: Guru Arjan Dev Ji** was responsible for the **compilation of the Adi Granth,** which later became the Guru Granth Sahib, the central religious scripture of Sikhism. He also **completed the construction of the Harmandir Sahib** (Golden Temple) in Amritsar.

Thus, option (c) is the correct answer.

97. *(c)* Guru Hargobind Sahib Ji

- **Guru Hargobind Sahib Ji,** the sixth Sikh Guru, is known as the '**Soldier Saint**'. He introduced the concept of **Miri and Piri**, which represents the dual aspects of temporal (Miri) and spiritual (Piri) authority. To embody this principle, Guru Hargobind wore two swords, symbolising the integration of spiritual and temporal leadership.
- He also constructed the **Akal Takht** (Throne of the Timeless One) in 1606, opposite the Harmandir Sahib (Golden Temple) in Amritsar. The Akal Takht served as the seat of Sikh temporal authority and was a place where the Sikh community could address both spiritual and temporal matters. This duality of power emphasised by Guru Hargobind played a crucial role in shaping the Sikh identity and its resistance to oppression.

Thus, option (c) is the correct answer.

98. *(d)* 1, 2 and 3

- **Statement 1 is correct: Guru Gobind Singh Ji**, the tenth Sikh Guru, founded the **Khalsa** in **1699** at Anandpur Sahib. The Khalsa was established as a collective body of initiated Sikhs who were committed to upholding the principles of Sikhism, including the defense of justice, equality and the Sikh faith. It is characterised by the Five Ks (Kesh, Kara, Kanga, Kachera and Kirpan).
- **Statement 2 is correct: Guru Arjan Dev Ji**, the fifth Sikh Guru, was indeed **executed by Mughal Emperor Jahangir** in **1606.** Guru Arjan was arrested, tortured and ultimately martyred for refusing to convert to Islam and for supporting the rebellious Prince Khusrau, Jahangir's son.
- **Statement 3 is correct: Guru Har Krishan Sahib Ji** was the **youngest Sikh Guru**, ascending to the position at the age of just five. He became the eighth Sikh Guru in 1661 and is remembered for his compassion and service to the sick during a smallpox epidemic in Delhi, where he eventually succumbed to the illness.

Thus, option (d) is the correct answer.

Past Learning (Answers)

1 (a)	**2** (b)	**3** (b)	**4** (a)	**5** (b)	**6** (c)	**7** (b)	**8** (c)	**9** (d)	**10** (c)
11 (b)	**12** (b)	**13** (d)	**14** (c)	**15** (b)	**16** (d)	**17** (d)	**18** (b)		

CHAPTER 03 Philosophy

Assessment Round

Topic 1 : Upanishadic Philosophy

1. With reference to the core ideas of Upanishadic philosophy, consider the following statements:

1. Atma is considered the only reality in an individual.
2. Moksha refers to the realisation of the oneness of Atma and Brahma.
3. Karma is considered a central concept in determining one's destiny.

How many of the statements given above is/are correct?

(a) Only one (b) Only two
(c) All three (d) None

2. With reference to the concept of Karma in Upanishadic philosophy, consider the following statements:

1. Karma refers to deeds that determine the present status of an individual.
2. Karma is directly related to one's past actions and future status.
3. Upanishads emphasise that desire is the root cause of Karma.

Which of the statements given above are correct?

(a) 1 and 2 only (b) 2 and 3 only
(c) 1 and 3 only (d) 1, 2 and 3

3. Identify the concept based on the following statements:

1. It refers to the ultimate reality within an individual.
2. It is identical to Brahma in Upanishadic philosophy.
3. The realisation of this concept leads to Moksha.

Choose the correct answer from the options given below:

(a) Samsara (b) Atma
(c) Maya (d) Karma

4. Which of the following describes the relationship between Atma and Brahma in Upanishadic philosophy?

(a) Atma is considered superior to Brahma.
(b) Atma and Brahma are seen as distinct entities with different roles.
(c) Atma and Brahma are identical, representing the oneness of individual and supreme reality.
(d) Atma is a creation of Brahma and is subordinate to it.

5. In the context of Upanishadic philosophy, which of the following actions would influence one's Samsara (cycle of life and death)?

1. Performing deeds (Karma) with attachment.
2. Realising the oneness of Atma and Brahma.
3. Accumulating desires and will leading to Karma.

Select the correct answer using the codes given below:

(a) 1, 2 and 3 (b) 1 and 3 only
(c) 2 only (d) 1 and 2 only

Topic 2 : Buddhist Philosophy

6. With reference to the Four Noble Truths in Buddhist philosophy, consider the following statements:

1. The truth of suffering is called 'Dukkha.'
2. Nirvana is the extinction of desire and sorrow, leading to absolute bliss.
3. The path to end suffering is through the Eightfold Path (Ashtangika Marga).

Which of the statements given above are correct?

(a) 1 and 2 only (b) 2 and 3 only
(c) 1 and 3 only (d) 1, 2 and 3

7. With reference to the Buddhist concept of Triratna, consider the following statements:

1. Triratna refers to the three jewels: Buddha, Dhamma and Sangha.
2. Buddha represents the monastic order.
3. Sangha represents the doctrine of Buddhism.

How many of the statements given above is/are incorrect?

(a) Only one (b) Only two
(c) All three (d) None

8. Which of the following statements is correct about Buddhist philosophy?

(a) Buddha believed in the permanence of the soul.
(b) Buddhism rejected the idea of Samsara.
(c) Buddhist philosophy describes Nirvana as a state of absolute bliss.
(d) Desire is considered a positive force in Buddhism.

9. Consider the following statements:

Statement I: According to Buddhist philosophy, nothing is permanent and everything is in a state of flux.

Statement II: This doctrine is known as the Doctrine of Transience, which forms a core belief in Buddhism.

Which one of the following is correct in respect of the above statements?

(a) Both Statement I and Statement II are correct and Statement II is the correct explanation for Statement I.
(b) Both Statement I and Statement II are correct, but Statement II is not the correct explanation for Statement I.
(c) Statement I is correct, but Statement I is incorrect.
(d) Statement I is incorrect, but Statement II is correct.

10. In the context of Buddhist philosophy, which of the following elements are associated with the cessation of suffering (Nirodha)?

1. Attaining Nirvana.
2. Following the Eightfold Path (Ashtangika Marga).
3. Accumulating good karma through deeds.

Select the correct answer using the codes given below:

(a) 1, 2 and 3 (b) 1 and 2 only
(c) 2 and 3 only (d) 1 only

11. Which of the following correctly describes the Doctrine of Pratisampyada in Buddhist philosophy?

(a) It refers to the belief that everything is permanent and unchanging.
(b) It refers to the idea that nothing exists in isolation and everything arises in dependence on conditions.
(c) It refers to the concept of the eternal soul being separate from the material world.
(d) It refers to the rejection of samsara and the belief in immediate enlightenment without following a path.

Topic 3 : Jaina Philosophy

12. In the context of Jainism, the five vows are fundamental to the practice of its followers. Which of the following are part of these five vows?

1. Ahimsa (Non-violence)
2. Satya (Truth)
3. Asteya (Non-stealing)
4. Brahmacharya (Celibacy)

Select the correct answer from the codes given below:

(a) 1 and 2 only (b) 1, 2 and 3 only
(c) 1, 2, 3 and 4 (d) 2 and 4 only

13. With reference to Jain philosophy, consider the following statements:

1. The process of Samvara involves stopping the influx of Karma through the practice of five vows.
2. Nirjara refers to the destruction of accumulated Karma by self-motivation.
3. Kevalya is the state of pure soul free from karmic matter.

How many of the statements given above is/are correct?

(a) Only one (b) Only two
(c) All three (d) None

14. With reference to the concept of 'Samvara' in Jainism, consider the following statements:

1. Samvara involves stopping the process of Asrava, which is the influx of Karma.
2. The process of Samvara can be achieved by following the five vows.
3. Samvara leads to the state of Samsara.

Which of the statements given above are correct?

(a) 1 and 2 only (b) 2 and 3 only
(c) 1 and 3 only (d) 1, 2 and 3

15. Identify the concept based on the following statements:

1. It is a practice in Jainism that involves fasting until death.
2. This practice is considered an art but not suicide in Jain philosophy.
3. It is traditionally known as Santhara.

Choose the correct answer from the codes given below:

(a) Nirjara (b) Samvara
(c) Kevalya (d) Sallekhana

16. Which of the following best describes the 'Three Jewels' (Tri-ratna) in Jain philosophy?

(a) They refer to the right beliefs, right conduct and right knowledge that lead to liberation.
(b) They represent the three main deities in Jainism.
(c) They symbolise the three vows taken by Jain monks.
(d) They are the three stages of enlightenment in Jainism.

17. With reference to the Doctrine of Anekantavada in Jainism, consider the following statements:

1. It asserts that an object of knowledge can be perceived differently by different individuals.
2. Anekantavada rejects the idea of absolute truth.
3. The doctrine emphasises the importance of understanding multiple viewpoints.

Which of the statements given above are correct?

(a) 1 and 2 only
(b) 2 and 3 only
(c) 1 and 3 only
(d) 1, 2 and 3

18. With reference to the doctrines of Jainism, consider the following statements:

1. The Doctrine of Syadvada states that an object of knowledge is conditioned and should be approached with caution.
2. The Doctrine of Nyayavada emphasises that knowledge is perceived through a particular viewpoint.
3. The Doctrine of Saptabhangi explains that an object of knowledge can be understood in seven different ways.

How many of the statements given above is/are incorrect?

(a) Only one
(b) Only two
(c) All three
(d) None

19. Which of the following statements is correct regarding the Doctrine of Syadvada in Jainism?

(a) It asserts that an object of knowledge is fixed and unchanging.
(b) It emphasises the need for cautious judgement due to the conditional nature of knowledge.
(c) It denies the existence of multiple perspectives on a single object.
(d) It advocates for the absolute truth of all knowledge.

20. Consider the following statements:

Statement I: According to Jainism, the Doctrine of Anekantavada emphasises the relativity and diversity of perspectives.

Statement II: This doctrine forms the basis of Jain epistemology, allowing for multiple truths.

Which one of the following is correct in respect of the above statements?

(a) Both Statement I and Statement II are correct and Statement II is the correct explanation for Statement I.

(b) Both Statement I and Statement II are correct, but Statement II is not the correct explanation for Statement I.

(c) Statement I is correct, but Statement II is incorrect.

(d) Statement I is incorrect, but Statement II is correct.

Topic 4 : Other Ancient Key Philosophies

21. With reference to Uchchedavada, consider the following statements:

1. Uchchedavada was founded by Ajit Kesakambalin, who is considered the earliest proponent of materialism in Indian philosophy.
2. The philosophy of Uchchedavada emphasises that everything ends with death, denying any form of afterlife or rebirth.
3. The Charvaka/Lokayata school of thought emerged from the ideas of Uchchedavada, focusing on materialism and the pursuit of pleasure as the ultimate goal of life.

How many of the statements given above is/are correct?

(a) Only one (b) Only two

(c) All three (d) None

22. With reference to the Niyativad/Ajivika philosophy, consider the following statements:

1. Niyativad asserts that everything in the world is pre-determined, rejecting the theory of karma.
2. The Ajivikas practiced complete nudity and rigorous asceticism as part of their spiritual discipline.
3. The philosophy flourished during the Pre-Mauryan and Mauryan ages, with Bimbisara being one of its followers.

Which of the statements given above are correct?

(a) 1 and 2 only

(b) 2 and 3 only

(c) 1 and 3 only

(d) 1, 2 and 3

23. With reference to the Charvaka/Lokayata school of thought, consider the following statements:

1. The Charvakas believed in living well as long as one is alive, even if it meant borrowing to enjoy life.
2. They accepted only perception (Pratyaksha) as a valid source of knowledge, rejecting the authority of the Vedas.
3. The Charvaka philosophy advocated for the existence of five fundamental elements-fire, earth, water, air and the concept of ether.

Which of the statements given above are correct?

(a) 1 and 2 only

(b) 2 and 3 only

(c) 1 and 3 only

(d) 1, 2 and 3

24. With reference to Akriyavada, consider the following statements:

1. This philosophy was founded by Purana Kashyap, who taught that the soul is different from the body and remains unaffected by physical actions.
2. Akriyavada believes in the doctrine of non-action, where actions do not result in either merit or demerit.
3. The philosophy later merged with Ajivikas and the Samkhya school of philosophy emerged from it.

How many of the statements given above is/are correct?

(a) Only one

(b) Only two

(c) All three

(d) None

25. With reference to Asasvatavada/Akrivavada, consider the following statements:

1. The core philosophy of Asasvatavada states that seven elements (Nikayas) constitute the universe.
2. These elements are considered fundamental and they can neither be created nor destroyed.
3. The Vaisheshika school of philosophy later emerged from the Asasvatavada philosophy.

Which of the statements given above are correct?

(a) 1 and 2 only
(b) 2 and 3 only
(c) 1 and 3 only
(d) 1, 2 and 3

26. Identify the philosophy based on the following statements:

1. It was established by Sanjay Vetiputta.
2. The core philosophy emphasises the theory of uncertainty, stating that nothing is certain in this world.
3. The doctrine of non-denial and non-approval are central to this philosophy.

Choose the correct answer from the codes given below:

(a) Anekantvada
(b) Asasvatavada
(c) Anichchitvada
(d) Niyativad/Ajivika

Topic 5 : Six System of Philosophies

27. With reference to Samkhya philosophy, consider the following statements:

1. Samkhya philosophy accepts the dualism of Prakriti (nature) and Purusha (soul), viewing them as separate entities.
2. In Samkhya philosophy, God is considered essential for the creation of the world.
3. Liberation in Samkhya is achieved when Purusha realises its distinction from Prakriti.

How many of the statements given above is/are correct?

(a) Only one (b) Only two
(c) All three (d) None

28. With reference to Mimansa philosophy, consider the following statements:

1. Mimansa believes in God as the guiding force of the universe.
2. The Mimansa system emphasises Vedic sacrifices as the means to attain salvation.
3. The Law of Karma is central to the Mimansa philosophy.

Which of the statements given above are correct?

(a) 1 and 2 only
(b) 2 and 3 only
(c) 1 and 3 only
(d) 1, 2 and 3

29. With reference to Vedanta/Uttar Mimansa, consider the following statements:

1. Vedanta emphasises the study of the Brahma Sutra and other Upanishadic texts.
2. The ultimate goal in Vedanta is to achieve Moksha through Brahmagyan (knowledge of Brahma).
3. Vedanta completely rejects the concepts of Atma and Maya.

How many of the statements given above is/are incorrect?

(a) Only one
(b) Only two
(c) All three
(d) None

30. With reference to the Yoga philosophy as described by Patanjali, consider the following statements:

1. Yoga accepts the synthesis of Purusha and Prakriti in the creation of the universe.
2. Liberation in Yoga is achieved by the release of Purusha from Prakriti through the practice of Ashtanga Yoga.
3. The eight limbs of Ashtanga Yoga include Yama, Niyama and Samadhi.

Which of the statements given above are correct?

(a) 1 and 2 only
(b) 2 and 3 only
(c) 1 and 3 only
(d) 1, 2 and 3

31. With reference to Nyaya philosophy, consider the following statements:

1. Nyaya's philosophy is based on logic and reasoning, emphasising the systematic analysis of knowledge.
2. According to Nyaya, liberation is achieved through the knowledge obtained via Pratyaksha (perception), Anumana (inference) and Shabda (testimony).
3. The Nyaya system rejects the existence of ideals and emotions as they are considered irrelevant to the pursuit of knowledge.

How many of the statements given above is/are correct?

(a) Only one
(b) Only two
(c) All three
(d) None

32. With reference to Vaisheshika philosophy, consider the following statements:

1. Vaisheshika's philosophy presents the idea of the atomic nature of the universe.
2. The Vaisheshika system accepts the dualism of matter and soul.
3. Vaisheshika emphasises the role of God in the creation and regulation of the universe.

Which of the statements given above are correct?

(a) 1 and 2 only
(b) 2 and 3 only
(c) 1 and 3 only
(d) 1, 2 and 3

33. Which of the following correctly describes the term 'Prasthanatrayi' in Vedanta philosophy?

(a) It refers to the three paths to salvation outlined in the Vedas.
(b) It denotes the three primary sources of knowledge in Vedanta: the Upanishads, the Bhagavad Gita and the Brahma Sutras.
(c) It is the term used for the three stages of meditation in Yoga philosophy.
(d) It signifies the three principal deities in Hinduism.

Topic 6 : Philosophies in Medieval India

34. With reference to Advaita (Monism) philosophy as propagated by Shankaracharya, consider the following statements:

1. In Advaita philosophy, Brahma is considered the only reality and the soul (Atma) is identical to Brahma.
2. Liberation in Advaita is achieved through Bhakti Marg (path of devotion).
3. Prakriti (nature) is considered an illusion in Advaita philosophy.

How many of the statements given above is/are correct?

(a) Only one (b) Only two
(c) All three (d) None

35. With reference to the philosophy of Shuddh-Advaita (Pure non-dualism) as taught by Vallabhacharya, consider the following statements:

1. Vallabhacharya accepted only one reality, which is the supreme God Krishna.
2. Atma and Prakriti are considered manifestations of the supreme power in Shuddh-Advaita.
3. The followers of this school belong to the Pushtimarg Sampradaya.

Which of the statements given above are correct?

(a) 1 and 2 only (b) 2 and 3 only
(c) 1 and 3 only (d) 1, 2 and 3

36. With reference to Vishishtadvaita (Qualified Monism) philosophy as taught by Ramanujacharya, consider the following statements:

1. Vishishtadvaita considers Brahma as the supreme reality and Vishnu as the supreme power.
2. According to Vishishtadvaita, Atma and Prakriti are attributes of Vishnu.
3. The path to salvation in Vishishtadvaita is through the knowledge of Atma and Brahma.

How many of the statements given above is/are correct?

(a) Only one (b) Only two
(c) All three (d) None

37. With reference to Dvaitadvaita (Differential Monism) philosophy as taught by Nimbarkacharya, consider the following statements:

1. Dvaitadvaita teaches that humans are both different from and non-different from God.
2. The supreme power is believed to transform into Atma and Prakriti.
3. The path to salvation in Dvaitadvaita is through the knowledge of Atma and Brahma.

Which of the statements given above are correct?

(a) 1 and 2 only
(b) 2 and 3 only
(c) 1 and 3 only
(d) 1, 2 and 3

38. Consider the following pairs regarding different branches of Vedanta philosophy:

	Type of Philosophy	Description
1.	Dualist	Considers only the supreme power as reality and negates the existence of the soul and creation
2.	Dvaitavad	Accepts two realities: supreme power and soul, recognising their differences
3.	Advaita	Accepts the reality of supreme power, soul and creation (Prakriti)

How many pairs given above is/are correctly matched?

(a) Only one pair (b) Only two pairs
(c) All three pairs (d) None

Past Learning

1. "Souls are not only the property of animal and plant life, but also of rocks, running water and many other natural objects not looked on as living by other religious sects."

The above statement reflects one of the core beliefs of which one of the following religious sects of ancient India? **(2023)**

(a) Buddhism
(b) Jainism
(c) Shaivism
(d) Vaishnavism

2. Which one of the following pairs does not form part of the six systems of Indian philosophy? **(2014)**

(a) Mimamsa and Vedanta
(b) Nyaya and Vaisheshika
(c) Lokayata and Kapalika
(d) Samkhya and Yoga

3. With reference to the history of philosophical thought in India, consider the following statements regarding Samkhya School. **(2013)**

1. Samkhya does not accept the theory of rebirth or transmigration of soul.
2. Samkhya holds that it is self-knowledge that leads to liberation and not any exterior influence or agent.

Which of the statement(s) given above is/are correct?

(a) Only 1 (b) Only 2
(c) Both 1 and 2 (d) Neither 1 nor 2

4. According to Mimamsa's system of philosophy, liberation is possible by means of **(1995)**

(a) Jnana (b) Bhakti
(c) Yoga (d) Karma

OMR SHEET

Assessment Round

1	a	b	c	d	31	a	b	c	d	61	a	b	c	d	91	a	b	c	d
2	a	b	c	d	32	a	b	c	d	62	a	b	c	d	92	a	b	c	d
3	a	b	c	d	33	a	b	c	d	63	a	b	c	d	93	a	b	c	d
4	a	b	c	d	34	a	b	c	d	64	a	b	c	d	94	a	b	c	d
5	a	b	c	d	35	a	b	c	d	65	a	b	c	d	95	a	b	c	d
6	a	b	c	d	36	a	b	c	d	66	a	b	c	d	96	a	b	c	d
7	a	b	c	d	37	a	b	c	d	67	a	b	c	d	97	a	b	c	d
8	a	b	c	d	38	a	b	c	d	68	a	b	c	d	98	a	b	c	d
9	a	b	c	d	39	a	b	c	d	69	a	b	c	d	99	a	b	c	d
10	a	b	c	d	40	a	b	c	d	70	a	b	c	d	100	a	b	c	d
11	a	b	c	d	41	a	b	c	d	71	a	b	c	d	101	a	b	c	d
12	a	b	c	d	42	a	b	c	d	72	a	b	c	d	102	a	b	c	d
13	a	b	c	d	43	a	b	c	d	73	a	b	c	d	103	a	b	c	d
14	a	b	c	d	44	a	b	c	d	74	a	b	c	d	104	a	b	c	d
15	a	b	c	d	45	a	b	c	d	75	a	b	c	d	105	a	b	c	d
16	a	b	c	d	46	a	b	c	d	76	a	b	c	d	106	a	b	c	d
17	a	b	c	d	47	a	b	c	d	77	a	b	c	d	107	a	b	c	d
18	a	b	c	d	48	a	b	c	d	78	a	b	c	d	108	a	b	c	d
19	a	b	c	d	49	a	b	c	d	79	a	b	c	d	109	a	b	c	d
20	a	b	c	d	50	a	b	c	d	80	a	b	c	d	110	a	b	c	d
21	a	b	c	d	51	a	b	c	d	81	a	b	c	d	111	a	b	c	d
22	a	b	c	d	52	a	b	c	d	82	a	b	c	d	112	a	b	c	d
23	a	b	c	d	53	a	b	c	d	83	a	b	c	d	113	a	b	c	d
24	a	b	c	d	54	a	b	c	d	84	a	b	c	d	114	a	b	c	d
25	a	b	c	d	55	a	b	c	d	85	a	b	c	d	115	a	b	c	d
26	a	b	c	d	56	a	b	c	d	86	a	b	c	d	116	a	b	c	d
27	a	b	c	d	57	a	b	c	d	87	a	b	c	d	117	a	b	c	d
28	a	b	c	d	58	a	b	c	d	88	a	b	c	d	118	a	b	c	d
29	a	b	c	d	59	a	b	c	d	89	a	b	c	d	119	a	b	c	d
30	a	b	c	d	60	a	b	c	d	90	a	b	c	d	120	a	b	c	d

Calculate Your Score

Correct (✓)	
Incorrect (✓)	
Unattempted	
Total Score	
Accuracy (%)	

Reasons for Incorrect Answers?

1. Lack of Knowledge/Existing Source Insufficient	
2. Lack of Multiple Revision	
3. Common Sense Mistakes	

Note :

1. Calculate total score as correct answers carry 2 marks each 1/3rd marks will deducted for **Incorrect** Answers.
2. Calculate Accuracy (%) by dividing the number of correct answers to the total number of attempted questions.

Detailed Solutions

Assessment Round

1. *(c)* All three

- **Statement 1 is correct:** In Upanishadic philosophy, **Atma** refers to the **inner self or soul**, considered an individual's true essence. Unlike the physical body or the mind, which are transient, Atma is eternal and unchanging. It is believed that this **Atma** is not different from **Brahma**.
- **Statement 2 is correct: Moksha** is the ultimate goal in Upanishadic teachings, representing liberation from the cycle of birth and death (Samsara). This liberation is achieved by realising that **Atma** (individual self) and **Brahma** (universal self) are the same.
- **Statement 3 is correct: Karma** refers to the law of cause and effect. Every action, thought, or deed generates Karma, which influences the individual's current and future life circumstances. The accumulated Karma from past lives, combined with the actions in the present life, determines one's destiny and the conditions of future rebirths.

Thus, option (c) is the correct answer.

2. *(d)* 1, 2 and 3

- **Statement 1 is correct: Karma** refers to all actions **performed by an individual**, whether **physical, mental or verbal**. These actions, whether good or bad, directly influence the individual's current state of life. The current favourable or unfavourable circumstances are seen as the result of past **Karma**.
- **Statement 2 is correct:** The Upanishads also teach that **Karma** is a cumulative process. The actions performed in past lives contribute to the **Karma** that manifests in the present. Likewise, the actions performed in the present will affect future births and conditions.
- **Statement 3 is correct:** According to the Upanishads, **desire** (Kama) is the root cause of **Karma**. Desires lead to actions aimed at fulfilling them and these actions generate **Karma**. The Upanishads advocate for the abandonment of desires and the pursuit of knowledge (**Jnana**) as the path to overcoming **Karma** and achieving **Moksha**.

Thus, option (d) is the correct answer.

3. *(b)* Atma

- In the Upanishadic tradition, **Atma** is the innermost essence or soul of an individual. It is considered the true self, distinct from the physical body and mind. The **Atma** is eternal, unchanging and is the same in all beings, reflecting the unity of all life.
- The Upanishads describe **Atma** as being identical to **Brahma**, the ultimate reality that pervades the entire universe. This realisation, known as **Brahma-Atma** Aikyam, is the key to attaining Moksha.
- **Moksha** is the liberation from the cycle of Samsara, achieved through the realisation of the oneness of **Atma** and **Brahma**. This realisation leads to the dissolution of the ego and the cessation of all desires, which binds the soul to the physical world.

Thus, option (b) is the correct answer.

4. *(c)* Atma and Brahma are identical, representing the oneness of individual and supreme reality.

- The relationship between **Atma** (individual soul) and **Brahma** (universal reality) is a cornerstone of Upanishadic philosophy. The Upanishads assert that while **Atma** appears to be an individual entity, separate from other beings, it is, in fact, the same as **Brahma**.
- Belief in the oneness of **Atma** and **Brahma** is a profound philosophical concept that challenges the perception of duality or separation in the world. According to the Upanishads, the distinctions we observe in the material world are due to ignorance (**Avidya**).
- The realisation that **Atma** is **Brahma** leads to liberation from the **cycle of birth and death**. This liberation, known as Moksha, is not a place but a state of consciousness where one experiences unity with the entire cosmos and eternal bliss.

Thus, option (c) is the correct answer.

5. *(b)* 1 and 3 only

- **Statement 1 is correct:** The Upanishads emphasise that performing actions with attachment (desire for the fruits of action) generates **Karma**. This **Karma** binds the soul to the cycle of **Samsara** (the cycle of birth and rebirth). The goal is to perform actions selflessly, without attachment, to avoid generating new **Karma** that would result in further rebirths.
- **Statement 2 is incorrect:** This realisation leads to **Moksha** (liberation) and the end of **Samsara**. When an individual understands that their **Atma** is the same as **Brahma**, they transcend the cycle of **Samsara** and achieve eternal freedom. This realisation does not contribute to Samsara but instead dissolves it.
- **Statement 3 is correct:** Desires are the root cause of **Karma** in Upanishadic philosophy. The will to act based on desires leads to actions that generate **Karma**. This accumulated **Karma** determines the conditions of one's future births, thereby perpetuating the cycle of **Samsara**.

Thus, option (b) is the correct answer.

6. *(d)* 1, 2 and 3

- **Statement 1 is correct:** The first of the Four Noble Truths in Buddhism is **Dukkha**, which acknowledges the pervasive nature of suffering in human existence. **Dukkha** is not just physical pain or mental distress but also the existential suffering that arises from the impermanent nature of life.
- **Statement 2 is correct:** The third Noble Truth describes the cessation of suffering, known as **Nirodha**, which is achieved through the attainment of **Nirvana**. This state of absolute bliss is free from the cycle of birth and death (Samsara) and represents the complete liberation of the mind from suffering.
- **Statement 3 is correct:** The fourth Noble Truth outlines the path to the cessation of suffering, known as the **Eightfold Path**. This path comprises eight practices that are divided into three main categories: ethical conduct (right speech, right action, right livelihood), mental discipline (right effort, right mindfulness, right concentration) and wisdom (right understanding, right intention).

Thus, option (d) is the correct answer.

7. *(b)* Only two

- **Statement 1 is correct:** The term **Triratna** in Buddhism refers to the three jewels or refuges that Buddhists take refuge in **Buddha** (the enlightened one), **Dhamma** (the teachings or doctrine) and Sangha (the monastic community).
- **Statement 2 is incorrect:** In this context, **Buddha** does not represent the monastic order but rather the historical Buddha, Siddhartha Gautama, who attained enlightenment and shared his insights with the world. The term also symbolises the ideal of enlightenment that all beings can achieve.
- **Statement 3 is incorrect: Sangha** refers to the community of monks, nuns and lay followers who practice the teachings of the Buddha. It is not the doctrine itself, but rather the collective of those who live according to the **Dhamma**.

Thus, option (b) is the correct answer.

8. *(c)* Buddhist philosophy describes Nirvana as a state of absolute bliss.

- **Statement (a) is incorrect:** Buddhism explicitly rejects the notion of an eternal, unchanging soul (atman). Instead, it teaches the doctrine of **Anatta** (no-self), where the concept of a permanent self is considered an illusion that leads to attachment and suffering.
- **Statement (b) is incorrect:** Rather than rejecting **Samsara**, Buddhism acknowledges its existence and seeks to transcend it. **Samsara** is the cycle of birth, death and rebirth that individuals undergo until they attain **Nirvana**.
- **Statement (c) is correct:** In Buddhism, **Nirvana** is described as the ultimate goal of spiritual practice, where the cycle of suffering (**Samsara**) is completely transcended. **Nirvana** represents the cessation of all forms of suffering and the attainment of a state of absolute bliss and peace.

- **Statement (d) is incorrect:** In Buddhism, desire (**Tanha**) is seen as the root cause of suffering. It leads to attachment, craving and ultimately, the perpetuation of the cycle of **Samsara.** The cessation of desire is essential for achieving **Nirvana.**

Thus, option (c) is the correct answer.

9. *(a)* Both Statement I and Statement II are correct and Statement II is the correct explanation for Statement I.

- **Statement I is correct:** The concept of **Anicca** (impermanence) is one of the three marks of existence in Buddhist philosophy, alongside Dukkha (suffering) and **Anatta** (no-self). **Anicca** teaches that all conditioned phenomena, including physical forms, thoughts, emotions and even the self are transient and subject to change.
- **Statement II is correct:** The **Doctrine of Transience** is directly related to the concept of Anicca. It emphasises that because all things are in a constant state of flux, they cannot provide lasting happiness or fulfillment.

Thus, option (a) is the correct answer.

10. *(b)* 1 and 2 only

- **Statement 1 is correct:** Nirvana is the ultimate goal in Buddhism and represents the cessation of all forms of suffering. It is a state of liberation where the cycle of birth and death (Samsara) is transcended and the individual is free from all desires, attachments and ignorance.
- **Statement 2 is correct:** The **Eightfold Path** is the practical guide to achieving **Nirvana.** It consists of eight interconnected practices: **right understanding, right intention, right speech, right action, right livelihood, right effort, right mindfulness and right concentration.**
- **Statement 3 is incorrect:** While accumulating good Karma (positive actions) is important in Buddhism for achieving favorable rebirths, **it does not directly lead to the cessation of suffering (Nirodha). Nirvana** is achieved through the eradication of all **Karma**—both good and bad by following the path of enlightenment.

Thus, option (b) is the correct answer.

11. *(b)* It refers to the idea that nothing exists in isolation and everything arises in dependence on conditions.

- **Pratisampyada (Dependent Origination):** The Doctrine of **Pratisampyada,** also known as Dependent Origination or Dependent Co-arising, is a fundamental concept in Buddhist philosophy. It explains that all phenomena arise in dependence on other phenomena; nothing exists independently or in isolation.
- **Twelve Links of Dependent Origination:** The concept of Dependent Origination is often illustrated through the Twelve Links (Nidanas) of Dependent Origination, which describe the cyclical process of Samsara (the cycle of birth, death and rebirth). Each link conditions the next, creating a continuous cycle of existence. Understanding and breaking this chain is essential for achieving Nirvana and escaping the cycle of **Samsara.**

Thus, option (b) is the correct answer.

12. *(c)* 1, 2, 3 and 4

- **Five Vows in Jainism:** The five major vows, known as **Anuvratas** for lay followers and **Mahavratas** for monks, are the cornerstone of Jain's ethical practice. These vows are:
- **Option 1 is correct: Ahimsa (Non-violence)** emphasises non-violence in thought, word and deed. It extends beyond human beings to include all living creatures.
- **Option 2 is correct:** Satya (Truth): The vow of Satya involves always speaking the truth. Jains are also taught to speak truthfully in a manner that does not cause harm to others.
- **Option 3 is correct: Asteya (Non- stealing):** Asteya involves refraining from taking anything that is not willingly given.
- **Option 4 is correct: Brahmacharya (Celibacy):** For lay followers, Brahmacharya typically means fidelity to one's spouse, while for monks, it entails complete celibacy. This

vow emphasises the control of desires and passions **to maintain spiritual purity.**

- **Aparigraha (Non-possession):** This vow involves the renunciation of material wealth and possessions. It encourages detachment from material goods and a life of simplicity.

Thus, option (c) is the correct answer.

13. *(c)* All three

- **Statement 1 is correct:** In Jain philosophy, **Samvara** refers to the process of stopping the influx of new Karma into the soul. This is achieved through the practice of the five vows (Ahimsa, Satya, Asteya, Brahmacharya and Aparigraha) along with other disciplines such as control of the senses, meditation and penance.
- **Statement 2 is correct: Nirjara** refers to the process of shedding or eliminating the accumulated Karma that has already been attached to the soul. This process involves intense spiritual practices such as fasting, meditation, repentance and self-discipline.
- **Statement 3 is correct: Kevalya** is the state of absolute knowledge and liberation in Jainism, where the soul is free from all karmic impurities. **Kevalya** is the final goal of Jain spiritual practice, where the soul transcends the cycle of birth and death and remains in a state of eternal peace.

Thus, option (c) is the correct answer.

14. *(a)* 1 and 2 only

- **Statement 1 is correct: Samvara** is the process in Jainism that involves stopping or blocking the influx of Asrava (karmic particles) into the soul which happens due to actions driven by passions, desires and attachments. By practicing **Samvara**, individuals prevent new karma from attaching to their souls, thereby stopping the cycle of karmic accumulation.
- **Statement 2 is correct:** The practice of **Samvara** is closely associated with the observance of the five major vows (Ahimsa, Satya, Asteya, Brahmacharya and Aparigraha). These vows help in controlling the passions and desires that lead to the inflow of karmic particles.
- **Statement 3 is incorrect: Samvara** is a process that helps in breaking free from **Samsara**. By preventing the influx of new karma and shedding existing karma through **Nirjara**, one moves closer to achieving **Kevalya** (liberation) and escaping the cycle of **Samsara.**

Thus, option (a) is the correct answer.

15. *(d)* Sallekhana

- **Sallekhana** (also known as **Santhara**) is a deeply revered practice in Jainism where an individual voluntarily fasts until death. This practice is undertaken with a sense of serenity and detachment, as a final act of renunciation and spiritual purification.
- **Art, Not Suicide:** In Jain philosophy, **Sallekhana** is distinguished from suicide by its underlying motivation and emotional state. It is seen as an art because it is conducted with great care, mindfulness and adherence to religious principles.
- **Traditional Practice: Sallekhana** is traditionally accepted within the Jain community, particularly among monks and nuns, but also by devout laypersons. It is considered the final vow of non-attachment and non-violence, as the individual minimises harm to themselves and others by withdrawing from the consumption of food and water.

Thus, option (d) is the correct answer.

16. *(a)* They refer to the right beliefs, right conduct and right knowledge that lead to liberation.

- **Three Jewels (Tri-ratna):** The **Three Jewels** or **Tri-ratna** in Jain philosophy are the three essential principles that guide a person on the path to spiritual liberation. These are:
  1. **Samyak Darshana (Right Belief):** This refers to the correct understanding and acceptance of the fundamental truths of Jainism, such as the belief in the soul, the law of karma and the potential for liberation.
  2. **Samyak Jnana (Right Knowledge):** Right knowledge involves understanding the nature of reality as it is, without any distortions or misconceptions. It includes knowledge of the self, the universe and the principles of karma and ethics.
  3. **Samyak Charitra (Right Conduct):** Right conduct is the practice of ethical and

moral behaviour by Jain teachings. It involves the observance of the five vows and living a life of non-violence, truthfulness and detachment.

Thus, option (a) is the correct answer.

17. *(d)* 1, 2 and 3

- **Statement 1 is correct:** The Doctrine of **Anekantavada** is a core principle in Jain philosophy that asserts the multiplicity of viewpoints. It teaches that reality is complex and multifaceted. According to **Anekantavada**, different individuals may perceive the same object or concept in different ways, depending on their perspective, knowledge and experiences.
- **Statement 2 is incorrect: Anekantavada rejects the idea of absolute truth because it suggests that reality is complex and multifaceted and there is no single, definitive way to understand it. Instead, truth is relative and can be understood from multiple perspectives therefore cannot be comprehended fully from a single perspective.**
- **Statement 3 is correct: Anekantavada** emphasises the importance of considering multiple viewpoints to arrive at a more holistic understanding of reality. This doctrine encourages intellectual humility and the acceptance that one's perspective is limited and that others may hold equally valid but different perspectives.

Thus, option (d) is the correct answer.

18. *(d)* None

- **Statement 1 is correct:** The Doctrine of **Syadvada** is also known as the doctrine of conditioned predication. According to it, no statement can be true or false because it depends on various factors, including time, place and the observer's perspective. This doctrine encourages **cautious judgement** and emphasises that truth is always **conditional and context-dependent.**
- **Statement 2 is correct:** The Doctrine of **Nyayavada** suggests that knowledge is perceived from a particular viewpoint or angle. This doctrine is about the methodology of knowing, asserting that one's perspective shapes one's understanding of reality.
- **Statement 3 is correct:** According to **Saptabhangi**, an object or concept can be understood in seven different ways, each providing a partial truth. The seven ways include statements like it is, it is not, it is and it is not and so on, capturing the nuanced and multifaceted nature of truth.

Thus, option (d) is the correct answer.

19. *(b)* It emphasises the need for cautious judgment due to the conditional nature of knowledge.

- The Doctrine of **Syadvada** in Jain philosophy is also known as the doctrine of "maybe" or conditional predication. It is a logical framework that suggests that any assertion about reality can only be conditionally true. **Syadvada** underscores the importance of cautious judgement and humility in making claims about reality.
- While **Syadvada** does not deny the possibility of knowing the truth, it does assert that our knowledge is always influenced by specific conditions and contexts. This doctrine aligns with the broader Jain principle of **Anekantavada**, which teaches that reality is multifaceted and cannot be fully understood from a single viewpoint.

Thus, option (b) is the correct answer.

20. *(a)* Both Statement I and Statement II are correct and Statement II is the correct explanation for Statement I.

- **Statement I is correct:** The Doctrine of **Anekantavada** encourages the recognition of multiple perspectives, asserting that no single view can encompass the entire truth. This doctrine fosters intellectual humility and tolerance, as it acknowledges that different people may hold different, yet valid, viewpoints about the same reality.
- **Statement II is the correct and also correct explanation of Statement II: Anekantavada** forms the foundation of Jain epistemology

(the study of knowledge). It leads to the development of two other key doctrines: **Syadvada** (the theory of conditional predication) and Saptabhangi (the theory of sevenfold predication). **Anekantavada** thus allows for the **coexistence of multiple truths**, each valid within its context.

Thus, option (a) is the correct answer.

21. *(c)* All three

- **Statement 1 is correct**: Ajit Kesakambalin is recognised as one of the earliest proponents of materialism in ancient Indian philosophy. He is known for founding **Uchchedavada**, a philosophy that fundamentally denies the existence of any afterlife or spiritual continuity after death.
- **Statement 2 is correct**: The core belief of **Uchchedavada** is that everything ends with death, body and soul perish entirely upon death and there is no afterlife, reincarnation, or spiritual survival. Uchchedavada rejects the **notions of sin, virtue and the moral consequences** that would typically follow in an afterlife.
- **Statement 3 is correct**: The **Charvaka or Lokayata** school of thought is often considered an extension or evolution of the materialist ideas presented in Uchchedavada. The **Charvakas** adopted and expanded upon the materialistic outlook, advocating for a philosophy that prioritises sensory experience and the pursuit of pleasure as the ultimate goals of life.

Thus, option (c) is the correct answer.

22. *(d)* 1, 2 and 3

- **Statement 1 is correct: Niyativad** (also known as Ajivika philosophy) is based on the belief in **Niyati** or fate, which posits that everything in the world is pre-determined and governed by an immutable cosmic order. This philosophy rejects the **theory of karma**-arguing instead that all events are predestined and cannot be altered by human actions.
- **Statement 2 is correct**: The **Ajivikas** were known for their extreme ascetic practices, which included complete nudity and rigorous physical discipline. They believed that by renouncing all worldly attachments and enduring severe hardships, they could align themselves with the preordained cosmic order and ultimately attain liberation.
- **Statement 3 is correct**: The Ajivika sect flourished during the Pre-Mauryan and Mauryan periods, particularly under the patronage of King **Bimbisara**, who is often listed as a follower of the sect. Their influence began to wane after the Mauryan period, as other religions gained prominence.

Thus, option (d) is the correct answer.

23. *(a)* 1 and 2 only

- **Statement 1 is correct**: The **Charvaka** or **Lokayata** school is known for its hedonistic approach to life. They famously advocated for the enjoyment of worldly pleasures, encapsulated in the maxim 'Eat, drink and be merry, for tomorrow we die'. The Charvakas were materialists who believed that the ultimate goal of life is to maximise pleasure and minimise pain.
- **Statement 2 is correct**: The **Charvakas** accepted only **Pratyaksha** (direct perception) as a reliable source of knowledge, rejecting other means such as inference and testimony (**eg-Vedas**), which are considered valid in other Indian philosophical schools.
- **Statement 3 is incorrect**: In their cosmology, the Charvakas recognised only four fundamental elements-**fire, earth, water and air-as the building blocks of the universe. They rejected the concept of ether (akasha)**, which was accepted by other Indian philosophical schools because it could not be perceived directly through the senses.

Thus, option (a) is the correct answer.

24. *(b)* Only two

- **Statement 1 is correct: Akriyavada** was founded by **Purana Kashyap**. He proposed that the soul is separate from the body and is unaffected by the physical actions performed by the body. This detachment suggests that the soul **remains pure and untouched**, regardless of the moral or immoral acts committed by the individual.
- **Statement 2 is correct: Akriyavada** is associated with the doctrine of non-action

(**Akriya**), which argues that actions do not produce any merit (punya) or demerit (paap). This view contrasts sharply with the karmic theory prevalent in many other Indian philosophical traditions, which holds that every action has consequences that influence future rebirths.

- **Statement 3 is incorrect**: The **Samkhya** school is one of the six classical systems of Indian philosophy and is more closely related to the **Yoga** tradition. It has its distinct origins and philosophies, focusing on dualism. **Akriyavada**, on the other hand, is more closely related to other heterodox traditions like **Ajivika** but did not directly influence the development of Samkhya.

Thus, option (b) is the correct answer.

25. *(d)* 1, 2 and 3

- **Statement 1 is correct: Asasvatavada**, also known as **Akrivavada**, is a philosophical system that posits the existence of seven fundamental elements, known as **Nikayas**, which constitute the entire universe. These elements are viewed as the building blocks of reality.
- **Statement 2 is correct**: The **Asasvatavada** doctrine emphasises that the seven elements are indestructible. This means that while the forms they compose may change, the elements themselves remain unchanged.
- **Statement 3 is correct**: While Vaisheshika developed its distinct system, it was influenced by earlier ideas like those found in **Asasvatavada.** This emphasis on fundamental elements in **Asasvatavada** provided a conceptual framework that may have influenced the later development of atomic theory in Vaisheshika.

Thus, option (d) is the correct answer.

26. *(c)* Anichchitvada

- **Anichchitvada** established by **Sanjay Vetiputta**, is characterised by its emphasis on uncertainty and skepticism. Anichchitvada teaches that nothing is certain in this world and as such, it is impossible to make definitive statements about the nature of reality, morality, or knowledge.
- The core of **Anichchitvada** is the idea that all claims about reality are subject to doubt. This leads to a position of non-commitment or non-attachment to any particular viewpoint.
- **Anichchitvada** incorporates a doctrine of **non-denial** (where one does not outright reject any claim) and non-approval (where one does not fully accept any claim either). This approach reflects the philosophy's commitment to uncertainty and skepticism, promoting intellectual humility and openness to new perspectives.

Thus, option (c) is the correct answer.

27. *(b)* Only two

- **Statement 1 is correct: Samkhya** is known for its dualistic framework. **Prakriti** is considered the material cause of the universe, while **Purusha** represents pure consciousness. The philosophy posits that these two principles are fundamentally different and independent of each other.
- **Statement 2 is incorrect**: Contrary to many other Indian philosophical systems, **Samkhya** does not consider God as essential or even relevant to the creation of the world. The universe is seen as a product of the interaction between Prakriti and Purusha without the need for a divine creator.
- **Statement 3 is correct:** Liberation, or **Moksha**, in Samkhya, is achieved when **Purusha** (the individual self) realises its complete distinction from Prakriti. This realisation leads to the cessation of all suffering, as Purusha becomes detached from the material world.

Thus, option (b) is the correct answer.

28. *(d)* 1, 2 and 3

- **Statement 1 is correct**: The **Mimansa** school of philosophy, particularly **Purva Mimansa**, is primarily concerned with the interpretation and ritualistic aspects of the Vedas. While Purva Mimansa acknowledged the existence of divine forces that are invoked through rituals. However, Uttar Mimansa (Vedanta) later incorporated a more explicit belief in a personal God, particularly in the context of guiding the universe.

- **Statement 2 is correct**: One of the central tenets of **Mimansa** is the belief in the efficacy of **Vedic sacrifices** (Yajnas). Salvation or **Moksha** in **Purva Mimansa** is not the cessation of rebirth but rather the accumulation of positive karmic results through the faithful execution of one's duties as outlined in the Vedas.
- **Statement 3 is correct**: The **Law of Karma** is integral to the Mimansa philosophy. It posits that every action has consequences and these are determined by the performance of Vedic duties. **Mimansa** emphasises that by following the Vedic injunctions, individuals can influence their karma and secure favourable outcomes.

Thus, option (d) is the correct answer.

29. *(a)* Only one

- **Statement 1 is correct**: Vedanta, also known as **Uttar Mimansa**, primarily focuses on the teachings of the Upanishads, the Brahma Sutra and the Bhagavad Gita. The study of these texts is central to Vedanta's philosophical inquiry, as they provide the basis for understanding the non-dualistic nature of existence.
- **Statement 2 is correct**: The ultimate goal in Vedanta is **Moksha**, which is the liberation from the cycle of birth and death. This liberation is achieved through **Brahmagyan**, (the knowledge of Brahma), the ultimate reality.
- **Statement 3 is incorrect**: Vedanta does not reject the concepts of **Atma** and **Maya**. These concepts are central to its teachings. **Atma** is the true self, which is identical to Brahma, while **Maya** refers to the illusory nature of the material world that obscures the true nature of reality.

Thus, option (a) is the correct answer.

30. *(d)* 1, 2 and 3

- **Statement 1 is correct**: In the **Yoga** philosophy, as described by Patanjali, the creation of the universe is understood as the result of the interaction between **Purusha** (consciousness) and **Prakriti** (matter). The goal of Yoga is to transcend this interaction and realise the pure state of Purusha.
- **Statement 2 is correct: Ashtanga Yoga** (the eightfold path) is the practical framework provided by Patanjali to achieve liberation (Moksha). Liberation is attained when Purusha is released from its identification with Prakriti accomplished through disciplined practice.
- **Statement 3 is correct**: The eight limbs of Ashtanga Yoga are **Yama** (ethical restraints), **Niyama** (observances), Asana (postures), **Pranayama** (breath control), **Pratyahara** (withdrawal of the senses), **Dharana** (concentration), **Dhyana** (meditation) and **Samadhi** (absorption or union).

Thus, option (d) is the correct answer.

31. *(b)* Only two

- **Statement 1 is correct: Nyaya** is a school of Indian philosophy that is primarily concerned with logic, epistemology and reasoning. The **Nyaya Sutras**, attributed to **Akshapada Gautama**, form the foundation of this system, which systematically categorises different types of knowledge and the means to acquire it.
- **Statement 2 is correct**: In Nyaya, liberation (**Moksha**) is believed to be attainable through the correct knowledge of reality. This knowledge is acquired through three primary means: **Pratyaksha** (perception), **Anumana** (inference) and **Shabda** (testimony).
- **Statement 3 is incorrect**: The Nyaya system does not reject the existence of ideals, beliefs, or emotions. Instead, it acknowledges that these mental states are dependent on the mind and are subject to logical analysis.

Thus, option (b) is the correct answer.

32. *(a)* 1 and 2 only

- **Statement 1 is correct**: The **Vaisheshika** school, founded by **Uluk Kanada** in the 6th century BCE, is renowned for its pioneering atomic theory. This school posits that all material objects in the universe are composed of indivisible and eternal particles known as **paramanus** (atoms).
- **Statement 2 is correct: Vaisheshika** is a dualistic philosophy that recognises the distinction between **Dravya** (substance), which includes both material elements like atoms and non-material entities like **Atma** (soul).

- **Statement 3 is incorrect**: While **Vaisheshika** discusses the natural laws governing the universe, the role of God is not central to its original doctrine. The system primarily focuses on explaining the physical world through the interactions of atoms and other substances.

Thus, option (a) is the correct answer.

33. *(b)* It denotes the three primary sources of knowledge in Vedanta: the Upanishads, the Bhagavad Gita and the Brahma Sutras.

- **Prasthanatrayi**: The term Prasthanatrayi means 'the three sources' or the 'three points of departure.' In Vedanta philosophy, it refers to the three foundational texts that are considered the primary sources of knowledge. These texts are:
  1. **The Upanishads**: These are ancient texts that form the philosophical basis of Hinduism. They explore the nature of reality, the self (Atma) and the ultimate reality (Brahma).
  2. **The Bhagavad Gita**: A 700-verse dialogue between Lord Krishna and the warrior Arjuna, synthesises various paths to spiritual realisation, including the paths of devotion (bhakti), knowledge (jnana) and disciplined action (karma).
  3. **The Brahma Sutras**: Also known as the Vedanta Sutras, these texts were written by the sage **Badarayana** to systematically summarise and interpret the teachings of the Upanishads. The Brahma Sutras play a crucial role in establishing the philosophical foundations of Vedanta.

Thus, option (b) is the correct answer.

34. *(b)* Only two

- **Statement 1 is correct: Advaita Vedanta**, as taught by **Shankaracharya**, posits that **Brahma** is the only ultimate reality. According to this philosophy, **Atma** (the individual soul) is not different from **Brahma**; they are the same.
- **Statement 2 is incorrect: Advaita** primarily advocates **Jnana Marg** (the path of knowledge) as the means to liberation. It teaches that through self-inquiry and the realisation of the non-dual nature of the self and Brahma, one can attain Moksha (liberation).
- **Statement 3 is correct**: In **Advaita Vedanta, Prakriti** (the material world) is considered **Maya**—an illusion that veils the true nature of reality. However, once the illusion of Maya is transcended, one realises that only Brahma is real and all distinctions are illusory.

Thus, option (b) is the correct answer.

35. *(d)* 1, 2 and 3

- **Statement 1 is correct: Vallabhacharya**, the proponent of **Shuddh-Advaita** (Pure non-dualism), taught that the supreme reality is **Krishna.** He posited that Krishna is the ultimate and only reality and everything else is a manifestation of his divine will.
- **Statement 2 is correct**: In **Shuddh-Advaita**, both **Atma** (soul) and **Prakriti** (nature) are considered real and are seen as manifestations of the supreme power, Krishna. This perspective allows for a non-dualistic understanding of reality, where everything is an aspect of Krishna, yet retains its distinct existence.
- **Statement 3 is correct:** The followers of **Vallabhacharya's** teachings form the **Pushtimarg Sampradaya**, a devotional sect dedicated to the worship of Krishna. The Pushtimarg emphasises grace (Pushti) as the means to attain divine favour.

Thus, option (d) is the correct answer.

36. *(b)* Only two

- **Statement 1 is correct: Vishishtadvaita**, or qualified non-dualism, as taught by **Ramanujacharya**, holds that **Brahma** is the supreme reality and Vishnu (or Narayana) is the supreme manifestation of Brahma. In this philosophy, Brahma is seen as having distinct attributes, which include the sentient souls (Atma) and the non-sentiment matter (Prakriti).
- **Statement 2 is correct**: According to **Vishishtadvaita**, **Atma** and **Prakriti** are considered to be real and are seen as attributes (or modes) of **Vishnu**. This contrasts with the pure monism of Advaita, where everything is seen as one without attributes. **Vishishtadvaita** acknowledges a qualified oneness, where the souls and matter are distinct but inseparable from the divine.

- **Statement 3 is incorrect: Vishishtadvaita** emphasises **Bhakti Marg** (the path of devotion) as the primary means to attain salvation. Ramanujacharya taught that through intense devotion and surrender to Vishnu, one can attain grace and ultimately achieve Moksha. While knowledge of Atma and Brahma is important, it is the grace of Vishnu, attained through devotion, that leads to liberation in **Vishishtadvaita.**

Thus, option (b) is the correct answer.

37. *(a)* 1 and 2 only

- **Statement 1 is correct: Nimbarkacharya** founded the Dvaitadvaita or **'Differential Monism'** school of thought. This philosophy asserts that the individual soul (Atma) and God (Brahma or Vishnu) are both distinct and non-distinct from each other i.e. there is a difference between the soul and God, but there is also an inseparable relationship that binds them.
- **Statement 2 is correct**: In **Dvaitadvaita,** it is believed that the **Supreme Power** (Vishnu) manifests or transforms into both **Atma** (soul) and **Prakriti** (nature). This idea aligns with the notion that everything in existence is connected to and derived from the supreme deity.
- **Statement 3 is incorrect**: While the knowledge of **Atma** and **Brahma** is important, **Nimbarkacharya** emphasised **Bhakti Marg** (the path of devotion) as the primary means to attain liberation. Devotion to Vishnu or Krishna, along with the grace of the deity, is seen as essential for achieving Moksha.

Thus, option (a) is the correct answer.

38. *(a)* Only one pair

- **Pair 1 is incorrectly matched: Dvaita,** or **Dualism,** is a philosophy attributed to **Madhvacharya.** It asserts the fundamental distinction between the supreme power (Vishnu) and the individual soul (Atma). Both are real, but they are eternally different. **Dvaita** does not consider Prakriti (the material world) as an illusion but as a distinct reality created by Vishnu.
- **Pair 2 is correctly matched: Dvaitadvaita,** or Differential Monism, is a philosophy taught by **Nimbarkacharya.** It holds that the supreme power (Vishnu), the soul (Atma) and creation (Prakriti) are all distinct yet interrelated realities. The philosophy acknowledges the reality of all three entities, recognising both their unity and their differences.
- **Pair 3 is incorrectly matched: Advaita** philosophy, primarily associated with **Shankaracharya,** teaches that **Brahma** (the supreme power) is the only reality. It denies the existence of the soul (Atma) and creation (Prakriti) as separate entities, considering them as mere illusions (Maya). In Advaita, everything is one with Brahma and the perception of duality is due to ignorance.

Thus, option (a) is the correct answer.

Past Learning (Answers)

1 (b) **2** (c) **3** (b) **4** (d)

CHAPTER 04 Bhakti and Sufi Movements

Assessment Round

Topic 1 : Bhakti Movement

1. With reference to the Alvars, consider the following statements:

1. Alvars were Vaishnava poet-saints who composed songs in praise of Lord Vishnu and Krishna.
2. The collection of hymns composed by the Alvars is called 'Tevaram'.
3. Andal was the only female Alvar, also referred to as 'Meera of the South'.

Which of the statements given above are correct?

(a) 1 and 2 only (b) 2 and 3 only
(c) 1 and 3 only (d) 1, 2 and 3

2. With reference to the Nayanars, consider the following statements:

1. The Nayanars were Tamil saints devoted to Lord Vishnu.
2. The Nayanars included Brahmins, nobles, as well as oil-mongers and Vellalars.
3. Tevaram is a collection of poems compiled by the Nayanar saints Appar, Sundarar and Sambandar.

Which of the statements given above is/are correct?

(a) 1 and 2 only (b) 2 and 3 only
(c) 1 and 3 only (d) 2 only

3. With reference to the Virashaiva/Lingayat sect, consider the following statements:

1. The Virashaiva sect was founded by Basavacharya during the Kalachuri dynasty in the 12th century CE.
2. The followers of this sect were called Virashaivas or Lingayats, known for wearing a Shivalinga on their left shoulder.
3. The Virashaivas accepted the idea of the caste system and upheld Brahminical orthodoxy.

How many of the statements given above is/are correct?

(a) Only one (b) Only two
(c) All three (d) None

4. With reference to the Haridasas, consider the following statements:

1. The Haridasas were a Shaivite sect that emphasised devotion to Lord Shiva.
2. The Haridasas were centered around Udupi, Karnataka and represented the Vaishnavite cult founded by Madhavacharya.
3. Prominent saints of the Haridasa tradition include Sripadaraya, Vyasaraya and Kanaka Dasa.

How many of the statements given above is/are correct?

(a) Only one (b) Only two
(c) All three (d) None

5. Identify the philosopher based on the following statements:

1. He was a philosopher and social reformer who founded the tradition of Lingayatism.
2. He advocated the principles of Arivu (true knowledge), Achara (right conduct), and Anubhava (divine experience).
3. He established the Anubhava Mandapa, considered the first Parliament of India.

Choose the correct answer from the options given below :

(a) Ramanujacharya (b) Basaveshwara
(c) Madhavacharya (d) Vallabhacharya

6. In the context of the Varkari sect, which of the following saints are associated with this tradition?

1. Eknath 2. Tukaram 3. Ramdas

Select the correct answer using the codes given below:

(a) 1 and 2 only (b) 2 and 3 only
(c) 1 and 3 only (d) 1, 2 and 3

7. With reference to the philosophy and contributions of Eknath, consider the following statements:

1. Eknath was a follower of the Saguna tradition and wrote under the pen name 'Eka Janardana.'
2. He composed the 'Mantra Gita,' a Marathi translation of the Bhagavad Gita.
3. Eknath popularised Vedanta philosophy and was associated with the Dharkari sect.

Which of the statements given above is/are incorrect?

(a) 1 and 2 only (b) 2 and 3 only
(c) 1 and 3 only (d) 1 only

8. With reference to the contributions of Namdev, consider the following statements:

1. Namdev was a disciple of Jnaneshwar and associated with the Varkari sect.
2. His philosophy combines both Nirguna and Saguna Bhakti traditions.
3. Namdev's Abhangas are thought to have been incorporated into the Guru Granth Sahib.

How many of the statements given above is/are correct?

(a) Only one (b) Only two
(c) All three (d) None

9. With reference to the Bhakti movement, consider the following statements:

1. Kabir was one of the greatest disciples of Ramananda and advocated the idea of one God.
2. Guru Nanak met Kabir at the age of 27 and was influenced by his teachings.
3. Kabir was known for his works 'Bijak', 'Sakhis', and 'Rekhta', which were later compiled into the Guru Granth Sahib.

How many of the statements given above is/are correct?

(a) Only one (b) Only two
(c) All three (d) None

10. With reference to the life and teachings of Guru Nanak, consider the following statements:

1. Guru Nanak was born in Talwandi, which is in present-day, Pakistan.
2. He conceptualised God as Nirguna (formless) and emphasised the middle path between asceticism and satisfaction of senses.
3. Guru Nanak's teachings were compiled into the Adi Granth, later known as the Guru Granth Sahib.

How many of the statements given above is/are incorrect?

(a) Only one (b) Only two
(c) All three (d) None

11. With reference to the teachings of Kabir, consider the following statements:

1. Kabir strongly criticised the meaningless rituals and ceremonies of both Hinduism and Islam.
2. Kabir's verses are found in the Guru Granth Sahib, where he is also credited with composing the Dasam Granth.
3. Kabir's followers are known as Kabirpanthis, and they uphold his teachings of monism and social equality.

Which of the statements given above are correct?

(a) 1 and 2 only (b) 2 and 3 only
(c) 1 and 3 only (d) 1, 2 and 3

12. With reference to the contributions of Guru Nanak to Sikhism, consider the following statements:

1. Guru Nanak was the founder of Sikhism and initiated the practice of Langar (community kitchen).
2. He emphasised a form of worship that combined elements of both Hinduism and Islam.
3. Guru Nanak was persecuted by Sikandar Lodhi for his teachings.

How many of the statements given above is/are correct?

(a) Only one (b) Only two
(c) All three (d) None

13. With reference to the Bhakti movement in South India, consider the following statements:

1. The Nalayira Divya Prabandham is a collection of hymns composed by the Nayanars in praise of Lord Shiva.
2. The Nayanars were a group of 63 Tamil saints who opposed the philosophy of Jainism and Buddhism.
3. Both the Alvars and the Nayanars included female saints who played a significant role in their respective traditions.

Which of the statements given above is/are correct?

(a) 1 and 2 only (b) 2 and 3 only
(c) 3 only (d) 1, 2 and 3

14. With reference to the contributions of Ramananda, consider the following statements:

1. Ramananda was a prominent Rama worshipper who played a significant role in the Bhakti movement in North India.
2. He preached in Sanskrit to make his teachings accessible and understandable to all.
3. Ramananda is credited with establishing the Sant Parampara.

Which of the statements given above are correct?

(a) 1 and 2 only (b) 2 and 3 only
(c) 1 and 3 only (d) 1, 2 and 3

15. With reference to the disciples of Ramananda, consider the following statements:

1. Kabir, a Muslim weaver, was one of the disciples of Ramananda.
2. Ravidas, a cobbler, was also one of Ramananda's prominent disciples.
3. Dhanna, a Rajput prince, was known for his association with Ramananda.

Which of the statements given above are correct?

(a) 1 and 2 only (b) 2 and 3 only
(c) 1 and 3 only (d) 1, 2 and 3

16. Identify the Bhakti saint based on the following statements:

1. He was born blind but fled at the age of 6 and became a disciple of Vallabha Acharya.
2. He was part of Ashtachap, a group of 8 devotees of Lord Krishna.
3. His works include 'Sahitya Lahiri', 'Sur Sagar', and 'Sur Saravali'.

Choose the correct answer from the options given below:

(a) Tulsidas
(b) Surdas
(c) Ravidas
(d) Vallabhacharya

17. Which of the following describes the philosophy of Vallabhacharya?

(a) He founded the philosophy of Dvaitadvaita, emphasising the distinction and non-distinction between God and soul.
(b) Vallabhacharya established the philosophy of Shuddhadvaita, or pure non-dualism, also known as the Pushti Marg.
(c) He was a proponent of Advaita Vedanta, focusing on the oneness of Atma and Brahma.
(d) Vallabhacharya propagated the Dvaita philosophy, advocating dualism between the individual soul and the supreme God.

18. With reference to Chaitanya Mahaprabhu's contributions to the Bhakti movement, consider the following statements:

1. Chaitanya Mahaprabhu popularised the chant of Hare Rama, Hare Krishna.
2. He was a Nirguna Bhakti saint who rejected the worship of deities with form.
3. Chaitanya Mahaprabhu founded ISKCON (International Society for Krishna Consciousness).

How many of the statements given above is/are correct?

(a) Only one
(b) Only two
(c) All three
(d) None

19. With reference to the contributions of Sankardeva, consider the following statements:

1. Sankardeva founded the Ekasarana Dharma, a neo-Vaishnavite movement in Assam.
2. He was known for creating a new type of music called Kirtan Ghosha.
3. Sankardeva's literary works were composed in the Assamese language.

Which of the statements given above are correct?

(a) 1 and 2 only (b) 2 and 3 only
(c) 1 and 3 only (d) 1, 2 and 3

20. In the context of Vaishnava Bhakti in Gujarat-Rajasthan, which of the following saints are associated with this region?

1. Narsi Mehta
2. Mirabai
3. Dadu Dayal

Select the correct answer using the codes given below:

(a) 1 and 2 only
(b) 2 and 3 only
(c) 1 and 3 only
(d) 1, 2 and 3

21. With reference to the contributions of Mirabai, consider the following statements:

1. Mirabai composed devotional songs in Rajasthani and Braj Bhasha praising Krishna.
2. She was married to Rana Sanga's son, Bhojraj, and treated Krishna as her husband.
3. Guru Ravidas was the teacher of Mirabai.

Which of the statements given above are correct?

(a) 1 and 2 only (b) 2 and 3 only
(c) 1 and 3 only (d) 1, 2 and 3

22. With reference to Dadu Dayal, consider the following statements:

1. Dadu Dayal was a Nirguna Bhakti saint from Ahmedabad.
2. He focused on the worship of Rama and Hanuman, rejecting the worship of Krishna.
3. Dadu Dayal established the Brahma Sampradaya or Parabrahma Sampradaya.

How many of the statements given above is/are correct?

(a) Only one
(b) Only two
(c) All three
(d) None

23. Which of the following describes the contributions of Lal Ded (Lalleshwari)?

(a) She was a Shaivite Bhakti saint from Kashmir, known for her compositions in the Kashmiri language called Vatsun or Vakh.
(b) Lal Ded was a Vaishnava Bhakti saint from Bengal who popularised Kirtans as a form of worship.
(c) She founded the Varkari tradition in Maharashtra, emphasising the worship of Vithoba.
(d) Lal Ded was a follower of Kabir and composed poetry in Hindi and Punjabi.

24. With reference to the nature of the Bhakti movement, consider the following statements:

1. The Bhakti movement was characterised by simple, non-philosophical teachings aimed at the masses.
2. It was reformist, rejecting rituals and ceremonies.
3. The movement emphasised intense love and devotion as the means to attain salvation.

How many of the statements given above is/are not correct?

(a) Only one (b) Only two
(c) All three (d) None

25. Regarding the Saguna and Nirguna aspects of the Bhakti movement, consider the following statements:

1. Saguna Bhakti involves the worship of God with form, while Nirguna Bhakti focuses on the worship of a formless God.
2. Prominent figures of Saguna Bhakti include Kabir and Guru Nanak.
3. Mirabai and Ramananda were associated with the Saguna Bhakti tradition.

How many of the statements given above is/are correct?

(a) Only one (b) Only two
(c) All three (d) None

Topic 2 : Sufi Movement

26. With reference to the introduction of Sufism in India, consider the following statements:

1. Sufism is a mystical movement that originated in the Arab world.
2. Sufism represents a liberal form of Islam.
3. Sufi saints entered India with the advent of Muslims during medieval times.

How many of the statements given above is/are correct?

(a) Only one (b) Only two
(c) All three (d) None

27. Consider the following pairs:

	Term	Meaning
1.	Urs	Head of a Wilayat (spiritual territory)
2.	Khalifa	Successor of Wali, appointed by Wali himself
3.	Pir	Disciple in the Sufi tradition

How many pairs given above is/are correctly matched?

(a) Only one (b) Only two
(c) All three (d) None

28. Consider the following pairs:

	Type of Sufi Saints	Characteristic
1.	Ba-Shara Sufi	Accepted Sharia (Islamic law)
2.	Be-sara Sufi	Rejected Sharia
3.	Vali	A mystic saint who attains union with God

How many pairs given above is/are correctly matched?

(a) Only one (b) Only two
(c) All three (d) None

29. Which of the following statements is correct about the Sufi concept of 'Fana'?

(a) Fana refers to the remembrance of God through Zikr.
(b) Fana involves the negation of all worldly things, focusing solely on the idea of God.
(c) Fana refers to the climax of the mystical union through Sama.
(d) Fana refers to the annihilation of the self, leading to union with God.

30. Consider the following pairs:

	Term	Explanation
1.	Marifat	Union with God or attainment of mystical knowledge
2.	Tauhid-i-Wajudi	Belief in one God for the whole universe
3.	Zikr	The practice of ending individuality/self

How many pairs given above is/are correctly matched?

(a) Only one
(b) Only two
(c) All three
(d) None

31. With reference to the Sufi orders (Silsilah) in India, consider the following statements:

1. The Chishti order was known for its liberal approach and emphasis on Wahdat-ul-Wujud (unity of existence).
2. The Suhrawardi order was orthodox and closely associated with political power.
3. The Firdausi order was known for its association with Wahdat-ul-Shuhud (unity of witness).

Which of the statements given above are correct?

(a) 1 and 2 only
(b) 2 and 3 only
(c) 1 and 3 only
(d) 1, 2 and 3

32. With reference to the Suhrawardi Sufi order, consider the following statements:

1. The Suhrawardi order was orthodox in its beliefs and practices.
2. Sheikh Shihab-ud-din Suhrawardi is considered the founder of this order.
3. This order had close connections with the political authorities and rulers of the time.

Which of the statements given above are correct?

(a) 1 and 2 only
(b) 2 and 3 only
(c) 1 and 3 only
(d) 1, 2 and 3

33. With reference to the Naqshbandi Sufi order, consider the following statements:

1. The Naqshbandi order was known for its liberal approach and was closely associated with the Mughal emperor Akbar.
2. Sheikh Ahmed Sirhindi, a prominent figure in the Naqshbandi order, opposed Akbar's liberal policies.
3. The Naqshbandi order emphasised strict adherence to Islamic law (Sharia).

How many of the statements given above is/are correct?

(a) Only one (b) Only two
(c) All three (d) None

34. Which of the following best describes the contribution of Lal Ded (Lalleshwari) to Sufism?

(a) She introduced the concept of Alakh Niranjan to Sufi saints.
(b) Lal Ded translated Persian Sufi texts into Sanskrit.
(c) She popularised the practice of Zikr among Sufi saints.
(d) Lal Ded's teachings emphasised the idea of Tauhid-i-Wajudi.

35. Which of the following Hindu ideas were adopted by Sufi saints in medieval India?

(a) Yogic posture and controlled breathing.
(b) Worship of idols and practice of Yajna.
(c) Study of Vedic scriptures and practice of Brahmacharya.
(d) Pilgrimage to Hindu temples and fasting on Ekadashi.

36. With reference to the influence of Hindu ideas on Sufism, consider the following statements:

1. The practice of Yogic postures was adopted by Sufi saints in medieval India.
2. Pranayam, or controlled breathing, became a common practice among Sufi mystics.
3. The concept of Alakh Niranjan, an imperceptible Lord, was integrated into Sufi theology.

How many of the statements given above is/are correct?

(a) Only one
(b) Only two
(c) All three
(d) None

OMR SHEET

Assessment Round

1	a	b	c	d	31	a	b	c	d	61	a	b	c	d	91	a	b	c	d
2	a	b	c	d	32	a	b	c	d	62	a	b	c	d	92	a	b	c	d
3	a	b	c	d	33	a	b	c	d	63	a	b	c	d	93	a	b	c	d
4	a	b	c	d	34	a	b	c	d	64	a	b	c	d	94	a	b	c	d
5	a	b	c	d	35	a	b	c	d	65	a	b	c	d	95	a	b	c	d
6	a	b	c	d	36	a	b	c	d	66	a	b	c	d	96	a	b	c	d
7	a	b	c	d	37	a	b	c	d	67	a	b	c	d	97	a	b	c	d
8	a	b	c	d	38	a	b	c	d	68	a	b	c	d	98	a	b	c	d
9	a	b	c	d	39	a	b	c	d	69	a	b	c	d	99	a	b	c	d
10	a	b	c	d	40	a	b	c	d	70	a	b	c	d	100	a	b	c	d
11	a	b	c	d	41	a	b	c	d	71	a	b	c	d	101	a	b	c	d
12	a	b	c	d	42	a	b	c	d	72	a	b	c	d	102	a	b	c	d
13	a	b	c	d	43	a	b	c	d	73	a	b	c	d	103	a	b	c	d
14	a	b	c	d	44	a	b	c	d	74	a	b	c	d	104	a	b	c	d
15	a	b	c	d	45	a	b	c	d	75	a	b	c	d	105	a	b	c	d
16	a	b	c	d	46	a	b	c	d	76	a	b	c	d	106	a	b	c	d
17	a	b	c	d	47	a	b	c	d	77	a	b	c	d	107	a	b	c	d
18	a	b	c	d	48	a	b	c	d	78	a	b	c	d	108	a	b	c	d
19	a	b	c	d	49	a	b	c	d	79	a	b	c	d	109	a	b	c	d
20	a	b	c	d	50	a	b	c	d	80	a	b	c	d	110	a	b	c	d
21	a	b	c	d	51	a	b	c	d	81	a	b	c	d	111	a	b	c	d
22	a	b	c	d	52	a	b	c	d	82	a	b	c	d	112	a	b	c	d
23	a	b	c	d	53	a	b	c	d	83	a	b	c	d	113	a	b	c	d
24	a	b	c	d	54	a	b	c	d	84	a	b	c	d	114	a	b	c	d
25	a	b	c	d	55	a	b	c	d	85	a	b	c	d	115	a	b	c	d
26	a	b	c	d	56	a	b	c	d	86	a	b	c	d	116	a	b	c	d
27	a	b	c	d	57	a	b	c	d	87	a	b	c	d	117	a	b	c	d
28	a	b	c	d	58	a	b	c	d	88	a	b	c	d	118	a	b	c	d
29	a	b	c	d	59	a	b	c	d	89	a	b	c	d	119	a	b	c	d
30	a	b	c	d	60	a	b	c	d	90	a	b	c	d	120	a	b	c	d

Calculate Your Score

Correct (✓)	
Incorrect (✓)	
Unattempted	
Total Score	
Accuracy (%)	

Reasons for Incorrect Answers?

1. Lack of Knowledge/Existing Source Insufficient	
2. Lack of Multiple Revision	
3. Common Sense Mistakes	

Note :

1. Calculate total score as correct answers carry 2 marks each 1/3rd marks will deducted for **Incorrect** Answers.
2. Calculate Accuracy (%) by dividing the number of correct answers to the total number of attempted questions.

Past Learning

1. Consider the following statements. **(2019)**

1. Saint Nimbarka was a contemporary of Akbar.
2. Saint Kabir was greatly influenced by Sheikh Ahmad Sirhindi.

Which of the statement(s) given above is/are correct?

(a) Only 1 (b) Only 2
(c) Both 1 and 2 (d) Neither 1 nor 2

2. Consider the following statements : **(2014)**

1. 'Bijak' is a composition of the teachings of Saint Dadu Dayal.
2. The philosophy of Pushti Marg was propounded by Madhvacharya.

Which of the statements given above is/are correct?

(a) Only 1 (b) Only 2
(c) Both 1 and 2 (d) Neither 1 nor 2

3. With reference to the religious history of medieval India, the Sufi mystics were known to pursue which of the following practices?

1. Meditation and control of breath. **(2013)**
2. Severe ascetic exercises in a lonely place.
3. Recitation of holy songs to arouse a state of ecstasy in their audience.

Select the correct answer using the codes given below.

(a) 1 and 2 (b) 2 and 3
(c) Only 3 (d) 1, 2 and 3

4. Consider the following bhakti saints. **(2013)**

1. Dadu Dayal 2. Guru Nanak
3. Tyagaraja

Who among the above was/were preaching when the Lodhi dynasty fell and Babur took over?

(a) 1 and 3 (b) 2 and 3
(c) Only 2 (d) 1, 2 and 3

5. Among the following, who was not a proponent of bhakti cult? **(2009)**

(a) Tukaram (b) Nagarjuna
(c) Vallabhacharya (d) Tyagaraja

6. Which one of the following sequences indicates the correct chronological order? **(2004)**

(a) Shankaracharya, Ramanuja, Chaitanya
(b) Ramanuja, Shankaracharya, Chaitanya
(c) Ramanuja, Chaitanya, Shankaracharya
(d) Shankaracharya, Chaitanya, Ramanuja

7. With reference to Sufism in Indian history, consider the following statements. **(2002)**

1. Sheikh Ahmad contemporary of Ibrahim Lodhi.
2. Sheikh Nasiruddin Chiragh-I-Dehlavi was disciple of Sheikh Nizamuddin Auliya.
3. Aurangzeb was a contemporary Chisti of Sheikh Salim.
4. The Qadiri order of Sufis was first introduced in India by Sheikh Niamutullah and Mohammad Jilani.

Which of the statements given above are correct?

(a) 1 and 2 (b) 1 and 3
(c) 2 and 3 (d) 2 and 4

8. Who among the following was the first Bhakti saint to use Hindi for the propagation of his message? **(2002)**

(a) Dadu (b) Kabir
(c) Ramananda (d) Tulsidas

9. Match List I with List II and select the correct answer using the codes given below the lists. **(2001)**

List I (Bhakti Saints)	List II (Professions)
A. Namdev	1. Barber
B. Kabir	2. Weaver
C. Ravidas	3. Tailor
D. Sena	4. Cobbler

Codes

	A	B	C	D
(a)	2	3	1	4
(b)	3	2	4	1
(c)	3	2	1	4
(d)	2	3	4	1

Detailed Solutions

Assessment Round

1. *(c)* 1 and 3 only
   - **Statement 1 is correct**: The **Alvars** were indeed Vaishnava poet saints from South India, particularly revered in Tamil regions. Devoted to **Lord Vishnu**, they composed devotional hymns and songs in praise of Vishnu and his incarnations, especially Krishna.
   - **Statement 2 is incorrect**: The collection of hymns composed by the Alvars is known as the **Nalayira Divya Prabandham**, not Tevaram (a collection of hymns composed by the Nayanars, who were devoted to Lord Shiva).
   - **Statement 3 is correct: Andal** is the only female Alvar and is highly venerated in the Tamil Vaishnava tradition. She is often referred to as the '**Meera of the South**' due to her deep devotion to Lord Vishnu, similar to the devotion of Meera Bai in North India.

   Thus, option (c) is the correct answer.

2. *(b)* 2 and 3 only
   - **Statement 1 is incorrect**: The **Nayanars** were Tamil saints who were devoted to **Lord Shiva**, not Vishnu. They played a crucial role in the Bhakti movement in South India, focusing their devotion on Shiva and composing hymns and songs in his praise.
   - **Statement 2 is correct**: The Nayanars came from diverse social backgrounds, including **Brahmins, nobles, oil-mongers and Vellalars** (agricultural community). This diversity reflected the inclusive nature of the Bhakti movement, which transcended caste and social barriers.
   - **Statement 3 is correct**: The **Tevaram** is a collection of devotional poems dedicated to Lord Shiva, compiled by the Nayanar saints **Appar, Sundarar and Sambandar** in the 10th century CE.

   Thus, option (b) is the correct answer.

3. *(b)* Only two
   - **Statement 1 is correct**: The **Virashaiva** sect, also known as the **Lingayat** movement, was founded by Basavacharya (or Basavanna) in the 12th century CE during the reign of the **Kalachuri dynasty** in Karnataka.
   - **Statement 2 is correct**: The followers of this sect were known as Virashaivas (heroes of Shiva) or Lingayats (wearers of the Shivalinga). They were distinctive for wearing a **Shivalinga** on their left shoulder, symbolising their devotion to Lord Shiva.
   - **Statement 3 is incorrect**: The Virashaiva/ Lingayat movement explicitly **rejected the caste system** and Brahminical orthodoxy. It was a reformist movement that advocated for the equality of all individuals, regardless of caste and promoted social reforms.

   Thus, option (b) is the correct answer.

4. *(b)* Only two
   - **Statement 1 is incorrect**: The **Haridasas** were not a Shaivite sect, but rather **a Vaishnavite** tradition that emphasised devotion to Lord **Vishnu**, particularly in his incarnation as **Krishna**.
   - **Statement 2 is correct**: The **Haridasa** movement was indeed centered around **Udupi, Karnataka and** was closely associated with the **Madhavacharya** tradition of **Dvaita Vedanta.**
   - **Statement 3 is correct:** Some of the prominent saints in the Haridasa tradition include **Sripadaraya, Vyasaraya, Purandaradasa** (known as the father of Carnatic music) and **Kanaka Dasa.**

   Thus, option (b) is the correct answer.

5. *(b)* Basaveshwara
   - **Basaveshwara**, also known as **Basavanna**, was a 12th-century philosopher, poet and social reformer who founded the **Lingayat** tradition, also known as **Virashaivism**. This movement was characterised by its opposition to the caste system and Brahminical orthodoxy, advocating for equality and social justice.

- Basaveshwara promoted the principles of **Arivu** (true knowledge), **Achara** (right conduct) and Anubhava (divine experience) as the foundation of spiritual life.
- **Anubhava Mandapa:** Basaveshwara established the **Anubhava Mandapa**, a unique institution that served as a common forum for discussion among his followers. It is often regarded as the **first democratic Parliament in India**, where spiritual and social issues were openly discussed and debated.

Thus, option (b) is the correct answer.

6. *(a)* 1 and 2 only

- The **Varkari sect** is a prominent Bhakti movement in Maharashtra that emphasizes the worship of Vithoba (a form of Lord Krishna) as the supreme deity. The followers of this tradition, known as Varkaris, are known for their devotion, which includes singing devotional songs known as **Abhangas** and participating in the annual pilgrimage to **Pandharpur**, the main temple of Vithoba.
- **Eknath** was a significant figure in the Varkari tradition. He was a Marathi saint, poet and scholar who contributed extensively to the Bhakti literature.
- **Tukaram** is another central figure in the Varkari sect. Tukaram's poetry is known for its deep emotional expression of devotion to Vithoba, as well as its social and ethical messages.
- **Ramdas** was a contemporary of Shivaji and was known for his teachings on physical and spiritual discipline. He was associated with the **Samarth sect**, which focused on the worship of Lord Rama and Hanuman.

Thus, option (a) is the correct answer.

7. *(b)* 2 and 3 only

- **Statement 1 is correct: Eknath** was indeed a follower of the **Saguna tradition**, which emphasisses the worship of a deity with form, in this case, Vithoba (a form of Krishna). Eknath' also wrote under the pen name **Eka Janardana**, which reflects his deep devotion.
- **Statement 2 is incorrect: 'Mantra Gita'** was composed by Tukaram, not Eknath. **Eknath** is known for other significant works, such as the Eknathi Bhagavata, a commentary on the **Bhagavata Purana** and the **Bhavarth Ramayana**, a Marathi version of the Ramayana.
- **Statement 3 is incorrect:** While Eknath was influenced by Vedanta philosophy, his main contribution was to the Bhakti movement within the Varkari sect. The **Dharkari sect** is not related to Eknath.

Thus, option (b) is the correct answer.

8. *(c)* All three

- **Statement 1 is correct: Namdev** was closely associated with the Varkari sect and was a contemporary of **Jnaneshwar.** While he is often linked to Jnaneshwar, it is important to note that their relationship was more of a mutual spiritual influence rather than a formal guru-disciple relationship.
- **Statement 2 is correct: Namdev's** philosophy is unique in that it embraces both **Nirguna Bhakti** (worship of a formless God) and **Saguna Bhakti** (worship of God with form). He worshiped Vithoba (a form of Krishna) as a Saguna deity, but his teachings also acknowledged the formless aspect of the divine.
- **Statement 3 is correct:** Namdev's **Abhangas** (devotional songs) are indeed thought to have been incorporated into the **Guru Granth Sahib**, the holy scripture of Sikhism.

Thus, option (c) is the correct answer.

9. *(b)* Only two

- **Statement 1 is correct: Kabir** was indeed one of the greatest disciples of Ramananda and is known for advocating the idea of **one God** (monotheism). He rejected the rigidities of both Hinduism and Islam and promoted a **universal spiritual message** that transcended religious boundaries. His teachings emphasised the unity of all religions and the importance of inner devotion over external rituals.
- **Statement 2 is incorrect:** There is no historical evidence regarding Guru Nanak's age when he met Kabir, but Kabir's teachings had a significant influence on **Guru Nanak's spiritual ideas.** Traditions hold that Guru Nanak and Kabir met and both saints shared similar spiritual messages, emphasising the oneness of God and the **rejection of ritualism.**

- **Statement 3 is correct: Kabir** is known for his works such as the **'Bijak'**, **'Sakhis'** and **'Rekhta'**. These compositions are central to the Kabirpanthi tradition and are revered by his followers.

Thus, option (b) is the correct answer.

10. *(d)* None

- **Statement 1 is correct: Guru Nanak**, the founder of Sikhism, was born in **1469** in **Talwandi**, which is now known as **Nankana Sahib** in present-day, **Pakistan**. His birthplace is a major pilgrimage site for Sikhs.
- **Statement 2 is correct: Guru Nanak** conceptualised God as **Nirguna**, meaning **formless, attributeless and beyond human comprehension**. He also advocated for a balanced life, emphasising the middle path between extreme asceticism and indulgence in worldly pleasures, encouraging his followers to live a life of honest work, devotion and service to humanity.
- **Statement 3 is correct:** Guru Nanak's teachings were compiled by his successors into the **Adi Granth**, which later became the **Guru Granth Sahib**, the central religious scripture of Sikhism.

Thus, option (d) is the correct answer.

11. *(c)* 1 and 3 only

- **Statement 1 is correct: Kabir** was a staunch critic of the ritualistic practices prevalent in both Hinduism and Islam. Kabir's poetry often highlighted the futility of rituals and the importance of inner purity and devotion.
- **Statement 2 is incorrect:** The **Dasam Granth** is attributed to **Guru Gobind Singh**, the tenth Sikh Guru and is not related to Kabir's works. Kabir's compositions in the Guru Granth Sahib are part of the broader collection of hymns from various saints and are revered for their deep spiritual insights.
- **Statement 3 is correct: Kabirpanthis** are followers of Kabir who uphold his teachings, which emphasise monism (the belief in one God) and social equality.

Thus, option (c) is the correct answer.

12. *(a)* Only one

- **Statement 1 is correct: Guru Nanak** is indeed the founder of **Sikhism** and is credited with initiating the practice of **Langar**, or the community kitchen, where free meals are provided to all, regardless of caste, religion, or social status.
- **Statement 2 is incorrect:** While **Guru Nanak** emphasized the unity of God and the importance of devotion, his teachings **did not aim to combine Hinduism and Islam.** Instead, he sought to transcend the divisions between these religions by advocating a spiritual path that focused on the worship of a formless God (Nirankar).
- **Statement 3 is incorrect:** There is no historical evidence that **Guru Nanak** was persecuted by **Sikandar Lodhi**. While Guru Nanak faced challenges and opposition during his travels, he was generally respected by the people he encountered, including leaders of different faiths.

Thus, option (a) is the correct answer.

13. *(c)* 3 only

- **Statement 1 is incorrect:** The **Nalayira Divya Prabandham** is a collection of hymns composed by the **Alvars**, not the Nayanars. These hymns are in praise of **Lord Vishnu**, not Lord Shiva. This collection is central to the Tamil Vaishnavite tradition.
- **Statement 2 is incorrect:** The **Nayanars** were devoted to Lord Shiva and focused on Shaivism, but their primary opposition was to Brahminical orthodoxy rather than Jainism and Buddhism.
- **Statement 3 is correct:** Both traditions included female saints who are highly revered. Among the **Alvars andal** is the most notable female saint, often referred to as 'Meera of the South'. Among the Nayanars, there were three notable female saints: **Karaikkal Ammaiyar, Mangayarkkarasiyar and Isaignaniyar.**

Thus, option (c) is the correct answer.

14. *(c)* 1 and 3 only

- **Statement 1 is correct: Ramananda** was indeed a prominent Rama worshipper and one of the key figures in the **Bhakti movement in North India.** His devotion to **Rama** was central to his teachings and he spread the message of devotion (Bhakti) to Rama.

- **Statement 2 is incorrect:** Ramananda preached in **Hindi and other local languages**, making his teachings accessible and understandable to the common people. His use of the vernacular was instrumental in spreading the Bhakti movement among the masses.
- **Statement 3 is correct: Ramananda** is credited with establishing the **Sant Parampara** (tradition of saints) in North India. His disciples included notable saints like Kabir, Ravidas and others who carried forward his teachings and further developed the Bhakti movement.

Thus, option (c) is the correct answer.

15. *(a)* 1 and 2 only

- **Statement 1 is correct: Kabir** was one of the most famous **disciples of Ramananda.** Born into a Muslim family of weavers, known for his poetry and teachings that emphasised the oneness of God and the futility of religious rituals.
- **Statement 2 is correct: Ravidas**, a cobbler by profession, was another prominent disciple of Ramananda. His teachings focused on the **idea of a casteless society** and the importance of devotion (Bhakti) over social status. Ravidas's hymns are included in the Guru Granth Sahib, the holy scripture of Sikhism.
- **Statement 3 is incorrect: Dhanna** was not a Rajput prince but rather a **Jat peasant** known for his devotion to Lord Krishna. He is often associated with the Bhakti movement but was not a direct disciple of Ramananda.

Thus, option (a) is the correct answer.

16. *(b)* Surdas

- **Surdas** was born blind and, according to tradition, left his home at the age of 6 to become a devotee of Lord Krishna. He later became a disciple of **Vallabhacharya**, the founder of the **Pushti Marg** tradition.
- Surdas was one of the eight poets known as the **Ashtachap**, who were devoted followers of Lord Krishna and prominent figures in the **Pushti Marg** tradition. These poets composed devotional songs that are still sung in Vaishnava temples today.
- Surdas is renowned for his poetic compositions, including **'Sur Sagar'**, **'Sur Saravali'** and **'Sahitya Lahiri'**. His works are celebrated for their lyrical beauty and deep devotion to Lord Krishna.

Thus, option (b) is the correct answer.

17. *(b)* Vallabhacharya established the philosophy of Shuddhadvaita, or Pure Non-dualism, also known as the Pushti Marg.

- **Vallabhacharya** was a prominent theologian and philosopher who founded the Shuddhadvaita (Pure Non-dualism) school of thought. This philosophy is also known as **Pushti Marg** (the Path of Grace).
- **Shuddhadvaita** emphasises that the individual soul (Atma) and the supreme God (Brahma) are essentially one, but unlike Advaita Vedanta, it acknowledges the reality of the world and the existence of God in a personal form.
- **Pushti Marg** is particularly known for its emphasis on Bhakti (devotion) to Lord Krishna, with a focus on loving surrender to God.

Thus, option (b) is the correct answer.

18. *(a)* Only one

- **Statement 1 is correct:** Chaitanya Mahaprabhu is widely recognised for popularising the chant of **'Hare Rama, Hare Krishna'**, which is a significant mantra in the Gaudiya Vaishnavism tradition.
- **Statement 2 is incorrect:** Chaitanya Mahaprabhu was a **Saguna Bhakti** saint, which means he promoted the worship of God with form, particularly in the form of Lord Krishna. Chaitanya Mahaprabhu taught the philosophy of **Achintya Bheda Abheda**, which supports the worship of Krishna as a personal deity.
- **Statement 3 is incorrect:** ISKCON (International Society for Krishna Consciousness) was founded much later, in the 20th century, by **A.C. Bhaktivedanta Swami Prabhupada**. While ISKCON is deeply influenced by Chaitanya Mahaprabhu's teachings, he did not establish the organisation.

Thus, option (a) is the correct answer.

19. *(a)* 1 and 2 only

- **Statement 1 is correct: Sankardeva** was a key figure in the religious and cultural life of Assam and is credited with founding the **Ekasarana Dharma**, a neo-Vaishnavite movement. This movement emphasised devotion to one God i.e. Krishna.
- **Statement 2 is correct:** Sankardeva is renowned for his literary and musical contributions. He composed the '**Kirtan Ghosha**,' a collection of devotional songs that became central to the religious practices of his followers.
- **Statement 3 is incorrect:** Although he contributed significantly to the cultural heritage of Assam, his literary works were primarily composed in **Brajavali**, a language that blends elements of Assamese and Maithili.

Thus, option (a) is the correct answer.

20. *(d)* 1, 2 and 3

- **Option 1 is correct:** Narsi Mehta was one of the earliest and most prominent Bhakti saints in Gujarat. He is often referred to as the **Adi Kavi** (first poet) of Gujarati literature and is best known for his composition '**Vaishnava Jana To**', a hymn that later became closely associated with Mahatma Gandhi.
- **Option 2 is correct: Mirabai** was a Rajput princess from Rajasthan who is celebrated for her deep devotion to Lord Krishna. Her compositions, written in **Rajasthani** and **Braj Bhasha**, are considered some of the finest examples of devotional poetry in India.
- **Option 3 is correct: Dadu Dayal** was a Nirguna Bhakti saint from **Ahmedabad**, Gujarat. He rejected the caste system and the ritualistic practices of both Hinduism and Islam. He founded the **Dadu Panth**, a sect that continues to follow his teachings.

Thus, option (d) is the correct answer.

21. *(d)* 1, 2 and 3

- **Statement 1 is correct: Mirabai** is celebrated for her devotional songs, which she composed in Rajasthani and **Braj Bhasha**. These songs express her deep love and devotion to Lord Krishna, whom she worshipped as her divine consort.
- **Statement 2 is correct:** Mirabai was married to **Bhojraj**, the son of **Rana Sanga** of Mewar. Despite her marriage, she remained completely devoted to Krishna, whom she regarded as her true husband. This spiritual devotion often led to conflicts with her in-laws.
- **Statement 3 is correct: Guru Ravidas** was a significant influence on Mirabai. She considered him her spiritual guru and often mentioned him in her poems.

Thus, option (d) is the correct answer.

22. *(a)* Only one

- **Statement 1 is correct:** Dadu Dayal was indeed a **Nirguna Bhakti** saint from **Ahmedabad**. He emphasised the worship of a formless God (Nirguna) and rejected the rituals and caste divisions of orthodox Hinduism.
- **Statement 2 is incorrect:** As a Nirguna Bhakti saint, Dadu Dayal did not emphasise the worship of specific deities with form (Saguna). Instead, his teachings were centered around devotion to a formless God.
- **Statement 3 is incorrect:** Dadu Dayal established the **Dadu Panth**, which follows his teachings, the Brahma Sampradaya is a different tradition within Hinduism and is not associated with Dadu Dayal.

Thus, option (a) is the correct answer.

23. *(a)* She was a Shaivite Bhakti saint from Kashmir, known for her compositions in the Kashmiri language called Vatsun or Vakh.

- **Lal Ded**, also known as **Lalleshwari**, **Lal Diddi** and **Yogeshwari**, was a revered Shaivite Bhakti saint and mystic poet from Kashmir. She lived during the 14th century and is one of the most influential figures in Kashmiri spiritual and literary history.
- Lal Ded is particularly known for her poetic compositions called **Vatsun** or **Vakh**, which are mystical verses written in the Kashmiri language. These poems are characterised by their deep spiritual insight and their focus on the inner experience of the divine.

- Her teachings also bridge the gap between the Shaivite and Sufi traditions, making her a unifying figure in the region's diverse religious landscape.

Thus, option (a) is the correct answer.

24. *(d)* None

- **Statement 1 is correct:** The **Bhakti movement** was characterised by simple, non-philosophical teachings that were accessible to the common people. The teachings were conveyed through devotional songs, poems and stories, making them easily understandable by people of all social strata.
- **Statement 2 is correct:** The Bhakti movement was inherently reformist. It rejected the ritualistic practices and rigid social hierarchies that were prevalent in Hindu society at the time.
- **Statement 3 is correct:** Central to the Bhakti movement was the concept of Bhakti, which means intense love and devotion to God. This devotion was seen as the primary means to attain salvation (Moksha).

Thus, option (d) is the correct answer.

25. *(b)* Only two

- **Statement 1 is correct: Saguna Bhakti** involves the worship of God with form (Saguna), meaning devotees worship deities like Krishna, Rama, or Vishnu, who are believed to have tangible, human-like forms. On the other hand, **Nirguna Bhakti** focuses on the worship of a formless, attribute-less God (Nirguna), where God is considered beyond physical form and human comprehension.
- **Statement 2 is incorrect:** Both Kabir and Guru Nanak are more closely associated with **Nirguna Bhakti**. They emphasised the worship of a formless God and often criticised the ritualistic practices associated with the worship of deities in physical form.
- **Statement 3 is correct: Mirabai** and **Ramananda** were indeed associated with the **Saguna Bhakti** tradition. Mirabai was a devotee of Lord Krishna, whom she worshipped as her divine husband. Ramananda, on the other hand, was a prominent figure in the Bhakti movement in North India and was a devotee of Lord Rama.

Thus, option (b) is the correct answer.

26. *(c)* All three

- **Statement 1 is correct: Sufism** is a mystical movement that originated in the **Arab world,** as a reaction to the perceived materialism and legalism within mainstream Islam and focused on the inner, spiritual dimension of the faith.
- **Statement 2 is correct:** Sufism is often described as a **liberal form of Islam** because it emphasises a personal relationship with God over strict adherence to religious laws (Sharia). Sufis are known for their inclusive approach, accepting people of different backgrounds and beliefs into their spiritual fold.
- **Statement 3 is correct:** Sufi saints entered India along with the spread of Islam during the **medieval period.** The arrival of Sufism in India was closely linked to the movements of Muslim traders, scholars and conquerors.

Thus, option (c) is the correct answer.

27. *(a)* Only one

- **Pair 1 is incorrectly matched:** In Sufi tradition, Urs refers to the annual commemoration of the death of a Sufi saint. It is considered a celebration of the saint's union with God and is often marked by large gatherings, prayers, recitations of poetry and music.
- **Pair 2 is correctly matched:** A **Khalifa** is a person chosen by a Sufi saint (Wali) to continue their spiritual lineage and teachings after their death. The Khalifa carries on the responsibilities of guiding the disciples (Murid) and maintaining the spiritual practices and traditions of the order.
- **Pair 3 is incorrectly matched:** Pir is a spiritual mentor or guide in Sufism, not a disciple. The **Murid** is the disciple who follows the teachings of the Pir. The Pir plays a crucial role in the spiritual development of the Murid, providing guidance and support on their path to spiritual enlightenment.

Thus, option (a) is the correct answer.

28. *(b)* Only two

- **Pair 1 is correctly matched: Ba-shara Sufi** saints are those who **accepted Sharia** (Islamic law). These Sufis integrated their mystical practices with the formal legal framework of Islam, adhering to the religious laws while pursuing their spiritual goals.
- **Pair 2 is correctly matched: Be-sara Sufi** saints are those who **rejected Sharia**. These Sufis focused entirely on the mystical and spiritual aspects of Islam, often disregarding the formal religious laws.
- **Pair 3 is incorrectly matched**: The specific characteristic of attaining union with God is more accurately associated with the concept of **Fana** or **Marifat** within Sufism. The **Vali** is more broadly recognised as a saintly figure who leads a Wilayat and guides followers, but the term does not specifically denote a saint who has attained mystical union.

Thus, option (b) is the correct answer.

29. *(d)* Fana refers to the annihilation of the self, leading to union with God.

- **Fana** is a central concept in Sufi mysticism, referring to the **annihilation of the self** or ego. This spiritual process involves transcending the individual self to achieve a union with God.
- The idea of **Fana** is closely linked to the Sufi goal of attaining **Marifat** (mystical knowledge) or **Itisal** (union with God). By annihilating the self, the Sufi becomes one with God, losing all sense of individual existence and achieving a state of divine presence.
- Zikr (remembrance of God) and Sama (mystical music and dance) are practices that can lead to the state of Fana, but they are not synonymous with it. Fana is the outcome of these practices, where the individual no longer perceives themselves as separate from the divine.

Thus, option (d) is the correct answer.

30. *(b)* Only two

- **Pair 1 is correctly matched: Marifat** refers to the **attainment of mystical knowledge** or **union with God.** Marifat is considered a higher level of spiritual understanding, beyond the ordinary knowledge of religious texts.
- **Pair 2 is correctly matched: Tauhid-i-Wajudi** refers to the belief in **one God** who encompasses the entire universe. This concept emphasises the oneness of existence, where all creation is seen as a manifestation of the divine.
- **Pair 3 is incorrectly matched: Zikr** refers to the **remembrance of God** through the repetition of divine names or phrases. It is a common Sufi practice aimed at keeping the consciousness focused on God at all times. The practice of ending individuality/self is more aligned with the concept of **Fana** rather than Zikr.

Thus, option (b) is the correct answer.

31. *(a)* 1 and 2 only

- **Statement 1 is correct**: The **Chishti order** in India was known for its **liberal approach** to Islam and its emphasis on **Wahdat-ul-Wujud**, which means **unity of existence**. This concept, popularised by Ibn al-Arabi, suggests that all of existence is a manifestation of God and there is no real separation between the creator and the creation.
- **Statement 2 is correct**: The **Suhrawardi order** was more **orthodox** in its beliefs and practices compared to the Chishti order. Their teachings emphasised adherence to Sharia (Islamic law) and they played a significant role in the political and religious life of the regions where they were active.
- **Statement 3 is incorrect**: The **Firdausi order** was known for its association with **Wahdat-ul-Wujud** (unity of existence) rather than **Wahdat-ul-Shuhud** (unity of witness). Wahdat-ul-Shuhud is a concept that suggests that the experience of God's presence is a matter of witnessing rather than a reflection of the oneness of all existence.

Thus, option (a) is the correct answer.

32. *(d)* 1, 2 and 3

- **Statement 1 is correct: The Suhrawardi order** is known for its **orthodox beliefs** and practices. Suhrawardis emphasised strict adherence to Islamic law (Sharia) and were more aligned with traditional Islamic teachings. Their practices were less liberal compared to the Chishti order, focusing more on the jurisprudence and doctrinal aspects of Islam.

- **Statement 2 is correct: Sheikh Shihab-ud-din Suhrawardi** is recognised as the **founder** of the Suhrawardi order. He established the order in Baghdad and it later spread to various parts of the Islamic world, including India.
- **Statement 3 is correct:** The Suhrawardi order maintained **close connections with political authorities** and rulers of the time. The Sufis of this order were often involved in state affairs and they received patronage from rulers.

Thus, option (d) is the correct answer.

33. *(b)* Only two

- **Statement 1 is incorrect:** Naqshbandi's order was **orthodox** and opposed Akbar's liberal policies, particularly his efforts to promote a syncretic religion known as Din-i-Ilahi, which sought to blend elements of different religions.
- **Statement 2 is correct: Sheikh Ahmed Sirhindi**, a prominent figure in the Naqshbandi order, is well-known for his **opposition to Akbar's liberal policies.** Sirhindi was a strong advocate for the preservation of Islamic orthodoxy and criticized Akbar's attempts to dilute Islamic principles by incorporating elements from other religions.
- **Statement 3 is correct:** The **Naqshbandi order** emphasised strict **adherence to Islamic law (Sharia).** The order was known for its conservative approach to religious practices and its insistence on following the principles of Sharia without compromise.

Thus, option (b) is the correct answer.

34. *(a)* She introduced the concept of Alakh Niranjan to Sufi saints.

- **Lal Ded** (Lalleshwari) was a 14th-century Kashmiri mystic whose teachings had a profound influence on both Hinduism and Sufism in the Kashmir region. She is known for her spiritual poetry, which expressed deep mystical insights and the quest for union with the divine.
- The concept of **Alakh Niranjan** refers to the **imperceptible, formless Lord.** This concept, which originated from the Nathpanthi tradition, was adopted by Sufi saints under the influence of Lal Ded's teachings. The term **'Alakh' means 'unseen' or 'formless'**, while 'Niranjan' signifies 'purity'. Together, they reflect the idea of a God who is beyond physical form and attributes.

Thus, option (a) is the correct answer.

35. *(a)* Yogic posture and controlled breathing.

Sufi saints adopted certain practices from Hindu yoga, including **Yogic postures and controlled breathing (Pranayam).** These practices were seen as effective methods for disciplining the body and mind, helping the practitioner attain a state of spiritual focus and union with God. The adoption of such practices highlights the **syncretic nature of Sufism** in India, where elements of different traditions were blended to create a unique spiritual path.

Thus, option (a) is the correct answer.

36. *(c)* All three

- **Statement 1 is correct:** The practice of **Yogic postures** was adopted by Sufi saints during medieval India. Sufi mystics recognised the value of these physical exercises in achieving mental concentration and preparing the body for long periods of meditation and spiritual contemplation.
- **Statement 2 is correct: Pranayam,** or controlled breathing, is another element of Hindu yoga that found its way into Sufi practices.
- **Statement 3 is correct:** The concept of **Alakh Niranjan** was integrated into Sufi theology, particularly under the influence of mystics like **Lal Ded** (Lalleshwari).

Thus, option (c) is the correct answer.

Past Learning (Answers)

1 (d)	2 (d)	3 (d)	4 (b)	5 (b)	6 (a)	7 (d)	8 (c)	9 (b)

CHAPTER 05 Paintings

Assessment Round

Topic 1 : Paintings in Ancient India

1. With reference to the 'Six Limbs of Paintings' in Indian art, consider the following elements.

1. Roopbhedah 2. Sadrisyam
3. Bhava

Which of the following elements is related to the expression of emotions in paintings?

(a) Roopbhedah,Bhava
(b) Sadrisyam, Roopbhedah
(c) Bhava
(d) Pramanam, Sadrisyam

2. What is the primary difference between Mural Paintings and Miniature Paintings in Indian art?

(a) Mural paintings are small in size, whereas miniature paintings are large.
(b) Mural paintings are created on walls or solid structures, while miniature paintings are small and delicate, often not larger than 25 cm.
(c) Mural paintings use brushwork techniques, and miniature paintings use fresco techniques.
(d) Mural paintings typically depict stories from epics, and miniature paintings focus on scenes of daily life.

3. With reference to fresco painting techniques, consider the following statements:

1. Buon fresco involves painting on a dry surface.
2. Secco fresco is less durable than Buon fresco.
3. Buon fresco is also known as 'true fresco.'

How many of the above statements is/are correct?

(a) Only one
(b) Only two
(c) All three
(d) None

4. Which of the following caves is known for its prehistoric paintings depicting scenes of everyday life, including animals and human figures?

(a) Ellora Caves
(b) Bhimbetka Caves
(c) Ajanta Caves
(d) Badami Caves

5. With reference to Bagh Caves, consider the following statements.

1. The Bagh Caves are located in Madhya Pradesh.
2. The themes of Bagh Cave paintings are generally non-religious, depicting dancers, musicians, and trees.
3. The caves were carved out of red sandstone cliffs.

How many of the statements given above is/are not correct?

(a) Only one
(b) Only two
(c) All three
(d) None

6. Identify the cave painting based on the following statements:

1. These paintings were patronised by the Chalukya king Mangalesha.
2. The themes mainly revolve around Brahmanical subjects, especially Shaivite themes.
3. One cave painting depicts a scene of Brahma sitting on his swan.
4. This cave is located in Karnataka.

Choose the correct answer from the options given below.

(a) Ajanta Caves
(b) Badami Caves
(c) Ellora Caves
(d) Bagh Caves

7. Consider the following features of the Sittanavasal Cave paintings:

1. The paintings are visible on the ceilings of shrines and verandas.
2. The themes predominantly include Jaina religious scenes, apsara dancing scenes, and natural scenery.
3. These caves are located in the Pudukkottai district of Tamil Nadu.

Which of the above statements are correct?

(a) 1 and 2 only
(b) 2 and 3 only
(c) 1, 2 and 3
(d) None

8. Consider the following pairs:

Cave Site	Location
1. Kanheri Caves	Odisha
2. Lenyadri Caves	Junnar
3. Saspol Caves	Ladakh
4. Udayagiri Caves	Tamil Nadu

Which of the pairs given above is/are correctly matched?

(a) Only one pair
(b) Only two pairs
(c) Only three pairs
(d) All four pairs

9. Consider the following pairs:

Cave Site	Location
1. Ravan Chhaya	Maharashtra
2. Pitalkhora Caves	Odisha
3. Undavalli Caves	Andhra Pradesh
4. Gawilgarh Caves	Tamil Nadu

How many pairs given above is/are correctly matched?

(a) Only one pair
(b) Only two pairs
(c) Only three pairs
(d) All four pairs

Topic 2 : Paintings in Medieval India

10. Identify the cave site based on the following statements:

1. The outline of these paintings is done in red ochre colour, with contouring in brown, black and dark red.
2. Scenes from Jataka stories, Buddha's life, and Bodhisattvas are prominently depicted.

Which of the following caves does this description fit?

(a) Ajanta Caves
(b) Badami Caves
(c) Ellora Caves
(d) Alchi Caves

11. Identify the cave paintings based on the following statements:

1. These paintings are found in Buddhist temples and monasteries dating back to the 11th-13th centuries CE.
2. The themes of these paintings are mainly Tantric Buddhism.
3. The paintings are done in multicolour, often depicting Mandala and deities like Tara.
4. These paintings are associated with Ladakh.

Choose the correct answer from the options given below :

(a) Ajanta Caves
(b) Alchi Monastery
(c) Ellora Caves
(d) Badami Caves

12. Identify the Paintings based on the following statements:

1. These paintings were primarily created during the Chola Empire in Tamil Nadu.
2. They often depict narratives and aspects related to Lord Shiva, including themes like Shiva as Nataraja.
3. The paintings are known for their use of vibrant colours and gold leaf detailing.
4. These paintings are associated with the temples of Tamil Nadu.

Choose the correct answer from the options given below :
(a) Lepakshi Paintings
(b) Tanjore Paintings
(c) Hampi Paintings
(d) Rajput Murals

13. With reference to the Cochin Murals, consider the following statements:

1. Cochin Murals, also known as Kerala Murals, painted between the 16th to 18th centuries CE.
2. The paintings are characterised by their luminous, bright and vivid colours.
3. These murals often depict Hindu mythology, including episodes from the Ramayana and Mahabharata.

How many of the above statements is/are correct?
(a) Only one (b) Only two
(c) All three (d) None

14. Identify the cave paintings based on the following statements:

1. These paintings are found in five caves located in Aurangabad, Maharashtra.
2. The paintings depict scenes of court life, festivals, and processions.
3. A remarkable feature of these paintings is the use of the blue colour and wide-open eyes in the depictions.
4. These caves are associated with the Rashtrakuta dynasty.

Select the correct answer from the options given below :
(a) Ajanta Caves (b) Ellora Caves
(c) Alchi Monastery (d) Badami Caves

15. Identify the Miniature style based on the following statements.

1. Developed during the 11th-12th century CE under the rule of the Palas in the Bengal and Bihar region.
2. It was significant for Buddhist art and was essentially represented as a manuscript illustration.
3. Prominent painters of this school were Dhimman and Vitapala.
4. This manuscript style involved the use of palm leaves.

Which manuscript style does this describe?
(a) Apabhramsa Miniature
(b) Pala Miniature
(c) Rajput Miniature
(d) Sultanate Paintings

16. With reference to Apabhramsa Miniature, consider the following statements:

1. It originated in the Gujarat and Mewar regions of Rajasthan during the 12th to 16th century CE.
2. The early phase was characterised by Jaina themes, and later Vaishnavite themes were used.
3. Faces in these paintings were shown with fish-shaped bulging eyes and a double chin.
4. The paintings were typically done on parchment.

How many of the statements given above is/are correct?
(a) Only one (b) Only two
(c) Only three (d) All four

17. Identify the painting style based on the following characteristics:

1. Patronised by Rajput rulers and flourished during the 15th to 18th centuries.
2. The style is known for its depiction of nature in vivid forms, including trees, rivers, and clouds.
3. Themes often include Krishna Bhakti, romantic scenes, and royal pursuits like hunting.
4. Various regional forms like Bundi, Mewar and Kishangarh emerged from this style.

Which painting style does this describe?
(a) Kangra Paintings (b) Rajput Paintings
(c) Mughal Paintings (d) Pahari Paintings

18. With reference to the Mewar School of Painting, consider the following statements:
1. It flourished during the 17th century and had significant contributions from painter Sahibdin.
2. The paintings often depicted literary works like the Ragamala, Ramayana and Bhagavata Purana.
3. The most important feature of this school was its use of realistic shading and perspective.
4. Substyles of Mewar paintings include Nathdwara, Deogarh, and Shahpura.

Which of the statements given above are correct?
(a) 1, 2 and 3 only
(b) 2, 3 and 4 only
(c) 1, 2 and 4 only
(d) 1, 2, 3 and 4

19. Identify the painting school based on the following statements:
1. Some legendary painters of this school include Sawant Singh and Nihal Chand.
2. Paintings from this school are known for their depiction of devotion and love between Radha and Krishna.
3. The most famous painting from this school is 'Bani Thani.'
4. This painting school originated in Rajasthan.

Which painting school does this describe?
(a) Kishangarh School
(b) Bundi School
(c) Pahari School
(d) Mewar School

20. Identify the painting style based on the following statements:
1. It flourished in Bundi and Kota, and its main themes revolved around Lord Krishna.
2. The most famous painting from this school is 'Baramasa' by Keshav Das.
3. These paintings highlighted local vegetation and night skies.
4. The school is known for its depiction of village life and rural scenes.

Which painting style does this describe?
(a) Kishangarh School
(b) Kangra School
(c) Bundi School
(d) Mewar School

21. Consider the following pairs:

	Painting School	Famous Painting
1.	Basholi	Baramasa
2.	Kangra	12-months painting
3.	Kishangarh	Bani Thani

How many of the above pairs is/are correctly matched?
(a) Only one (b) Only two
(c) All three (d) None

22. With reference to the Sultanate Paintings, consider the following statements:
1. These paintings represent a synthesis of indigenous and Persian styles.
2. The Nimatnama, a cookery manuscript, was illustrated under Nasir Shah's rule.
3. Paintings from this period primarily focused on scenes from the Quran.
4. Sultanate paintings flourished in South India during the Chola period.

Which of the statements given above are correct?
(a) 1 and 2 only
(b) 2 and 3 only
(c) 1, 2 and 3 only
(d) 1, 3 and 4 only

23. Consider the following pairs:

	Painting School	Region
1.	Basholi	Jammu and Kashmir
2.	Kangra	Rajasthan
3.	Mewar	Madhya Pradesh

How many of the above pairs is/are correctly matched?
(a) Only one
(b) Only two
(c) All three
(d) None

24. With reference to Mughal Paintings, consider the following statements:

1. The Mughal painting style reflects a blend of indigenous and Persian influences.
2. Babur employed several painters to create illustrations for his autobiography.
3. Akbar established a separate department for paintings known as Tasvirkhana.
4. Humayun's return from Persia introduced Iranian influence into Mughal paintings.

How many of the above statements is/are not correct?

(a) Only one (b) Only two
(c) Only three (d) None

25. What was a significant feature introduced during Akbar's reign in Mughal painting?

(a) The use of oil paints in miniatures
(b) The development of three-dimensional figures
(c) The emphasis on landscape painting
(d) The inclusion of calligraphy in paintings

26. Identify the Mughal ruler who established the Tasvirkhana (Department of Paintings):

(a) Babur (b) Humayun
(c) Akbar (d) Shah Jahan

27. Identify the Mughal ruler associated with the following features:

1. Illustrated manuscripts declined and naturalistic paintings rose in prominence.
2. Depictions of birds, animals, and flora became the key theme.
3. The use of decorated margins in paintings began during this reign.
4. The ruler was a good artist himself with his workshop.

Which Mughal ruler does this describe?

(a) Akbar
(b) Jahangir
(c) Shah Jahan
(d) Aurangzeb

28. Regarding European influence on Mughal paintings, consider the following statements:

1. Perspectives and foreshortening techniques were introduced.
2. The use of light and shade effects became prominent in battle scenes.
3. European dress patterns were depicted in some miniatures.
4. The motif of roaming clouds was a common feature.

How many of the above statements is/are correct?

(a) Only one (b) Only two
(c) Only three (d) All four

Topic 3 : Paintings in Modern India

29. Identify the region based on the following features of Company Paintings:

1. The paintings were influenced by European elements and often depicted the social life of Indians.
2. Watercolour was used, and linear perspective along with shading was observable.
3. The patrons were officials of the East India Company and affluent Indians.
4. This style of painting was known as Murshidabad Kalam in a specific region.

Which region does this painting style belong to?

(a) Kolkata (b) Murshidabad
(c) Patna (d) Lucknow

30. With reference to Western Influence on Indian Paintings, consider the following statements:

1. Western influence on Indian paintings grew significantly between the 1840s and 1900s.
2. Raja Ravi Varma, belonging to the royal family of Travancore, was a prominent figure during this period.
3. Painters during this period were mostly amateurs with little formal training.
4. This period is also known for the emergence of oil paintings in Indian art.

Which of the statements given above are correct?

(a) 1 and 2 only
(b) 2 and 3 only
(c) 1, 2 and 4 only
(d) 3 and 4 only

31. With reference to the Bengal School of Paintings, consider the following statements:

1. The Bengal School of Paintings was pioneered by Abanindranath Tagore during the 1900s-1920s.
2. It was inspired by Swadeshi concepts and sought to influence the national movement.
3. The school embraced Western formats and techniques to depict Indian culture.
4. Nandalal Bose, a key figure in this movement, used techniques from the Ajanta and Bagh cave paintings.

How many of the above statements is/are correct?

(a) Only one (b) Only two
(c) Only three (d) All four

32. Consider the following pairs related to Modern Trends in Indian art:

	Art Form	Associated Artist
1.	Primitivism	Rabindranath Tagore
2.	Cubism	Gaganendranath Tagore
3.	Surrealism	Jamini Roy

How many of the above pairs is/are incorrectly matched?

(a) Only one pair
(b) Only two pairs
(c) All three pairs
(d) None

33. With reference to the Modern Trends in Indian art, consider the following statements:

1. Rabindranath Tagore was associated with the use of Cubism to create a unique style.
2. Gaganendranath Tagore used Primitivism to portray rural life and women.
3. Jamini Roy introduced a European style in his work, later assimilating Indian traditions.
4. Amrita Shergill initially used an Indian style but later adopted European techniques.

How many of the statements given above is/are correct?

(a) Only one (b) Only two
(c) All three (d) None

Topic 4 : Folk Paintings

34. Consider the following statements regarding Thang Ka Paintings:

1. It is a Tibetan Buddhist painting primarily practiced in Assam and Meghalaya.
2. It is usually painted on cotton and silk featuring Hindu and Jaina deities.
3. Pigments are mixed with water-soluble mediums to create vibrant colours.
4. Each colour used in the painting has specific significance, such as white for serenity and black for depicting anger.

Which of the above given statements are correct?

(a) 1 and 2 only (b) 3 and 4 only
(c) 2 and 3 only (d) 1 and 4 only

35. Consider the following statements about Madhubani Paintings:

1. Madhubani paintings are traditionally done by men in Madhubani town.
2. The paintings use vibrant colours derived from natural sources and are made from rice paste and vegetable colours.
3. Madhubani paintings with frequent use of shading techniques often feature double-line borders.
4. These paintings have been awarded a GI tag.

Which of the above given statements are correct?

(a) 1 and 4 only (b) 3 and 4 only
(c) 2 and 3 only (d) 2 and 4 only

36. With reference to Manjusha Paintings, consider the following statements:

1. Manjusha Paintings originated in the Bhagalpur region of Bihar.
2. These paintings are traditionally done by the Kumbhakar and Malakar communities.
3. The paintings prominently feature three colours: Pink, Green and Blue.
4. The primary motif in these paintings is the swirling image of a snake.

Which of the following statements is/are correct?

(a) Only one (b) Only two
(c) Only three (d) All four

37. Consider the following statements regarding Pichhwai Paintings:

1. Pichhwai Paintings originate from Rajasthan, primarily Nathdwara.
2. The main theme is the depiction of Lord Krishna (Shreenath Ji).
3. They are typically done on paper and are placed behind the idol of Shreenath Ji.

Which of the following statements is/are correct?

(a) Only one (b) Only two
(c) Only three (d) None

38. Identify the correct statements about Kalamkari Paintings:

1. Kalamkari is a traditional art form of hand painting done on wall.
2. The term 'Kalamkari' is derived from 'Kalam', meaning pen, used for intricate designs.
3. The two main styles are Srikalahasti and Machilipatnam.
4. These paintings are known for their use of synthetic dyes and have received a GI tag.

Choose the correct answer from the options given below:

(a) 1 and 3 only
(b) 2 and 3 only
(c) 1 and 4 only
(d) 2 and 4 only

39. With reference to Warli Paintings, consider the following statements:

1. Warli Paintings are practiced by the Warli tribe indigenous to the Sahyadri region in Maharashtra.
2. The paintings predominantly use basic geometric shapes like circles, triangles and squares, often associated with the cave paintings at Bhimbetka.
3. The themes include scenes of hunting, fishing, farming, festivals, and dances, often depicting the goddess of fertility, Palaghata.

How many of the above statements is/are incorrect?

(a) Only one (b) Only two
(c) All three (d) None

40. Identify the painting style based on the following statements:

1. It is a type of scroll painting from Rajasthan, painted on long pieces of cloth called Phad, typically 15 to 30 feet long.
2. The themes of this paintings revolve around the heroic deeds of local deities and heroes, as well as scenes from rural life, flora, and fauna.
3. Subjects involve in this type of paintings are characterised by large eyes and round faces.

Which of the following painting styles is described above?

(a) Warli Painting (b) Phad Painting
(c) Pithora Painting (d) Saura Painting

41. With reference to Saura Paintings, consider the following statements:

1. Saura Paintings were created by the Lanjia Saura tribes of Odisha and are a form of ritualistic mural painting.
2. The paintings are also known as Idital, and the person who creates them is called iditalma.
3. The colours used in Saura Paintings are typically derived from natural sources, with red earth (geru) and white being the most common.

How many of the above statements is/are correct?

(a) Only one (b) Only two
(c) All three (d) None

42. Consider the following statements about Pithora Paintings:

1. Pithora Paintings are tribal paintings from Gujarat and Madhya Pradesh, characterised by the depiction of seven horses.
2. These paintings are typically created on walls to bring peace and prosperity to households.
3. Pithora artists, known as Lakhara, use a vibrant colour palette, including white (clay), orange, green, blue, red and yellow.

How many of the above statements is/are correct?

(a) Only one (b) Only two
(c) All three (d) None

OMR SHEET

Assessment Round

1	(a) (b) (c) (d)	31	(a) (b) (c) (d)	61	(a) (b) (c) (d)	91	(a) (b) (c) (d)
2	(a) (b) (c) (d)	32	(a) (b) (c) (d)	62	(a) (b) (c) (d)	92	(a) (b) (c) (d)
3	(a) (b) (c) (d)	33	(a) (b) (c) (d)	63	(a) (b) (c) (d)	93	(a) (b) (c) (d)
4	(a) (b) (c) (d)	34	(a) (b) (c) (d)	64	(a) (b) (c) (d)	94	(a) (b) (c) (d)
5	(a) (b) (c) (d)	35	(a) (b) (c) (d)	65	(a) (b) (c) (d)	95	(a) (b) (c) (d)
6	(a) (b) (c) (d)	36	(a) (b) (c) (d)	66	(a) (b) (c) (d)	96	(a) (b) (c) (d)
7	(a) (b) (c) (d)	37	(a) (b) (c) (d)	67	(a) (b) (c) (d)	97	(a) (b) (c) (d)
8	(a) (b) (c) (d)	38	(a) (b) (c) (d)	68	(a) (b) (c) (d)	98	(a) (b) (c) (d)
9	(a) (b) (c) (d)	39	(a) (b) (c) (d)	69	(a) (b) (c) (d)	99	(a) (b) (c) (d)
10	(a) (b) (c) (d)	40	(a) (b) (c) (d)	70	(a) (b) (c) (d)	100	(a) (b) (c) (d)
11	(a) (b) (c) (d)	41	(a) (b) (c) (d)	71	(a) (b) (c) (d)	101	(a) (b) (c) (d)
12	(a) (b) (c) (d)	42	(a) (b) (c) (d)	72	(a) (b) (c) (d)	102	(a) (b) (c) (d)
13	(a) (b) (c) (d)	43	(a) (b) (c) (d)	73	(a) (b) (c) (d)	103	(a) (b) (c) (d)
14	(a) (b) (c) (d)	44	(a) (b) (c) (d)	74	(a) (b) (c) (d)	104	(a) (b) (c) (d)
15	(a) (b) (c) (d)	45	(a) (b) (c) (d)	75	(a) (b) (c) (d)	105	(a) (b) (c) (d)
16	(a) (b) (c) (d)	46	(a) (b) (c) (d)	76	(a) (b) (c) (d)	106	(a) (b) (c) (d)
17	(a) (b) (c) (d)	47	(a) (b) (c) (d)	77	(a) (b) (c) (d)	107	(a) (b) (c) (d)
18	(a) (b) (c) (d)	48	(a) (b) (c) (d)	78	(a) (b) (c) (d)	108	(a) (b) (c) (d)
19	(a) (b) (c) (d)	49	(a) (b) (c) (d)	79	(a) (b) (c) (d)	109	(a) (b) (c) (d)
20	(a) (b) (c) (d)	50	(a) (b) (c) (d)	80	(a) (b) (c) (d)	110	(a) (b) (c) (d)
21	(a) (b) (c) (d)	51	(a) (b) (c) (d)	81	(a) (b) (c) (d)	111	(a) (b) (c) (d)
22	(a) (b) (c) (d)	52	(a) (b) (c) (d)	82	(a) (b) (c) (d)	112	(a) (b) (c) (d)
23	(a) (b) (c) (d)	53	(a) (b) (c) (d)	83	(a) (b) (c) (d)	113	(a) (b) (c) (d)
24	(a) (b) (c) (d)	54	(a) (b) (c) (d)	84	(a) (b) (c) (d)	114	(a) (b) (c) (d)
25	(a) (b) (c) (d)	55	(a) (b) (c) (d)	85	(a) (b) (c) (d)	115	(a) (b) (c) (d)
26	(a) (b) (c) (d)	56	(a) (b) (c) (d)	86	(a) (b) (c) (d)	116	(a) (b) (c) (d)
27	(a) (b) (c) (d)	57	(a) (b) (c) (d)	87	(a) (b) (c) (d)	117	(a) (b) (c) (d)
28	(a) (b) (c) (d)	58	(a) (b) (c) (d)	88	(a) (b) (c) (d)	118	(a) (b) (c) (d)
29	(a) (b) (c) (d)	59	(a) (b) (c) (d)	89	(a) (b) (c) (d)	119	(a) (b) (c) (d)
30	(a) (b) (c) (d)	60	(a) (b) (c) (d)	90	(a) (b) (c) (d)	120	(a) (b) (c) (d)

Calculate Your Score

Correct (✓)	
Incorrect (✓)	
Unattempted	
Total Score	
Accuracy (%)	

Reasons for Incorrect Answers?

1. Lack of Knowledge/Existing Source Insufficient	
2. Lack of Multiple Revision	
3. Common Sense Mistakes	

Note :

1. Calculate total score as correct answers carry 2 marks each 1/3rd marks will deducted for **Incorrect** Answers.
2. Calculate Accuracy (%) by dividing the number of correct answers to the total number of attempted questions.

Past Learning

1. Consider the following pairs. **(2023)**

	Site	Well known for
1.	Besnagar	Shaivite cave shrine
2.	Bhaja	Buddhist cave shrine
3.	Sittanawasal	Jain cave shrine

How many of the above pairs is/are correctly matched?
(a) Only one
(b) Only two
(c) All three
(d) None

2. Who among the following Mughal Emperors shifted emphasis from illustrated manuscripts to the album and individual portrait? **(2019)**
(a) Humayun
(b) Akbar
(c) Jahangir
(d) Shah Jahan

3. The well-known painting 'Bani Thani' belongs to the **(2018)**
(a) Bundi school
(b) Jaipur school
(c) Kangra school
(d) Kishangarh school

4. The painting of Bodhisattva Padmapani is one of the most famous and often-illustrated paintings: **(2017)**
(a) Ajanta
(b) Badami
(c) Bagh
(d) Ellora

5. Kalamkari painting refers to **(2015)**
(a) a hand-painted cotton textile in South India
(b) a handmade drawing on bamboo handicrafts in North-East India
(c) a block-painted woollen cloth in Western Himalayan region of India
(d) a hand-painted decorative silk cloth in North-Western India

6. Consider the following famous names. **(2009)**
1. Amrita Shergil
2. Bikash Bhattacharjee
3. NS Bendre
4. Subodh Gupta

Who of the above is/are well-known as artist(s)?
(a) Only 1
(b) 1 and 4
(c) 2, 3 and 4
(d) All of the above

7. The paintings of Abanindranath Tagore are classified as **(1999)**
(a) Realistic
(b) Socialistic
(c) Revivalistic
(d) Impressionistic

8. The Mughal school of painting formed the spinal column of the various schools of Indian miniature art. Which one of the following painting styles was not affected by Mughal painting? **(1995)**
(a) Pahari
(b) Rajasthani
(c) Kangra
(d) Kalighat

Detailed Solutions

Assessment Round

1. *(c)* Bhava

The 'Six Limbs of Painting' (Shadanga) are foundational principles that were first detailed in ancient Indian texts on art and aesthetics, particularly in the Vishnudharmottara Purana. These six limbs are considered the guiding principles for creating a successful and expressive painting:

- **Roopbhedah :** This refers to the knowledge of form or **appearance,** which is essential in creating visual distinctions between different subjects within a painting.
- **Sadrisyam :** Sadrisyam involves the **accuracy of resemblance,** ensuring that the depicted subjects in the painting are lifelike and true to their real-world counterparts.
- **Bhava :** Bhava is the **expression of emotion, mood, or sentiment** in a painting. It is one of the most crucial aspects as it breathes life into the artwork, allowing the viewer to connect emotionally with the scene depicted.
- **Lavanya Yojanam :** This limb refers to the infusion of **grace and beauty** in the painting, ensuring that the artwork not only represents its subjects accurately but also does so with elegance and aesthetic appeal.
- **Pramanam :** Pramanam deals with **proportion and scale,** ensuring that all elements within the painting are in correct proportion to one another.
- **Varnika Bhanga :** This refers to the appropriate **use of colours and brush techniques** to enhance the overall impact of the painting.

Thus, option (c) is the correct answer.

2. *(b)* Mural paintings are created on walls or solid structures, while miniature paintings are small and delicate, often not larger than 25 cm.

- Two prominent forms of Indian art are Mural Paintings and Miniature Paintings.
- **Mural Paintings** are **large artworks** created directly on **walls, ceilings, or other solid surfaces.** The most famous examples of mural paintings in India are found in the Ajanta Caves and Ellora Caves in Maharashtra. Murals are typically created using fresco techniques, where pigments are applied onto wet plaster, allowing the colours to integrate with the wall surface as it dries.
- **Miniature Paintings :** In contrast, miniature paintings are **small, detailed works of art,** typically created on materials like paper, cloth, or ivory. A key characteristic of miniature paintings is their small size, generally not exceeding 25 cm in any dimension, allowing them to be easily portable and often used in manuscripts or albums.

Thus, option (b) is the correct answer.

3. *(b)* Only two

Fresco painting is an ancient method of mural painting applied on freshly laid lime plaster, primarily used in large-scale wall paintings found in historical and religious sites.

- **Statement 1 is incorrect :** Buon fresco (true fresco) involves applying pigments onto wet, freshly laid plaster, not a dry surface. As the plaster dries, the pigments become an integral part of the wall, ensuring the durability of the artwork.
- **Statement 2 is correct** Secco fresco involves painting on **a dry plaster surface.** Since the pigments do not chemically bond with the wall, secco fresco is less durable compared to buon fresco.
- **Statement 3 is correct :** Buon fresco is indeed also known as **true fresco** because of its longevity and the method of application, which ensures that the colours are deeply embedded in the wall surface, making the artwork resistant to environmental damage.

Thus, option (b) is the correct answer.

4. *(b)* Bhimbetka Caves

- The **Bhimbetka Caves,** located in the **Raisen District of Madhya Pradesh,** India, are renowned for their prehistoric rock art that dates back to the Paleolithic, Mesolithic and Neolithic periods.

- The Bhimbetka rock shelters are considered one of the oldest known sites of human habitation in India. The paintings depict scenes **of everyday life, such as hunting, dancing, communal gatherings and rituals.**
- The paintings were created using **natural pigments** made from minerals like ochre, hematite and lime. These pigments were mixed with water, and sometimes with animal fat or plant sap, to create a paint that was applied to the rock surfaces.
- The Bhimbetka rock shelters were declared a **UNESCO World Heritage Site in 2003,** recognising their outstanding universal value as a cultural property.

Thus, option (b) is the correct answer.

5. *(d)* None

- **Statement 1 is correct :** The **Bagh Caves** are indeed located in **Madhya Pradesh,** along the banks of the **Baghani River,** about 97 kilometers from the city of Dhar. The caves were created during the late **4th to 6th century** CE and are an excellent example of ancient Indian rock-cut architecture.
- **Statement 2 is correct :** The mural paintings of the Bagh Caves are primarily **secular,** focusing on themes from everyday life, including depictions of dancers, musicians, flora, and fauna.
- **Statement 3 is correct :** The Bagh Caves were carved out of **red sandstone cliffs.** The natural reddish-brown hue of the sandstone provided a unique canvas for the artists, who adorned the interiors of the caves with vibrant paintings.

Thus, option (d) is the correct answer.

6. *(b)* Badami Caves

- The **Badami Caves** were patronised by the **Chalukya dynasty,** specifically by **King Mangalesha,** who ruled during the 6th century CE.
- The **themes** of the paintings and sculptures in the Badami Caves primarily revolve around **Brahmanical subjects,** with a significant emphasis on Shaivism (worship of Lord Shiva).
- One of the notable paintings in the cave depicts Brahma sitting on his swan, or Hamsa. This scene is one of the many intricate and detailed artworks found in the Badami Caves, showcasing the artistic skills of the Chalukyan period.
- The Badami Caves are located in **Karnataka,** and they are among the most important historical sites in the state. The caves are set against a backdrop of rugged red sandstone cliffs, which add to their visual and architectural appeal.

Thus, option (b) is the correct answer.

7. *(c)* 1, 2 and 3

- **Statement 1 is correct:** The paintings in the **Sittanavasal Caves** are found on the ceilings of shrines and verandas, as well as on the pillars and walls of the cave. The cave's layout, including the shrines, verandas, and meditation halls, is typical of ancient rock-cut Jain temples.
- **Statement 2 is correct:** The themes of the Sittanavasal paintings are **predominantly Jain**, reflecting the religious practices and beliefs of the time. The murals include depictions of Jaina Tirthankaras, apsaras (celestial dancers), lotus ponds, and other natural elements. These paintings are often praised for their delicate brushwork, the use of natural pigments, and the intricate detailing of figures.
- **Statement 3 is correct:** The Sittanavasal Caves are situated in the **Pudukkottai district** of **Tamil Nadu,** an area rich in history and archaeological significance. These caves date back to the 7**th century CE** and are one of the most important examples of Jain art and architecture in South India.

Thus, option (c) is the correct answer.

8. *(b)* Only two pairs

- **Pair 1 is incorrectly matched :** The **Kanheri Caves** are located in **Maharashtra**, not Odisha. These caves are an extensive network of rock-cut structures in the **Sanjay Gandhi National Park, Mumbai.** They date back to the 1st century BCE and continued to be developed until the 10th century CE.

- **Pair 2 is correctly matched :** The **Lenyadri Caves** are located in **Junnar in Maharashtra.** This group of caves consists of about 30 rock-cut Buddhist caves, with Cave 7 being particularly famous as one of the **Ashtavinayak shrines dedicated to Lord Ganesha.**
- **Pair 3 is correctly matched :** The **Saspol Caves** are located in **Ladakh**. These caves are located near Saspol village and are famous for their well-preserved Buddhist murals that depict various deities, including Buddha, Bodhisattvas, and guardian deities.
- **Pair 4 is incorrectly matched :** The **Udayagiri Caves** are located in **Madhya Pradesh,** not Tamil Nadu. These rock-cut caves are notable for their association with the Gupta period, particularly for the sculpture of **Vishnu in his Varaha (boar) avatar rescuing the Earth.**

Thus, option (b) is the correct answer.

9. *(a)* Only one pair

- **Pair 1 is incorrectly matched : Ravan Chhaya** is a rock shelter in **Odisha**, known for its ancient rock art. The site is located in the **Angul district** and is famous for its carvings and the depiction of the mythical demon king Ravana.
- **Pair 2 is incorrectly matched: Pitalkhora Caves** are located in **Maharashtra**, in the Satmala Range of the Western Ghats. They are among the earliest examples of rock-cut architecture in India, dating back to the 3rd century BCE, and contain both Chaitya (prayer halls) and Viharas (monasteries) with Buddhist relics.
- **Pair 3 is correctly matched: Undavalli Caves** are located near **Vijayawada** (Andhra Pradesh) and are notable examples of Indian rock-cut architecture. They were initially Buddhist caves and later became associated with Hinduism. The largest cave has a huge reclining statue of Vishnu sculpted from a single block of granite.
- **Pair 4 is incorrectly matched : Gawilgarh Caves** are located in **Madhya Pradesh,** near the Gawilgarh Fort. These caves have significant historical importance but are often confused with other cave sites in the region.

Thus, option (a) is the correct answer.

10. *(a)* Ajanta Caves

- The **Ajanta Caves,** a UNESCO World Heritage Site located in the **Aurangabad district of Maharashtra,** India, are one of the most celebrated examples of ancient Indian art. These rock-cut caves date back to the **2nd century BCE to about 480 CE** and were primarily used as a monastic retreat for Buddhist monks.
- The paintings in the Ajanta Caves are remarkable for their intricate and vibrant colours, which have survived centuries. The outline of these paintings is typically done using **red ochre,** with contouring in **brown, black and dark red.**
- The content of these murals is profoundly religious and narrative, focusing on the **Jataka tales,** which recount the previous lives of the Buddha, emphasising moral lessons and the path to enlightenment. Additionally, the murals depict scenes from the **life of Gautama Buddha** and various **Bodhisattvas**-enlightened beings who have postponed their own Nirvana to help others achieve enlightenment.

Thus, option (a) is the correct answer.

11. *(b)* Alchi Monastery

- The **Alchi Monastery,** situated in the Ladakh region of Jammu and Kashmir, India, is an exceptional site that represents one of the oldest surviving Buddhist monastic complexes in the region. The monastery dates back to the **11th-13th centuries CE** and is particularly famous for its well-preserved murals and paintings, which are a **testament to the region's rich Buddhist heritage.**
- The paintings at Alchi Monastery are primarily influenced by **Tantric Buddhism,** a complex and esoteric branch of Buddhism that emphasises rituals, meditation, and visualisation practices. This is evident in the depiction of **Mandalas**-geometric patterns **symbolising** the universe-and various **Buddhist deities** such as **Tara,** who is considered a Bodhisattva of compassion and action. These deities are intricately painted, often shown in their cosmic and wrathful

forms, reflecting the deep spiritual symbolism of Tantric practices.

Thus, option (b) **is the correct answer.**

12. *(b)* Tanjore Paintings

- **Tanjore Paintings,** also known as **Thanjavur Paintings,** is a classical South Indian painting style that originated during the **Chola Empire** (9th to 13th centuries CE) in the region of Tamil Nadu. This art form continued to flourish under the patronage of the Maratha rulers, who ruled Thanjavur after the decline of the Cholas. The depiction of **Hindu gods and goddesses** is a central theme in Tanjore paintings, with a particular emphasis on Lord Shiva in various forms, including the popular representation of **Shiva as Nataraja,** the cosmic dancer.
- One of the most distinctive features of Tanjore Paintings is the use of **gold leaf** to embellish the figures and enhance the opulence of the artwork. This gold leaf is often used alongside **semi-precious stones** and **glass beads,** which add to the richness and three-dimensionality of the paintings. The paintings are typically executed on wooden panels, which are coated with a mixture of chalk powder and a binding medium to create a smooth surface. The **Tanjore Paintings** are also significant for their artistic technique, which has been passed down through generations of artists, known as **Chitrakaras.** These paintings are traditionally associated with the temples of Tamil Nadu, where they are often found adorning the walls of sanctums and shrines.

Thus, option (b) is the correct answer.

13. *(c)* All three

- **Statement 1 is correct :** Cochin Murals, which are a part of the broader tradition of **Kerala Murals,** represent one of the finest examples of classical Indian mural art. These murals were predominantly created between the **16th and 18th centuries CE,** during the rule of various Hindu kingdoms in Kerala, including the Zamorin of Calicut and the Kochi kings.
- **Statement 2 is correct :** The **Cochin Murals** are particularly celebrated for their use of luminous, **bright, and vivid colours.** The artists employed natural pigments derived from minerals, plants, and other organic sources, creating a palette that includes **vibrant reds, greens, blues and yellows.** These colours were applied with meticulous attention to detail, resulting in paintings that are not only visually striking but also imbued with a sense of divine energy.
- **Statement 3 is correct :** The subject matter of these murals predominantly revolves around Hindu mythology, with extensive depictions of stories from the **Ramayana, Mahabharata** and **Puranas.** Scenes of gods and goddesses, celestial beings, and mythical creatures are portrayed with intricate detail, often accompanied by floral and geometric patterns that frame the central figures. The Cochin Murals are found in various temples across Kerala, such as the Mattancherry Palace (also known as the Dutch Palace), where they adorn the walls of the royal chambers.

Thus, option (c) is the correct answer.

14. *(b)* Ellora Caves

- The **Ellora Caves,** located in the **Aurangabad district of Maharashtra,** India, are one of the largest rock-cut monastery-temple cave complexes in the world and a UNESCO World Heritage Site. The caves were excavated between the **6th and 10th centuries CE** and are notable for their extensive carvings and **paintings** that reflect the religious harmony of the time, as they include Buddhist, Hindu, and Jain monuments.
- Out of the 34 caves at Ellora, five are specifically known for their **paintings,** which are found in the Hindu caves. These paintings are especially remarkable for their depiction of **court life, festivals and processions,** providing a vivid glimpse into the socio-cultural life of the period.
- One of the most striking features of the paintings at Ellora is the use of **blue colour.** The pigment used for this blue colour, believed to be derived from lapis lazuli, was highly valued and rare, indicating the importance of these murals. The use of **wide-open eyes** in the depictions is another

notable characteristic, adding a sense of life and dynamism to the figures.

- The Ellora Caves are particularly associated with the **Rashtrakuta dynasty,** which ruled a large part of the Deccan region in India from the 8th to the 10th centuries. The most famous monument at Ellora is the Kailasa temple (Cave 16), which was commissioned by King Krishna I of the Rashtrakuta dynasty.

Thus, option (b) is the correct answer.

15. *(b)* Pala Miniature

- The Pala Miniature style developed during the **11th-12th century** CE under the Pala dynasty, which ruled over the Bengal and Bihar regions. The Pala rulers were great patrons of Buddhism, and during their reign, the art of miniature painting flourished as part of the broader Buddhist cultural renaissance.
- These miniatures were primarily used for manuscript illustrations, especially on palm leaves. The paintings depicted Buddhist deities, monks, and scenes from Buddhist texts. Prominent painters of this school include **Dhimman and Vitapala,** who were recognised for their expertise in this intricate art form. The miniatures were typically inscribed on **palm leaves, known as pothi format,** which were cut into specific shapes and secured with wooden covers at the top, and bottom.

Thus, option (b) is the correct answer.

16. *(c)* Only three

- **Statement 1 is correct :** The **Apabhramsa Miniature** style originated in the **Gujarat and Mewar regions of Rajasthan** during the 12th to 16th century CE.
- **Statement 2 is correct :** Initially, these paintings were deeply influenced by Jaina themes, reflecting the religious and cultural landscape of the time. Over time, the themes expanded to include Vaishnavite subjects, such as the stories from Gita Govinda.
- **Statement 3 is correct :** The distinctive artistic features of Apabhramsa paintings include faces with fish-shaped bulging eyes, pointed noses, and double chins.
- **Statement 4 is incorrect :** The paintings were not typically done on parchment; instead, they were initially created on palm leaves in the pothi format and later on paper in a vertical pothi format.

Thus, option (c) is the correct answer.

17. *(b)* Rajput Paintings

- The **Rajput Paintings** were patronised by the Rajput rulers and flourished from the 15th to 18th centuries. These paintings are a reflection of the Rajput courtly life and religious devotion, particularly towards Hindu deities like Krishna.
- The style is renowned for its **vivid depiction of nature.** Trees, rivers, clouds, and other elements are painted with great detail and vibrancy, reflecting the artists deep connection with the natural world. The depiction of women in graceful and **stylised** forms is another characteristic of this style.
- The themes of Rajput paintings often include **Krishna Bhakti** (devotion to Lord Krishna), romantic scenes between Krishna and Radha, and royal pursuits such as hunting and courtroom scenes. These themes were not only religious but also celebrated the royal lifestyle.
- The Rajput style gave rise to several regional forms, such as **Bundi, Mewar and Kishangarh,** each with its unique characteristics but all rooted in the broader Rajput tradition.

Thus, option (b) is the correct answer.

18. *(c)* 1, 2 and 4 only

- **Statement 1 is correct:** The **Mewar School of painting** flourished during the **17th century,** with notable contributions from the painter **Sahibdin.** Sahibdin was a master artist who significantly contributed to the development of the Mewar style, particularly in the depiction of religious and courtly themes.
- **Statement 2 is correct:** The Mewar School is renowned for its illustrations of literary works such as the **Ragamala, Ramayana and Bhagavata Purana.** These texts were often illustrated in vivid colours and intricate details, reflecting the spiritual and cultural life of the region.

- **Statement 3 is incorrect:** The Mewar School is not particularly known for the use of realistic shading and perspective, which are more characteristic of Mughal paintings. The Mewar style is **more stylised, focusing on bright colours and detailed figures** rather than realistic portrayals.
- **Statement 4 is correct:** The **Mewar School** gave rise to various substyles, including **Nathdwara, Deogarh and Shahpura**. Each of these substyles had its unique characteristics while retaining the overall aesthetic of the Mewar tradition.

Thus, option (c) is the correct answer.

19. *(a)* Kishangarh School

- The Kishangarh School is renowned for its depiction of themes related to the divine love between **Radha and Krishna**. These paintings **are characterised** by the delicate portrayal of emotions, with Radha and Krishna often depicted in romantic settings, surrounded by lush landscapes. The painting **'Bani Thani'** created by Nihal Chand, is one of the most famous works from the Kishangarh School. Bani Thani is often referred to as the '**Mona Lisa of India**' due to her stylised and idealised facial features, including arched eyebrows, elongated eyes, and a sharp nose, all of which became distinctive features of the Kishangarh style.
- The Kishangarh School originated in **Rajasthan** and it flourished under the patronage of the rulers of Kishangarh. The school is recognised for blending Mughal influences with traditional Rajput art, creating a unique and sophisticated style. Legendary painters like **Sawant Singh and Nihal Chand** were associated with this school of painting.

Thus, option (a) is the correct answer.

20. *(c)* Bundi School

- The **Bundi School of Painting** flourished in the regions of **Bundi and Kota in Rajasthan**. The paintings from this school often revolve around the life and legends of **Lord Krishna,** depicting him in various forms, including as a divine lover, a child, and a protector. The most famous painting from the Bundi School is **'Baramasa,'** created by Keshav Das. 'Baramasa' refers to the depiction of the **12 months of the year,** showing the effects of seasonal changes on human emotions, which was a popular theme in Indian art.
- The Bundi School is known for its detailed portrayal of **local vegetation, night skies and seasonal changes**. The artists used a vivid palette to bring out the natural beauty of the landscapes, often juxtaposed with scenes **from village life.** The Bundi School often depicted scenes of village life and rural activities, such as farming, cattle herding, and festive celebrations. These elements were integrated into the religious and royal themes, providing a glimpse into the everyday life of the people.

Thus, option (c) is the correct answer.

21. *(b)* Only two

- **Pair 1 is incorrectly matched :** The **Basholi School** is not associated with the painting **'Baramasa'**. This painting is linked to the **Bundi School.** The Basholi School is known for its vibrant use of colours and distinctive facial features, such as large expressive eyes. It is famous for its portrayal of Hindu deities, particularly those from the Puranic traditions.
- **Pair 2 is correctly matched :** The **Kangra School** is indeed associated with the **'12-month painting'**. This painting depicts the impact of the twelve months on human emotions and nature, a theme that was popular in Kangra and other Pahari schools.
- **Pair 3 is correctly matched :** The **Kishangarh School** is famous for the painting **'Bani Thani'** which is often compared to the Mona Lisa due to its idealised and stylised portrayal of feminine beauty.

Thus, option (b) is the correct answer.

22. *(a)* 1 and 2 only

- **Statement 1 is correct :** Sultanate Paintings represent a blend of indigenous Indian and Persian artistic styles. This synthesis resulted from the cultural interactions between the Indian subcontinent and the Persianate world, particularly during the period of the Delhi Sultanate.

- **Statement 2 is correct :** The **Nimatnama, a manuscript on cookery,** was indeed illustrated under the rule of **Nasir Shah, the Sultan of Mandu.** This manuscript is notable not only for its recipes but also for its richly detailed illustrations that reflect a unique blend of Indian and Persian art traditions.
- **Statement 3 is incorrect :** While Islamic art in general, especially in regions like Persia, often focused on Quranic themes, Sultanate Paintings in India were more diverse. They included a wide range of themes, including courtly life, romantic stories, and even scenes from Indian epics like the Ramayana and Mahabharata.
- **Statement 4 is incorrect :** Sultanate paintings did not flourish in South India during the Chola period. The Chola period is much earlier and is known for its bronze sculptures and temple architecture rather than Sultanate paintings.

Thus, option (a) is the correct answer.

23. *(a)* Only one

- **Pair 1 is correctly matched:** The **Basholi School** is associated with Jammu and Kashmir. It developed in the **17th century** and is famous for its vibrant use of colours, bold and expressive features, and devotional themes, particularly those depicting Hindu gods and goddesses like Krishna and Shiva.
- **Pair 2 is incorrectly matched :** Kangra School belongs to the **Himachal Pradesh** region, particularly the Kangra Valley. It flourished in the mid-18th century under the patronage of Rajput rulers and is known for its delicate lines, naturalistic landscapes, and romantic themes, particularly those related to the life of Krishna.
- **Pair 3 is incorrectly matched :** The Mewar School is from Rajasthan, particularly associated with the region around Udaipur. It is one of the oldest schools of Rajput painting and is known for its vivid colours and depictions of religious and courtly themes.

Thus, option (a) is the correct answer.

24. *(d)* None

- **Statement 1 is correct :** The **Mughal painting** style indeed reflects a blend of indigenous Indian and Persian influences. This fusion began with the arrival of Persian artists at the Mughal court, particularly under the reigns of Babur and Humayun, and continued to develop through the subsequent rulers.
- **Statement 2 is correct : Babur,** the founder of the Mughal Empire, was a keen naturalist and had an interest in recording his observations of nature. According to historical sources, he employed painters to illustrate his autobiography, the **Baburnama,** which included detailed depictions of the flora, fauna, and landscapes that he encountered.
- **Statement 3 is correct : Akbar** established a separate department for paintings known as Tasvirkhana. This department became the center of Mughal artistic activity, where numerous artists worked on illustrating manuscripts, painting portraits, and developing the distinctive Mughal style.
- **Statement 4 is correct : Humayun,** after being exiled to Persia, returned to India with two Persian artists, **Abdus Samad, and Mir Sayyid Ali.** Their influence led to the introduction of Iranian styles into the Mughal court, which had a lasting impact on Mughal paintings.

Thus, option (d) is the correct answer.

25. *(b)* The development of three-dimensional figures

- A significant innovation during Akbar's reign was the development of **three-dimensional figures** in Mughal paintings. This was achieved through the **use of perspective and foreshortening techniques,** which were relatively new to Indian art at the time. These techniques were likely influenced by European art, which was being introduced to the Mughal court through European missionaries and traders.
- **Other Features :** Akbar's reign also saw the **promotion of calligraphy** and a focus on narrative scenes.

Thus, option (b) is the correct answer.

26. *(c)* Akbar

- The **Tasvirkhana, or Department of Paintings,** was established by Akbar, the third Mughal emperor. The Tasvirkhana was a **specialised** workshop where a large number of painters worked under the guidance of master artists. They produced manuscripts, portraits, and other forms of paintings that combined Persian, Indian, and European influences.
- The creation of the Tasvirkhana not only **centralised** artistic production but also allowed for the systematic development of the Mughal style. It became the hub of innovation where artists were encouraged to experiment with new techniques, themes, and styles.

Thus, option (c) is the correct answer.

27. *(b)* Jahangir

- The reign of **Jahangir** marked a shift in Mughal painting from the narrative, manuscript-based works of Akbar's time to a more **naturalistic and detailed approach.** These paintings often included **lifelike portraits of specific species,** reflecting Jahangir's scientific curiosity.
- Another innovation during **Jahangir's** reign was the introduction of **decorated margins** in paintings. These margins were often **filled with intricate floral and geometric designs,** enhancing the overall aesthetic appeal of the artworks.
- **Jahangir** was known to be a skilled artist himself and took an active role in the artistic production of his court. His reign saw the **zenith of Mughal painting,** with artists like **Ustad Mansur and Abul Hasan** achieving great fame for their work.

Thus, option (b) is the correct answer.

28. *(c)* Only three

- **Statement 1 is correct :** The introduction of perspective and foreshortening techniques into Mughal paintings is one of the most significant influences on European art. These techniques allowed Mughal artists to create a more **three-dimensional effect** in their works, making the figures and objects appear more realistic.
- **Statement 2 is correct :** The use of **light and shade effects,** also known as **chiaroscuro,** became prominent in Mughal paintings, especially in scenes depicting battles or other dynamic events. This technique was borrowed from European art and was used to enhance the drama, and realism of the paintings.
- **Statement 3 is correct :** European dress patterns began to appear in Mughal miniatures, reflecting the Mughal court's interactions with European traders and missionaries. These miniatures sometimes depicted European figures or Mughal courtiers dressed in European-style clothing.
- **Statement 4 is incorrect :** While clouds and other natural elements were common in Mughal paintings, the motif of roaming clouds is not specifically attributed to European influence. Instead, this was more of a stylistic choice that developed within the Indian tradition, although European influence did encourage greater realism in these depictions.

Thus, option (c) is the correct answer.

29. *(b)* Murshidabad

- Company Paintings, also known as **Kampani Kalam,** emerged during the British colonial period in India, particularly in the late **18th and early 19th centuries.** These paintings reflected a **blend of Indian and European styles,** as Indian artists adopted Western techniques such as **watercolour,** linear perspective and shading.
- The **themes** of Company Paintings often depicted the **social life of Indians,** including scenes of daily life, local customs and rituals, which were of interest to European patrons. The patrons of these paintings were often officials of the East India Company and other affluent foreigners who wanted to document the local culture.
- **Murshidabad Kalam** refers to the style of Company Paintings that originated in Murshidabad. The artists of this region were known for their delicate brushwork and detailed depictions of everyday life.

Thus, option (b) is the correct answer.

30. *(c)* 1, 2 and 4 only

- **Statement 1 is correct :** The period from the **1840s to the 1900s** indeed witnessed a growing Western influence on Indian paintings. This was a time when European styles, techniques and subjects began to be adopted by Indian artists, particularly those trained in art schools established by the British in major cities like Calcutta, Bombay, and Madras.
- **Statement 2 is correct : Raja Ravi Varma (1848-1906),** a member of the royal family of Travancore, was one of the most prominent figures of this period. He is often referred to as the **'father of modern Indian art'** for his pioneering work in blending European realism with Indian subjects.
- **Statement 3 is incorrect :** Unlike the earlier Company style painters, who were often self-taught or learned through apprenticeships, these artists were trained in Western methods, including the use of perspective, anatomy and light and shade.
- **Statement 4 is correct :** This period saw the **emergence of oil painting in Indian art.** Before this, Indian art was primarily based on frescoes, murals and miniatures. Raja Ravi Varma, in particular, is credited with **popularising** the use of oil paints, which allowed for greater detail, texture, and realism in his works.

Thus, option (c) is the correct answer.

31. *(c)* Only three

- **Statement 1 is correct :** The Bengal School of Paintings was indeed pioneered by **Abanindranath Tagore** during the early 20th century, specifically from the 1900s to the 1920s. Abanindranath Tagore sought to revive Indian art by rejecting the Western styles that were dominant at the time.
- **Statement 2 is correct :** The **Bengal School** was closely aligned with the **Swadeshi movement,** which was part of India's struggle for independence. The school's artists aimed to create art that was uniquely Indian, drawing inspiration from India's rich cultural heritage, including its classical texts, epics, and ancient art forms.
- **Statement 3 is incorrect :** The **Bengal School rejected Western formats** and techniques. Instead, it embraced Indian themes and techniques, such as those found in Ajanta, and Bagh cave paintings, Rajput miniatures, and Mughal art.
- **Statement 4 is correct : Nandalal Bose,** one of the most important figures of the Bengal School, drew heavily on techniques from ancient Indian art, particularly the Ajanta and Bagh cave paintings.

Thus, option (c) is the correct answer.

32. *(b)* Only one pair

- **Pair 1 is incorrectly matched :** Rabindranath Tagore is not specifically associated with Primitivism. Instead, Jamini Roy is more closely associated with Primitivism, which is characterised by simplicity and a focus on the culture of indigenous or rural communities.
- **Pair 2 is correctly matched : Gaganendranath Tagore,** a prominent figure in Indian art, is indeed associated with Cubism. He used the language of Cubism, which involves depicting objects in geometric shapes and multiple perspectives, to create a unique style that blended Western and Indian elements.
- **Pair 3 is incorrectly matched :** Jamini Roy is not associated with Surrealism. **Surrealism,** which involves **depicting dream-like, illogical scenes,** is not typically linked to any of the artists mentioned in the list.

Thus, option (b) is the correct answer.

33. *(d)* None

- **Statement 1 is incorrect :** Rabindranath Tagore was **not** associated with Cubism. While he made significant contributions to the world of art, particularly through his establishment of **Kala Bhawan at Santiniketan,** his work did not align with Cubism.
- **Statement 2 is incorrect :** It was **Jamini Roy,** not Gaganendranath Tagore, who used **Primitivism.** Jamini Roy was known for his distinctive style that drew inspiration from folk art and tribal traditions, portraying themes of rural life, women, and children.

- **Statement 3 is incorrect : Jamini Roy** did not introduce a European style; rather, he consciously rejected European influences in his work, focusing instead on creating art that was rooted in Indian traditions. He was a major proponent of Primitivism in Indian art, emphasising indigenous techniques and themes over Western styles.
- **Statement 4 is incorrect :** Amrita Shergill is known for the opposite progression-initially, she was trained in European academic styles but later turned towards Indian subjects and techniques.

Thus, option (d) is the correct answer.

34. *(b)* 3 and 4 only

- **Statement 1 is incorrect :** Thang Ka paintings are a traditional form of Tibetan Buddhist painting, but they are primarily practiced in **Ladakh, Sikkim, and parts of Himachal Pradesh,** particularly in the Kangra region. These paintings are religious, often depicting Buddhist deities, scenes, and mandalas.
- **Statement 2 is incorrect :** Thang Ka paintings are typically **done on cotton or silk fabric.** The subjects of these paintings often include intricate depictions of Buddhist **deities, scenes from Buddhist texts, or symbolic mandalas.**
- **Statement 3 is correct :** The pigments used in Thang Ka paintings are **mixed with water-soluble mediums,** often combined with animal glue, to create vibrant and lasting colours.
- **Statement 4 is correct :** In Thang Ka paintings, each colour holds symbolic significance. For instance, white represents serenity, **red represents passion,** black can represent anger or destruction, and so on. These colours are not just decorative but also carry deep symbolic meanings in the Buddhist tradition.

Thus, option (b) is the correct answer.

35. *(d)* 2 and 4 only

- **Statement 1 is incorrect :** Traditionally, Madhubani paintings have been **pre-dominantly done by women,** particularly those in the **Madhubani region of Bihar.** This art form is passed down through generations, with women typically decorating walls and floors of their homes during festivals and special occasions.
- **Statement 2 is correct :** Madhubani paintings are known for their vibrant use of natural colours, including **rice paste and vegetable dyes.** These colours are often derived from sources such as turmeric, indigo, and flowers.
- **Statement 3 is incorrect :** A distinctive feature of Madhubani paintings is the **absence of shading.** Instead, artists use double lines to create borders, often filling the gaps with diagonal or parallel lines, making the figures and motifs stand out clearly.
- **Statement 4 is correct :** Madhubani paintings have been **awarded the Geographical Indication (GI)** tag, which helps preserve the traditional art form and ensures that only authentic Madhubani paintings from the specified region can be labelled as such.

Thus, option (d) is the correct answer.

36. *(c)* Only three

- **Statement 1 is correct :** Manjusha paintings are indigenous to the **Bhagalpur region of Bihar.** They are a unique form of art that has historical and cultural significance, particularly in the context of the **Anga Mahajanapada.**
- **Statement 2 is correct :** Traditionally, Manjusha paintings were created by the **Kumbhakar (potter)** and Malakar **(maker of garlands) communities.** These communities would use these paintings in various rituals and religious practices.
- **Statement 3 is incorrect :** While Manjusha paintings do use vibrant colours, the traditional palette primarily includes **Pink, Green and Yellow.** The use of these colours is symbolic and adds to the distinctiveness of the artwork.
- **Statement 4 is correct :** The swirling snake, often depicted in vibrant colours, is a recurring motif in Manjusha paintings. It is a significant symbol, often associated with the ancient folklore and religious practices of the region.

Thus, option (c) is the correct answer.

37. *(b)* Two Only

- **Statement 1 is correct :** Pichhwai paintings are a traditional art form that originated in Nathdwara, Rajasthan. These paintings are typically created as large, elaborate cloth paintings hung behind the **idol of Shreenath Ji.**
- **Statement 2 is correct :** The central theme of Pichhwai paintings is the **depiction of Shreenath Ji,** the local form of **Lord Krishna.** These paintings illustrate various episodes from the life of Krishna, particularly those related to his childhood and youth.
- **Statement 3 is incorrect :** Pichhwai paintings are not typically done on paper; they are usually created on cloth or fabric. These large cloth paintings are then hung behind the idol of Shreenath Ji in temples. These paintings were introduced by Vallabhacharya in the 16th century.

Thus, option (b) is the correct answer.

38. *(b)* 2 and 3 only

- **Statement 1 is incorrect :** Kalamkari is an ancient style of hand painting done on **cotton or silk fabric with** a **tamarind pen** along with natural dyes not on walls. They are primarily practiced in **Andhra Pradesh**, particularly in the regions of **Srikalahasti and Machilipatnam.**
- **Statement 2 is correct :** The name 'Kalamkari' indeed comes from the word 'Kalam', which means pen. This pen is used by artists to draw intricate designs freehand on fabric, a distinctive feature of this art form.
- **Statement 3 is correct :** There are two main styles of Kalamkari painting: Srikalahasti, which is done entirely by hand, and Machilipatnam, which involves block printing along with hand painting.
- **Statement 4 is incorrect :** Traditional Kalamkari paintings use natural dyes, not synthetic ones. The art form has indeed received a GI tag, but the use of synthetic dyes is not typical in authentic Kalamkari.

Thus, option (b) is the correct answer.

39. *(d)* None

- **Statement 1 is correct :** Warli Paintings are one of the oldest forms of tribal art in India, dating back to around 3000 BC. The Warli tribe, predominantly residing in the **mountainous and coastal areas of Maharashtra in the Sahyadri region,** developed this unique art form. Warli tribe has passed down the tradition of Warli Painting through generations, making it an intrinsic part of their cultural heritage.
- **Statement 2 is correct :** Warli Paintings are distinctive for their use of basic geometric shapes such as circles, triangles, and squares. These shapes are symbolic; for instance, circles represent the sun and moon, triangles represent mountains and pointed trees, and squares symbolise sacred enclosures or land. This simplicity in design has led to comparisons with prehistoric cave paintings, particularly **those found at Bhimbetka,** which also use geometric shapes to depict human and animal figures.
- **Statement 3 is correct :** The themes of Warli's Paintings are drawn from the daily life and natural surroundings of the tribe. **Scenes of hunting, fishing, farming, and dancing are common,** reflecting the Warli's deep connection to nature and their agrarian lifestyle. The fertility goddess Palaghata is a significant figure in Warli art, often depicted to invoke blessings for a bountiful harvest.

Thus, option (d) is the correct answer.

40. *(b)* Phad Painting

- Phad Painting is a vibrant and historical art form that originates from the state of Rajasthan, specifically from the regions of Bhilwara and Shahpura. This traditional form of painting has been practiced for over 700 years and is deeply embedded in the local culture and religious practices. Phad Paintings are created on a **long piece of cloth** or canvas known as Phad, which can range in length from **15 to 30 feet**. These scrolls are unique because they are used in traditional storytelling performances.

- The Phad is unrolled gradually as the narrative of the story unfolds, often accompanied by music and dance. The themes depicted in Phad Paintings typically **focus on the heroic tales of local deities** such as **Pabuji and Devnarayan,** who are revered as **incarnations of Vishnu and protectors of the community.** These stories often include scenes of battle, valor, and divine intervention. In addition to these mythological themes, Phad Paintings also **portray everyday rural life, including agricultural activities, festivals, and the natural environment**, capturing the essence of life in Rajasthan.
- One of the most recognisable features of Phad Paintings is the **depiction of characters with large, expressive eyes and round faces.** This stylistic choice helps convey emotion and drama, which are essential in storytelling.

Thus, option (b) is the correct answer.

41. *(c)* All three

- **Statement 1 is correct :** Saura Paintings are an ancient and sacred art form practiced by the **Lanjia Saura tribe,** one of the oldest tribes in India, residing primarily in the **hilly regions of Odisha.** The Saura tribe has been creating these murals for centuries as part of their religious and social rituals.
- **Statement 2 is correct :** In the Saura tradition, the term Idital refers to both the paintings and the deity they represent. The person who creates these paintings is **known as iditalma,** a role that is usually passed down through generations within families.
- **Statement 3 is correct :** The colours used in Saura Paintings are derived from natural sources, reflecting the tribe's close connection with nature. **Red earth (geru) and white are the primary colours used,** symbolising the earth and purity, respectively. The use of these natural colours not only adds to the aesthetic appeal of the paintings but also reinforces the tribe's respect for and reliance on their natural environment. The motifs in these paintings include stick figures representing **humans and animals, trees, the sun, and other elements of nature,** all depicted in a stylised yet simple manner.

Thus, option (c) is the correct answer.

42. *(c)* All three

- **Statement 1 is correct :** Pithora Paintings are a **vibrant and ritualistic** art form practiced by the **Rathwa and Bhilala** tribes in the regions of **Gujarat and Madhya Pradesh.** These paintings are not just art but are deeply rooted in the cultural and spiritual practices of the tribes. One of the most distinctive features of Pithora Paintings is the **depiction of seven horses,** which are believed to symbolise the seven hills that surround the areas where these tribes live.
- **Statement 2 is correct :** Pithora Paintings are created on the walls of homes as part of a ritual to **ensure peace, prosperity, and protection** for the family and community. These paintings are typically commissioned by families to fulfill vows made to the deities in exchange for blessings.
- **Statement 3 is correct :** The artists, known as **Lakhara,** use a wide array of colours about the vibrant colour palette used by Pithora artists, known as Lakhara, is indeed accurate. The use of colours in Pithora Paintings is both symbolic and celebratory. White (clay) is often used as the base, while other colours such as **orange, green, blue, red, and yellow** are applied to create vivid depictions of deities, animals, and natural elements. These colours are not just decorative; they carry spiritual significance, with each colour representing different aspects of life and nature.

Thus, option (c) is the correct answer.

Past Learning (Answers)

1 (b)	2 (c)	3 (d)	4 (a)	5 (a)	6 (d)	7 (c)	8 (d)

CHAPTER 06 Literature

Assessment Round

Topic 1 : Sanskrit and Brahmanical Literature

1. With reference to ancient Indian drama, consider the following statements:

1. The drama 'Sariputra Prakarna' is attributed to Ashvaghosha and deals with Sariputra, a disciple of Buddha.
2. 'Mudrarakshasa' by Vishakhadutta deals with the story of King Chandragupta Maurya's ascension to the throne.
3. Kalidasa's 'Abhijnana Shakuntalam' is based on the love story of King Dushyant and Shakuntala.

How many of the statements given above is/are correct?

(a) Only one (b) Only two
(c) All three (d) None

2. Consider the following playwrights:

1. Kalidasa
2. Bhavabhuti
3. Sudraka
4. Mahendravarman

How many of the above are known for contributing to ancient Indian dramas?

(a) Only one
(b) Only two
(c) Only three
(d) All four

3. With reference to ancient Indian playwrights, consider the following statements:

1. Kalidasa's works include 'Raghuvamsa' and 'Meghaduta,' which are poems.
2. Vishakhadutta is the author of 'Mudrarakshasa.'
3. Bhavabhuti's dramas were known for their focus on romantic themes, especially in 'Malti Madhava.'

Which of the given above statements is/are correct?

(a) 1 and 2 only (b) 2 only
(c) 3 only (d) 1, 2 and 3

4. In the context of ancient Indian literature, which of the following works focus on the historical accounts of kings?

1. Harivamsa by Bhasa
2. Vikramorvashiyam by Kalidasa
3. Devichandraguptam by Vishakhadutta

Select the correct answer using the codes given below:

(a) 1 and 2 only (b) 2 only
(c) 2 and 3 only (d) 3 only

5. Identify the playwright based on the following statements:

1. He authored 'Uttararamacharita,' based on the later life of Lord Rama after his return to Ayodhya.
2. His work 'Malti Madhava' is a love story of the minister's daughter and Madhava.

Choose the correct answer from the codes given below:

(a) Bhasa
(b) Kalidasa
(c) Bhavabhuti
(d) Vishakhadatta

6. Consider the following pairs:

	Playwright	Contribution
1.	Sudraka	Mrichchhakatika
2.	Kalidasa	Malavikagnimitra
3.	Mahendravarman	Mattavilasa Prahasana

How many pairs given above is/are incorrectly matched?
(a) Only one pair
(b) Only two pairs
(c) Only three pairs
(d) None

7. Consider the following pairs:

	Writer	Work
1.	Aryabhatta	Aryabhatiya
2.	Patanjali	Mahabhasya
3.	Vatsyayana	Brihatsamhita

How many pairs given above is/are correctly matched?
(a) Only one pair
(b) Only two pairs
(c) Only three pairs
(d) None

8. With reference to ancient Indian texts, consider the following statements:
1. Vatsyayana authors Kamasutra and is a treatise on human sensual behaviour.
2. Charaksamhita by Charak is a treatise on ancient medical systems.
3. Natyashastra by Bharat focuses on drama, music, and dance.

How many of the statements given above is/are correct?
(a) Only one (b) Only two
(c) All three (d) None

9. Some ancient Indian texts are classified as Sruti, while others are classified as Smriti. What is the difference between the two?
(a) Sruti is considered a divine revelation, while Smriti is based on human knowledge.
(b) Smriti includes Vedic literature, while Sruti includes the epics.
(c) Sruti texts are known for their secular aspects, while Smriti texts are purely philosophical.
(d) There is no material difference between the two.

10. Regarding the Vedas, consider the following statements:
1. The Vedas are composed of four parts: Samhita, Brahmanas, Aranyakas and Upanishads.
2. Aranyakas represent the philosophical aspects of the rituals.
3. Upanishads are also known as Vedanta, which is the last part of the Vedas.

Which of the statements given above are correct?
(a) 1 and 2 only
(b) 2 and 3 only
(c) 1 and 3 only
(d) 1, 2 and 3

11. With reference to the Rigveda, consider the following statements:
1. Rigveda is the oldest among the four Vedas and is considered the first testament of mankind.
2. The Gayatri Mantra is found in Mandala III of the Rigveda.
3. The Rigveda is written in Brahmi script.

How many of the statements given above is/are not correct?
(a) Only one (b) Only two
(c) All three (d) None

12. Regarding the Rigveda, consider the following statements:
1. It contains a collection of 1028 hymns placed in 10 mandalas.
2. Mandala X of Rigveda includes the Purusha Sukta, which mentions the four-class Varna system.
3. It expresses the presence of monotheistic beliefs.

Which of the statements given above are correct?
(a) 1 and 2 only (b) 2 and 3 only
(c) 1 and 3 only (d) 1, 2 and 3

13. Identify the Veda based on the following statements:

1. It is further classified into Krishna (black) and Shukla (white).
2. Krishna Yajurveda is known for its disorganised and confusing structure, whereas Shukla Yajurveda is well-organised.

Choose the correct answer from the options given below.

(a) Rigveda (b) Yajurveda
(c) Samaveda (d) Atharvaveda

14. Identify the Veda based on the following statements:

1. It contains a collection of melodies and chants, also called the 'Book of Chants.'
2. Its hymns are sung by a special class of Brahmans called Udgataris.

Choose the correct answer from the options given below.

(a) Rigveda (b) Yajurveda
(c) Samaveda (d) Atharvaveda

15. With reference to the Atharvaveda, consider the following statements:

1. It is the latest of the four Vedas and is attributed to Atharvan and Angirasa.
2. The Mundaka Upanishad, from which the phrase 'satyamev Jayate' is taken, is associated with the Atharvaveda.
3. It focuses on peace, prosperity and everyday problems.

How many of the statements given above is/are correct?

(a) Only one
(b) Only two
(c) All three
(d) None

16. With reference to the Upanishads, consider the following statements:

1. The Brihadaranyaka Upanishad is the oldest among the Upanishads and contains the first reference to the transmigration of the soul.
2. The Upanishads are known as Vedanta because they mark the conclusion phase of Vedic literature.
3. The Muktika Upanishad was translated into Persian by Dara Shikoh in 1656.

How many of the statements given above is/are correct?

(a) Only one (b) Only two
(c) All three (d) None

17. How do you distinguish between Aranyakas and Upanishads in the context of Vedic literature?

1. Aranyakas emphasised mysticism and philosophy, serving as a bridge between Karma Marg and Jnana Marg.
2. Upanishads focus on philosophical ideas about the universe, Brahman, and Atman, transitioning Vedic rituals into new religious ideas.

Which of the statements given above is/are correct?

(a) 1 only (b) 2 only
(c) Both 1 and 2 (d) Neither 1 nor 2

18. Consider the following pairs:

	Upanishad	Key Theme
1.	Katha Upanishad	The Secret of Death
2.	Chandogya Upanishad	References to the four ashramas
3.	Mandaka Upanishad	The shortest Upanishad, focusing on the mystic syllable Om

How many pairs given above is/are correctly matched?

(a) Only one pair (b) Only two pairs
(c) All three pairs (d) None

19. With reference to the Aranyakas, consider the following statements:

1. They are the concluding part of the Brahmanas and were written in the forests.
2. Aranyakas stress moral values and form a bridge between Karma Marg and Jnana Marg.
3. They emphasise sacrifice rituals over philosophical contemplation.

How many of the statements given above is/are correct?

(a) Only one (b) Only two
(c) All three (d) None

20. Consider the following pairs:

	Vedanga	Subject
1.	Shiksha	Phonetics
2.	Vyakarana	Astronomy
3.	Kalpa	Ritual Ceremonies

How many pairs given above is/are correctly matched?

(a) Only one pair (b) Only two pairs
(c) All three pairs (d) None

21. With reference to Kalpa Sutras, consider the following statements:

1. The Grihasutras deal with the performance of small-scale rituals within households.
2. The Sulvasutras focus on the construction of fire altars and are significant for the development of geometry.
3. The Dharmasutras deal with customs, duties, and laws, forming the basis of judicial systems in ancient India.

How many of the statements given above is/are correct?

(a) Only one (b) Only two
(c) All three (d) None

22. Consider the following pairs regarding the types of marriages according to Grihasutras:

	Type of Marriage	Description
1.	Brahma	Marriage of a daughter to the most eligible man
2.	Gandharva	Marriage by purchasing the bride
3.	Asura	Love marriage

How many pairs given above is/are incorrectly matched?

(a) Only one pair (b) Only two pairs
(c) All three pairs (d) None

23. Which of the following best describes the term Dharmashastra?

(a) It is a collection of hymns dedicated to various deities.
(b) It is an ancient Sanskrit text that includes codes of conduct, ethics and social norms.
(c) It is a guide for performing rituals and sacrifices during religious ceremonies.
(d) It is a commentary on the mystic syllable Om and other Vedic concepts.

24. With reference to Dharmashastras, consider the following statements:

1. Manusmriti is considered one of the oldest Dharmashastras and has significantly influenced Hindu law.
2. Dharmashastras include Bhasyas, which are critical commentaries on the idea of Dharma.
3. Yajnavalkya Smriti deals with legal maxims related to the topic of Dharma.

How many of the statements given above is/are correct?

(a) Only one
(b) Only two
(c) All three
(d) None

25. Some ancient Indian texts are classified as Dharmashastras, while others are classified as Grihasutras. What is the difference between the two?

(a) Dharmashastras focus on laws and ethical conduct, while Grihasutras provide guidelines for household rituals and ceremonies.
(b) Grihasutras are concerned with societal norms and duties, whereas Dharmashastras focus exclusively on religious rituals.
(c) Dharmashastras and Grihasutras serve the same purpose with no significant difference.
(d) Grihasutras are limited to a specific region, while Dharmashastras are pan-Indian texts.

26. Which of the following best describes the concept of 'Bhasyas' in ancient Indian texts?

(a) They are ritual manuals detailing the procedures for sacrifices.
(b) They are critical and detailed commentaries on the ideas of Dharmashastra, providing interpretations and explanations.
(c) They are texts focused on the ethical and moral values of society.
(d) They are narratives describing the lives of deities and legendary heroes.

27. With reference to the Dharmashastra texts, consider the following statements:

1. The Manusmriti and Yajnavalkya Smriti are key Dharmashastra texts that shaped the socio-religious and legal framework in ancient India.
2. Bhaśyas are critical interpretations and commentaries that explain and clarify the Dharmashastra texts.
3. Dharmashastra texts, including the Manusmriti, were composed entirely in verse and prose form, offering detailed rules of conduct.

How many of the statements given above is/are correct?

(a) Only one
(b) Only two
(c) All three
(d) None

28. With reference to the Arthashastra, consider the following statements:

1. The Arthashastra is divided into 15 Adhikaranas (parts) and 150 Prakarnas (chapters).
2. It provides a comprehensive outline of statecraft, including functions of executive authorities, administration of justice and foreign policy.

Which of the statements given above is/are correct?

(a) 1 only (b) 2 only
(c) Both 1 and 2 (d) Neither 1 nor 2

29. Regarding the Arthashastra's stance on slavery, consider the following statements:

1. The Arthashastra states that a person cannot be enslaved by birth or by voluntarily selling themselves.
2. It recognises the institution of slavery but provides specific rules for the treatment of female slaves and their children.
3. Violation of the rules regarding slavery attracted a fine of 12 panas.

How many of the statements given above is/are not correct?

(a) Only one (b) Only two
(c) All three (d) None

30. Regarding the Ramayana, consider the following statements:

1. The Ramayana was written by Maharishi Valmiki, who is often referred to as the Adikavi.
2. The Ramayana is divided into 7 Kandas, with the first and seventh Kandas being the latest additions.
3. According to the Ramayana, the fourfold objectives of mankind are Dharma, Artha, Kama and Moksha.

Which of the statements given above are correct?

(a) 1 and 2 only
(b) 2 and 3 only
(c) 1 and 3 only
(d) 1, 2 and 3

31. In the context of the Mahabharata, which of the following events or concepts are included in the epic?

1. Nishkama Karma: The idea of performing one's duty without attachment to the results.
2. Bhishma Parva: The parva from which the Bhagavad Gita is extracted.
3. Shanti Parva: The largest parva in the Mahabharata.

Select the correct answer using the codes given below:

(a) 1 and 2 only (b) 2 only
(c) 1 and 3 only (d) 1, 2 and 3

32. With reference to the Puranas, consider the following statements:

1. The Puranas consist of ancient lores and narrative stories in poetic form, existing in both Vedic and post-Vedic ages.
2. There are 18 Mahapuranas and 19 Upapuranas.
3. The Matsya Purana is considered the oldest of the Puranas and discusses Vishnu's 10 incarnations.

How many of the statements given above is/are correct?

(a) Only one
(b) Only two
(c) All three
(d) None

33. Parables and fables are both forms of short stories. What is the key difference between the two?

(a) Parables are short stories illustrating a spiritual or moral lesson, usually featuring human characters, while fables feature animals, humans, or mythical characters to illustrate a moral.

(b) Fables focus on religious teachings, while parables are more concerned with social norms.

(c) Parables are always written in prose, while fables are written in verse.

(d) There is no significant difference between parables and fables.

Topic 2 : Prakrit and Pali Literature

34. With reference to Buddhist literature, consider the following statements:

1. The Sutta Pitaka was written by Ananda and is divided into five subparts known as Nikayas.
2. The Vinaya Pitaka, compiled by Upali, contains the monastic rules of conduct for monks and nuns.
3. The Abhidhamma Pitaka was compiled during the 3rd Buddhist Council by Moggaliputta Tissa.

How many of the statements given above is/are correct?

(a) Only one (b) Only two
(c) All three (d) None

35. What is the primary difference between Canonical and Non-Canonical Buddhist literature?

(a) Canonical literature includes texts that define religious tenets, while non-canonical literature does not.

(b) Canonical literature focuses on the life of Buddha, while non-canonical literature focuses on the lives of Bodhisattvas.

(c) Canonical literature is written in Pali, while non-canonical literature is written in Sanskrit.

(d) There is no significant difference between the two.

36. How do the Jataka tales differ from the Lalitavistara Sutra in Buddhist literature?

(a) Jataka tales are written in Pali and focus on the previous births of Buddha, while Lalitavistara Sutra is a Mahayana text related to Buddha's life.

(b) Lalitavistara Sutra contains philosophical teachings, while Jataka tales are purely stories.

(c) Jataka tales are part of canonical literature, while Lalitavistara Sutra is non-canonical.

(d) Both are considered as canonical literature with no difference in focus.

37. Consider the following pairs:

Buddhist Text	Focus
1. Dipavamsa	Buddhist chronicle of Sri Lanka
2. Mahavamsa	Epic poem detailing Buddha's visit to Ceylon (Sri Lanka)
3. Milind Panho	Dialogue between King Menander and monk Nagasena

How many pairs given above is/are correctly matched?

(a) Only one (b) Only two
(c) All three (d) None

38. With reference to Jain literature, consider the following statements:

1. The Agamas are the canonical texts of Jainism, compiled by Gandharas who were the disciples of Mahavira.
2. The Svetambara sect rejected the authority of the Angas, leading to their recomposition during the Vallabhi Council.
3. The Digambara sect gives sacred status to texts like Karmaprabhrta and Kashayaprabhrta.

How many of the statements given above is/are correct?

(a) Only one
(b) Only two
(c) All three
(d) None

39. What is the key difference between canonical and non-canonical texts in Jain literature?
(a) Canonical texts are written in Prakrit, while non-canonical texts are written in Sanskrit.
(b) Canonical texts are composed of the teachings of Mahavira, while non-canonical texts include biographies and commentaries.
(c) Non-canonical texts are not recognised by the Digambara sect, while canonical texts are universally accepted.
(d) Canonical texts focus on rituals, while non-canonical texts focus on philosophy.

40. How do the contributions of Samantabhadra differ from those of Umaswami in Jain literature?
(a) Samantabhadra focused on the life of Jain householders, while Umaswami focused on Jain philosophy.
(b) Umaswami wrote in Prakrit, while Samantabhadra wrote in Sanskrit.
(c) Samantabhadra is known for the Tattvarthasutra, while Umaswami is known for the Ratna-Karanda.
(d) Both contributed to the explanation of Karma theory in Jainism.

41. Consider the following pairs:

Jain Scholar	Contribution
1. Bhadrabahu	Kalpa Sutra
2. Acharya Kundkunda	Samayasara
3. Haribhadra Suri	Samaraichchakaha

How many pairs given above is/are correctly matched?
(a) Only one (b) Only two
(c) All three (d) None

Topic 3 : Tamil Literature

42. With reference to Tamil literature, consider the following statements:
1. Tamil Sangam literature consists of over 2000 poems composed by poets from various social classes.
2. Sangam literature is divided into Puram and Aham, focusing on material and emotional themes respectively.
3. The Sangam period was under the patronage of the Chola dynasty.

How many of the statements given above is/are correct?
(a) Only one (b) Only two (c) All three (d) None

43. Consider the following pairs regarding social classes mentioned in Tamil Sangam literature:

Social Class	Role
1. Arashar	Kings
2. Velalar	Priests
3. Vaishiyar	Traders

How many pairs given above is/are incorrectly matched?
(a) Only one (b) Only two
(c) All three (d) None

44. With reference to the Three Sangams in Tamil history, consider the following statements:
1. The first Sangam was presided over by Agastya and was held in Madurai.
2. The second Sangam is known for the composition of Tolkappiyam, the oldest surviving Tamil text.
3. The third Sangam was held in Alvai, where texts like Silapaddigaram were written.

How many of the statements given above is/are correct?
(a) Only one (b) Only two
(c) All three (d) None

45. With reference to prominent Sangam literature, consider the following statements:
1. Manimekalai, composed by Sittalai Sattanar, is focused on the themes of chastity and conversion to Buddhism.
2. Tolkappiyam is a Tamil text that deals primarily with grammar and is considered a key text in understanding ancient Tamil society.
3. Tirukkural, authored by Thiruvalluvar, is often referred to as the 'Bible of Tamil Land' and is a treatise on ethics, polity, and social norms.

How many of the statements given above is/are correct?
(a) Only one (b) Only two
(c) All three (d) None

46. Identify the author of the following Tamil epic based on the provided statements:

1. The epic narrates the story of Kovalan and Madhavi, and includes elements of Jainism.
2. The story emphasises the idea of justice and moral values, with Kannagi performing Sati to prove the innocence of her husband Kovalan.

Choose the correct answer from the options given below.

(a) Sittalai Sattanar
(b) Ilango Adigal
(c) Tolkappiyar
(d) Thiruvalluvar

47. How do the contributions of Tolkappiyar differ from those of Thiruvalluvar in Tamil literature?

(a) Tolkappiyar focused on Tamil grammar and social history, while Thiruvalluvar wrote on ethics, and polity.
(b) Thiruvalluvar composed the earliest Tamil epic, while Tolkappiyar wrote on political norms.
(c) Tolkappiyar's works are more focused on love and war, while Thiruvalluvar's work is purely grammatical.
(d) Both are primarily known for their contributions to religious texts in Tamil literature.

Topic 4 : Literature in Medieval India

48. With reference to Persian literature in India, consider the following statements:

1. Tawarikh is a form of history writing characterised by proper organisation, a chronological approach and a systematic way of writing.
2. Amir Khusro developed a new style of poetry known as Sabq-i-Hindi.
3. The Mahabharata was translated into Persian as Razmnama by Badayuni during the Mughal period.

How many of the statements given above is/are not correct?

(a) Only one (b) Only two
(c) All three (d) None

49. With reference to Persian translations, which of the following texts were translated into Persian during the Mughal period?

1. Atharvaveda by Haji Ibrahim Sirhindi
2. Leelavati by Faizi
3. Ramayana by Abdul Rahim

Select the correct answer using the codes given below:

(a) 1 and 2 only
(b) 2 and 3 only
(c) 1 and 3 only
(d) 1, 2 and 3

50. About Non-Islamic historical writings in India, consider the following statements:

1. Bakhar was a form of historical narrative written in Marathi.
2. Janamsakhis are historical accounts written in Sanskrit and Hindi, chronicling the lives of Sikh Gurus.
3. Prabandhas, written in Sanskrit, were historical narratives used to chronicle the achievements of kings and warriors.

How many of the statements given above is/are correct?

(a) Only one
(b) Only two
(c) All three
(d) None

51. Regarding Non-Islamic historical writings, consider the following pairs:

Historical Narrative	Region/Languages
1. Bakhar	Marathi
2. Buranji	Assamese
3. Khayt	Persian

How many pairs given above is/are correctly matched?

(a) Only one pair
(b) Only two pairs
(c) All three pairs
(d) None

52. With reference to Qaseeda, Ginans and Shahr Ashob, consider the following statements:

1. Qaseeda is a narrative form often used in Persian and Arabic literature to praise kings or heroes.
2. Ginans are devotional hymns recited by Nizari Ismaili Muslim communities, commonly found in South Asia.
3. Shahr Ashob refers to Urdu narrative poems that reflect the emotional thoughts of poets during the Mughal Empire.

How many of the statements given above is/are not correct?

(a) Only one
(b) Only two
(c) All three
(d) None

53. Regarding the Rajatarangini, consider the following statements:

1. It was written by Kalhan during the reign of Jaisimha in the 12th century CE.
2. It is the first pure historical text of Kashmir, providing a detailed account of the socio-political and economic conditions of the region.
3. Rajatarangini describes the reigns of various kings, including the misrule during the reign of King Kalash, the son of Ananta Deva.

Which of the statements given above are correct?

(a) 1 and 2 only (b) 2 and 3 only
(c) 1 and 3 only (d) 1, 2 and 3

54. How does Rajatarangini differ from other historical texts of its time?

(a) Rajatarangini was the first historical text to use a chronological approach in narrating the history of a region.
(b) Unlike other texts, Rajatarangini was written in the form of a poem with 7826 verses.
(c) Rajatarangini focused on the moral and ethical aspects of kingship, which was uncommon in other historical narratives.
(d) There is no significant difference between Rajatarangini and other contemporary historical texts.

55. Consider the following pairs:

Rajatarangini Observations	Descriptions
1. King Kalash's misrule	During the reign, common people ate rice and a wild vegetable called utpala saka.
2. King Harsha's reforms	Introduced a general dress for the king, which included a long coat.

Which of the pairs given above is/are correctly matched?

(a) 1 only
(b) 2 only
(c) Both 1 and 2
(d) Neither 1 nor 2

56. Identify the regional literature based on the following features:

1. Amuktamalyada, written in Telugu by Jinasena, focuses on the wedding of Vishnu and the female Vaishnava saint Andal.
2. Pampa's Adipurana is a Kannada version of the work by Krishnadeva Raya, focusing on the life of Rishabhanatha, the first Tirthankara in Jainism.

How many statements given above is/are correctly matched?

(a) 1 only (b) 2 only
(c) Both 1 and 2 (d) Neither 1 nor 2

57. Consider the following pairs:

Regional Literature	Features
1. Vachanas	Shaivite Bhakti poetry written in Kannada
2. Bhakti Ratnavali	Historical chronicles written in Assamese
3. Kamba Ramayan	Tamil Ramayana written by Kamban

How many pairs given above is/are correctly matched?

(a) Only one
(b) Only two
(c) All three
(d) None

58. Consider the following pairs:

Regional Literature	Language/Region
1. Abhanga	Marathi
2. Chandidasi Vaishnavite Poetry	Tamil
3. Buranjis	Assamese

How many pairs given above is/are correctly matched?

(a) Only one (b) Only two
(c) All three (d) None

59. With reference to Arabic literature in India, consider the following statements:

1. Kitab-ul-Hind, written by Al-Biruni, provides a highly analytical and critical view of Indian life during the time of Mahmud Ghazni's invasion.
2. Rehla, written by Ibn Battuta during the reign of Muhammad-bin-Tughlaq, details the political, social and economic conditions of India, with specific mentions of the slavery system, and market prices.
3. Arabic literature in India was more confined to scholars and academicians, and wasn't as widespread as Persian literature.

How many of the statements given above is/are not correct?

(a) Only one (b) Only two
(c) All three (d) None

60. Consider the following pairs regarding forms of Sufi literature:

Form	Description
1. Risalah	A short book on a specific topic
2. Mansavi	Narrative poems, often dealing with spiritual themes
3. Maktubat	Accounts of saints, including their teachings and philosophies

How many pairs given above is/are correctly matched?

(a) Only one
(b) Only two
(c) All three
(d) None

61. With reference to writings by rulers, consider the following statements:

1. Futuhaat-i-Firozshahi, written by Firoz Shah Tughlaq in Persian, focuses on governance and his benevolent work.
2. Tuzuk-i-Babri, the autobiography of Babur, is written in Chagatai-Turkish language and details his conquest of India.
3. Amuktamalyada is a Telugu text written by Krishnadeva Raya, focusing on the wedding of God Vishnu with the female Alvar saint Andal.

How many of the statements given above is/are correct?

(a) Only one
(b) Only two
(c) All three
(d) None

62. Consider the following pairs regarding works by rulers:

Work	Language/Region
1. Tuzuk-i-Jahangiri	Persian
2. Humayun Nama	Chagatai-Turkish
3. Badshah Nama	Persian

How many pairs given above is/are correctly matched?

(a) Only one
(b) Only two
(c) All three
(d) None

OMR SHEET

Assessment Round

1	(a) (b) (c) (d)	31	(a) (b) (c) (d)	61	(a) (b) (c) (d)	91	(a) (b) (c) (d)
2	(a) (b) (c) (d)	32	(a) (b) (c) (d)	62	(a) (b) (c) (d)	92	(a) (b) (c) (d)
3	(a) (b) (c) (d)	33	(a) (b) (c) (d)	63	(a) (b) (c) (d)	93	(a) (b) (c) (d)
4	(a) (b) (c) (d)	34	(a) (b) (c) (d)	64	(a) (b) (c) (d)	94	(a) (b) (c) (d)
5	(a) (b) (c) (d)	35	(a) (b) (c) (d)	65	(a) (b) (c) (d)	95	(a) (b) (c) (d)
6	(a) (b) (c) (d)	36	(a) (b) (c) (d)	66	(a) (b) (c) (d)	96	(a) (b) (c) (d)
7	(a) (b) (c) (d)	37	(a) (b) (c) (d)	67	(a) (b) (c) (d)	97	(a) (b) (c) (d)
8	(a) (b) (c) (d)	38	(a) (b) (c) (d)	68	(a) (b) (c) (d)	98	(a) (b) (c) (d)
9	(a) (b) (c) (d)	39	(a) (b) (c) (d)	69	(a) (b) (c) (d)	99	(a) (b) (c) (d)
10	(a) (b) (c) (d)	40	(a) (b) (c) (d)	70	(a) (b) (c) (d)	100	(a) (b) (c) (d)
11	(a) (b) (c) (d)	41	(a) (b) (c) (d)	71	(a) (b) (c) (d)	101	(a) (b) (c) (d)
12	(a) (b) (c) (d)	42	(a) (b) (c) (d)	72	(a) (b) (c) (d)	102	(a) (b) (c) (d)
13	(a) (b) (c) (d)	43	(a) (b) (c) (d)	73	(a) (b) (c) (d)	103	(a) (b) (c) (d)
14	(a) (b) (c) (d)	44	(a) (b) (c) (d)	74	(a) (b) (c) (d)	104	(a) (b) (c) (d)
15	(a) (b) (c) (d)	45	(a) (b) (c) (d)	75	(a) (b) (c) (d)	105	(a) (b) (c) (d)
16	(a) (b) (c) (d)	46	(a) (b) (c) (d)	76	(a) (b) (c) (d)	106	(a) (b) (c) (d)
17	(a) (b) (c) (d)	47	(a) (b) (c) (d)	77	(a) (b) (c) (d)	107	(a) (b) (c) (d)
18	(a) (b) (c) (d)	48	(a) (b) (c) (d)	78	(a) (b) (c) (d)	108	(a) (b) (c) (d)
19	(a) (b) (c) (d)	49	(a) (b) (c) (d)	79	(a) (b) (c) (d)	109	(a) (b) (c) (d)
20	(a) (b) (c) (d)	50	(a) (b) (c) (d)	80	(a) (b) (c) (d)	110	(a) (b) (c) (d)
21	(a) (b) (c) (d)	51	(a) (b) (c) (d)	81	(a) (b) (c) (d)	111	(a) (b) (c) (d)
22	(a) (b) (c) (d)	52	(a) (b) (c) (d)	82	(a) (b) (c) (d)	112	(a) (b) (c) (d)
23	(a) (b) (c) (d)	53	(a) (b) (c) (d)	83	(a) (b) (c) (d)	113	(a) (b) (c) (d)
24	(a) (b) (c) (d)	54	(a) (b) (c) (d)	84	(a) (b) (c) (d)	114	(a) (b) (c) (d)
25	(a) (b) (c) (d)	55	(a) (b) (c) (d)	85	(a) (b) (c) (d)	115	(a) (b) (c) (d)
26	(a) (b) (c) (d)	56	(a) (b) (c) (d)	86	(a) (b) (c) (d)	116	(a) (b) (c) (d)
27	(a) (b) (c) (d)	57	(a) (b) (c) (d)	87	(a) (b) (c) (d)	117	(a) (b) (c) (d)
28	(a) (b) (c) (d)	58	(a) (b) (c) (d)	88	(a) (b) (c) (d)	118	(a) (b) (c) (d)
29	(a) (b) (c) (d)	59	(a) (b) (c) (d)	89	(a) (b) (c) (d)	119	(a) (b) (c) (d)
30	(a) (b) (c) (d)	60	(a) (b) (c) (d)	90	(a) (b) (c) (d)	120	(a) (b) (c) (d)

Calculate Your Score

Correct (✓)	
Incorrect (✓)	
Unattempted	
Total Score	
Accuracy (%)	

Reasons for Incorrect Answers?

1. Lack of Knowledge/Existing Source Insufficient	
2. Lack of Multiple Revision	
3. Common Sense Mistakes	

Note :

1. Calculate total score as correct answers carry 2 marks each 1/3rd marks will deducted for **Incorrect** Answers.
2. Calculate Accuracy (%) by dividing the number of correct answers to the total number of attempted questions.

Past Learning

1. Which one of the following is a work attributed to playwright Bhasa? **(2024)**
(a) Kavyalankara
(b) Natyashastra
(c) Madhyama - vyayoga
(d) Mahabhashya

2. Sanghabhuti, an Indian Buddhist monk, who travelled to China at the end of the fourth century AD, was the author of a commentary on **(2024)**
(a) Prajnaparamita Sutra
(b) Visuddhimagga
(c) Sarvastivada Vinaya
(d) Lalitavistara

3. With reference to the scholars/literatures of ancient India, consider the following statements. **(2020)**
1. Panini is associated with Pushyamitra Shunga.
2. Amarasimha is associated with Harshavardhana.
3. Kalidasa is associated with Chandragupta II.

Which of the statements given above is/are correct?
(a) 1 and 2 only (b) 2 and 3 only
(c) Only 3 (d) 1, 2 and 3

4. With reference to the cultural history of India, the memorising of chronicles, dynastic histories and epic tales was the profession of who of the following? **(2016)**
(a) Shramana (b) Parivraajaka
(c) Agrahaarika (d) Magadha

5. Which one of the following books of ancient India has the love story of the son of the founder of Shunga dynasty? **(2016)**
(a) Svapnavasavadattam
(b) Malavikagnimitra
(c) Meghadoot
(d) Ratnavali

6. Which one of the following was given classical language status recently? **(2015)**
(a) Odia
(b) Konkani
(c) Bhojpuri
(d) Assamese

7. Consider the following languages. **(2014)**
1. Gujarati
2. Kannada
3. Telugu

Which of the above has/have been declared as 'Classical Language/Languages' by the Government?
(a) 1 and 2 only
(b) Only 3
(c) 2 and 3 only
(d) All of the above

8. Who of the following is the author of a collection of poem called 'Golden Threshold'? **(2009)**
(a) Aruna Asaf Ali
(b) Annie Besant
(c) Sarojini Naidu
(d) Vijaya Lakshmi Pandit

9. Mahamastakabhisheka, a great religious event, is associated with and done for who of the following? **(2009)**
(a) Bahubali
(c) Mahavirji
(b) Buddha
(d) Nataraja

10. Recently, the manuscripts of which one of the following have been included in the UNESCO's Memory of World Register?
(a) Abhidhamma Pitaka **(2008)**
(b) Mahabharata
(c) Ramayana
(d) Rig-Veda

11. Match List I with List II and select the correct answer using the codes given below the lists. **(2008)**

List I (Authors)		List II (Works)	
A.	Bankim Chandra	1.	Shatranj Ke Khilari
B.	Dinabandhu Mitra	2.	Devi Chaudhurani
C.	Prem Chand	3.	Nil Darpan
		4.	Chandrakanta

Codes

	A	B	C
(a)	2	4	1
(b)	3	4	2
(c)	2	3	1
(d)	3	1	4

12. Who among the following wrote the poem, Subh-e Azadi? **(2008)**

(a) Sahir Ludhiyanvi
(b) Faiz Ahmed Faiz
(c) Mohammad Iqbal
(d) Maulana Abul Kalam Azad

13. The song 'Amar Sonar Bangla' written during the Swadeshi Movement of India inspired the liberation struggle of Bangladesh and was adopted as the National Anthem of Bangladesh. Who wrote this song? **(2007)**

(a) Rajni Kanta Sen
(b) Dwijendralal Roy
(c) Mukunda Das
(d) Rabindranath Tagore

14. Who wrote the book 'The Story of The Integration of the Indian States'? **(2007)**

(a) B. N. Rao
(b) C. Rajagopalachari
(c) Krishna Menon
(d) V. P. Menon

15. Who among the following, wrote the book 'Bahubivah'? **(2007)**

(a) Raja Rammohan Roy
(b) Ishwar Chandra Vidyasagar
(c) Pandita Ramabai
(d) Rabindranath Tagore

16. 'Mrichchhakatika' an ancient Indian book written by Shudraka deals with **(2003)**

(a) the love affair of a rich merchant with the daughter of a courtesan
(b) the victory of Chandragupta II over the Shaka Kshatrapas of Western India
(c) the military expeditions and exploits of Samudragupta
(d) the love affairs between a Gupta King and a princess of Kamarupa

17. Who amongst the following Englishmen, first translated Bhagavad Gita into English? **(2001)**

(a) William Jones
(b) Charles Wilkins
(c) Alexander Cunningham
(d) John Marshall

18. The following persons came to India at one time or another. **(1999)**

1. Megasthenese
2. Fa- Hien
3. I-Tsing
4. Hiuen-Tsang

The correct chronological sequence of their visits.

(a) 3, 2, 1, 4
(b) 3, 1, 2, 4
(c) 1, 3, 2, 4
(d) 1, 3, 4, 2

19. Which of the following pairs are correctly matched? **(1998)**

List I	List II
1. Mrichchhakatika	Shudraka
2. Buddhacharita	Vasubandhu
3. Mudrarakshasa	Vishakhadatta
4. Harshacharita	Banabhatta

Select the correct answer using the codes given below.

(a) 1, 2, 3 and 4
(b) 1, 3 and 4
(c) 1 and 4
(d) 2 and 3

20. Match List I with List II and select the correct answer using the codes given below the lists. **(1997)**

List I (Authors)		List II (Texts)
A. Varahamihira	1.	Prabandha Chintamani
B. Visakhadatta	2.	Mrichchhakatika
C. Shudraka	3.	Brihat-Samhita
D. Bilhana	4.	Devi Chandraguptam
	5.	Vikramankadeva - Charita

Codes

	A	B	C	D
(a)	3	4	5	2
(b)	3	4	2	5
(c)	5	3	4	1
(d)	1	3	5	2

21. Which one of the following pairs of composers in different languages and their works on the Mahabharata theme is correctly matched? **(1997)**

(a)	Sarladasa	Bengali
(b)	Kasirama	Oriya
(c)	Tikkana	Marathi
(d)	Pampa	Kannada

22. Which one of the following scripts of ancient India was written from right to left? **(1997)**

(a) Brahmi
(b) Nandinagari
(c) Sharada
(d) Kharoshti

23. Nastaliq was **(1996)**

(a) a Persian script used in medieval India
(b) a raga composed by Tansen
(c) a cess levied by the Mughal rulers
(d) a manual of code of conduct for the Ulemas

24. Which one of the following texts of ancient India allows divorce to a wife deserted by her husband? **(1996)**

(a) Kamasutra
(b) Manavadharmashastra
(c) Sukra Nitisara
(d) Arthashastra

25. The term 'apabhramsa' was used in medieval Sanskrit texts to denote **(1996)**

(a) Outcastes among the Rajputs
(b) Deviations from Vedic rituals
(c) early forms of some of the modern Indian languages
(d) non-Sanskrit verse metres

Detailed Solutions

Assessment Round

1. *(c)* All three

- **Statement 1 is correct:** 'Sariputra Prakarna' is indeed attributed to the Buddhist scholar **Ashvaghosha,** which explores themes related to the life and teachings of Buddha, with a focus on Sariputra, one of Buddha's chief disciples known for his wisdom and leadership in spreading Buddhism.
- **Statement 2 is correct:** 'Mudrarakshasa,' a play by **Vishakhadutta,** is a classical Sanskrit drama which deals with the cunning strategies of **Chanakya** (Kautilya), the advisor to **Chandragupta Maurya,** as he secures the throne for Chandragupta by defeating the Nanda dynasty.
- **Statement 3 is correct: Kalidasa's 'Abhijnana Shakuntalam'** is classical Sanskrit play based on a story from the Mahabharata and revolves around the romantic saga of **King Dushyant and Shakuntala,** the daughter of sage Vishwamitra, and the celestial nymph Menaka.

Thus, option (c) is the correct answer.

2. *(d)* All four

- **Kalidasa** is often regarded as the greatest classical Sanskrit poet and dramatist of ancient India. His works, such as **'Shakuntala,' 'Vikramorvashiyam'** and **'Malavikagnimitra,'** have left an indelible mark on Indian literature.
- **Bhavabhuti** was another eminent dramatist, best known for his three plays: **'Malti Madhava,' 'Uttararamcharita'** and **'Mahaviracharita.'** His works often focused on heroic themes and deep emotional conflicts, with **'Uttararamcharita'** being particularly famous for depicting the later life of Lord Rama, post his return to Ayodhya.
- **Sudraka** was a king and playwright known for his only surviving play, **'Mrichchhakatika'** (The Little Clay Cart). This play is a complex narrative involving love, intrigue and social commentary, set against the backdrop of urban life in ancient India.
- **Mahendravarman I** was a Pallava king who authored the farcical play **'Mattavilasa Prahasana'** (The Delight of the Drunken Sport). This satirical drama pokes fun at various religious sects of the time, particularly the Kapalikas and Pasupatas, reflecting the cultural, and religious diversity of South India during his reign.

Thus, option (d) is the correct answer.

3. *(d)* 1, 2 and 3

- **Statement 1 is correct: Kalidasa,** often hailed as the **Shakespeare of India. 'Raghuvamsa'** is a mahakavya (epic poem) that chronicles the lineage of the Raghu dynasty, to which Lord Rama belonged. **'Meghaduta',** another masterpiece, is a lyric poem that tells the story of a yaksha (demigod) who, exiled by his master, sends a message to his wife through a passing cloud.
- **Statement 2 is correct: 'Mudrarakshasa'** by **Vishakhadutta** is a historical drama that explores the political machinations and strategies employed by Chanakya to establish Chandragupta Maurya on the throne.
- **Statement 3 is correct: Bhavabhuti's 'Malti Madhava'** is a romantic drama set in the backdrop of Ujjain, involving the love story of Malati and Madhava. The play is rich in emotional content, exploring themes of love, duty and sacrifice.

Thus, option (d) is the correct answer.

4. *(d)* 3 only

- **Statement 1 is incorrect : Harivamsa** is not authored by Bhasa but is an appendix to the Mahabharata, traditionally attributed to Vyasa. It focuses on the genealogy and history of the Yadava, and Kuru dynasties, tracing the lineage of Lord Krishna, and the Pandavas.
- **Statement 2 is incorrect: Vikramorvashiyam** by Kalidasa is a romantic drama and does not focus on historical accounts of kings. It tells the love story of King Pururavas and the celestial nymph Urvashi, blending

mythological themes with poetic expression, making it a work of fiction rather than historical narration.

- **StStatement 3 is correct: Devichandraguptam** by Vishakhadutta is believed to be a lost drama that depicted the story of King Chandragupta II (Vikramaditya) and his victory over the Shakas. .

Thus, option (d) is the correct answer.

5. *(c)* Bhavabhuti

- **Bhavabhuti** is the playwright in question here. He was a **7th century Sanskrit scholar** and dramatist known for his profound work **'Uttararamcharita'** which is a play that portrays the later years of Lord Rama's life, focusing on his exile of Sita, and the reunion with his sons.
- In **'Malti Madhava'**, Bhavabhuti crafts a romantic narrative set against the social and political backdrop of ancient India. The play showcases his ability to blend romance with social commentary, making it one of his most enduring works.

Thus, option (c) is the correct answer.

6. *(d)* None

- **Pair 1 is correctly matched: Sudraka,** a king and dramatist, is credited with the play **'Mrichchhakatika'** (The Little Clay Cart). This play is a complex narrative involving love, poverty and social justice, set against the urban life of ancient India.
- **Pair 2 is correctly matched:** Kalidasa, one of the greatest playwrights and poets of ancient India, authored several significant works, including **'Malavikagnimitra'**. This play revolves around the love story of King Agnimitra of the Shunga dynasty and Malavika, a beautiful dancer.
- **Pair 3 is correctly matched: Mahendravarman I,** a Pallava king, authored 'Mattavilasa Prahasana' (The Delight of the Drunken Sport), a satirical play that ridicules the religious practices of various sects, particularly the Kapalikas and Pasupatas.

Thus, option (d) is the correct answer.

7. *(b)* Only two pairs

- **Pair 1 is correctly matched: Aryabhatta** was an ancient Indian mathematician and astronomer who wrote **'Aryabhatiya'**, a seminal work in mathematics, and astronomy. It includes discussions on arithmetic, algebra, trigonometry and celestial calculations.
- **Pair 2 is correctly matched: Patanjali** is traditionally recognised as the author of the **'Mahabhasya'**, a comprehensive commentary on **Panini's grammar treatise,** the **'Ashtadhyayi.'** The **'Mahabhasya'** is one of the most important works on Sanskrit grammar, elaborating on the rules established by Panini and providing a deep insight into the structure of the Sanskrit language.
- **Pair 3 is incorrectly matched: Vatsyayana** is best known for authoring the **'Kamasutra,'** a treatise on human sensuality and the art of love. However, **'Brihatsamhita,'** a significant work in astrology and divination, was written by Varahamihira, not Vatsyayana.

Thus, option (b) is the correct answer.

8. *(c)* All three

- **Statement 1 is correct:** The **'Kamasutra'** is authored by **Vatsyayana.** It is an ancient Indian text on human sexual behaviour, love and social conduct. The text is divided into seven parts, each dealing with different aspects of love, relationships and social life, making it one of the most famous works of ancient Indian literature.
- **Statement 2 is correct:** The **'Charaksamhita'** is a foundational text in **Ayurveda,** authored by Charaka. This ancient medical treatise discusses various aspects of medicine, including diagnosis, treatment and the prevention of diseases.
- **Statement 3 is correct:** The **'Natyashastra'** is attributed to **Bharata Muni** and is an ancient Indian treatise on the performing arts, encompassing drama, music, dance, and other theatrical elements.

Thus, option (c) is the correct answer.

9. *(a)* Sruti is considered a divine revelation, while Smriti is based on human knowledge.

- **Sruti** refers to the body of texts that are considered to be **divinely revealed and are thus regarded as eternal, and unquestionable.** The Vedas and Upanishads fall into this category. These texts were passed down orally through generations before being written down and they form the core of **Hindu religious thought.**
- Smriti, on the other hand, refers to texts that are remembered and are considered to be of human authorship. These texts provide **guidelines on social, ethical and legal matters,** and have been subject to interpretation, and adaptation over time. Eg- Dharmashastras, Itihasas (like the Ramayana and Mahabharata), and Puranas.

Thus, option (a) is the correct answer.

10. *(d)* 1, 2 and 3

- **Statement 1 is correct:** The Vedas, the oldest sacred texts of Hinduism, are divided into four main parts.
- **Samhitas** are collections of hymns and prayers.
- **Brahmanas** are prose texts that provide explanations of the rituals and the symbolism behind them.
- **Aranyakas** serve as a bridge between the ritualistic Brahmanas and the philosophical Upanishads, focusing on the inner meaning of rituals.
- **Upanishads,** also known as Vedanta (the end of the Vedas), deal with philosophical concepts such as the nature of the self (Atman), the nature of ultimate reality (Brahman), and the relationship between the two.
- **Statement 2 is correct:** Aranyakas are considered the philosophical treatises that explore the deeper, esoteric meanings of the rituals described in the Brahmanas.
- **Statement 3 is correct:** The Upanishads are rightly called Vedanta because they represent the concluding portions of the Vedas. They emphasise metaphysical knowledge (Jnana) over ritual action (Karma) and are considered the foundation of Vedantic philosophy.

Thus, option (d) is the correct answer.

11. *(b)* Only two

- **Statement 1 is correct:** The **Rigveda** is collection of hymns and is the oldest of the four Vedas, composed around 1500 BCE. It is often regarded as the **'first testament of mankind'** due to its antiquity and foundational role in Hinduism.
- **Statement 2 is correct:** The **Gayatri Mantra,** one of the most revered mantras in Hinduism, is found in **Mandala III of the Rigveda.** It is a hymn dedicated to Savitri, the sun deity and is chanted for spiritual enlightenment, and wisdom.
- **Statement 3 is incorrect:** The Rigveda was originally composed in **Vedic Sanskrit and transmitted orally.** The earliest scripts used for writing the Vedas were Brahmi and Kharosthi, but the Rigveda itself was not originally written in Brahmi script.

Thus, option (b) is the correct answer.

12. *(a)* 1 and 2 only

- **Statement 1 is correct:** The **Rigveda** consists of **1028 hymns (Suktas)** organised into 10 books or Mandalas. These hymns are dedicated to various deities like Agni, Indra and Soma, and are used in rituals, and sacrifices.
- **Statement 2 is correct : Mandala X** of the Rigveda is significant for containing the **Purusha Sukta,** a hymn that describes the cosmic giant Purusha and his sacrifice, which led to the creation of the four Varnas (Brahmin, Kshatriya, Vaishya, and Shudra).
- **Statement 3 is incorrect:** While the Rigveda does contain some hymns that emphasise a single deity as supreme in different contexts (a concept known as Henotheism), it predominantly reflects a **polytheistic belief system.** The deities in the Rigveda are often invoked for their specific powers-Agni (fire), Indra (rain and war), Varuna (cosmic order), and so on.

Thus, option (a) is the correct answer.

13. *(b)* Yajurveda

- **The Yajurveda** is one of the four Vedas and **is** primarily focused on the **liturgy (rituals) associated with sacrifices.** The Yajurveda **is** divided into two major recensions-**Krishna Yajurveda (Black Yajurveda) and Shukla Yajurveda (White Yajurveda).** The distinction between these two lies in their organisation and the inclusion of Brahmana portions.

- The Krishna Yajurveda is considered **more archaic and disorganised,** containing a mixture of prose and verse, with the Brahmana portions embedded within the Samhitas. On the other hand, the **Shukla Yajurveda,** also known as the Vajasaneyi Samhita, is **more systematically arranged,** with the Samhita and Brahmana texts clearly separated. This structured organisation of the Shukla Yajurveda makes it easier to understand and use in rituals.

Thus, option (b) is the correct answer.

14. *(c)* Samaveda

- The **Samaveda,** often referred to as the '**Book of Chants**' is one of the four Vedas and is distinguished by its focus on musical aspects of Vedic rituals. The Samaveda consists mainly of hymns from the Rigveda, set to a melody and intended to be sung during the performance of sacrifices.
- The hymns of the Samaveda are sung by a special class of priests called **Udgataris.** These priests play a crucial role in Vedic rituals, where the chanting of Samaveda hymns is believed to please the deities and ensure the success of the rituals.

Thus, option (c) is the correct answer.

15. *(c)* All three

- **Statement 1 is correct:** The **Atharvaveda** is indeed the last of the four Vedas and is often attributed to the sages **Atharvan** and **Angirasa.** Atharvaveda includes hymns, spells, and incantations that deal with everyday concerns, such as health, prosperity, and protection from evil.
- **Statement 2 is correct:** The phrase '**Satyamev Jayate**' (Truth alone triumphs) is derived from the **Mundaka Upanishad,** which is associated with the Atharvaveda. This phrase is a significant part of the Indian national emblem and reflects the enduring influence of Vedic literature on Indian culture and values.
- **Statement 3 is correct:** The Atharvaveda is known for its practical approach to life, addressing issues like healing, longevity and societal well-being. It contains hymns and spells aimed at ensuring peace and prosperity, dealing with illnesses, resolving conflicts, and addressing other daily life concerns.

Thus, option (c) is the correct answer.

16. *(c)* All three

- **Statement 1 is correct:** The Brihadaranyaka Upanishad, one of the oldest and most significant Upanishads, is one of the earliest texts to discuss the concept of the transmigration of the soul (reincarnation).
- **Statement 2 is correct:** The term '**Vedanta**' literally means 'the end of the Vedas' and refers to the Upanishads, which are considered the concluding part of Vedic literature. The Upanishads focus on philosophical inquiry and metaphysical knowledge.
- **Statement 3 is correct:** The **Muktika Upanishad** is a later Upanishad and it was translated into Persian by the Mughal prince Dara Shikoh in 1656, known as the '**Sirr-e-Akbar**' (The Great Secret).

Thus, option (c) is the correct answer.

17. *(c)* Both 1 and 2

- **Statement 1 is correct:** The **Aranyakas** are a category of Vedic texts that form a bridge between the ritual-focused **Brahmanas and the philosophical Upanishads.** They discuss the symbolic meaning of rituals and are seen as moving away from the physical performance of sacrifices (Karma Marg) towards a more mystical, and philosophical understanding (Jnana Marg).
- **Statement 2 is correct:** The **Upanishads,** also known as **Vedanta,** represent the culmination of Vedic thought. They focus on deep philosophical concepts, such as the nature of the **self (Atman),** the **ultimate reality (Brahman)** and the relationship between the two.

Thus, option (c) is the correct answer.

18. *(b)* Only two pairs

- **Pair 1 is correctly matched:** The **Katha Upanishad** is centered around the theme of death and the afterlife. It is a dialogue between the young boy Nachiketa and Yama, the god of death, where profound discussions on the **nature of the self,** the universe, and the concept of liberation (**Moksha**) take place.
- **Pair 2 is incorrectly matched:** The **Chandogya Upanishad** is one of the oldest Upanishads and contains a wide array of philosophical discussions, including the concept of **Tat Tvam Asi ('That Thou Art').** However, it does not focus on the four ashramas (stages of life); this concept is more elaborated in the Manusmriti and other Smriti texts.
- **Pair 3 is correctly matched:** The **Mandukya Upanishad** is the **shortest** of the Upanishads, consisting of just 12 verses. It is highly significant in Vedanta philosophy because it explicates the syllable Om as the sound symbolising the entirety of consciousness, divided into four states: waking, dreaming, deep sleep and the fourth state of transcendental consciousness (Turiya).

Thus, option (b) is the correct answer.

19. *(b)* Only two

- **Statement 1 is correct:** The Aranyakas are considered as the concluding part of the Brahmanas. The term **'Aranyaka'** means 'pertaining to the forest,' suggesting that these texts were intended for study and contemplation by ascetics living in the wilderness, away from the distractions of societal life.
- **Statement 2 is correct:** Aranyakas are known for their focus on esoteric and mystical interpretations of rituals. They mark a shift from the external rituals (Karma Marg) emphasised in the Brahmanas to the internal, contemplative path (Jnana Marg) that is fully developed in the Upanishads.
- **Statement 3 is incorrect:** The Aranyakas do not emphasize ritual action as much as the Brahmanas do; instead, they focus on the symbolic and philosophical aspects of rituals.

Thus, option (b) is the correct answer.

20. *(b)* Only two pairs

- **Pair 1 is correctly matched:** Shiksha is the Vedanga concerned with Phonetics. It deals with the correct pronunciation and intonation of Vedic texts, which was crucial for the accurate performance of rituals and recitations.
- **Pair 2 is incorrectly matched:** Vyakarana is actually the Vedanga concerned with Grammar, not Astronomy. It includes works like Panini's 'Ashtadhyayi,' which is a comprehensive treatise on Sanskrit grammar, essential for preserving the purity of the language used in the Vedas.
- **Pair 3 is correctly matched:** Kalpa is correctly matched with Ritual Ceremonies. It deals with the guidelines for performing rituals, sacrifices, and other religious ceremonies, including the Grihasutras, Dharmasutras, and Shrautasutras.

Thus, option (b) is the correct answer.

21. *(c)* All three

- **Statement 1 is correct:** The **Grihasutras** are manuals that provide detailed instructions on the performance of domestic rituals, such as marriage ceremonies, the Upanayana (sacred thread ceremony) and other rites of passage within the household.
- **Statement 2 is correct:** The **Sulvasutras** are specialised texts within the Kalpa Sutras that deal with the geometry and measurements required for constructing sacrificial altars (Yajnas).
- **Statement 3 is correct:** The **Dharmasutras** are indeed concerned with the rules of conduct, ethics and duties (Dharma) that individuals must follow in society. These texts lay down the legal and moral framework for various aspects of life, including marriage, inheritance, and the duties of different social classes.

Thus, option (c) is the correct answer.

22. *(b)* Only two pairs

- **Pair 1 is correctly matched:** The **Brahma marriage** is correctly described as the marriage of a daughter to the most eligible and suitable groom. In this type of marriage, the father of the bride willingly gives her away to a man of good character and virtues, often without expecting anything in return.

- **Pair 2 is incorrectly matched:** In the Grihasutras, Gandharva marriage is a union based on mutual attraction and love, often without the formal consent of the families. It is essentially a love marriage and does not involve purchasing the bride.
- **Pair 3 is incorrectly matched:** Asura marriage involves the groom giving wealth or valuables to the bride's family in exchange for the bride. It is generally considered less prestigious than Brahma or Gandharva marriage and is often associated with the buying of the bride.

Thus, option (b) is the correct answer.

23. *(b)* It is an ancient Sanskrit text that includes codes of conduct, ethics and social norms.

- The **Dharmashastras** are ancient Indian texts that **deal with law, ethics and moral codes,** providing a comprehensive guide on how individuals should conduct themselves in various aspects of life. These texts cover topics such as the duties of kings (Rajadharma), the responsibilities of different social classes (Varna Dharma), inheritance laws and the rights, and duties of individuals within society.
- The most famous Dharmashastras include **Manusmriti, Yajnavalkya Smriti and Narada Smriti.**

Thus, option (b) is the correct answer.

24. *(b)* Only two

- **Statement 1 is correct: Manusmriti,** also known as the **Laws of Manu,** is one of the oldest and most influential Dharmashastras. It provides detailed guidelines on social conduct, laws and ethics. Manusmriti has played a crucial role in **shaping Hindu law and social practices** over the centuries.
- **Statement 2 is incorrect: Bhasyas** are critical commentaries on various texts, including the Dharmashastras. However, Bhasyas are not part of the Dharmashastras themselves but are later scholarly interpretations and analyses of these texts.
- **Statement 3 is correct:** The **Yajnavalkya Smriti** is another important Dharmashastra that deals with legal maxims and principles related to Dharma. It is considered more progressive and systematic compared to Manusmriti and includes discussions on civil, and criminal law, property rights, and family law.

Thus, option (b) is the correct answer.

25. *(a)* Dharmashastras focus on laws and ethical conduct, while Grihasutras provide guidelines for household rituals and ceremonies.

- **Dharmashastras** are a body of literature that deal primarily with law, ethics and social duties. They provide comprehensive guidelines on various aspects of life, including the duties of individuals according to their varna (social class), the rights and responsibilities within the family, property laws, and role of the king and state.
- **Grihasutras** are manuals that focus on the domestic rituals and ceremonies to be performed by a householder (Grihastha). They include detailed instructions on rites of passage such as birth ceremonies, initiation (Upanayana), marriage, and funeral rites.

Thus, option (a) is the correct answer.

26. *(b)* They are critical and detailed commentaries on the ideas of Dharmashastra, providing interpretations, and explanations.

- **Bhasyas** are detailed and **critical commentaries** on ancient texts such as the Vedas, Upanishads, Dharmashastras and philosophical works like the Brahma Sutras. These commentaries are written by scholars to elucidate, interpret and sometimes debate the meanings of the original texts.
- The most famous **Bhasyas include those by Adi Shankaracharya,** who wrote extensive commentaries on the **Upanishads, the Bhagavad Gita and the Brahma Sutras,** helping to establish the Advaita Vedanta school of thought.

Thus, option (b) is the correct answer.

27. *(b)* Only two

- **Statement 1 is correct:** The **Manusmriti** and **Yajnavalkya Smriti** are among the most influential Dharmashastra texts. Manusmriti is traditionally regarded as foundational text of Hindu law, while **Yajnavalkya Smriti** is known for its systematic and comprehensive treatment of legal principles, covering both **civil, and criminal law.**

- **Statement 2 is correct: Bhasyas** are indeed critical interpretations and commentaries on these Dharmashastra texts. Scholars like Medhatithi and Vijnaneshwara wrote Bhasyas on the Manusmriti, and Yajnavalkya Smriti, respectively, providing explanations, interpretations of complex or ambiguous passages.
- **Statement 3 is incorrect: Dharmashastra** texts like Manusmriti are primarily composed in verse (Shlokas), which makes them accessible and easier to memorise. However, they are **not written in prose form**; instead, the prose is often found in the Bhasyas and other commentaries that explain these verses.

Thus, option (b) is the correct answer.

28. *(c)* Both 1 and 2

- **Statement 1 is correct:** The **Arthashastra,** attributed to **Kautilya** (also known as Chanakya), is an ancient Indian treatise on statecraft, economic policy and military strategy. It is divided into 15 Adhikaranas (books or sections), which are further subdivided into 150 Prakarnas (chapters).
- **Statement 2 is correct:** The Arthashastra is one of the most comprehensive texts on statecraft from ancient India. It provides detailed instructions on the functioning of various executive authorities, the administration of justice, foreign relations, economic policies and even the organisation of society.

Thus, option (c) is the correct answer.

29. *(d)* None

- **Statement 1 is correct:** The Arthashastra does not categorically prohibit slavery but it does regulate it. It acknowledges that a person could become a slave through various means, such as being captured in war, by judicial punishment, or by selling oneself into slavery.
- **Statement 2 is correct:** The Arthashastra does recognise slavery and includes detailed provisions regarding the rights, and treatment of slaves. For instance, it specifies that if a female slave gives birth to a child by her master, both the child and the mother are to be set free.
- **Statement 3 is correct:** The **Arthashastra** does prescribe fines and other punishments for the violation of these rules, including a fine of 12 panas for certain offenses. This reflects the text's attempt to regulate the institution of slavery within the framework of ancient Indian society.

Thus, option (d) is the correct answer.

30. *(d)* 1, 2 and 3

- **Statement 1 is correct:** The **Ramayana** is indeed attributed to Maharishi Valmiki, who is often hailed as the '**Adikavi**' or the first poet of India. It narrates the life and adventures of **Lord Rama,** focusing on his exile, the abduction of his wife Sita by Ravana, the demon king of Lanka, and her eventual rescue.
- **Statement 2 is correct:** The Ramayana is traditionally divided into 7 Kandas (books). These include the **Bala Kanda, Ayodhya Kanda, Aranya Kanda, Kishkindha Kanda, Sundara Kanda, Yuddha Kanda and Uttara Kanda.** Scholars believe that the Bala Kanda (first) and Uttara Kanda (seventh) were laters additions to the original text.
- **Statement 3 is correct:** The Ramayana indeed discusses the four Purusharthas or objectives of human life-**Dharma** (righteousness), **Artha** (material prosperity), **Kama** (desire) and **Moksha** (liberation).

Thus, option (d) is the correct answer

31. *(d)* 1, 2 and 3

- **Pair 1 is correctly matched: Nishkama Karma,** or the idea of performing one's duty without attachment to the results, is a central concept in the Bhagavad Gita, which is part of the Mahabharata.
- **Pair 2 is correctly matched: Bhishma Parva** is the **sixth book** of the Mahabharata and includes the Bhagavad Gita, where Lord Krishna delivers his discourse on Dharma, Yoga, and Bhakti to Arjuna on the battlefield of Kurukshetra.

- **Pair 3 is correctly matched: Shanti Parva** is indeed the largest parva in the Mahabharata. It follows the conclusion of the Kurukshetra war and is largely concerned with the duties of a king (Rajadharma), and the responsibilities of a ruler towards his subjects.

Thus, option (d) is the correct answer.

32. *(b)* Only two

- **Statement 1 is correct:** The Puranas are a genre of ancient Indian literature that blend mythological stories, historical narratives and religious teachings. They were composed over a long period, spanning both the Vedic and post-Vedic ages.
- **Statement 2 is incorrect:** There are traditionally **18 Mahapuranas and 18 Upapuranas, not 19.** The Mahapuranas are considered major texts, while the Upapuranas are secondary or lesser-known texts.
- **Statement 3 is correct:** The **Matsya Purana** is one of the oldest Puranas and it does discuss the **10** incarnations **(Dashavatara)** of Vishnu, with a particular focus on the Matsya (fish) incarnation.

Thus, option (b) is the correct answer.

33. *(a)* Parables are short stories illustrating a spiritual or moral lesson, usually featuring human characters, while fables feature animals, humans, or mythical characters to illustrate a moral.

- **Parables** are short, didactic stories that **illustrate a moral or spiritual lesson.** These stories usually feature human characters and are often used in religious contexts to teach ethical principles or spiritual truths.
- Fables, on the other hand, are short stories that **typically feature animals, mythical creatures** or inanimate objects that are anthropomorphised (given human characteristics). The primary purpose of fables is to convey a moral lesson, often through clever and witty storytelling.

Thus, option (a) is the correct answer.

34. *(b)* Only two

- **Statement 1 is incorrect:** The **Sutta Pitaka** is one of the three main divisions of the Tripitaka (the Buddhist Canon). The Sutta Pitaka is divided into five Nikayas (collections), but it was not written by Ananda. Ananda played a significant role in reciting the discourses at the First Buddhist Council, but the texts themselves were not written by him.
- **Statement 2 is correct:** The **Vinaya Pitaka** is the section of the Buddhist Canon that deals with the rules of discipline (Vinaya) governing the Sangha (monastic community of monks and nuns). It was indeed compiled by Upali, who was a prominent disciple of the Buddha, particularly renowned for his expertise in the Vinaya.
- **Statement 3 is correct:** The **Abhidhamma Pitaka** is a collection of texts that present the doctrinal teachings of Buddhism in a systematic, analytical framework. It is believed to have been compiled during the Third Buddhist Council, which was convened by **Emperor Ashoka** and presided over by the monk **Moggaliputta Tissa.**

Thus, option (b) is the correct answer.

35. *(a)* Canonical literature includes texts that define religious tenets, while non-canonical literature does not.

- **Canonical Buddhist literature** consists of the texts that are recognised as the authoritative scriptures of Buddhism, which include the Tripitaka (Pali Canon). These texts form the core teachings and doctrinal foundations of Buddhism, defining religious tenets and practices.
- **Non-Canonical Buddhist literature** includes texts that are not considered part of the official canon but are still influential in Buddhist teachings. These may include Jataka tales, commentaries and various Mahayana sutras that expand upon the original doctrines.

Thus, option (a) is the correct answer.

36. *(a)* Jataka tales are written in Pali and focus on the previous births of Buddha, while Lalitavistara Sutra is a Mahayana text related to Buddha's life.

- **Jataka tales** are part of the **Khuddaka Nikaya** within the Sutta Pitaka in the **Pali** Canon and focus on recounting the previous lives of the Buddha. These stories highlight the moral virtues and karmic deeds that contributed to the Buddha's path to enlightenment.

- The **Lalitavistara Sutra** is a **Sanskrit Mahayana** text that provides an elaborate account of the Buddha's life, from his descent from the Tushita heaven to his first sermon at Sarnath. They focuses on the Buddha's final life and his journey to enlightenment, providing a mix of biography and doctrinal teachings.

Thus, option (a) is the correct answer.

37. *(b)* Only two

- **Pair 1 is correctly matched: Dipavamsa** is the oldest extant chronicle of Sri Lanka, written in Pali. It primarily focuses on the history of Buddhism in Sri Lanka, detailing the island's history from its legendary origins to the introduction of Buddhism by Mahinda, the son of Emperor Ashoka.
- **Pair 2 is incorrectly matched: Mahavamsa** is another **Pali** chronicle that continues the historical narrative from the Dipavamsa. While it discusses many aspects of Buddhism in Sri Lanka, it is not specifically an epic poem detailing the Buddha's visit to Sri Lanka.
- **Pair 3 is correctly matched: Milind Panho** is a text that records a dialogue between the Greek King **Menander I (Milinda)** and the Buddhist monk **Nagasena.** This text is significant for its exploration of Buddhist doctrine and philosophy through a question, and answer format.

Thus, option (b) is the correct answer.

38. *(b)* Only two

- **Statement 1 is correct:** The **Agamas** are indeed the principal scriptures of the **Svetambara** sect of Jainism, believed to have been orally transmitted by Mahavira's immediate disciples, the Gandharas. These texts cover various aspects of Jain doctrine, ethics and monastic discipline.
- **Statement 2 is incorrect:** The **Svetambara** sect preserved the **Angas** (which are part of the Agamas) and did not reject their authority. In fact, it was during the Vallabhi Council (c. 5th century CE) that these texts were compiled into written form to preserve them, as oral transmission was becoming unreliable.
- **Statement 3 is correct:** The **Digambara** sect, which does not accept the Agamas preserved by the Svetambaras, considers texts like **Karmaprabhrta** and **Kashayaprabhrta** as important scriptures. These texts discuss the nature of karma and passions, and are integral to Digambara doctrine.

Thus, option (b) is the correct answer.

39. *(b)* Canonical texts are composed of the teachings of Mahavira, while non-canonical texts include biographies and commentaries.

- **Canonical texts** in Jainism, particularly within the Svetambara sect, include the **Agamas** and their various components like the Angas, Upangas, and Mulasutras. These texts are written in Prakrit and are believed to be the direct teachings of **Mahavira,** transmitted through his disciples.
- **Non-canonical texts** include works that were composed later, such as commentaries, philosophical treatises and biographies of Jain Tirthankaras and saints. These texts are often written in **Sanskrit** or regional languages and expand upon the ideas found in the canonical scriptures, offering interpretations, and additional insights.

Thus, option (b) is the correct answer.

40. *(a)* Samantabhadra focused on the life of Jain householders, while Umaswami focused on Jain philosophy.

- **Samantabhadra** was an early Jain philosopher and author associated with the **Digambara** tradition. He wrote in **Sanskrit** and is well-known for works like **Ratnakaranda Shravakachara,** which is a treatise on the conduct of Jain laypersons (Shravakas), and **Apta-Mimamsa,** which defends Jain doctrines against criticisms from other Indian philosophical schools.
- **Umaswami** (also known as Umasvati) is traditionally recognised for his work **Tattvarthasutra,** a key text that systematises Jain philosophy in a logical and accessible manner. It outlines the main principles of Jain metaphysics, ethics and epistemology.

Thus, option (a) is the correct answer.

41. *(c)* All three

- **Pair 1 is correctly matched: Bhadrabahu** is credited with the **Kalpa Sutra,** an important Jain text in the **Svetambara** tradition that provides biographies of the Jain Tirthankaras, especially Mahavira and lays down the rules for monastic life, particularly for the Paryushana festival.
- **Pair 2 is correctly matched: Acharya Kundkunda** is a prominent figure in Jainism, particularly in the Digambara tradition. He is known for writing the **Samayasara,** a philosophical text that explores the nature of the soul and its relationship with karma.
- **Pair 3 is correctly matched: Haribhadra Suri** was a Svetambara scholar known for his contributions to Jain literature, including **Samaraichchakaha,** which is a narrative poem or katha that explores moral and ethical dilemmas.

Thus, option (c) is the correct answer.

42. *(b)* Only two

- **Statement 1 is correct:** Tamil Sangam literature is a rich and ancient body of work dating back to between 300 BCE and 300 CE. This literary corpus is a remarkable collection that comprises **2,381 poems** contributed by 473 **poets,** representing a wide spectrum of society.
- **Statement 2 is correct:** Sangam literature indeed classifies its content into two distinct categories: **Puram** and **Aham. Puram** (external) poems deal with themes related to public life, such as war, heroism, governance, and community ethics. **Aham** (internal) poetry is introspective, focusing on the personal emotions and relationships of individuals.
- **Statement 3 is incorrect:** The Sangam period is traditionally associated with the **Pandya dynasty,** which provided significant patronage to the arts, literature, and culture during this time. The Pandyas ruled from Madurai, which was the center of the Sangam assemblies.

Thus, option (b) is the correct answer.

43. *(a)* Only one

- **Pair 1 is correctly matched: Arashar** refers to **kings or rulers** in Sangam literature. They were considered the highest in the social hierarchy and were responsible for governance, maintaining justice, and protecting the land.
- **Pair 2 is incorrectly matched: Velalar** were primarily **agricultural landlords** and farmers, not priests. They played a significant role in the agrarian economy of ancient Tamil society, managing large tracts of land and employing labourers.
- **Pair 3 is correctly matched: Vaishiyar** refers to the merchant class, who were engaged in trade and commerce. The Vaishiyar were crucial to the economy, facilitating trade not just within the Tamil regions but also with foreign lands, including Rome, South-East Asia and the rest of the Indian sub-continent.

Thus, option (a) is the correct answer.

44. *(b)* Only two

- **Statement 1 is correct:** According to Tamil tradition, the **First Sangam,** also known as the **Mudharchangam,** was indeed presided over by the sage **Agastya,** who is revered as the father of Tamil literature and grammar. This Sangam was said to be held in **Madurai,** the ancient capital of the Pandya kings.
- **Statement 2 is correct:** The **Second Sangam,** also known as the **Idaichangam,** is said to have been held at Kapatapuram, another ancient city believed to be submerged. The **Tolkappiyam,** attributed to the scholar Tolkappiyar, is considered the earliest extant Tamil literary work.
- **Statement 3 is incorrect:** The **Third Sangam** or **Kadaichangam,** was held in Madurai, not Alvai (also known as Alavay, an ancient city near Korkai). Many of the classical Tamil texts, including **Silapaddigaram,** were composed during it.

Thus, option (b) is the correct answer.

45. *(c)* All three

- **Statement 1 is correct: Manimekalai** is composed by **Sittalai Sattanar,** it is the sequel to **Silapaddikaram** and focuses on the life of

Manimekalai, the daughter of Kovalan and Madhavi. The text explores themes of chastity, as Manimekalai chooses a life of celibacy, renouncing worldly pleasures to pursue spiritual enlightenment.

- **Statement 2 is correct: Tolkappiyam** is indeed the oldest surviving Tamil text and it is primarily a work on Tamil grammar, covering phonetics, morphology, syntax, and semantics. It also provides a comprehensive account of the social structure, customs and cultural practices of the time.
- **Statement 3 is correct: Tirukkural** is one of the most revered texts in Tamil literature, written by the poet-philosopher **Thiruvalluvar**. It is often referred to as the **'Bible of Tamil Land'** due to its universal appeal and the breadth of topics it covers, including ethics (Aram), wealth (Porul), and love (Inbam).

Thus, option (c) is the correct answer.

46. *(b)* Ilango Adigal

- The epic described is **Silapaddigaram** (Silappatikaram), which was composed by **Ilango Adigal**, a Jain monk and the brother of Chera king Senguttuvan. The story revolves around **Kovalan**, a wealthy merchant, and his wife **Kannagi**.
- After being wrongfully accused of theft and executed, Kannagi proves his innocence, and in her rage, burns down the city of Madurai by invoking the power of justice. The epic intertwines themes of love, betrayal and justice, and also reflects Jain moral values, such as the emphasis on non-violence, and truth.

Thus, option (b) is the correct answer.

47. *(a)* Tolkappiyar focused on Tamil grammar and social history, while Thiruvalluvar wrote on ethics and polity.

- **Tolkappiyar** is credited with writing the **Tolkappiyam**, the oldest extant Tamil grammatical work. Tolkappiyam is a comprehensive treatise that not only deals with Tamil grammar and linguistic norms but also provides insights into the social, cultural, and ethical aspects of early Tamil society.
- **Thiruvalluvar** is the author of the **Tirukkural**, a work that focuses on ethics, politics and love. Thiruvalluvar's work is not a grammatical treatise but a guide on leading a virtuous and ethical life. Tirukkural is structured into three sections: Aram (virtue), Porul (wealth and polity) and Inbam (love).

Thus, option (a) is the correct answer.

48. *(d)* None

- **Statement 1 is correct: Tawarikh** were typically written in Persian and followed a systematic, and chronological approach to documenting events, rulers, and significant occurrences. Tawarikh often served as official records of the reigns of various rulers, providing insights into political, military and administrative activities.
- **Statement 2 is correct: Amir Khusro** (1253-1325) was a prolific Persian poet, musician and scholar associated with the Delhi Sultanate. Khusro is credited with developing a unique style of poetry called Sabq-i-Hindi (literally, 'the Indian style'), which blended Persian literary forms with Indian themes, imagery and expressions.
- **Statement 3 is correct:** The **Mahabharata** was translated into Persian during the reign of the Mughal Emperor **Akbar**. The translation, known as **Razmnama** (Book of War), was part of Akbar's project of translating important Hindu texts into Persian, **Abdual-Qadir Bada'uni** was involved in this translation project.

Thus, option (d) is the correct answer.

49. *(d)* 1, 2 and 3

- **Statement 1 is correct: Atharvaveda** was translated into Persian by **Haji Ibrahim Sirhindi** during the reign of Akbar. This translation was part of Akbar's larger initiative to make Hindu religious texts available in Persian.
- **Statement 2 is correct: Leelavati,** a renowned Sanskrit text on mathematics by **Bhaskaracharya,** was translated into Persian by Faizi, a scholar and poet who was also one of Akbar's Navaratnas (Nine Jewels).
- **Statement 3 is correct: Ramayana** was translated into Persian by **Abdul Rahim**

Khan-i-Khana, another of Akbar's Navaratnas. Rahim was a poet, scholar and noble who contributed significantly to the cultural, and literary life of Akbar's court.

Thus, option (d) is the correct answer.

50. *(b)* Only two

- **Statement 1 is correct: Bakhar** is a form of historical narrative that emerged in the Maratha region, primarily written in Marathi. These narratives documented the history of the Maratha Empire, its rulers, military campaigns and significant events.
- **Statement 2 is incorrect: Janamsakhis** are biographical accounts of the lives of the Sikh Gurus, especially Guru Nanak. However, they were not written in Sanskrit and Hindi; rather, they were primarily composed in **Punjabi,** and **Braj Bhasha.**
- **Statement 3 is correct: Prabandhas** are a genre of narrative literature written in **Sanskrit** and other regional languages, mainly during the medieval period. These texts are semi-historical and often combine factual events with legend and folklore.

Thus, option (b) is the correct answer.

51. *(b)* Only two

- **Pair 1 is correct:** As mentioned earlier, **Bakhar** is a historical narrative written in **Marathi,** chronicling the history of the Maratha Empire.
- **Pair 2 is correct: Buranji** is a historical chronicle written in **Assamese.** The Buranjis were court chronicles of the Ahom kings in Assam, documenting political, social and economic conditions.
- **Pair 3 is incorrect:** The term **Khayt** here might be a confusing with **Khyat,** which refers to historical chronicles written in **Marwari** in the region of Rajasthan, not in Persian.

Thus, option (b) is the correct answer.

52. *(d)* None

- **Statement 1 is correct: Qaseeda** is indeed a classical form of Arabic and Persian poetry that is typically a panegyric, or a poem of praise, often directed towards kings, nobles, or heroes. The form is known for its elaborate structure and use of ornate language.
- **Statement 2 is correct: Ginans** are indeed devotional hymns that are recited by the Nizari Ismaili Muslim community, particularly in South Asia. These hymns are part of the religious tradition of the Ismailis and are sung in various languages, including Gujarati, Sindhi, and Khojki.
- **Statement 3 is correct: Shahr Ashob** is a genre of **Urdu poetry** that literally means 'The City's Lament'. These poems emerged during the Mughal period and were particularly used to express the poets' anguish, and sorrow over social, political, and economic disruptions, such as the decline of cities or the moral decay of society.

Thus, option (d) is the correct answer.

53. *(d)* 1, 2 and 3

- **Statement 1 is correct: Rajatarangini,** which means 'The River of Kings', is written by the Kashmiri Brahmin scholar **Kalhan** in the 12th century CE. It provides a detailed, chronological account of the history of Kashmir composed in **Sanskrit** and consists of nearly **7,826 verses** divided into eight books or **Tarangas.**
- **Statement 2 is correct: Rajatarangini** is indeed considered the first historical text of its kind in India, focusing on the history of Kashmir with an emphasis on the socio-political and economic conditions of the region.
- **Statement 3 is correct: Kalhan's Rajatarangini** indeed describes the reigns of various kings of Kashmir, including the misrule of King **Kalash,** the son of King **Ananta Deva.** Kalash's reign is characterised by corruption, moral decline and administrative inefficiency, which Kalhan documents in his work.

Thus, option (d) is the correct answer.

54. *(a)* Rajatarangini was the first historical text to use a chronological approach in narrating the history of a region.

- **Rajatarangini** is distinct from other historical texts of its era due to its comprehensive and chronological approach to documenting history. Written by **Kalhan** in the 12th century CE, Rajatarangini is a unique work in

Indian historiography. It is composed in Sanskrit and presents a detailed history of the kings of Kashmir, tracing the lineage of rulers from mythical times to Kalhan's contemporary period.

- His work is structured in eight books or **Tarangas** (waves), each detailing different periods in Kashmir's history. Rajatarangini is written in verse, which is uncommon for historical texts that are typically composed in prose.

Thus, option (a) is the correct answer.

55. *(c)* Both 1 and 2

- **Pair 1 is correctly matched:** In Kalhan's Rajatarangini , Kalash's rule is described as a period of moral decline and corruption, which led to widespread suffering among the people. The common people were so impoverished that they were forced to subsist on rice and a wild vegetable called **utpala saka.**
- **Pair 2 is correctly matched:** Kalhan describes **Harsha** as a ruler who, despite his initial promise, became despotic. One of the reforms introduced by Harsha included a change in the royal attire, where he mandated a **general dress for the king,** which included a long coat.

Thus, option (c) is the correct answer.

56. *(d)* None

- **Statement 1 is incorrect: Amuktamalyada** was written by **Krishnadeva Raya,** not Jinasena. It is a significant work in Telugu literature that tells the story of **Andal,** a female Vaishnava saint and her deep devotion to Lord Vishnu.
- **Statement 2 is incorrect: Adi Pampa's Adipurana** is a Kannada version of the Sanskrit work by **Jinasena,** not by Krishnadeva Raya. Adipurana is a Jain text that narrates the life of **Rishabhanatha,** the first Tirthankara.

Thus, option (d) is the correct answer.

57. *(b)* Only two

- **Pair 1 is correctly matched:** Vachanas are **Shaivite Bhakti** poems written in **Kannada,** associated with the Virashaiva movement or Lingayatism, which was led by Basava and other saints like Allama Prabhu, and Akka Mahadevi in the 12th century.
- **Pair 2 is incorrectly matched: Bhakti Ratnavali** is not a historical chronicle but rather a compilation of devotional hymns or Bhakti poetry. It was composed by **Madhavadeva,** a key figure in the Bhakti movement in Assam and reflects the spiritual, and devotional ethos of the region.
- **Pair 3 is correctly matched: Kamba Ramayan** is the **Tamil** adaptation of the **Ramayana,** written by the poet **Kamban.** It is a significant literary work in Tamil literature, known for its poetic beauty and the way it integrates Tamil cultural elements into the traditional Ramayana narrative.

Thus, option (b) is the correct answer.

58. *(b)* Only two

- **Pair 1 is correctly matched: Abhanga** are devotional songs dedicated to the god **Vithoba** and are written in **Marathi.** Abhangas are a significant form of Bhakti literature in Marathi language, popularised by saints like Tukaram, Namdev,etc.
- **Pair 2 is incorrectly matched: Chandidas** was a medieval Bengali poet known for his **Vaishnavite** devotional songs. Therefore, Chandidasi poetry is in **Bengali,** not Tamil.
- **Pair 3 is correctly matched: Buranjis** are historical chronicles written in **Assamese.** They were originally composed in the Ahom language, later translated into Assamese and documented the history, and culture of Assam, particularly during the Ahom rule.

Thus, option (b) is the correct answer.

59. *(d)* None

- **Statement 1 is correct: Kitab-ul-Hind (or Tahqiq ma li'l-Hind)** was written by **Al-Biruni,** a renowned Persian scholar who accompanied Mahmud of Ghazni during his invasions of India. Al-Biruni's work is one of the earliest comprehensive studies of Indian society, culture, religion and science from an outsider's perspective.
- **Statement 2 is correct: Rehla** is the travelogue of **Ibn Battuta,** written during the reign of **Muhammad-bin-Tughlaq** and

served as a Qadi (judge) in his court. Rehla provides a vivid account of the socio-political and economic conditions of India at that time, including details on the administrative practices, the justice system, the market economy, and the prevalence of slavery.

- **Statement 3 is correct:** Arabic was the language of religious and scholarly works, **Persian** became the language of administration, literature, and culture under the Delhi Sultanate, and the Mughals. Therefore, Persian literature was far more widespread and influential in India than Arabic literature.

Thus, option (d) is the correct answer.

60. *(b)* Only two

- **Pair 1 is correctly matched:** In Sufi literature, Risalah often refers to treatises that focus on specific aspects of **Islamic mysticism, theology or practice.** These are concise, authoritative texts that discuss matters such as **Sufi ethics, practices or spiritual guidance.**
- **Pair 2 is correctly matched: Mansavi** (also spelled Masnavi) refers to **narrative poems** that are often spiritual in nature. A famous example is **Rumi's Masnavi,** which is a collection of Sufi spiritual teachings written in verse.
- **Pair 3 is incorrectly matched: Maktubat** refers to **collections of letters** written by Sufi saints to their disciples or peers, offering spiritual guidance, advice and teachings. They are not accounts of saints or their philosophies, but rather correspondences that convey personal insights and spiritual instruction.

Thus, option (b) is the correct answer.

61. *(c)* All three

- **Statement 1 is correct: Futuhaat-i-Firozshahi** is a text written by **Firoz Shah Tughlaq** in Persian. The text reflects Firoz Shah's concern with good governance, his benevolent attitude towards his subjects and his efforts to ensure justice, and social welfare.
- **Statement 2 is correct: Tuzuk-i-Babri,** also known as the **Baburnama,** is the autobiography of Babur, the founder of the Mughal Empire in India. Written in **Chagatai-Turkish,** Babur's mother tongue, the text is a detailed account of his life, including his early years, military campaigns and eventual conquest of India.
- **Statement 3 is correct: Amuktamalyada** is indeed a Telugu text written by **Krishnadeva Raya,** the famous Vijayanagara emperor. The text is an epic poem that describes the wedding of the god Vishnu (often referred to as Ranganatha) with Andal, a revered female Alvar saint known for her deep devotion to Vishnu.

Thus, option (c) is the correct answer.

62. *(b)* Only two

- **Pair 1 is correctly matched: Tuzuk-i-Jahangiri,** also known as the Jahangirnama, is the autobiography of Mughal Emperor **Jahangir,** written in **Persian.** The text provides a detailed account of Jahangir's reign, including his reflections on governance, his love for art and nature, his administration, and his military campaigns.
- **Pair 2 is incorrectly matched: The Humayun Nama** was written by **Gulbadan Begum,** Humayun's sister, in **Persian,** not Chagatai-Turkish. It is a biographical account of Emperor Humayun's life, documenting his struggles, achievements and the challenges he faced.
- **Pair 3 is correctly matched:** The **Badshah Nama** is a chronicle of the reign of Mughal Emperor **Shah Jahan,** written in **Persian** by **Abdul Hamid Lahori.** It provides detailed accounts of Shah Jahan's administration, military campaigns and architectural achievements.

Thus, option (b) is the correct answer.

Past Learning (Answers)

1 (c)	2 (c)	3 (c)	4 (d)	5 (b)	6 (a)	7 (c)	8 (c)	9 (a)	10 (d)
11 (c)	12 (b)	13 (d)	14 (d)	15 (b)	16 (a)	17 (b)	18 (b)	19 (b)	20 (b)
21 (d)	22 (d)	23 (a)	24 (d)	25 (c)					

CHAPTER 07 Dance

Assessment Round

Topic 1 : Conceptual Aspect

1. With reference to ancient Indian texts, consider the following statements:

1. The Natyashastra is the first formal mention of dance found in Indian literature.
2. The Natyashastra contains chapters on dance and drama.
3. The Natyashastra was written by Sage Nandikesvara.

How many of the statements given above is/are correct?

(a) Only one (b) Only two
(c) All three (d) None

2. Consider the following aspects of dance as per Natyashastra and Abhinaya Darpan:

1. Nritta involves abstract rhythmic movement with no message or story.
2. Nritta and Natya both depict pure dance steps without any narrative.
3. Natya is an amalgamation of dance, drama, and music, including aspects from various Vedas.

Which of the statements given above are correct?

(a) 1 and 3 only (b) 1, 2 and 3 only
(c) 1 and 2 only (d) 2 and 3 only

3. In the context of dance forms, which of the following elements relate to the dance movements in Indian classical dance?

1. Mudra refers to the hand gestures used during the dance.
2. Chari involves both hand and leg movements together.
3. Karna refers to specific dance poses created by the position of hands and legs together.

Select the correct answer using the codes given below:

(a) 1, 2 and 3 (b) 1 only
(c) 2 and 3 only (d) 1 and 3 only

4. Consider the following pairs of conceptual aspects of drama:

1.	Characters	Describe various attributes of characters, including appearance and status.
2.	Bhava	Represents the aesthetic experience of the audience.
3.	Rasa	Reveals the core characteristics of drama, typically focusing on emotions.

How many pairs given above is/are not correctly matched?

(a) Only one pair (b) Only two pairs
(c) All three pairs (d) None

5. Which of the following best describes the difference between the dance forms Tandava and Lasya?

(a) Tandava represents graceful rhythmic movements, while Lasya is violent and forceful.
(b) Tandava has a vigorous masculine aspect, whereas Lasya is gentle, calm, and graceful.
(c) Tandava is associated with Parvati, and Lasya is associated with Shiva.
(d) There is no significant difference between the two.

6. Regarding the Sangeet Natak Academy, consider the following statements:

1. It was created by a resolution of the Ministry of Culture in 1952.
2. The Academy supervises institutions and projects of national importance related to performing arts.
3. It has an autonomous status under the Ministry of Education.

Which of the statements given above are correct?

(a) 1 and 2 only
(b) 2 and 3 only
(c) 1 and 3 only
(d) 1, 2 and 3

7. How do you distinguish between Agama Nartanam and Carnatakam dance forms?

1. Agama Nartanam is performed under royal patronage, while Carnatakam is performed in temple rituals.
2. Agama Nartanam involves rituals, while Carnatakam is associated with ceremonial occasions only.

Which of the statements given above is/are not correct?

(a) 1 only
(b) 2 only
(c) Both 1 and 2
(d) Neither 1 nor 2

Topic 2 : Classical Dance Forms

8. With reference to Bharatanatyam, consider the following statements:

1. Bharatanatyam evolved as a significant aspect of rituals in temples.
2. The theoretical base of Bharatanatyam can be traced back to Kuchipudi.
3. Tanjore Quartet played a crucial role in defining the elements of Bharatanatyam.

How many of the statements given above is/are correct?

(a) Only one
(b) Only two
(c) All three
(d) None

9. Consider the following elements of Bharatanatyam:

1. Alarippu 2. Shabdam
3. Jatiswaram 4. Tillana

Which of the above are the correct elements of Bharatanatyam?

(a) 1 and 2 only (b) 1, 2 and 3 only
(c) 1, 2, 3 and 4 (d) 2 and 4 only

10. Consider the following statements about a classical dance form:

1. It is characterised by graceful swaying body movements with no abrupt jerks.
2. The dancers wear a white or off-white saree with golden brocade.
3. It is performed in symphony with Carnatic music.

Identify the dance form based on the given statements.

(a) Kathak (b) Mohiniyattam
(c) Odissi (d) Sattriya

11. Regarding Kathakali, consider the following statements:

1. Kathakali is also known as the 'Ballad of the East'.
2. The language used in Kathakali songs is Manipravalam.
3. It is usually performed by a female troupe.

Which of the statements given above are correct?

(a) 1 and 2 only
(b) 2 and 3 only
(c) 1 and 3 only
(d) 1, 2 and 3

12. With reference to Kathakali, consider the following statements:

1. It is a dance form native to Kerala.
2. Characters in Kathakali use elaborate facial makeup and costumes.
3. The dance emphasises the representation of Rasas through the movement of eyes and eyebrows.

How many of the statements given above is/are correct?

(a) Only one (b) Only two
(c) All three (d) None

13. Regarding Kuchipudi, consider the following statements:

1. Kuchipudi is named after a village in Andhra Pradesh.
2. It developed as a result of the Bhakti movement.
3. It is performed in both Tamil and Telugu languages.

Which of the statements given above are correct?

(a) 1 and 2 only (b) 2 and 3 only
(c) 1 and 3 only (d) 1, 2 and 3

14. With reference to Kuchipudi, consider the following statements:

1. It involves both dance and drama elements.
2. Kuchipudi performers often combine the role of a singer into themselves.
3. The dance form includes demonstrative eye movements and fast footwork.

How many of the statements given above is/are not correct?

(a) Only one (b) Only two
(c) All three (d) None

15. With reference to Kathak, consider the following statements:

1. Kathak can trace its roots to Ras Leela of Brajbhumi.
2. It developed under the influence of Persian dressing and style.
3. Kathak is known for its vigorous footwork and elaborate facial expressions.

How many of the statements given above is/are correct?

(a) Only one (b) Only two
(c) All three (d) None

16. Consider the following Gharanas of Kathak:

1. Lucknow
2. Jaipur
3. Banaras

Which of the above Gharanas are known for their emphasis on expression and grace?

(a) 1 only
(b) 1 and 3 only
(c) 2 and 3 only
(d) 1, 2 and 3

17. Consider the following statements about a classical dance form:

1. It uses Thaat, Jugalbandi, and Tarana as key elements.
2. It is performed in both traditional male and female costumes, including ghungroos.
3. The music associated with this dance form is Dhrupad.

Identify the dance form based on the given statements.

(a) Kathak (b) Bharatnatyam
(c) Odissi (d) Manipuri

18. With reference to Odissi, consider the following statements:

1. Odissi is derived from the ancient dance form Odra Nritya.
2. It primarily involves symmetric body postures called Bhanga.
3. The dance form is associated with Vaishnavism.

How many of the statements given above is/are not correct?

(a) Only one (b) Only two
(c) All three (d) None

19. Consider the following features of Odissi:

1. It uses instruments like Pakhawaj and cymbals.
2. The dance involves themes from Vaishnavism.
3. It includes elements of both Nritta and Abhinaya.

Which of the above are the correct elements of Odissi?

(a) 1 and 2 only (b) 2 and 3 only
(d) 1 and 3 only (c) 1, 2 and 3

20. Identify the dance form based on the following statements:

1. The dance is performed as a solo female performance.
2. It is characterised by the swaying movements of the body.
3. The costume includes a white saree with golden brocade.

Select the correct option from below:

(a) Manipuri (b) Kathak
(c) Mohiniyattam (d) Odissi

21. In the context of Indian dance forms, which of the following transactions or actions will be recorded as an element in Manipuri dance?

1. Use of Nagabhadra mudra
2. Performance of Rasleela Sankirtan
3. Costume involving peacock feathers for male dancers

Select the correct answer using the codes given below:

(a) 1 only (b) 1 and 3 only
(c) 2 and 3 only (d) 1, 2 and 3

22. With reference to Sattriya, consider the following statements:

1. Sattriya includes elements of Nritta, Natya, and Nritya.
2. It is performed by monks known as 'Bhokots'.
3. Sattriya was founded in the medieval period by the Bhakti saint Sankaradev.

How many of the statements given above is/are correct?

(a) Only one (b) Only two
(c) All three (d) None

23. With reference to Indian classical dance forms, consider the following statements:

1. Bharatanatyam is often performed in the Carnatic music style.
2. Kathakali primarily uses Manipravalam as the language for its songs.
3. Kuchipudi dancers traditionally wear a crown known as Tahiya.

How many of the statements given above is/are correct?

(a) Only one (b) Only two
(c) All three (d) None

24. Consider the following dance forms:

1. Kathak 2. Manipuri
3. Mohiniyattam 4. Odissi

Which of the above are performed predominantly by female dancers?

(a) 1 and 2 only
(b) 3 and 4 only
(c) 2 and 4 only
(d) 1, 2, 3 and 4

25. Regarding the dance form Sattriya, consider the following statements:

1. Sattriya was propagated through the Bhakti movement.
2. The themes of Sattriya are primarily based on the stories of Radha-Krishna.
3. It was traditionally performed in open-air spaces after sunset.

Which of the statements given above are correct?

(a) 1 and 2 only (b) 2 and 3 only
(c) 1 and 3 only (d) 1, 2 and 3

26. Match the following Indian classical dance forms with their associated famous personalities:

	Dance Form		Famous Personality
A.	Bharatanatyam	1.	Rukmini Devi Arundale
B.	Kathakali	2.	Guru Kunchu Kurup
C.	Odissi	3.	Guru Kelucharan Mohapatra
D.	Manipuri	4.	Guru Singhajit Singh

Select the correct match using the codes given below:

(a) A-1, B-2, C-3, D-4
(b) A-2, B-3, C-1, D-4
(c) A-1, B-3, C-2, D-4
(d) A-3, B-1, C-2, D-4

27. Match the following Indian classical dance forms with the states they are traditionally associated with:

	Dance Form		State
A.	Kathak	1.	Uttar Pradesh
B.	Mohiniyattam	2.	Kerala
C.	Sattriya	3.	Assam
D.	Bharatanatyam	4.	Tamil Nadu

Select the correct match using the codes given below:

(a) A-1, B-2, C-3, D-4
(b) A-2, B-3, C-1, D-4
(c) A-3, B-4, C-1, D-2
(d) A-4, B-1, C-2, D-3

28. Match the following Indian classical dance forms with the unique instruments associated with them:

	Dance Form		Unique Instrument
A.	Kathak	1.	Tabla
B.	Odissi	2.	Pakhawaj
C.	Manipuri	3.	Pena
D.	Bharatanatyam	4.	Mridangam

Select the correct match using the codes given below:
(a) A-1, B-2, C-3, D-4
(b) A-2, B-3, C-4, D-1
(c) A-3, B-4, C-1, D-2
(d) A-4, B-1, C-2, D-3

Topic 3 : Folk Dances

29. Identify the folk dance based on the following statements:
1. It is performed with a trident and involves vigorous movements symbolising destruction.
2. The dance is associated with the worship of Lord Shiva and is performed during festivals like Mahashivratri.
3. The performers often depict the mythological story of Veerabhadra, an incarnation of Lord Shiva.
4. This dance is associated with the state of Andhra Pradesh.

Choose the correct option from the below:
(a) Veeranatyam (b) Raut Nacha
(c) Ka Shad Suk (d) Bihu

30. Identify the folk dance based on the following statements:
1. It is performed by the Yadav (cowherd) community during the Diwali festival.
2. The dance involves men carrying sticks and performing synchronised movements to the beats of traditional music.
3. It is a form of worship to honour Lord Krishna, the protector of cattle.
4. This dance is associated with the state of Chhattisgarh.

Choose the correct option from the below:
(a) Veeranatyam
(b) Raut Nacha
(c) Gethinglim
(d) Charkula

31. With reference to the folk dances of India, consider the following statements:
1. Burrakatha is a narrative dance form from Andhra Pradesh.
2. Dumhal is performed by the Wattal tribe of Jammu and Kashmir.
3. Kaikottikali is a temple dance performed in Kerala during Onam.

How many of the statements given above is/are incorrect?
(a) Only one
(b) Only two
(c) All three
(d) None

32. With reference to the folk dances of India, consider the following statements:
1. Ghoomar is a dance associated with the women of the Bhil tribe in Rajasthan.
2. Bhangra is the male counterpart of Giddha, both popular in Punjab.
3. Cheraw is a traditional dance performed in Nagaland.

How many of the statements given above is/are correct?
(a) Only one (b) Only two
(c) All three (d) None

33. With reference to the folk dances of India, consider the following statements:
1. Butta Bommalu involves dancers wearing masks resembling toy-like shapes.
2. Paika is a martial dance form from Odisha.
3. Jawara is a harvest dance from Madhya Pradesh.

How many of the statements given above is/are correct?
(a) Only one
(b) Only two
(c) All three
(d) None

34. Consider the following folk dances and their respective states:

1.	Dumhal	Jammu and Kashmir
2.	Raut Naach	Chhattisgarh
3.	Fugdi	Goa

How many of the pairs given above is/are correctly matched?

(a) Only one (b) Only two
(c) All three (d) None

35. Consider the following folk dances and their respective regions:

1.	Mayilattam	Kerala
2.	Chakyar Koothu	Tamil Nadu
3.	Pata Kunitha	Karnataka

How many of the pairs given above is/are incorrectly matched?

(a) Only one (b) Only two
(c) All three (d) None

36. Identify the folk dance based on the following statements:

1. This is a harvest dance performed by the Jaintia tribe.
2. The dance involves rhythmic movements accompanied by the beats of traditional drums.
3. It is performed during the Shad Suk Mynsiem festival, celebrating the harvest and the arrival of spring.
4. This dance is associated with the state of Meghalaya.

Choose the correct option from the below:

(a) Ka Shad Suk Mynsiem
(b) Rauf
(c) Veeranatyam
(d) Koodiyattam

37. Consider the following pairs:

1.	Gaur Maria	Chhattisgarh
2.	Bhootha Aradhane	Karnataka
3.	Alkap	West Bengal

Which of the above pairs are correctly matched?

(a) 1 and 2 only (b) 2 and 3 only
(c) 1 and 3 only (d) 1, 2 and 3

38. In the context of Indian folk dances, which of the following are ritualistic?

1.	Gaur Maria	Chhattisgarh
2.	Padayani	Kerala
3.	Thang Ta	Manipur

Select the correct answer using the codes given below:

(a) 1 only (b) 1 and 2 only
(c) 2 and 3 only (d) 1, 2 and 3

39. Identify the folk dance based on the following statements:

1. This dance is performed by the women of the Angami tribe during festivals.
2. It involves slow, graceful movements and is accompanied by traditional songs.
3. The dance is a celebration of the rich cultural heritage of the Angami community.
4. This dance is associated with the state of Nagaland.

Choose the correct option from the below:

(a) Gethinglim (b) Raut Nacha
(c) Veeranatyam (d) Bihu

40. In the context of Indian dance forms, which of the following are performed during festivals or celebrations?

1.	Fugdi	Goa during Ganesh Chaturthi
2.	Kaikottikali	Kerala during Onam festival
3.	Dumhal	Jammu and Kashmir on ceremonial days

Select the correct answer using the codes given below:

(a) 1 and 2 only (b) 2 and 3 only
(c) 1, 2 and 3 (d) None

41. Identify the state based on the following folk dances:

1. Burrakatha
2. Butta Bommalu
3. Kolatam

Which of the following states does this list of dances belong to?

(a) Tamil Nadu (b) Andhra Pradesh
(c) Karnataka (d) Telangana

42. Identify the region based on the following folk dances:

1. Padayani
2. Kolkali
3. Kaikottikali

Which state is known for these dances?

(a) Tamil Nadu
(b) Kerala
(c) Karnataka
(d) Andhra Pradesh

43. Identify the folk dance based on the following statements:

1. This is a harvest dance that is performed to celebrate the Assamese New Year, Bohag Bihu.
2. The dance is characterised by brisk steps, rapid hand movements, and rhythmic drumming.
3. It is performed by both men and women, often in open fields, celebrating the joy of the harvest.
4. This dance is associated with the state of Assam.

Choose the correct option from the below:

(a) Bihu
(b) Charkula
(c) Yakshagana
(d) Ka Shad Suk Mynsiem

44. Identify the folk dance based on the following statements:

1. This dance is performed with a large, circular wooden contraption that is balanced on the head.
2. It symbolises the dance of Radha as she welcomes Lord Krishna to her village.
3. The dance is typically performed during the festival of Holi in the Braj region.
4. This dance is associated with the state of Uttar Pradesh.

Choose the correct option from the below:

(a) Charkula (b) Rauf
(c) Bihu (d) Gethinglim

45. Identify the region based on the following dances:

1. Bhootha Aradhane
2. Pata Kunitha
3. Yakshagana

Which state is associated with these folk dances?

(a) Andhra Pradesh
(b) Karnataka
(c) Tamil Nadu
(d) Kerala

46. Identify the region based on the following traditional dances:

1. Raut Naach
2. Panthi
3. Karma Naach

Which state is known for these dances?

(a) Odisha
(b) Chhattisgarh
(c) Jharkhand
(d) Madhya Pradesh

47. Identify the folk dance based on the following statements:

1. It is one of the oldest surviving Sanskrit theatre traditions in India.
2. The dance form includes a combination of dance, drama, and music, often depicting stories from Hindu epics.
3. The performance involves elaborate costumes, makeup and precise facial expressions (Abhinaya).
4. This dance is associated with the state of Kerala.

Choose the correct option from the below:

(a) Koodiyattam (b) Yakshagana
(c) Bihu (d) Veeranatyam

OMR SHEET

Assessment Round

1	a	b	c	d	31	a	b	c	d	61	a	b	c	d	91	a	b	c	d
2	a	b	c	d	32	a	b	c	d	62	a	b	c	d	92	a	b	c	d
3	a	b	c	d	33	a	b	c	d	63	a	b	c	d	93	a	b	c	d
4	a	b	c	d	34	a	b	c	d	64	a	b	c	d	94	a	b	c	d
5	a	b	c	d	35	a	b	c	d	65	a	b	c	d	95	a	b	c	d
6	a	b	c	d	36	a	b	c	d	66	a	b	c	d	96	a	b	c	d
7	a	b	c	d	37	a	b	c	d	67	a	b	c	d	97	a	b	c	d
8	a	b	c	d	38	a	b	c	d	68	a	b	c	d	98	a	b	c	d
9	a	b	c	d	39	a	b	c	d	69	a	b	c	d	99	a	b	c	d
10	a	b	c	d	40	a	b	c	d	70	a	b	c	d	100	a	b	c	d
11	a	b	c	d	41	a	b	c	d	71	a	b	c	d	101	a	b	c	d
12	a	b	c	d	42	a	b	c	d	72	a	b	c	d	102	a	b	c	d
13	a	b	c	d	43	a	b	c	d	73	a	b	c	d	103	a	b	c	d
14	a	b	c	d	44	a	b	c	d	74	a	b	c	d	104	a	b	c	d
15	a	b	c	d	45	a	b	c	d	75	a	b	c	d	105	a	b	c	d
16	a	b	c	d	46	a	b	c	d	76	a	b	c	d	106	a	b	c	d
17	a	b	c	d	47	a	b	c	d	77	a	b	c	d	107	a	b	c	d
18	a	b	c	d	48	a	b	c	d	78	a	b	c	d	108	a	b	c	d
19	a	b	c	d	49	a	b	c	d	79	a	b	c	d	109	a	b	c	d
20	a	b	c	d	50	a	b	c	d	80	a	b	c	d	110	a	b	c	d
21	a	b	c	d	51	a	b	c	d	81	a	b	c	d	111	a	b	c	d
22	a	b	c	d	52	a	b	c	d	82	a	b	c	d	112	a	b	c	d
23	a	b	c	d	53	a	b	c	d	83	a	b	c	d	113	a	b	c	d
24	a	b	c	d	54	a	b	c	d	84	a	b	c	d	114	a	b	c	d
25	a	b	c	d	55	a	b	c	d	85	a	b	c	d	115	a	b	c	d
26	a	b	c	d	56	a	b	c	d	86	a	b	c	d	116	a	b	c	d
27	a	b	c	d	57	a	b	c	d	87	a	b	c	d	117	a	b	c	d
28	a	b	c	d	58	a	b	c	d	88	a	b	c	d	118	a	b	c	d
29	a	b	c	d	59	a	b	c	d	89	a	b	c	d	119	a	b	c	d
30	a	b	c	d	60	a	b	c	d	90	a	b	c	d	120	a	b	c	d

Calculate Your Score

Correct (✓)	
Incorrect (✓)	
Unattempted	
Total Score	
Accuracy (%)	

Reasons for Incorrect Answers?

1. Lack of Knowledge/Existing Source Insufficient	
2. Lack of Multiple Revision	
3. Common Sense Mistakes	

Note :

1. Calculate total score as correct answers carry 2 marks each 1/3rd marks will deducted for **Incorrect** Answers.
2. Calculate Accuracy (%) by dividing the number of correct answers to the total number of attempted questions.

Past Learning

1. Consider the following pairs: **(2018)**

Tradition	State
1. Chapchar Kut festival	Mizoram
2. Khongjom Parba ballad	Manipur
3. Thang-Ta dance	Sikkim

Which of the pairs given above is/are correct?

(a) 1 only (b) 1 and 2
(c) 3 only (d) 2 and 3

2. With reference to Manipuri Sankirtana, consider the following statements: **(2017)**

1. It is a song and dance performance.
2. Cymbals are the only musical instruments used in the performance.
3. It is performed to narrate the life and deeds of Lord Krishna.

Which of the statements given above is/are correct?

(a) 1, 2 and 3 (b) 1 and 3 only
(c) 2 and 3 only (d) 1 only

3. With reference to the famous Sattriya dance, consider the following statements: **(2014)**

1. Sattriya is a combination of music, dance and drama.
2. It is a centuries-old living tradition of Vaishnavites of Assam.
3. It is based on classical Ragas and Talas of devotional songs composed by Tulsidas, Kabir and Mirabai.

Which of the statements given above is/are correct?

(a) 1 only (b) 1 and 2 only
(c) 2 and 3 only (d) 1, 2 and 3

4. Consider the following pairs: **(2014)**

1. Garba	Gujarat
2. Mohiniyattam	Odisha
3. Yakshagana	Karnataka

Which of the pairs given above is/are correctly matched?

(a) 1 only (b) 2 and 3 only
(c) 1 and 3 only (d) 1, 2 and 3

5. In the context of the cultural history of India, a pose in dance and dramatics called 'Tribhanga' has been a favourite of Indian artists from ancient times till today. Which one of the following statements best describes this pose? **(2013)**

(a) One leg is bent and the body is slightly but oppositely curved at the waist and neck
(b) Facial expressions, hand gestures, and make-up are combined to symbolise certain epic or historic characters
(c) Movements of body, face, and hands are used to express oneself or to tell a story
(d) A little smile, slightly curved waist, and certain hand gestures are emphasised to express feelings of love or eroticism

6. How do you distinguish between Kuchipudi and Bharatanatyam dances? **(2012)**

1. Dancers occasionally speaking dialogues is found in Kuchipudi dance but not in Bharatanatyam.
2. Dancing on the brass plate by keeping the feet on its edges is a feature of Bharatanatyam but Kuchipudi dance does not have such a form of movement.

Which of the statements given above is/are correct?

(a) 1 only (b) 2 only
(c) Both 1 and 2 (d) Neither 1 nor 2

7. Match List I with List II and select the correct answer using the codes given below the lists. **(2009)**

List I (Famous Persons)	List II (Well-Known as)
A. Amrita Shergil	1. Dancer
B. Bhimsen Joshi	2. Painter
C. Rukmini Devi Arundale	3. Poet
D. Suryakant Tripathi 'Nirala'	4. Singer

Codes

	A	B	C	D
(a)	2	1	4	3
(b)	2	4	1	3
(c)	3	1	4	2
(d)	3	4	1	2

8. Bimbavati Devi is a well-known dancer of which type of dance? **(2008)**
(a) Manipuri (b) Bharatanatyam
(c) Kuchipudi (d) Odissi

9. Match List I with List II and select the correct answer by using the codes given below the lists. **(2007)**

List I (Person)	**List II** (Known as)
A. Bhajan Sopori	1. Bharatnatyam dancer
B. Birju Maharaj	2. Exponent of Santoor
C. Priyadarshini Govind	3. Mridangam maestro
D. Gopala Krishnan	4. Kathak dancer

Codes

	A	B	C	D
(a)	2	1	4	3
(b)	3	1	4	2
(c)	2	4	1	3
(d)	3	4	1	2

10. Who among the following was presented with the Sangeet Natak Akademi Ratna Award, in 2005 for her lifetime achievement in dance? **(2006)**
(a) Chandralekha
(b) Tanjavur Balasaraswati
(c) Uma Sharma
(d) Yamini Krishnamurthy

11. Consider the following statements regarding the Chakiarkoothu form of dance. **(2000)**
1. It is performed by the Chakiar caste.
2. It cannot be traditionally witnessed by the higher caste Hindus.
3. Mizhavu is the accompanying instrument.
4. Its theatre form is called Koothambalam.

Which of these statements are correct?
(a) 1, 3 and 4
(b) 1, 2 and 3
(c) 2, 3 and 4
(d) 1, 2 and 4

12. Which one of the following pairs of folk dance forms and states is not correctly matched? **(1999)**

(a)	Korku	Maharashtra
(b)	Jhumar	Haryana
(c)	Thali	Himachal Pradesh
(d)	Mukna	Manipur

13. Which one of the following dances involves solo performance? **(1997)**
(a) Bharatanatyam
(b) Kuchipudi
(c) Mohiniyattam
(d) Odissi

Detailed Solutions

Assessment Round

1. *(b)* Only two

- **Statement 1 is correct:** The **Natyashastra**, attributed to the **sage Bharata Muni**, is considered the earliest and most comprehensive treatise on performing arts, particularly on dance, music and drama. This text dates back to somewhere between 200 BCE and 200 CE, though the exact period is debated among scholars.
- **Statement 2 is correct:** The Natyashastra is a voluminous text divided into 36 chapters, covering various aspects of theatre, including dance and drama. The text provides detailed guidance on the execution of gestures, emotions (Bhava), and the resultant aesthetic experience (Rasa).
- **Statement 3 is incorrect:** Natyashastra is an ancient text on the performing arts, it was composed by **Bharata Muni**, not by Sage Nandikesvara. **Nandikesvara** is associated with another important text on dance called **Abhinaya Darpan**, which focuses specifically on the art of expression (Abhinaya) in dance.

Thus, option (b) is the correct answer.

2. *(a)* 1 and 3 only

- **Statement 1 is correct:** Nritta is a term used in Indian classical dance that refers **to pure dance movements.** It is characterised by intricate footwork, rhythmic sequences, and aesthetic beauty without any intended meaning or storyline.
- **Statement 2 is incorrect:** Nritta focuses on **pure dance movements devoid of storytelling, Natya** is a more comprehensive form that combines dance with drama. Natya encompasses the enactment of stories, often from mythology or religious texts, and involves characters, dialogue, and music.
- **Statement 3 is correct:** Natya is a **synthesis of dance (Nritta), dramatic expression (Abhinaya), and music (Sangita).** The Vedic influence is evident in the components of Natya: the Rigveda contributes the **pathya** (words), the Yajurveda provides **Abhinaya (gestures)**, the Samaveda offers the **Gita (music)**, and the Atharvaveda brings in the rasa (aesthetic experience).

Thus, option (a) is the correct answer.

3. *(d)* 1 and 3 only

- **Statement 1 is correct: Mudras** are **symbolic hand gestures** that play a crucial role in Indian classical dance. They are used to convey specific meanings, emotions, or aspects of storytelling.
- **Statement 2 is incorrect:** Chari specifically refers to the **movements of the feet in dance.** These movements are classified into various types based on how the feet are positioned and moved. Chari is crucial in creating rhythm and grace in a dance performance.
- **Statement 3 is correct:** Karna refers to **complex dance poses where the hands and legs are coordinated** to create specific shapes or stances. The Natyashastra describes 108 Karnas, which are not just physical poses but are also imbued with symbolic meaning.

Thus, option (d) is the correct answer.

4. *(a)* Only one pair

- **Pair 1 is correctly matched:** In the context of drama, characters are defined by various attributes such as **appearance, status, role, and personality.** The Natya Shastra provides detailed guidance on how characters should be portrayed to convey their essence effectively to the audience.
- **Pair 2 is incorrectly matched:** Bhava refers to the **emotions or feelings expressed** by the characters in a performance, which contribute to the audience's emotional experience but are not themselves the aesthetic experience. The Bhava is conveyed through various means such as facial expressions, body language, and dialogue delivery, and it is intended to evoke a specific response from the audience.

- **Pair 3 is incorrectly matched:** Rasa is not simply about the core characteristics of drama but about the **resultant aesthetic experience that the audience feels.** Rasa is the ultimate goal of any artistic performance, as it represents the emotional resonance that a well-executed drama or dance leaves with the audience.

Thus, option (a) is the correct answer.

5. *(b)* Tandava has a vigorous masculine aspect, whereas Lasya is gentle, calm, and graceful.

- **Tandava** is traditionally characterised by its forceful, vigorous, and masculine movements, often associated with the powerful and destructive aspects of Lord Shiva. In contrast, Lasya represents **soft, graceful, and feminine movements,** symbolising beauty, love, and tenderness, often associated with Goddess Parvati.
- **Tandav** is characterised by its powerful and **masculine energy.** Lasya, on the other hand, is the **feminine counterpart** of Tandava, often associated with **Parvati,** who is **Shiva's consort.** Lasya embodies the softer, gentler aspects of dance, representing grace, beauty, and the creative force.

Thus, option (b) is the correct answer.

6. *(a)* 1 and 2 only

- **Statement 1 is correct:** The **Sangeet Natak Academy,** also known as the National Academy of Music, Dance, and Drama, was **established in 1952** by a resolution of the then Ministry of Education, which later became the Ministry of Culture. The Academy was created to promote and preserve the diverse cultural heritage of India in the fields of music, dance, and drama.
- **Statement 2 is correct:** The Academy has a significant role in the preservation and promotion of India's rich cultural traditions. It supervises and supports various institutions of national importance, such as the National School of Drama, the Jawaharlal Nehru Manipur Dance Academy, and the Kathak Kendra in New Delhi.
- **Statement (3) is incorrect:** While it was initially established **under the Ministry of Education, it now functions as an autonomous body** under the Ministry of Culture. The Academy's autonomous status allows it to operate with a degree of independence, essential for fostering creativity and innovation in the arts.

Thus, option (a) is the correct answer.

7. *(c)* Both 1 and 2

- **Statement 1 is incorrect:** Agama Nartanam refers to the dance forms performed **in the sanctum sanctorum of temples during rituals and ceremonies.** Carnatakam, on the other hand, refers to dances performed under royal patronage.
- **Statement 2 is incorrect:** Agama Nartanam is associated with rituals, but Carnatakam is **not merely associated with ceremonial occasions;** it is more closely linked with **performances in royal courts.**

Thus, option (c) is the correct answer.

8. *(b)* Only two

- **Statement 1 is correct:** Bharatanatyam is one of the oldest classical dance forms of India, originating in the **temples of Tamil Nadu.** It was historically performed by **Devadasis,** who were dedicated to serving the deities through dance.
- **Statement 2 is incorrect:** Bharatanatyam's theoretical foundation is **rooted in the Natyashastra,** an ancient treatise on performing arts attributed to the **sage Bharata Muni.** Kuchipudi, on the other hand, developed in **Andhra Pradesh** and has its own unique set of traditions and practices.
- **Statement 3 is correct:** The **Tanjore Quartet,** composed of four brothers-**Chinniah, Ponniah, Sivanandam, and Vadivelu**-are credited with **refining and structuring Bharatanatyam** into its modern form. They were crucial in establishing the repertoire and pedagogical methods that are still followed by Bharatanatyam practitioners today.

Thus, option (b) is the correct answer.

9. (c) 1, 2, 3 and 4

- **Option 1 is correct:** Alarippu is the opening item in a Bharatanatyam recital. The term **Alarippu** means **flowering bud** and the dance symbolises the awakening of the body and mind. Alarippu is performed with rhythmic syllables called **Solkattu** and it combines facial expressions, hand gestures (mudras), and footwork in a simple, rhythmic pattern.

- **Option 2 is correct: Shabdam** is a more expressive piece that **combines dance and narrative.** It includes lyrics that praise a deity or a king and the dancer interprets these lyrics through a combination of Abhinaya (expressive gestures) and dance.
- **Option 3 is correct: Jatiswaram** is another non-narrative piece, focusing on the technical aspects of dance. It is characterised by intricate **footwork, complex rhythms and precise movements.** While it does not convey a story, it is crucial for demonstrating the dancer's skill and command over the art form.
- **Option 4 is correct: Tilana** is the concluding piece of a Bharatanatyam performance and is known for its **lively and rhythmic nature.** Tillana is typically fast-paced and involves intricate footwork, brisk movements, and dynamic poses.

Thus, option (c) is the correct answer.

10. *(b)* The dance form described here is **Mohiniyattam,** which originates from Kerala. This dance is named after the enchantress avatar of Lord Vishnu, Mohini. Mohiniyattam is known for smooth, flowing, and feminine movements, with an emphasis on **Lasya (grace) and Bhava (emotion) and avoiding any abrupt or jerky movements.**

- The traditional attire for Mohiniyattam dancers is a **white or off-white saree** with a broad golden border, known as **Kasavu.** The simplicity of the costume is meant to highlight the **dancer's expressions** and movements rather than distract with **elaborate ornamentation.**
- Mohiniyattam is performed in **Carnatic music,** which provides the rhythmic and melodic foundation for the dance, and the dancer's movements are closely aligned with the **tala (rhythm) and raga (melody) of the music.**

Thus, option (b) is the correct answer.

11. *(a)* 1 and 2 only

- **Statement 1 is correct: Kathakali,** a classical dance-drama form from **Kerala,** is often referred to as the **Ballad of the East** because of its elaborate and dramatic storytelling, which is similar to the ballad traditions in the West.
- **Statement 2 is correct: Manipravalam,** a blend of Sanskrit and Malayalam, is the language used in the lyrics of Kathakali songs. This language was historically used in literary works and religious texts in Kerala, making it suitable for Kathakali, which often draws on **religious and mythological themes.**
- **Statement 3 is incorrect:** Traditionally, Kathakali is performed by male artists, even in female roles. While there are **female Kathakali artists today, the tradition remains predominantly male,** particularly in its classical form.

Thus, option (a) is the correct answer.

12. *(c)* All three

- **Statement 1 is correct: Kathakali** is a classical dance-drama that originated in the state of **Kerala,** India. It is one of the most renowned cultural traditions of Kerala and is known for its elaborate performances that combine dance, drama, and music.
- **Statement 2 is correct:** One of the most distinctive features of Kathakali is its elaborate facial makeup and costumes. The makeup and costumes are designed to **exaggerate the facial expressions and movements of the dancers,** which is essential for conveying the emotions and narrative of the performance.
- **Statement 3 is correct:** Kathakali places significant emphasis on the **representation of Rasas, or emotions,** which are conveyed through the dancer's facial expressions and body movements. The eyes and eyebrows play a crucial role in this, with specific movements (**known as Nayanabhinaya**) used to express different emotions such as **anger, fear, love, etc.**

Thus, option (c) is the correct answer.

13. *(a)* 1 and 2 only

- **Statement 1 is correct: Kuchipudi** is named after the **village of Kuchipudi** in the Krishna district of **Andhra Pradesh**, where this classical dance form originated. Kuchipudi is known for its graceful movements, expressive storytelling, and dramatic elements.
- **Statement 2 is correct**: Kuchipudi, like many other classical dance forms in India, was **influenced by the Bhakti movement**, which emphasised devotion to a personal god and the expression of this devotion through art.
- **Statement 3 is incorrect**: Kuchipudi is **traditionally performed in Telugu,** the language of Andhra Pradesh. While there may be instances where Kuchipudi is performed in other languages for specific audiences, it is primarily associated **with Telugu.**

Thus, option (a) is the correct answer.

14. (d) None

- **Statement 1 is correct**: Kuchipudi is a dance-drama tradition that blends classical dance with theatrical elements. The dance is highly expressive, using facial expressions (Abhinaya) to convey emotions and tell stories.
- **Statement 2 is correct:** In Kuchipudi, it is not uncommon for performers to sing while dancing, especially in solo performances where the dancer must portray multiple **characters and narrate the story.** This unique feature distinguishes **Kuchipudi** from other classical dance forms where singing is typically done by accompanying musicians.
- **Statement 3 is correct**: Kuchipudi often includes **intricate patterns of footwork** that are executed **in sync with the rhythm** of the accompanying music. The eye movements are particularly important in conveying emotions and connecting with the audience, as they enhance the narrative aspect of the performance.

Thus, option (d) is the correct answer.

15. *(b)* Only two

- **Statement 1 is correct**: Kathak is one of the eight classical dance forms of India, with roots that trace back to the ancient **Ras Leela performances of Brajbhumi**, which depicted the life and exploits of Lord Krishna. These performances were originally devotional, celebrating the divine love between Krishna and the Gopis (milkmaids).
- **Statement 2 is correct**: During the Mughal era, Kathak evolved significantly under Persian and Central Asian influences. The dance form adapted elements of Persian culture, including its intricate costumes, the use of courtly themes, and a more refined, sensual style of movement.
- **Statement 3 is incorrect**: Kathak is renowned for its intricate and vigorous footwork (**Tatkar**), which is performed with **rhythmic precision and often at a fast tempo**. However, Kathak is less focused on elaborate facial expressions compared to other dance forms.

Thus, option (b) is the correct answer.

16. *(b)* 1 and 3 only

- **Lucknow Gharana** of Kathak is known for its emphasis on grace, expression (Bhava), and subtlety. It focuses on delicate, refined movements and the **expressive storytelling aspect of Kathak.** The facial **expressions (Abhinaya)** and the emotive quality of the dance are given significant importance in this Gharana.
- **Jaipur Gharana** is characterised by its vigorous and complex footwork, rhythmic patterns, and extensive **use of spins (Chakkars)**. It is known for its robust and energetic style, which is influenced by the martial **traditions of Rajasthan**. The focus is more on the technical aspects of dance, such as intricate footwork and rhythm, rather than on expression and storytelling.
- **Banaras Gharana** emphasises grace and expression. It is particularly known for its devotional themes and is often performed in temples as part of religious ceremonies. The Banaras style is spiritual and serene, with a focus on Bhakti (devotion) and Rasas (emotional expressions).

Thus, option (b) is the correct answer.

17. *(a)* Kathak

- **Thaat, Jugalbandi and Tarana** are specific elements of Kathak.
- **Thaat** refers to the initial stance or posture that the dancer takes, setting the mood for the performance.
- **Jugalbandi** is a playful, competitive exchange between the dancer and the percussionist (usually the tabla player), where both attempt to outdo each other in complexity and speed of rhythms.
- **Tarana** is a rhythmic composition that often serves as the finale of a Kathak performance, characterised by fast-paced footwork and pirouettes (Chakkars).
- The use of **ghungroos** (ankle bells) is essential in Kathak. The costumes vary for men and women, with men typically wearing an angarkha (a type of tunic) and women wearing a lehenga or saree.
- **Dhrupad** is an ancient genre of Hindustani classical music that is often used as an accompaniment in Kathak performances, particularly in its more serious, devotional pieces.

Thus, option (a) is the correct answer.

18. *(d)* None

- **Statement 1 is correct**: Odissi is derived from the ancient dance traditions of **Odra Nritya,** which is mentioned in **classical Sanskrit texts like the Natyashastra.** Odra Nritya refers to the dance traditions of the region of Odisha, which evolved into what is now known as Odissi.
- **Statement 2 is correct: Bhanga** refers to the body postures used in Odissi, which are essential to the **dance's aesthetic and spiritual expression.** These postures include tribhangi (three bends) and chauka (square posture), which create a sense of symmetry and grace.
- **Statement 3 is correct**: Odissi is deeply connected to the religious traditions of Odisha, particularly **Vaishnavism,** which is the worship of Lord Vishnu. Many of the dance pieces in Odissi are dedicated to **Jagannath,** a form of Vishnu worshiped in Puri, Odisha.

Thus, option (d) is the correct answer.

19. *(d)* 1, 2 and 3

- **Statement 1 is correct**: The musical accompaniment in Odissi often includes traditional Indian instruments such as the **Pakhawaj** (a two-headed drum) and **cymbals.** The Pakhawaj provides the rhythmic base for the dance, while the cymbals (manjira) add to the percussive elements of the music.
- **Statement 2 is correct**: Odissi is closely associated with **Vaishnavism,** and many of its themes are devotional, centered around stories of Lord Vishnu, particularly in his incarnation as Krishna. The **Gita Govinda** is one of the most popular texts used in Odissi performances.
- **Statement 3 is correct: Nritta** and **Abhinaya** are two fundamental components of Odissi, as they are in most classical Indian dance forms.
- **Nritta** refers to pure dance movements that do not convey any specific meaning or story. It is purely decorative and focuses on the beauty of movement and rhythm.
- **Abhinaya** refers to the expressive aspect of dance, where the dancer conveys emotions, stories, and feelings through facial expressions, gestures, and movements.

Thus, option (d) is the correct answer.

20. *(c)* Mohiniyattam

- **Mohiniyattam is traditionally performed as a solo dance by female artists.** It is named after Mohini, the enchantress avatar of Lord Vishnu. The solo performance allows the dancer to fully express the emotional depth and grace associated with the dance form.
- Mohiniyattam is characterised by **soft, swaying movements** that reflect the gentle swaying of palm trees in the wind. The movements are fluid and feminine, embodying the Lasya style of dance, which is associated with grace and beauty.
- The traditional costume for Mohiniyattam is a white or off-white saree with a gold border (**Kasavu**). The costume is complemented by simple jewelley and flowers in the hair, maintaining the focus on the dance itself rather than on elaborate adornment.

Thus, option (c) is the correct answer.

21. *(d)* 1, 2 and 3

- **Statement 1 is correct:** The **Nagabhadra mudra** is a specific hand gesture used in Manipuri dance, which has symbolic significance. It is used to represent the serpent and is part of the intricate language of gestures that Manipuri dancers use to tell stories and convey emotions.
- **Statement 2 is correct: Rasleela Sankirtan** is a traditional performance in Manipuri dance, depicting the divine love of Krishna and Radha. Sankirtan involves singing and dancing in a circular formation, accompanied by the beat of the **Pung** (a traditional drum).
- **Statement 3 is correct:** The costume for male dancers in Manipuri often includes **a crown adorned with peacock feathers**, particularly in Rasleela performances, where the dancer represents Lord Krishna. The use of peacock feathers is symbolic of Krishna, who is often depicted wearing a crown with peacock feathers.

Thus, option (d) is the correct answer.

22. *(c)* All three

- **Statement 1 is correct**: Sattriya incorporates elements of **Nritta** (pure dance), **Natya** (drama) and **Nritya** (expressive dance). The dance form is known for its devotional content, and the performances are typically based on stories from the epics and Puranas, particularly those related to Lord Krishna.
- **Statement 2 is correct**: Sattriya was originally performed by male monks in the Sattras (Vaishnavite monasteries) of Assam. These monks are known as **Bhokots**. They danced as a part of their daily rituals and to propagate the teachings of Sankaradev.
- **Statement 3 is correct**: Srimanta Sankaradev, a saint-scholar, poet, playwright, and social-religious reformer, founded Sattriya in the medieval period. He used dance and drama as a means to spread the teachings of Bhakti (devotion).

Thus, option (c) is the correct answer.

23. *(b)* Only two

- **Statement 1 is correct: Bharatanatyam**, a classical dance form **from Tamil Nadu**, is closely associated with Carnatic music, which is the classical music tradition of Southern India. The compositions used in Bharatanatyam performances are typically set to classical ragas and talas of Carnatic music.
- **Statement 2 is correct: Kathakali**, a classical dance-drama from Kerala, indeed uses **Manipravalam, a blend of Sanskrit and Malayalam**, as the language for its songs and dialogues. **Manipravalam allows for a rich expression of the stories from epics and Puranas** that are depicted in Kathakali performances.
- **Statement 3 is incorrect: Tahiya** is a crown traditionally worn by **Odissi** dancers, not Kuchipudi dancers. In Kuchipudi, the dancers typically wear traditional South Indian attire such as the saree for women and dhoti for men, and their headgear is not specifically referred to as Tahiya.

Thus, option (b) is the correct answer.

24. *(b)* 3 and 4 only

- **Option 1 is incorrect**: While Kathak is performed **by both men and women**, it does not fall under the category of being predominantly a female dance form. The male performers often play a significant role, especially in the traditional Gharanas.
- **Option 2 is incorrect**: Manipuri dance, especially the Rasleela tradition, is often performed **by both male and female dancers.** However, in the context of the Sattriya tradition of Assam, it was predominantly performed by male monks.
- **Option 3 is correct**: Mohiniyattam is traditionally **performed by women and is characterised by its graceful and swaying movements.** The name itself is derived from the word 'Mohini', the female avatar of Vishnu, making it predominantly a female dance form.
- **Option 4 is correct**: Odissi is predominantly performed **by female dancers, although male dancers also perform it.** The dance's soft and lyrical movements, as well as the themes of love and devotion, lend themselves to performances by women.

Thus, option (b) is the correct answer.

25. *(a)* 1 and 2 only

- **Statement 1 is correct**: Sattriya was indeed propagated through the **Bhakti movement**, specifically through the neo-Vaishnavism movement led by **Srimanta Sankaradev in Assam.** Sattriya was developed within the monasteries of Assam (known as Sattras) as a means of teaching and spreading the Vaishnavite philosophy.
- **Statement 2 is correct**: The themes of Sattriya are based on the **stories of Radha-Krishna,** along with other tales from Hindu epics such as the Ramayana and Mahabharata. The Rasleela tradition, which depicts the divine love of Krishna and Radha, is a prominent theme in Sattriya performances.
- **Statement 3 is incorrect**: Sattriya was traditionally performed within the confines of the **Sattras (Vaishnavite monasteries), rather than in open-air spaces.** The performances were part of the religious rituals and ceremonies conducted by the monks and were not typically performed in public or open spaces, especially not after sunset.

Thus, option (a) is the correct answer.

26. *(a)* A-1, B-2, C-3, D-4

- **Bharatanatyam: Rukmini Devi Arundale** is a key figure in the revival of Bharatanatyam. She was instrumental in bringing this dance form from temple settings into mainstream performance venues and founded the Kalakshetra Foundation in Chennai to promote classical arts.
- **Kathakali: Guru Kunchu Kurup** was a legendary Kathakali artist known for his exceptional performances and contributions to the art form. He was awarded several honours for his work in promoting Kathakali.
- **Odissi: Guru Kelucharan Mohapatra** was one of the most renowned Odissi dancers and choreographers. He played a pivotal role in popularising Odissi dance and contributed significantly to its modern repertoire.
- **Manipuri: Guru Singhajit Singh** is renowned for his proficiency in Manipuri dance and has made a name for himself as a superb dancer, choreographer, scholar, and artist with exceptional creative talent.
  - He was born in Manipur on 1st May, 1935. He received the Padma Shri in 1986 and the Sangeet Natak Akademi Award in 1984 for his services to Manipuri dance.

Thus, option (a) is the correct answer.

27. *(a)* A-1, B-2, C-3, D-4.

- **Kathak:** Kathak is traditionally associated with Uttar Pradesh, particularly with regions like Lucknow, Jaipur, and Banaras, where different Gharanas (schools) of Kathak developed.
- **Mohiniyattam:** This dance form is native to Kerala and is known for its graceful, swaying movements that are symbolic of the feminine dance tradition of the state.
- **Sattriya:** Originating from the Vaishnavite monasteries of Assam, Sattriya is a dance-drama performance that is deeply connected to the religious practices of the region.
- **Bharatanatyam:** Bharatanatyam is the classical dance form of Tamil Nadu, with a rich tradition that dates back thousands of years. It is widely performed across the state and is considered one of the oldest dance forms in India.

Thus, option (a) is the correct answer.

28. *(a)* A-1, B-2, C-3, D-4

- **Kathak:** The **Tabla** is the most commonly used percussion instrument in Kathak performances. It provides the rhythmic foundation that is essential for the intricate footwork characteristic of Kathak.
- **Odissi: Pakhawaj** is the traditional drum used in Odissi dance performances. It provides the rhythmic accompaniment and is integral to the music that accompanies Odissi.
- **Manipuri: Pena** is a unique string instrument used in Manipuri dance. It is an ancient traditional instrument that has a distinct sound and is integral to Manipuri folk and classical music.
- **Bharatanatyam:** The **Mridangam** is a classical percussion instrument used in Bharatanatyam performances. It provides the

rhythmic structure for the dance and is central to the music of South Indian classical dance.

Thus, option (a) is the correct answer.

29. *(a)* Veeranatyam

- **Veeranatyam** is a traditional dance form from **Andhra Pradesh** that is closely associated with the worship of **Lord Shiva**, performed during religious festivals such as Mahashivratri. The dance is characterised by the use of a trident (**Trishul**) as a prop, symbolising the destructive aspect of Shiva. The performers engage in vigorous movements, often creating an intense and dramatic atmosphere.
- The dance often depicts the mythological story of **Veerabhadra**, an incarnation of Shiva created to avenge the insult to Shiva by Daksha, his father-in-law.

Thus, option (a) is the correct answer.

30. *(b)* Raut Nacha

- **Raut Nacha** is a traditional folk dance performed by the **Yadav community**, who are traditionally cowherds. It is associated with the state of **Chhattisgarh**. The dance is a way to celebrate and honor their profession and their devotion to **Lord Krishna**. It is primarily performed during the **Diwali** festival.
- The dance involves the use of sticks, which the dancers rhythmically strike together in time with the music. The dance is lively and energetic, with participants often performing in large groups.

Thus, option (b) is the correct answer.

31. *(d)* None

- **Statement 1 is correct: Burrakatha** is a traditional narrative dance form from **Andhra Pradesh** that evolved from the folk storytelling practices of the region. It is a form of oral tradition where a main storyteller (known as the Kathakudu) is accompanied by two assistants who provide musical and vocal support.
- **Statement 2 is correct: Dumhal** is a ceremonial folk dance performed by the **Wattal tribe** in **Jammu and Kashmir**. The dance is typically performed by men who wear long, flowing robes and tall conical caps decorated with beads and shells.
- **Statement 3 is correct: Kaikottikali**, also known as **Thiruvathirakali**, is a traditional dance performed by women in **Kerala** during the festival of Onam. Women dressed in traditional white sarees with gold borders (known as Kasavu sarees) perform Kaikottikali while clapping their hands and singing traditional folk songs.

Thus, option (d) is the correct answer.

32. *(b)* Only two

- **Statement 1 is correct: Ghoomar** is a traditional folk dance of **Rajasthan**, particularly associated with the women of the Bhil tribe. The dance is typically performed by women wearing flowing Ghagras (skirts) that create a mesmerizing visual effect as they spin in circles. Ghoomar is performed during various festive occasions such as weddings, Holi, and Teej.
- **Statement 2 is correct: Bhangra** is a lively and energetic dance form from Punjab, traditionally performed by men to celebrate the harvest season, particularly the festival of **Vaisakhi. Giddha** is the female counterpart of Bhangra, performed by women during similar festive occasions.
- **Statement 3 is incorrect: Cheraw**, also known as the **bamboo dance**, often performed during important festivals like Chapchar Kut and Christmas, is a traditional dance of **Mizoram**, not Nagaland. In Cheraw, dancers step in and out of clapping bamboo poles that are held horizontally at ground level.

Thus, option (b) is the correct answer.

33. *(c)* All three

- **Statement 1 is correct: Butta Bommalu** is a unique folk dance from Andhra Pradesh where performers wear large masks made of clay, wood, or papier-mâché, designed to resemble different characters or toy-like figures. The masks are elaborately decorated and are often inspired by mythological figures or local folklore.

- **Statement 2 is correct: Paika** is a traditional martial dance form from **Odisha**, named after the Paikas, the warrior class of the region. Paika dance is performed with traditional weapons like swords, shields, and spears, and it involves vigorous movements, jumps, and complex footwork.
- **Statement 3 is correct: Jawara** is a folk dance from **Madhya Pradesh**, specifically associated with the Bundelkhand region. It is performed by the farming community during the harvest season to celebrate the abundance of crops. The dance involves women balancing baskets filled with freshly harvested grain on their heads while performing intricate steps.

Thus, option (c) is the correct answer.

34. *(c)* All three

- **Pair 1 is correctly matched: Dumhal** is a ceremonial folk dance of the **Wattal tribe in Jammu and Kashmir**. This dance is performed exclusively by men who wear long, colourful robes and conical caps adorned with beads and shells. The dancers move rhythmically to the beat of drums and other traditional instruments.
- **Pair 2 is correctly matched: Raut Naach** is a traditional folk dance of the Yadav (cowherd) community in **Chhattisgarh**. The dance is performed during the festival of Diwali to honour Lord Krishna, who is believed to be the protector of cattle.
- **Pair 3 is correctly matched: Fugdi** is a popular folk dance performed by women in **Goa**. The dance is typically performed during religious and social celebrations, particularly during the Ganesh Chaturthi festival and at the onset of the monsoon season.

Thus, option (c) is the correct answer.

35. *(b)* Only two

- **Pair 1 is incorrectly matched: Mayilattam**, or the peacock dance, is a folk dance form from **Tamil Nadu**, that imitates the graceful movements of a peacock. Performers, often young girls, dress in costumes that resemble peacocks, complete with a large feathered tail that can be fanned out.
- **Pair 2 is incorrectly matched: Chakyar Koothu** is a classical dance and dramatic art form from Kerala, traditionally performed in temples **as a part of the Koodiyattam theatre.** It is a solo performance where the performer, known as the **Chakyar**, narrates stories from Hindu epics, particularly the **Mahabharata and Ramayana**, with satirical and humorous commentary.
- **Pair 3 is correctly matched: Pata Kunitha** is a traditional folk dance from **Karnataka**, particularly popular in the Mysore region. The dance is performed by men who carry large bamboo poles (Patas) decorated with colourful cloth and flowers. The performers dance energetically, spinning and twirling the poles in intricate patterns.

Thus, option (b) is the correct answer.

36. *(a)* Ka Shad Suk Mynsiem

- Ka Shad Suk Mynsiem is a traditional harvest dance performed by the **Jaintia tribe**, one of the indigenous communities in **Meghalaya.**
- The dance is characterised by rhythmic movements that are in harmony with the beats of traditional drums and other musical instruments.
- It is performed during the Shad Suk Mynsiem festival, which marks the end of the harvest season and the arrival of spring. The festival is a significant cultural event in Meghalaya, where the community comes together to celebrate nature's bounty and offer prayers for future prosperity.

Thus, option (a) is the correct answer.

37. *(d)* 1, 2 and 3

- **Pair 1 is correctly matched: Gaur Maria** is a traditional dance performed by the **Maria tribe** in **Chhattisgarh**. It is a ritualistic dance associated with the worship of deities and the spirits of ancestors. The dance is accompanied by traditional music played on instruments like the Mandar and Tumba.

- **Pair 2 is correctly matched: Bhootha Aradhane**, or spirit worship, is a ritualistic dance form from the coastal regions of **Karnataka.** It is performed to appease the spirits (Bhoothas) believed to protect the village. The dance is accompanied by drums, cymbals, and wind instruments, creating a dramatic and mystical atmosphere.
- **Pair 3 is correctly matched: Alkap** is a traditional folk dance-drama from **West Bengal**, particularly popular in the rural areas of the Malda and Murshidabad districts. It is performed during the Gajan festival in honour of Lord Shiva.

Thus, option (d) is the correct answer.

38. *(d)* 1, 2 and 3

- **Pair 1 is correctly matched: Gaur Maria** is a ritualistic dance performed by the Maria tribe in Chhattisgarh. It is performed during important ceremonies and festivals, often to seek blessings for protection, good harvests, and prosperity.
- **Pair 2 is correctly matched: Padayani** is a traditional ritualistic dance from **Kerala,** performed in honor of the goddess Bhadrakali. The dance is characterised by the use of large, colourful masks (Kolams) representing various divine and demonic characters.
- **Pair 3 is correctly matched: Thang Ta** is a traditional martial art and dance form from **Manipur** that incorporates ritualistic elements. Thang Ta is performed as a ceremonial dance during religious festivals and cultural events, symbolising the warrior spirit and the protection of the community.

Thus, option (d) is the correct answer.

39. *(a)* Gethinglim

- **Gethinglim** is a traditional folk dance performed by the **Angami tribe**, one of the major Naga tribes in **Nagaland.** The dance is typically performed by women during various festivals, which involves slow, graceful movements that are performed in harmony with traditional songs sung by the participants.
- Gethinglim is more than just a dance; it is a celebration of the cultural heritage and traditions of the Angami tribe. The dance is performed during important festivals, such as **Sekrenyi**, which is a major festival of the Angami people, marking the beginning of the new year.

Thus, option (a) is the correct answer.

40. *(c)* All three

- **Pair 1 is correctly matched: Fugdi** is a traditional folk dance performed by women in Goa, particularly during religious festivals like Ganesh Chaturthi and during the harvest season. The dance is known for its fast-paced, rhythmic movements, where women form circles or rows and clap their hands while singing folk songs.
- **Pair 2 is correctly matched: Kaikottikali**, also known as **Thiruvathirakali**, is a traditional group dance performed by women in **Kerala** during the **Onam** festival. Women dressed in traditional **Kasavu** sarees perform graceful, synchronised movements while clapping their hands and singing folk songs.
- **Pair 3 is correctly matched: Dumhal**, as mentioned earlier, is a ceremonial dance performed by the **Wattal tribe of Jammu and Kashmir.** The dance involves men wearing colourful robes and conical caps, and dancing in a circle around a planted banner while singing traditional songs.

Thus, option (c) is the correct answer.

41. *(b)* Andhra Pradesh

- **Burrakatha** is a narrative dance form from **Andhra Pradesh** that combines storytelling with music, dance, and drama. It is traditionally performed by a main storyteller and two assistants, who together narrate stories from epics, folklore, and social themes.
- **Butta Bommalu** is another folk dance from Andhra Pradesh, where performers wear large, colourful masks made of clay or wood, resembling toy-like figures. The term 'Butta Bommalu' translates to basket toys, reflecting the toy-like appearance of the masks worn by the dancers.

- **Kolatam,** also known as **Dandiya** in other regions, is a traditional stick dance performed in Andhra Pradesh. It involves rhythmic clapping of sticks, synchronised movements, and the singing of folk songs.

Thus, option (b) is the correct answer.

42. *(b)* Kerala

- **Padayani** is a traditional folk dance and ritualistic performance from Kerala, specifically performed in the temples of Central Kerala, particularly in the Pathanamthitta district. It is associated with the worship of Goddess Bhadrakali and is performed as part of temple festivals.
- **Kolkali** is another traditional dance form from Kerala, primarily performed by the Muslim community in the Malabar region. It is a group dance where participants use sticks (Kols) to create rhythmic beats while performing synchronized movements.
- **Kaikottikali**, also known as **Thiruvathirakali**, is a popular folk dance of Kerala, performed by women during the Onam festival. It is a graceful group dance where participants move in a circle around a lamp or floral arrangement, clapping their hands and singing traditional songs.

Thus, option (b) is the correct answer.

43. *(a)* Bihu

- **Bihu** is the most popular **folk dance** of **Assam**, performed during the Bohag Bihu festival, which marks the beginning of the **Assamese New Year**. Bohag Bihu is the most important festival in Assam, celebrating the **arrival of spring and the abundance of the harvest.**
- The Bihu dance is known for its brisk, energetic steps, rapid hand movements, and the rhythmic beats of the dhol **(drum) and Pepa** (horn). Both **men and women** participate in the dance, which is typically performed in **open fields or courtyards,** dressed in traditional Assamese attire, adding to the colourful spectacle.

Thus, option (a) is the correct answer.

44. *(a)* Charkula

- **Charkula** is a unique and traditional dance from the **Braj region of Uttar Pradesh**, where the dancer balances a large, circular wooden structure (Charkula) on her head. The Charkula is often decorated with oil lamps or flowers, and its weight requires exceptional skill and balance to dance.
- The dance symbolises the joy and devotion of Radha as she welcomes Lord Krishna to her village. The Charkula represents the prosperity and the light that Radha brings into Krishna's life, and the dance is a reenactment of this divine interaction.
- Charkula is primarily performed during the festival of Holi, a significant festival in the Braj region, which is closely associated with the legends of Radha and Krishna.

Thus, option (a) is the correct answer.

45. *(b)* Karnataka

- **Bhootha Aradhane**, also known as spirit worship, is a traditional ritualistic performance from the coastal regions of Karnataka, particularly in the **Tulu Nadu** region. It involves the invocation and worship of spirits (Bhoothas) that are believed to protect the village.
- **Pata Kunitha** is a folk dance from Karnataka, where performers carry large bamboo poles (Patas) adorned with colourful decorations. The dance is performed during religious festivals and processions, particularly in the **Mysore** region.
- **Yakshagana** is a traditional theater form that combines dance, music and drama, and it is native to the **coastal regions of Karnataka.** The performance is based on stories from Hindu epics such as the Mahabharata and Ramayana, and it involves elaborate costumes, makeup, and dramatic dialogues.

Thus, option (b) is the correct answer.

46. *(b)* Chhattisgarh

- **Raut Naach** is a traditional dance performed by the Yadav (cowherd) community in

Chhattisgarh. The dance is performed during the Diwali festival to honor Lord Krishna, who is considered the protector of cattle.

- **Panthi** is another traditional folk dance from Chhattisgarh, performed by the Satnami community during religious festivals and social gatherings. The dance is performed in **honour of Guru Ghasidas**, the founder of the Satnami sect, and it reflects the spiritual beliefs and practices of the community.
- **Karma Naach** is a traditional dance performed by the tribal communities of Chhattisgarh, Madhya Pradesh, and Odisha. The dance is associated with the Karma festival, which is celebrated to honour the Karma tree, believed to be a symbol of fertility and prosperity.

Thus, option (b) is the correct answer.

47. *(a)* Koodiyattam.

- **Koodiyattam** is one of the oldest surviving classical theatre traditions in India, associated with the state of Kerala, performed in temple theatres known as Kuttampalams. It is performed in the Sanskrit language and is considered one of the most ancient forms of theatre in the world. The art form is recognised by **UNESCO as a Masterpiece of the Oral and Intangible Heritage of Humanity.**
- Koodiyattam combines elements of dance, drama, and music, with performances that are often based on stories from Hindu epics such as the Ramayana and Mahabharata.
- The performers in Koodiyattam wear elaborate costumes and makeup, which are integral to their portrayal of various characters. The art form is known for its emphasis on Abhinaya, or expressive facial gestures, which are used to convey complex emotions and narratives. The performances are often slow and deliberate, allowing for a deep emotional connection with the audience.

Thus, option (a) is the correct answer.

Past Learning (Answers)

1 (b)	2 (b)	3 (b)	4 (c)	5 (a)	6 (a)	7 (b)	8 (a)	9 (c)	10 (a)
11 (a)	12 (c)	13 (c)							

CHAPTER 08

Drama, Theatre and Puppetry

Assessment Round

Topic 1 : Drama

1. With reference to Natyashastra, consider the following statements:

1. Natyashastra was the first source to enumerate detailed techniques and precautions for drama.
2. Brahma created Natyaveda to help the masses to overcome suffering.
3. Drama in ancient India was primarily a narrative art form without any performance elements.

Which of the above statements are correct?

(a) 1 and 2 only
(b) 2 and 3 only
(c) 1 and 3 only
(d) 1, 2 and 3

2. Which of the following statements about the classifications of Abhinaya in Natyashastra is incorrect?

(a) Angika Abhinaya refers to expression through limbs.
(b) Vachika Abhinaya is the expression through dialogues.
(c) Aharya Abhinaya is the expression through natural, realistic actions of daily life.
(d) Sattvika Abhinaya represents truthful expressions.

3. How do you distinguish between Lokadharmi and Natya Dharmi Abhinaya?

1. Lokadharmi Abhinaya is focused on the natural expression of things or events of daily life, while Natya Dharmi Abhinaya follows codified principles of emotions and themes.
2. Lokadharmi Abhinaya is poetic, while Natya Dharmi Abhinaya is more realistic and random.

Which of the statements given above is/are correct?

(a) 1 only (b) 2 only
(c) Both 1 and 2 (d) Neither 1 nor 2

4. Consider the following pairs:

	Terminologies	Components Associated
1.	Yavanika	Curtain dividing backstage and stage
2.	Vidushak	Hero-Heroine
3.	Nepathya	Backstage
4.	Sutradhaar	Clown, normally played by ugly Brahmin

How many pairs given above is/are incorrectly matched?

(a) Only one pair
(b) Only two pairs
(c) Only three pairs
(d) All four pairs

5. Consider the following pairs:

	Terminologies	Components Associated
1.	Natyagraha	Stage
2.	Sutradhar	Stage Manager
3.	Pratinayak	Villain
4.	Vidushak	Clown

How many pairs given above is/are correctly matched?
(a) Only one pair (b) Only two pairs
(c) Only three pairs (d) All four pairs

6. With reference to the works of Kalidasa, consider the following statements:
1. 'Abhijnana Shakuntalam' is considered one of the greatest Sanskrit plays.
2. 'Malvikagnimitra' is a work that deals with historical events.
3. 'Vikramorvasiya' is a drama composed in Prakrit.

How many of the statements given above is/are correct?
(a) Only one (b) Only two
(c) All three (d) None

7. Match the following work and their Author:

	Authors		Work
1.	Kalidasa	A.	Mrichchhakatika
2.	Bhasa	B.	Malvikagnimitra
3.	Sudraka	C.	Swapnavasavadattam
4.	Bhavabhuti	D.	Uttararamacharita

Codes
(a) 1-B, 2-C, 3-A, 4-D
(b) 1-C, 2-B, 3-D, 4-A
(c) 1-B, 2-A, 3-C, 4-D
(d) 1-D, 2-A, 3-B, 4-C

8. Consider the following pairs:

	Authors	Work
1.	Harshavardhana	Priyadarsika
2.	Vishakhadatta	Mudrarakshasa
3.	Mahendravarman	Mattavilasa Prahasana
4.	Bhavabhuti	Devichandraguptam

How many pairs given above is/are correctly matched?
(a) Only one pair
(b) Only two pairs
(c) Only three pairs
(d) All four pairs

9. What is the difference between the plays of Harshavardhana and Sudraka?
(a) Sudraka's plays are focused on social themes, while Harshavardhana's plays are more poetic in nature.
(b) Harshavardhana's works are entirely mythological, while Sudraka's works have a historical base.
(c) Harshavardhana's works were influenced by Greek drama, while Sudraka's works were purely Indian in style.
(d) There is no material difference between their works.

10. With reference to the National School of Drama, consider the following statements:
1. It was established in 1959 as an autonomous body.
2. It functions under the Ministry of Culture.
3. Its headquarters is located in Mumbai.

How many of the statements given above is/are not correct?
(a) Only one (b) Only two
(c) All three (d) None

Topic 2 : Theatre

11. Consider the following pairs:

	Folk	State
1.	Bhand Pather	Madhya Pradesh
2.	Maach	Jammu and Kashmir
3.	Powada	Maharashtra
4.	Dashavatar	Maharashtra

How many pairs given above is/are correctly matched?
(a) Only one pair (b) Only two pairs
(c) Only three pairs (d) All four pairs

12. With reference to Yakshagana, consider the following statements:

1. Yakshagana is a traditional theatre form from Kerala.
2. It primarily depicts mythological stories and Puranas.
3. Yakshagana performances often include themes from the Mahabharata, such as Draupadi Swayamvar and Abhimanyu Vadh.

How many of the statements given above is/are correct?

(a) Only one (b) Only two
(c) All three (d) None

13. With reference to Therukoothu, consider the following statements:

1. Therukoothu is a folk drama from Tamil Nadu that means 'street play.'
2. It is performed mainly during temple festivals dedicated to the goddess Mariamman.
3. Therukoothu performances are centered around historical events rather than mythological stories.

Which of the statements given above is/are correct?

(a) 1 and 2 only (b) 2 only
(c) 3 only (d) 1, 2 and 3

14. Identify the correct statement(s) about Mudiyettu:

1. It is a traditional folk theatre form of Tamil Nadu.
2. Mudiyettu is usually performed only in the Vishnu temples of Kerala.
3. The central theme of Mudiyettu is the triumph of the goddess Bhadrakali over the asura Darika.

Choose the correct answer from the codes given below:

(a) 1 only (b) 2 only
(c) 3 only (d) 2 and 3 only

15. What is the difference between Krishnattam and other traditional folk theatres of Kerala?

(a) Krishnattam is exclusively centered on the life and stories of Lord Rama, unlike other folk theatres.
(b) Krishnattam was patronised by the King of Travancore, while other theatres were supported by local temple communities.
(c) Krishnattam focuses on the theme of Lord Krishna and was patronised by King Manavada of Calicut.
(d) There is no material difference between Krishnattam and other traditional folk theatres in Kerala.

16. Match the following folk theatres with their corresponding states:

	Folk Theatre		State
1.	Nautanki	A.	West Bengal
2.	Ojhapali	B.	Madhya Pradesh
3.	Maach	C.	Assam
4.	Jatra	D.	North India

Choose the correct option from the codes given below:

(a) 1-D, 2-C, 3-A, 4-B
(b) 1-A, 2-D, 3-C, 4-B
(c) 1-D, 2-C, 3-B, 4-A
(d) 1-D, 2-C, 3-C, 4-A

17. Which of the following statements about Tal Maddale is incorrect?

(a) Tal Maddale is a dialogue-based performance without costume, dance, or acting.
(b) It is performed in the Malabar region of Kerala.
(c) The conversations in Tal Maddale are mainly drawn from mythology.
(d) It is a traditional theatre form of Karnataka and Kerala.

18. How do you distinguish between Kuruvanji and Bayalata?

1. Kuruvanji is centered around the love story of a heroine, while Bayalata focuses on epic poetry and stories from Ramayana and Mahabharata.
2. Bayalata is an open-air theatre to worship local deities, while Kuruvanji involves Bharatanatyam as the principal dance form.

Which of the statements given above is/are correct?

(a) 1 only (b) 2 only
(c) Both 1 and 2 (d) Neither 1 nor 2

19. With reference to Pagati Veshaalu, consider the following statements:

1. Pagati Veshaalu is performed by three to four individuals.
2. The performance revolves around a principal character called Vesham, who is a symbol of disguise.
3. Pagati Veshaalu is primarily performed in Tamil Nadu and Karnataka.

Which of the statements given above is/are correct?

(a) 1 and 2 only
(b) 2 and 3 only
(c) 3 only
(d) 1, 2 and 3

20. Match the following folk theatres with their corresponding states:

	Folk Theatre		State
1.	Kariyala	A.	Punjab
2.	Naqal/Bhand	B.	Assam
3.	Swaang/Saang	C.	Gujarat
4.	Ojapali	D.	Himachal Pradesh

Codes

(a) 1-D, 2-A, 3-B, 4-C
(b) 1-A, 2-D, 3-C, 4-B
(c) 1-D, 2-B, 3-A, 4-C
(d) 1-D, 2-A, 3-C, 4-B

Topic 3 : Puppetry

21. Consider the following pairs:

	Puppetry	State
1.	Tolpava Kuthu	West Bengal
2.	Tholu Bommalata	Andhra Pradesh
3.	Kathi Kandhe	Bihar
4.	Yampuri	Kerala

How many pairs given above is/are correctly matched?

(a) Only one pair
(b) Only two pairs
(c) Only three pairs
(d) All four pairs

22. With reference to Glove Puppetry, consider the following statements:

1. Glove puppetry is also known as hand puppetry or palm puppetry.
2. Puppets in this form generally have legs to enhance their mobility.
3. It is prominent in the states of Uttar Pradesh, Odisha, West Bengal and Kerala.

How many of the statements given above is/are correct?

(a) Only one
(b) Only two
(c) All three
(d) None

23. Identify the correct statement(s) about String Puppetry:

1. String puppetry is the most articulate form of puppetry, with puppets made from wood.
2. String puppets are controlled by attaching strings to various body parts like the head, hands and legs.
3. The regional forms of string puppetry include Kathputli, Kundhei, Gombeyatta and Bommalattam.

Choose the correct answer from the codes given below:

(a) 1 only
(b) 2 and 3 only
(c) 3 only
(d) 1, 2 and 3

24. With reference to Shadow Puppetry, consider the following statements:

1. Shadow puppets are made of flat opaque or translucent leather.
2. This form of puppetry thrives in Andhra Pradesh, Odisha, Karnataka, Kerala, and Maharashtra.
3. The shadows can be either silhouettes or coloured, depending on the puppet material and screen colour.

How many of the statements given above is/are incorrect?

(a) Only one
(b) Only two
(c) All three
(d) None

25. With reference to Rod Puppetry, consider the following statements:

1. Rod puppetry is an extension of glove puppetry where the puppet is controlled through rods attached to various body parts.
2. It is mainly popular in Eastern India, particularly in Bihar, Odisha and West Bengal.
3. The largest and heaviest rod puppets are found in Maharashtra.

Which of the statements given above is/are correct?

(a) 1 and 2 only (b) 2 only
(c) 3 only (d) 1, 2 and 3

26. With reference to Indian Puppetry, consider the following statements:

1. The first archaeological evidence of puppetry was found in the Indus Valley Civilisation at Mohenjodaro.
2. The earliest written reference to puppetry is found in the Tamil classic 'Silappadikaram' by Ilango Adigal.
3. The Bhagavad Gita describes the universe as being controlled by God (puppeteer) with three strings: Satta, Raja, and Tama.

How many of the statements given above is/are correct?

(a) Only one (b) Only two
(c) All three (d) None

27. Identify the correct statement(s) about Kathputli:

1. Kathputli is a form of string puppetry with no legs.
2. The term Kathputli is derived from the words Kath, meaning wood, and Putli, meaning doll.
3. Kathputli is believed to have been started by the Bhat community of Rajasthan.

Choose the correct answer from the codes given below:

(a) 1 only (b) 2 only
(c) 2 and 3 only (d) 1, 2 and 3

28. Match the following forms of puppetry with their corresponding states:

Puppetry		State	
1.	Chamadyacha Bahulya	A.	Kerala
2.	Pavakoothu	B.	Tamil Nadu
3.	Togalu Gombayatta	C.	Karnataka
4.	Ravanchhaya	D.	Odisha

Codes

(a) 1-D, 2-C, 3-A, 4-B
(b) 1-B, 2-A, 3-D, 4-C
(c) 1-C, 2-A, 3-D, 4-B
(d) 1-C, 2-D, 3-A, 4-B

OMR SHEET

Assessment Round

1	a	b	c	d	31	a	b	c	d	61	a	b	c	d	91	a	b	c	d
2	a	b	c	d	32	a	b	c	d	62	a	b	c	d	92	a	b	c	d
3	a	b	c	d	33	a	b	c	d	63	a	b	c	d	93	a	b	c	d
4	a	b	c	d	34	a	b	c	d	64	a	b	c	d	94	a	b	c	d
5	a	b	c	d	35	a	b	c	d	65	a	b	c	d	95	a	b	c	d
6	a	b	c	d	36	a	b	c	d	66	a	b	c	d	96	a	b	c	d
7	a	b	c	d	37	a	b	c	d	67	a	b	c	d	97	a	b	c	d
8	a	b	c	d	38	a	b	c	d	68	a	b	c	d	98	a	b	c	d
9	a	b	c	d	39	a	b	c	d	69	a	b	c	d	99	a	b	c	d
10	a	b	c	d	40	a	b	c	d	70	a	b	c	d	100	a	b	c	d
11	a	b	c	d	41	a	b	c	d	71	a	b	c	d	101	a	b	c	d
12	a	b	c	d	42	a	b	c	d	72	a	b	c	d	102	a	b	c	d
13	a	b	c	d	43	a	b	c	d	73	a	b	c	d	103	a	b	c	d
14	a	b	c	d	44	a	b	c	d	74	a	b	c	d	104	a	b	c	d
15	a	b	c	d	45	a	b	c	d	75	a	b	c	d	105	a	b	c	d
16	a	b	c	d	46	a	b	c	d	76	a	b	c	d	106	a	b	c	d
17	a	b	c	d	47	a	b	c	d	77	a	b	c	d	107	a	b	c	d
18	a	b	c	d	48	a	b	c	d	78	a	b	c	d	108	a	b	c	d
19	a	b	c	d	49	a	b	c	d	79	a	b	c	d	109	a	b	c	d
20	a	b	c	d	50	a	b	c	d	80	a	b	c	d	110	a	b	c	d
21	a	b	c	d	51	a	b	c	d	81	a	b	c	d	111	a	b	c	d
22	a	b	c	d	52	a	b	c	d	82	a	b	c	d	112	a	b	c	d
23	a	b	c	d	53	a	b	c	d	83	a	b	c	d	113	a	b	c	d
24	a	b	c	d	54	a	b	c	d	84	a	b	c	d	114	a	b	c	d
25	a	b	c	d	55	a	b	c	d	85	a	b	c	d	115	a	b	c	d
26	a	b	c	d	56	a	b	c	d	86	a	b	c	d	116	a	b	c	d
27	a	b	c	d	57	a	b	c	d	87	a	b	c	d	117	a	b	c	d
28	a	b	c	d	58	a	b	c	d	88	a	b	c	d	118	a	b	c	d
29	a	b	c	d	59	a	b	c	d	89	a	b	c	d	119	a	b	c	d
30	a	b	c	d	60	a	b	c	d	90	a	b	c	d	120	a	b	c	d

Calculate Your Score

Correct (✓)	
Incorrect (✓)	
Unattempted	
Total Score	
Accuracy (%)	

Reasons for Incorrect Answers?

1. Lack of Knowledge/Existing Source Insufficient	
2. Lack of Multiple Revision	
3. Common Sense Mistakes	

Note :

1. Calculate total score as correct answers carry 2 marks each 1/3rd marks will deducted for **Incorrect** Answers.
2. Calculate Accuracy (%) by dividing the number of correct answers to the total number of attempted questions.

Past Learning

1. With reference to ancient Indian History, consider the following pairs: **(2023)**

	Literary work	Authors
1.	Devichandragupta	Bilhana
2.	Hammira-Mahakavya	Nayachandra Suri
3.	Milinda-Panha	Nagarjuna
4.	Nitivakyamrita	Somadeva Suri

How many of the above pairs is/are correctly matched?

(a) Only one (b) Only two
(c) Only three (d) All four

2. With reference to the history of ancient India, Bhavabhuti, Hastimalla and Kshemeshvara were famous **(2021)**

(a) Jain monks (b) Playwrights
(c) Temple architects (d) Philosophers

3. Which one of the following books of Ancient India has the love story of the son of the founder of the Sunga Dynasty? **(2016)**

(a) Swapnavasavadatta (b) Malavikagnimitra
(c) Meghadoota (d) Ratnavali

4. Consider the following statements. **(2009)**

1. The National School of Drama was setup by Sangeet Natak Academy in 1959.
2. The highest honour conferred by the Sahitya Academy on a writer is by electing him its fellow.

Which of the statement(s) given above is/are correct?

(a) Only 1
(b) Only 2
(c) Both 1 and 2
(d) Neither 1 nor 2

5. Ebrahim Alkazi is an eminent personality in which one of the following areas? **(2008)**

(a) Heart surgery
(b) Civil aviation
(c) Theatre training
(d) Transport engineering

6. Which one of the following pairs is not correctly matched? **(2000)**

(a)	Bakti Itihas	Badal Sarkar
(b)	Sita Swayamvar	Vishnu Das Bhave
(c)	Yayati	Girish Karnad
(d)	Giddha	Jabbar Patel

7. The first feature film (talkie) to be produced in India was: **(1999)**

(a) Hatimtai
(b) Alam Ara
(c) Pundalik
(d) Raja Harishchandra

8. Which one of the following statements is not correct? **(1999)**

(a) 'Neel Darpan' was a play based on the exploitation of the indigo farmers.
(b) The author of the play 'Ghashiram Kotwal' is Vijay Tendulkar.
(c) The play 'Navanna' by Navin Chandra Das was based on the famine of Bengal.
(d) Urdu theatre used to depend heavily on Parsi theatre.

9. Which one of the following pairs is correctly matched? **(1996)**

(a)	Naqqual	Bihar
(b)	Tamasha	Orissa
(c)	Ankia Nat	Assam
(d)	Baha	Punjab

Detailed Solutions

Assessment Round

1. *(a)* 1 and 2 only

- **Statement 1 is correct**: The **Natyashastra** by **Bharata Muni** is a comprehensive and earliest surviving text on **Indian dramaturgy**, dating back to around **200 BCE to 200 CE**. It is the first source that provides detailed instructions on various aspects of drama, including stage design, music, dance, and acting techniques.
- **Statement 2 is correct**: According to the Natyashastra, the concept of **Natyaveda** (the Veda of theatre) was created by **Brahma as the fifth Veda.** It was intended to be an instrument of enlightenment and entertainment, helping people to **overcome the vicissitudes** of life by representing the world's sorrows and joys on stage.
- **Statement 3 is incorrect**: Indian drama, as described in the **Natyashastra**, was a highly developed performance art that **integrated narrative, dialogue, music, dance, and acting.** It was not merely a narrative art form; instead, it was a comprehensive spectacle involving various sensory elements.

Thus, option (a) is the correct answer.

2. *(c)* Aharya Abhinaya is the expression through natural, realistic actions of daily life.

- **Option (a) is correct: Angika Abhinaya** refers to the expression through physical movements, particularly those of the limbs and body. This includes gestures (mudras) and postures (sthanka) that communicate various emotions and actions.
- **Option (b) is correct: Vachika Abhinaya** is a type of Abhinaya that pertains to verbal expression, encompassing dialogue, song, and sound. The use of voice modulation, accent, and pitch plays a critical role in conveying the intended message and emotion.
- **Option (c) is incorrect: Aharya Abhinaya** involves the external appearance of a performer, including costumes, makeup, jewellery, and props. It is crucial in defining the character's role, status, and personality in the play.
- **Option (d) is correct: Sattvika Abhinaya** involves the genuine internal emotional response and its manifestation on stage, such as tears, blushes, or shivers, which are spontaneous reactions of the actor to the emotions being portrayed.

Thus, option (c) is the correct answer.

3. *(a)* 1 only

- **Statement 1 is correct: Lokadharmi Abhinaya** is rooted in the realistic portrayal of everyday life. It involves natural expressions, gestures, and actions that people use in daily interactions. Contrary to Lokadharmi, Natya Dharmi is highly stylised and symbolic. It follows codified gestures, expressions, and movements that may not be realistic but convey deeper, often spiritual or emotional, meanings.
- **Statement 2 is incorrect**: Lokadharmi Abhinaya is more **realistic** and random, focused on depicting daily life naturally, while Natya Dharmi is **poetic**, following a highly structured and codified approach. Natya Dharmi is more aligned with the traditional, classical Indian dance forms, where symbolism and stylization play a crucial role in performance.

Thus, option (a) is the correct answer.

4. *(b)* Only two pairs

- **Pair 1 is correctly matched**: In traditional Indian theatre, **Yavanika** refers to the curtain that separates the backstage from the main stage. This curtain is significant in the dramatic reveal of scenes or characters in a play, a common technique used to build suspense or introduce new elements to the audience.
- **Pair 2 is incorrectly matched: Vidushak** is typically a **comic character** who, despite his humorous role, often provides critical commentary on the events of the play, sometimes reflecting deeper truths or moral lessons.

- **Pair 3 is correctly matched:** Nepathya refers to the **backstage area**, where actors prepare before coming onto the stage. It is also the area where props and costumes are stored and where the technical aspects of the production, such as lighting and sound, are managed.
- **Pair 4 is incorrectly matched: Sutradhar** means the **holder of strings** and refers to the narrator or the stage manager in traditional Indian theatre. The Sutradhar introduces the play, provides commentary, and ensures a smooth transition between scenes.

Thus, option (b) is the correct answer.

5. *(d)* All four pairs

- **Pair 1 is correctly matched: Natyagraha** refers to the **entire stage or theatre** in Indian dramaturgy. The stage is where the performance takes place and is designed according to specific guidelines mentioned in the Natyashastra to optimise the visibility and audibility of the audience.
- **Pair 2 is correctly matched: Sutradhar** plays the role of the **stage manager or narrator**, who not only manages the flow of the performance but also guides the audience through the story.
- **Pair 3 is correctly matched:** The term **Pratinayak** refers to the **antagonist or villain** in a play. In Indian classical drama, the Pratinayak is an essential character who opposes the hero (Nayak) and creates conflict, driving the narrative forward.
- **Pair 4 is correctly matched:** The **Vidushak** is the **clown or jester** in Indian theatre, known for his witty remarks and comedic presence. Despite being a comic relief, the Vidushak often plays a critical role in conveying important messages to the audience through humour.

Thus, option (d) is the correct answer.

6. *(a)* Only one

- **Statement 1 is correct: Abhijnana Shakuntalam** is one of **Kalidasa**'s most celebrated works and is considered one of the greatest plays in Sanskrit literature. The play beautifully weaves together romance, drama, and mythology, and it has had a profound influence on Indian and Western literature and art.
- **Statement 2 is incorrect: Malvikagnimitra** is more of a **romantic** comedy than a historical play. It tells the story of the love between **King Agnimitra** and the maid **Malavika.** While it does involve historical figures, the focus is on the romantic plot rather than historical events.
- **Statement 3 is incorrect: Vikramorvasiya** is written in **Sanskrit**, not Prakrit. The play is another masterpiece by **Kalidasa**, focusing on the love story between the mortal king Pururavas and the celestial nymph Urvashi.

Thus, option (a) is the correct answer.

7. *(a)* 1-B, 2-C, 3-A, 4-D

- **(1-B): Kalidasa**, often regarded as the greatest poet and dramatist in Sanskrit literature, wrote **Malvikagnimitra**, a romantic play that narrates the story of King Agnimitra's love for the beautiful maid Malavika.
- **(2-C): Bhasa** is one of the earliest known Sanskrit dramatists, and his work **Swapn-avasavadattam** is a play that dramatizes the political and personal challenges faced by **Udayana**, the king of Vatsa, and his queen **Vasavadatta.**
- **(3-A): Sudraka's Mrichchhakatika**, also known as **The Little Clay Cart** is a ten-act Sanskrit drama that is celebrated for its realistic portrayal of urban life in ancient India. Mrichchhakatika tells the story of a noble but impoverished Brahmin, **Charudatta**, and his love for the courtesan **Vasantasena.**
- **(4-D): Bhavabhuti's Uttararamacharita** is a poignant retelling of the later life of **Lord Rama**, focusing on his moral dilemmas and the emotional turmoil following Sita's exile. The play is renowned for its deep emotional resonance and its exploration of dharma (righteousness) and personal duty, and it holds an esteemed place in Sanskrit literature.

Thus, option (a) is the correct answer.

8. *(c)* Only three pairs

- **Pair 1 is correctly matched:** Emperor **Harshavardhana**, who ruled North India in the 7th century, authored several plays, including **Priyadarsika**, a romantic drama. The play is a testament to Harsha's literary talents and his ability to weave complex narratives around love and royalty.

- **Pair 2 is correctly matched: Mudrarakshasa** is a historical play by **Vishakhadatta,** depicting the clever strategies employed by Chanakya to bring Chandragupta Maurya to power. The play is admired for its political intrigue, intricate plot, and portrayal of statecraft in ancient India.
- **Pair 3 is correctly matched: Mahendra-varman I, the Pallava king,** authored **Mattavilasa Prahasana,** a farcical play that satirizes the religious hypocrisy of certain sects. The play is notable for its humour and its sharp critique of contemporary religious practices.
- **Pair 4 is incorrectly matched: Devichandra-guptam** is often attributed to **Vishakhadatta,** and it is known for its depiction of the intrigue and battles surrounding the Gupta dynasty. **Bhavabhuti's** known works include **Malatimadhava, Mahaviracharita, and Uttararamacharita.**

Thus, option (c) **is the correct answer.**

9. *(a)* Sudraka's plays are focused on social themes, while Harshavardhana's plays are more poetic in nature.

- **Sudraka**: The works of Sudraka, particularly **Mrichchhakatika**, are celebrated for their focus on social issues, the depiction of the everyday life of the common people, and their vibrant, realistic portrayal of urban life in ancient India. Sudraka's plays often explore themes of love, poverty, and social justice, making them more accessible and relatable to the audience.
- In contrast, **Harshavardhana's** works like **Ratnavali** and **Priyadarsika** are known for their poetic elegance and sophisticated courtly themes. His plays often revolve around the lives of royalty and are marked by their refined language, intricate plots, and emphasis on romantic and moral ideals.

Thus, option (a) **is the correct answer.**

10. *(b)* Only two

- **Statement 1 is incorrect**: The **National School of Drama** (NSD) was established in 1959, but it was not immediately an autonomous body. Initially, it was part of the Sangeet Natak Akademi but became an autonomous organisation in 1975.
- **Statement 2 is correct**: The NSD operates under the **Ministry of Culture**, Government of India, and it is one of the foremost institutions dedicated to the training of theatre practitioners in India. The school offers a three-year full-time diploma course in Dramatic Arts and has been instrumental in promoting theatre across the country.
- **Statement 3 is incorrect:** The headquarters of the NSD is located in **New Delhi,** not Mumbai. The Delhi-based institution has also organised various theatre festivals and workshops to encourage the development and preservation of traditional and contemporary Indian theatre.

Thus, option (b) **is the correct answer.**

11. *(b)* Only two pairs

- **Pair 1 is incorrectly matched: Bhand Pather** is a traditional folk theatre form from **Jammu and Kashmir,** not Madhya Pradesh. It is known for its satirical humor and the integration of social and mythological themes, often performed in open spaces in rural areas.
- **Pair 2 is incorrectly matched**: Maach is a traditional folk theatre form of **Madhya Pradesh,** not Jammu and Kashmir. It is a musical drama where dialogues are often sung in the form of couplets, known as Rangat Dohas, and it is characterised by its strong connections to the region's folk traditions.
- **Pair 3 is correctly matched: Powada** is a traditional **Marathi ballad** that glorifies the deeds of the Maratha heroes, especially Shivaji Maharaj. The performances are energetic and patriotic, often accompanied by musical instruments like the dholki and tasha.
- **Pair 4 is correctly matched: Dashavatar** is a popular folk theatre form in **Maharashtra** that depicts the ten incarnations of **Lord Vishnu.** The performances are religious and are typically performed in temple courtyards during festivals.

Thus, option (b) **is the correct answer.**

12. *(b)* Only two

- **Statement 1 is incorrect: Yakshagana** is a traditional theatre form from **Karnataka**, not Kerala. This vibrant and colourful form of theatre is known for its elaborate costumes, vigorous dance movements, and powerful music, often performed overnight in open spaces.
- **Statement 2 is correct: Yakshagana** primarily depicts mythological stories and episodes from the Puranas, particularly focusing on the **Mahabharata** and **Ramayana**. The performances are deeply rooted in Hindu religious traditions and are known for their dramatisation of these epic tales.
- **Statement 3 is correct: Yakshagana** performances frequently include themes from the Mahabharata, such as **Draupadi Swayamvar, Abhimanyu Vadh**, and other significant episodes. These stories are dramatised with great intensity and are accompanied by a powerful musical score that enhances the emotional impact of the performance.

Thus, option (b) is the correct answer.

13. *(a)* 1 and 2 only

- **Statement 1 is correct: Therukoothu** is a traditional folk drama form from **Tamil Nadu**, and the name means **street play**. It is performed in open spaces, usually on streets or in temple courtyards, and is known for its lively and spontaneous style.
- **Statement 2 is correct: Therukoothu** performances are often linked to religious festivals, particularly those dedicated to the goddess **Mariamman**, the rain goddess, who is widely worshipped in Tamil Nadu. The performances are intended to invoke the goddess's blessings for a good harvest and protection from diseases.
- **Statement 3 is incorrect:** Therukoothu is typically centered around mythological stories, especially from the **Mahabharata**, rather than historical events. The performances are characterised by exaggerated expressions, high-pitched dialogue delivery, and energetic dance movements.

Thus, option (a) is the correct answer.

14. *(c)* 3 only

- **Statement 1 is incorrect: Mudiyettu** is not a traditional folk theatre form of Tamil Nadu; it belongs to **Kerala**. It is performed as a **ritualistic theatre** form in the Bhadrakali temples of Kerala and is considered a part of the region's intangible cultural heritage.
- **Statement 2 is incorrect: Mudiyettu** is not performed in Vishnu temples but is exclusively performed in **Bhadrakali temples in Kerala**. The ritualistic performance is conducted annually during the post-harvest season, and it reenacts the mythological battle between the **goddess Bhadrakali and the demon Darika**.
- **Statement 3 is correct:** The central theme of Mudiyettu is indeed the **triumph of goddess Bhadrakali over the asura Darika**. This theme is dramatised through elaborate dance movements, vibrant costumes, and vigorous drumming, which together create a powerful and immersive theatrical experience.

Thus, option (c) is the correct answer.

15. *(c)* Krishnattam focuses on the theme of Lord Krishna and was patronised by King Manavada of Calicut.

- **Krishnattam** is a unique form of dance-drama that originated in Kerala and was patronised by **King Manavada** of Calicut (also known as **Zamorin of Calicut**) in the 17th century. It is based on the life and exploits of **Lord Krishna** and is performed as a series of eight plays over eight consecutive nights, each depicting different episodes from Krishna's life, as described in the text **Krishnageeti** written by King Manavada himself. The performances are highly stylized, combining elements of dance, music, and drama, with elaborate costumes and intricate facial makeup.
- Unlike other folk theatres in Kerala, which may focus on a variety of themes, Krishnattam is exclusively centered on the stories of Krishna, making it unique in its devotional and thematic focus.

Thus, option (c) is the correct answer.

16. *(c)* **Nautanki** is a traditional folk theatre form from **North India**, especially popular in **Uttar Pradesh, Haryana,** and **Rajasthan.** The performances are characterised by their use of exaggerated acting, lively songs, and dramatic dialogue, making them highly engaging and entertaining for the audience.

- **Ojhapali** is a narrative folk theatre form from **Assam,** associated with the worship of the **goddess Manasha** (the serpent goddess). The performances involve a lead singer (Oja) who narrates the story, accompanied by assistants (**Palis**) who provide musical and vocal support.
- **Maach** is a traditional folk theatre form of **Madhya Pradesh,** especially popular in the Malwa region. It is a dramatic performance style that combines music, dialogue, and dance. The tunes of this theatrical style are known as **Rangat.**
- **Jatra** is a popular folk theatre form from **West Bengal,** known for its bold, direct style of storytelling. It traditionally combines elements of music, dance, and drama to narrate stories, often with a strong moral or religious message.

Thus, option (c) **is the correct answer.**

17. *(a)* Tal Maddale is a dialogue-based performance without costume, dance, or acting.

- **Tal Maddale** is a traditional form of dialogue-based performance from **Karnataka,** closely related to **Yakshagana** but without the **use of costumes, dance, or elaborate acting.** The performers sit in a semicircle, and the main narrator (**Bhagavatha**) leads the story with the help of other performers. The narratives are usually drawn from **mythological stories** and epics like the Mahabharata and Ramayana.
- While it shares similarities with Yakshagana, Tal Maddale is distinctive in its minimalist approach, focusing on verbal expression and dialogue rather than visual spectacle.

Thus, option (a) **is the correct answer.**

18. *(c)* Both 1 and 2

- **Statement 1 is correct: Kuruvanji** is a classical **Tamil dance-drama** that centers around the love story of a heroine, often depicted as a maiden who falls in love with a divine or royal figure. The name Kuruvanji refers to a **fortune-telling woman** who predicts the future of the heroine. The dance-drama is notable for its use of **Bharatanatyam,** which enhances the narrative through expressive gestures (mudras) and dance movements.
- **Statement 2 is correct: Bayalata** is an **open-air theatre** form from **Karnataka** that primarily focuses on epic poetry and stories from the **Ramayana** and **Mahabharata.** It is performed in **open spaces,** often during festivals, and involves a combination of dialogue, music, and dance.

Thus, option (c) **is the correct answer.**

19. *(a)* 1 and 2 only

- **Statement 1 is correct: Pagati Veshaalu** is a folk performance form from **Andhra Pradesh** and **Telangana,** where a **small group** of performers (usually three to four) enact satirical and social commentaries.
- **Statement 2 is correct:** Performs enact satirical and social commentaries through the character of **Vesham,** which means **disguise.** The performances are known for their humor, wit, and the use of disguise to critique social norms and behaviours.
- **Statement 3 is incorrect:** Pagati Veshaalu is a tradition specific to the **Telugu-speaking** regions. The performances are generally held in open spaces, and the themes often revolve around social reforms and moral teachings, making them an important cultural tradition in these states.

Thus, option (a) **is the correct answer.**

20. *(d)* 1-D, 2-A, 3-C, 4-B

- **(1-D): Kariyala** is a traditional folk theatre form from **Himachal Pradesh,** particularly prevalent in the **Shimla, Solan and Sirmaur districts.** It is usually performed during village fairs and festivals and is characterised by its satirical content, often poking fun at local politics, social issues, and human behaviours.
- **(2-A): Naqal or Bhand** is a form of mimicry-based folk theatre from **Punjab** (and also found in **Uttar Pradesh**), where

performers mimic local characters, politicians, and celebrities, often with a humorous twist. The performers, known as **Naqalchis** or Bhand, use satire to entertain and sometimes to critique social norms and behaviours.

- **(3-C): Swaang or Saang** is a popular form of musical drama that originated in the states of **Rajasthan, Haryana** and **Gujarat.** It involves a mix of dialogue, music, and dance, and the performances often depict episodes from local folklore, mythology, and history.
- **(4-B): Ojapali** is a traditional folk theatre form of **Assam**, deeply rooted in the region's cultural and religious practices. It is characterised by its unique blend of narrative storytelling, musical performance, and ritualistic elements. It involves a solo performer, known as the Ojapali or the narrator, who recites the story with the aid of a drum known as the **khol.**

Thus, option (d) is the correct answer.

21. *(a)* Only one pair

- **Pair 1 is incorrectly matched: Tolpava Kuthu** is a traditional **shadow puppetry** form from **Kerala,** specifically associated with the worship of the **goddess Bhadrakali.** The puppets are made of leather and are used to narrate episodes from the Ramayana, particularly the story of the battle between Rama and Ravana.
- **Pair 2 is correctly matched: Tholu Bommalata** is a form of **shadow puppetry** from **Andhra Pradesh.** The puppets are made from translucent leather and are used to tell stories from the Ramayana, Mahabharata, and other Puranic texts.
- **Pair 3 is incorrectly matched: Kathi Kandhe** is a **rod puppetry** form from **Odisha,** not Bihar. The puppets are manipulated using rods, and the performances often depict stories from the Ramayana, Mahabharata, and local legends. The puppets are typically made from wood and are dressed in colourful costumes.
- **Pair 4 is incorrectly matched: Yampuri** is a **rod puppetry** form from **Bihar,** not Kerala. The puppets are unique in that they are made from a single piece of wood and have no joints.

Thus, option (a) is the correct answer.

22. *(b)* Only two

- **Statement 1 is correct:** Glove puppetry is also known as **hand puppetry or palm puppetry,** where the puppeteer wears the puppet like a glove, controlling its head and arms with their fingers. These puppets are typically made of cloth, papier-mâché, or wood, and are used to narrate both mythological and social stories.
- **Statement 2 is incorrect:** In glove puppetry, the lower part of the puppet is usually a long flowing skirt or robe, and the puppets generally do not have legs. The focus is on the movement of the puppet's upper body and arms, which are manipulated by the fingers of the puppeteer.
- **Statement 3 is correct:** Glove puppetry is prominent in **Uttar Pradesh, Odisha, West Bengal and Kerala.** Eg- Pavakoothu in Kerala and Sakhi nach in Odisha.

Thus, option (b) is the correct answer.

23. *(d)* 1, 2 and 3

- **Statement 1 is correct: String puppetry,** also known as **marionette puppetry,** is one of the most complex and articulate forms of puppetry, where the puppets are manipulated using strings attached to various body parts such as the head, hands, legs, and even waist.
- **Statement 2 is correct:** Strings are attached to various body parts like the head, hands, and legs, which allows the puppeteer to create fluid and dynamic movements. The puppeteer typically manipulates the strings from above, often standing on a platform, giving the illusion that the puppets are moving on their own.
- **Statement 3 is correct:** The regional forms of string puppetry mentioned are Kathputli (Rajasthan), Kundhei (Odisha), Gombeyatta (Karnataka), and Bommalattam (Tamil Nadu). Each of these forms has its unique characteristics, influenced by local traditions, culture, and storytelling methods.

Thus, option (d) is the correct answer.

24. *(d)* None

- **Statement 1 is correct: Shadow puppetry** involves the use of flat, opaque, or translucent figures that are held against a translucent screen with a strong light source behind them, casting shadows that the audience views on the other side of the screen.
- **Statement 2 is correct:** Shadow puppets are made from materials like leather, which are often painted or dyed in vibrant colours. The tradition of shadow puppetry thrives in regions such as **Andhra Pradesh (Tholu Bommalata), Odisha (Ravanachhaya), Karnataka (Togalu Gombeyatta), Kerala (Tolpava Koothu)** and **Maharashtra.**
- **Statement 3 is correct:** The shadows can be silhouettes or coloured depending on the material of the puppets and the screen. For example, **Tholu Bommalata from Andhra** Pradesh uses **translucent leather puppets** that create coloured shadows, making the performances visually captivating.

Thus, option (d) is the correct answer.

25. *(a)* 1 and 2 only

- **Statement 1 is correct: Rod puppetry** is an extension of glove puppetry where the puppets are controlled using rods attached to various parts of the puppet's body. These rods allow the puppeteer to manipulate the puppets from below or behind, creating more complex and dynamic movements than are possible with glove puppets.
- **Statement 2 is correct:** Rod puppetry is mainly popular in Eastern India, particularly in **Bihar (Yampuri), Odisha (Kathi Kandhe), and West Bengal (Putul Nach)**. Each region has its distinct style and techniques.
- **Statement 3 is incorrect:** The heaviest and most complex puppets are typically found in **Tamil Nadu's Bommalattam,** which combines elements of rod and string puppetry. These puppets can be up to **4-5 feet tall** and are manipulated by multiple puppeteers using both rods and strings.

Thus, option (a) is the correct answer.

26. *(c)* All three

- **Statement 1 is correct:** The first archaeological evidence of puppetry in India was found at **Mohenjodaro**, one of the major cities of the **Indus Valley Civilisation, dating back to 2500 BCE.** Excavations at the site revealed small terracotta figurines with sockets attached to their limbs, suggesting that they were used as puppets.
- **Statement 2 is correct:** The earliest written reference to puppetry is found in the Tamil classic **Silappadikaram,** written by **Ilango Adigal.** This ancient Tamil epic mentions various forms of performing arts, including puppetry, which was an integral part of the cultural life in South India during that period.
- **Statement 3 is correct: The Bhagavad Gita** provides a metaphorical reference to puppetry, where the universe is described as being controlled by God, who is the supreme puppeteer with 3 strings -**Sattva** (goodness), **Rajas** (passion), and **Tamas** (ignorance). They represent 3 fundamental qualities influencing human behaviour and life.

Thus, option (c) is the correct answer.

27. *(d)* 1, 2 and 3

- **Statement 1 is correct: Kathputli** is a traditional string puppetry form from **Rajasthan.** One of the distinctive features of Kathputli puppets is that they **do not have legs;** instead, they have long, flowing skirts that cover the lower body, adding to the illusion of movement created by the strings.
- **Statement 2 is correct:** The word Kathputli indeed comes from **Kath** (wood) and **Putli** (doll). These puppets are intricately carved from wood and are usually around 1.5 to 2 feet tall. They are adorned with vibrant costumes and jewellery, reflecting the traditional Rajasthani attire.
- **Statement 3 is correct:** The **Kathputli** tradition is believed to have been started by the **Bhat community of Rajasthan,** who were itinerant performers and storytellers. They

travelled from village to village, using these puppets to narrate tales of valour, love, and mythology, often accompanied by music and songs.

Thus, option (d) is the correct answer.

28. *(c)* 1-C, 2-A, 3-D, 4-B

- (1-C): **Chamadyacha Bahulya** is a traditional shadow puppetry form from **Karnataka**. The puppets used in this form are made from animal hide, usually buffalo or deer skin, which is intricately cut and painted.
- (2-A): **Pavakoothu,** also known as **Nizhalattam,** is a traditional glove puppetry form from Kerala. This form of puppetry is influenced by the classical dance-drama Kathakali, evident in the elaborate costumes and makeup of the puppets.
- (3-D): **Togalu Gombayatta** is a traditional shadow puppetry form from **Karnataka**. The puppets are made from leather and are designed in various sizes, with larger puppets representing gods and smaller ones representing humans or demons.
- (4-B): **Ravanchhaya** is a distinctive form of shadow puppetry from **Odisha**. It means **shadow** of **Ravana** and the performances typically focus on episodes from the Ramayana, particularly the story of the demon king Ravana. Puppets in Ravanchhaya do not have joints and are carved from a single piece of hide, which gives them a unique and recognisable silhouette.

Thus, option (c) is the correct answer.

Past Learning (Answers)

1 (b) **2** (b) **3** (b) **4** (c) **5** (c) **6** (d) **7** (b) **8** (c) **9** (c)

CHAPTER 09 Music

Assessment Round

Topic 1 : Classical Music

1. With reference to the ancient texts related to music, consider the following statements:

1. Gandharva Veda, an Upaveda of Samaveda, is known for teaching the science of music.
2. Brihaddesi, written by Matanga, is a Tamil poem providing information about music during the Chola period.
3. Sangita Ratnakara is known as the 'ocean of music and dance.'

How many of the statements given above is/are correct?

(a) Only one (b) Only two
(c) All three (d) None

2. Identify the ancient text based on the following statements:

1. It was written by Narada and categorises Raga as male, female, and neuter.
2. It is one of the key texts in Indian classical music that delves into the emotional expressions of ragas.
3. It was referenced by both Hindustani and Carnatic music traditions.

Which of the following texts is best described by the statements above?

(a) Sangita Makaranda (b) Sangita Sudhakara
(c) Sangita Ratnakara (d) Natyashastra

3. Regarding the Natyashastra, consider the following statements:

1. It is the earliest literature that talks about music in Sanskrit.
2. It describes musical instruments, Swara, Jati, and musical compositions.
3. It was written by Bharat Muni.

Which of the statements given above are correct?

(a) 1 and 2 only (b) 2 and 3 only
(c) 1 and 3 only (d) 1, 2 and 3

4. Consider the following statements about the Sama Veda:

1. All seven notes of the raga Kharaharapriya can be found in the Sama Veda.
2. It primarily discusses dance and music collectively.
3. It includes the science of music as explained in Gandharva Veda.

Which of the statements given above are incorrect?

(a) 1 and 2 only (b) 2 and 3 only
(c) 1 and 3 only (d) 1, 2 and 3

5. With reference to ancient texts on music, consider the following statements:

1. Sangita Sudhakara was written by Someshwara, a Chalukyan king.
2. Gita Govinda, written by Jayadeva, describes Raga and Tala associated with the eight moods of the heroine.
3. Sangraha Choodamani deals with the system of Carnatic music.

How many of the statements given above is/are correct?

(a) Only one (b) Only two
(c) All three (d) None

6. With reference to the aspects of music as per Natyashastra, consider the following statements:

1. Swara refers to the smallest integral part of the pitch that the human ear can detect.
2. Shruti is the arrangement of Swaras in different sequences.
3. Tala is the cycle of beats performed by singers.

How many of the statements given above is/are correct?

(a) Only one
(b) Only two
(c) All three
(d) None

7. Match the following Ragas with their corresponding Rasa (mood):

	Ragas		Corresponding Rasa
1.	Bhairav	A.	Peace / Tranquility
2.	Deepak	B.	Courage
3.	Shree	C.	Satisfaction
4.	Malkaus	D.	Vir / Brave

Choose the correct option from the codes below:

(a) 1-A, 2-B, 3-C, 4-D
(b) 1-B, 2-C, 3-A, 4-D
(c) 1-A, 2-D, 3-C, 4-B
(d) 1-D, 2-A, 3-B, 4-C

8. With reference to Ragas, consider the following statements:

1. Audava Raga is a pentatonic raga containing five ragas.
2. Sampurna Raga is a heptatonic raga containing seven ragas.
3. Jatis are the basic elements for the working of Raga.

Which of the statements given above are correct?

(a) 1 and 2 only
(b) 2 and 3 only
(c) 1 and 3 only
(d) 1, 2 and 3

9. Regarding Vadya, the classification of musical instruments, consider the following statements:

1. Ghan Vadya produces sound through the vibration of the entire instrument.
2. Sushir Vadya produces sound through the vibration of stretched strings.
3. Tata Vadya produces sound through the flow of wind.

Which of the statements given above is/are correct?

(a) 1 only (b) 2 and 3 only
(c) 1 and 2 only (d) 1, 2 and 3

10. Consider the following statements about Tala and Shruti:

1. Tala is related to Laya, which means the repetitive nature of any activity.
2. Shruti is the arrangement of Swaras in different sequences.
3. Tala is the smallest integral part of the pitch.

Which of the statement(s) given above is/are correct?

(a) 1 only (b) 1 and 2 only
(c) 2 and 3 only (d) 1, 2 and 3

11. Identify the vocal style based on the following statements:

1. It is performed mostly by solo singers.
2. It was patronised by Akbar and Raja Man Singh of Gwalior.
3. It is the oldest vocal style in Indian classical music.

Which of the following vocal styles is described above?

(a) Tarana (b) Khayal
(c) Thumri (d) Dhrupad

12. Regarding Thumri, consider the following statements:

1. Thumri can be romantic or devotional.
2. It is usually performed at the end of Khayal concerts.
3. The language used in Thumri is Braj Bhasha.

Which of the statements given above are correct?

(a) 1 and 2 only (b) 2 and 3 only
(c) 1 and 3 only (d) 1, 2 and 3

13. Identify the vocal style based on the following statements:
1. It evolved out of the Qawwali singing style.
2. It was invented by Amir Khusrau.
3. It is flexible in nature and has two sections: Asthayi and Antara.

Which of the following vocal styles is described above?
(a) Dhrupad
(b) Khayal
(c) Thumri
(d) Tarana

14. How do you distinguish between Tarana and Tappa?
1. Tarana involves many words that are sung in a fast tempo, while Tappa compositions are quick, crisp, and volatile.
2. Tarana was invented by Amir Khusrau, while Tappa originated from folk songs of camel riders.

Which of the statements given above is/are correct?
(a) 1 only (b) 2 only
(c) Both 1 and 2 (d) Neither 1 nor 2

15. With reference to Carnatic music, consider the following statements:
1. Carnatic music emphasises the quality of lyrics.
2. It is based on textual standards and set to a fixed raga or tala with minimal improvisation.
3. Charana is the first part of any formal composition.

How many of the statements given above is/are correct?
(a) Only one (b) Only two
(c) All three (d) None

16. With reference to the Trinity of Carnatic Music, consider the following statements:
1. Tyagaraja composed the Panchratna Kritis in dedication to Lord Rama.
2. Muthuswami Dikshitar composed Kritis mostly in Telugu.
3. Syama Sastri composed three musical genres called Svarajati.

How many of the statements given above is/are correct?
(a) Only one
(b) Only two
(c) All three
(d) None

17. Identify the historical figure based on the following statements:
1. He was a Vaishnavite Saint during the Vijayanagar rule.
2. He codified the Carnatic musical system and recognised 84 ragas.
3. He is often referred to as the Father of Carnatic Music.

Which of the following figures is described above?
(a) Tyagaraja
(b) Purandara Dasa
(c) Muthuswami Dikshitar
(d) Syama Sastri

18. How do you distinguish between Hindustani and Carnatic music?
1. Hindustani music has many Gharanas, while Carnatic music has no Gharanas.
2. Hindustani music is more emotional, while Carnatic music is more philosophical.

Which of the statements given above is/are correct?
(a) 1 only
(b) 2 only
(c) Both 1 and 2
(d) Neither 1 nor 2

19. How do Hindustani and Carnatic music differ in their structural bondage?
1. Hindustani music has less structural bondage and allows for more innovation.
2. Carnatic music is more rigid with greater structural bondage.

Which of the statements given above is/are correct?
(a) 1 only (b) 2 only
(c) Both 1 and 2 (d) Neither 1 nor 2

20. With reference to the fusion of classical and folk music, consider the following statements:

1. Qawwali originated out of the Sufi tradition and was popularised by Amir Khusrau.
2. Rabindra Sangeet, which blends ragas with folk music, was initiated by Gurudev Rabindranath Tagore.
3. Ghazals were introduced by Chaitanya Mahaprabhu during the medieval period.

How many of the statements given above is/are correct?

(a) Only one (b) Only two
(c) All three (d) None

21. Consider the following statements about Gana Sangeet:

1. Gana Sangeet is sung in choirs or groups and reflects patriotism.
2. It is mostly composed of love songs.
3. It was started by Mirza Ghalib.

Which of the statements given above is/are correct?

(a) 1 only (b) 1 and 2 only
(c) 2 and 3 only (d) 1, 2 and 3

22. With reference to the Gharanas in Hindustani classical music, consider the following statements:

1. The Kirana Gharana focuses on expressing emotional moods.
2. The Gwalior Gharana is associated with the Khayal style of singing.
3. The Jaipur-Atrauli Gharana focuses primarily on rhythmic performances.

How many of the statements given above is/are correct?

(a) Only one (b) Only two
(c) All three (d) None

Topic 2 : Folk Music

23. With reference to the folk music style Pandavani, consider the following statements:

1. Pandavani involves the singing of tales from the Ramayana as a ballad.
2. The main singer in Pandavani performs with symbolic gestures while sitting throughout the performance.
3. Pandavani is traditionally performed in the state of Chhattisgarh.

How many of the statements given above is/are correct?

(a) Only one (b) Only two
(c) All three (d) None

24. Match the following regional music styles with their corresponding states:

1.	Pankhida	A.	Uttar Pradesh
2.	Mando	B.	Goa
3.	Hori	C.	Kashmir
4.	Chhakri	D.	Rajasthan

Choose the correct option from the codes below:

(a) 1-D, 2-B, 3-A, 4-C
(b) 1-C, 2-D, 3-B, 4-A
(c) 1-A, 2-B, 3-D, 4-C
(d) 1-B, 2-A, 3-C, 4-D

25. Which of the following statements about Rasiya Geet is incorrect?

(a) Rasiya Geet is traditionally sung in Braj, the sacred land of Lord Krishna's leelas.
(b) It is sung by peasants in Rajasthan while working in the fields.
(c) It is closely woven into the daily life and chores of the people in Braj.
(d) It is not confined to any particular festival.

26. Identify the folk music style based on the following statements:

1. It is a group song where girls and boys sing stanzas in response to each other, often from opposite hill peaks.
2. It is primarily sung in the Kullu Valley of Himachal Pradesh.
3. The participants rarely see each other's faces during the singing.

Which of the following folk music styles is described above?

(a) Laman (b) Chhakri
(c) Pandavani (d) Lotia

27. Identify the folk music style based on the following statements:

1. It is a folk song sung by women in Uttar Pradesh during the rainy season.
2. It is traditionally sung on the third day in the second half of the Bhadra month.
3. The women sing this style all night while dancing in a semi-circle.

Which of the following folk music styles is described above?
(a) Hori
(b) Kajri
(c) Teej Songs
(d) Burrakatha

28. With reference to the folk music style Shakunakhar, consider the following statements:

1. Shakunakhar songs are sung during religious ceremonies such as baby showers and childbirth.
2. These songs are performed exclusively by men without any instrumental accompaniment.
3. Shakunakhar is a traditional folk music style from Kumaon.

How many of the statements given above is/are correct?
(a) Only one (b) Only two
(c) All three (d) None

29. With reference to the folk music style Alha, consider the following statements:

1. Alha narrates the heroic deeds of Alha and Udal, two warrior brothers.
2. It is the most popular regional music of Bundelkhand.
3. Alha is primarily sung during the festival of Holi.

How many of the statements given above is/are correct?
(a) Only one
(b) Only two
(c) All three
(d) None

30. Match the following folk music styles with their descriptions:

1.	Powada	A.	A ballad form from Maharashtra narrating heroic deeds
2.	Teej Songs	B.	Festival songs sung by women in Rajasthan
3.	Tappa	C.	Semi-classical vocal music inspired by camel riders in Punjab
4.	Burrakatha	D.	A highly dramatic form of ballad from Andhra Pradesh

Choose the correct option from the codes below:
(a) 1-A, 2-B, 3-C, 4-D
(b) 1-B, 2-A, 3-D, 4-C
(c) 1-C, 2-D, 3-A, 4-B
(d) 1-D, 2-C, 3-B, 4-A

31. Match the following folk music styles with their regions:

1.	Bhakha	A.	Odisha
2.	Daskathia	B.	Mizoram
3.	Sana Lamok	C.	Jammu and Kashmir
4.	Saikuti Zai	D.	Manipur

Choose the correct option from the codes below:
(a) 1-C, 2-A, 3-D, 4-B
(b) 1-B, 2-C, 3-A, 4-D
(c) 1-A, 2-B, 3-C, 4-D
(d) 1-D, 2-A, 3-B, 4-C

32. With reference to the Basant Geet from Garhwal, consider the following statements:

1. Basant Geet is sung during the festival of Basant Panchmi.
2. The songs are sung to welcome the spring season, which is filled with colourful flowers.
3. The songs are performed exclusively by men while making floor designs with rice flour.

How many of the statements given above is/are correct?
(a) Only one (b) Only two
(c) All three (d) None

33. How do you distinguish between Chai Hia and Bhuta songs?

1. Chai Hia songs are associated with the Chapchar Kut festival in Mizoram, while Bhuta songs are sung during rituals to ward off evil spirits in Kerala.
2. Chai Hia songs are performed by both men and women, while Bhuta songs are primarily performed by men.

Which of the statements given above is/are incorrect?

(a) 1 only (b) 2 only
(c) Both 1 and 2 (d) Neither 1 nor 2

34. How do you distinguish between Ja-jin-ja and Nyioga songs from Arunachal Pradesh?

1. Ja-jin-ja is sung during the marriage ceremony, while Nyioga is sung at the end of the marriage ceremony.
2. Ja-jin-ja is associated with welcoming the bride, while Nyioga is associated with bidding farewell to the couple.

Which of the statements given above is/are incorrect?

(a) 1 only
(b) 2 only
(c) Both 1 and 2
(d) Neither 1 nor 2

35. How do you distinguish between Zikir and Borgeet songs from Assam?

1. Zikir embodies the teachings of Islam, while Borgeet is associated with Ekasarana Dharma.
2. Zikir is performed in groups, while Borgeet is usually a solo performance.

Which of the statements given above is/are correct?

(a) 1 only
(b) 2 only
(c) Both 1 and 2
(d) Neither 1 nor 2

36. How do you distinguish between Dollu Kunitha from Karnataka and other folk dances?

1. Dollu Kunitha is named after the percussion instrument 'dollu' and is performed by the Kuruba community.
2. It is a solo dance form, whereas most other folk dances from Karnataka are group performances.

Which of the statements given above is/are correct?

(a) 1 only
(b) 2 only
(c) Both 1 and 2
(d) Neither 1 nor 2

OMR SHEET

Assessment Round

1	(a) (b) (c) (d)	31	(a) (b) (c) (d)	61	(a) (b) (c) (d)	91	(a) (b) (c) (d)
2	(a) (b) (c) (d)	32	(a) (b) (c) (d)	62	(a) (b) (c) (d)	92	(a) (b) (c) (d)
3	(a) (b) (c) (d)	33	(a) (b) (c) (d)	63	(a) (b) (c) (d)	93	(a) (b) (c) (d)
4	(a) (b) (c) (d)	34	(a) (b) (c) (d)	64	(a) (b) (c) (d)	94	(a) (b) (c) (d)
5	(a) (b) (c) (d)	35	(a) (b) (c) (d)	65	(a) (b) (c) (d)	95	(a) (b) (c) (d)
6	(a) (b) (c) (d)	36	(a) (b) (c) (d)	66	(a) (b) (c) (d)	96	(a) (b) (c) (d)
7	(a) (b) (c) (d)	37	(a) (b) (c) (d)	67	(a) (b) (c) (d)	97	(a) (b) (c) (d)
8	(a) (b) (c) (d)	38	(a) (b) (c) (d)	68	(a) (b) (c) (d)	98	(a) (b) (c) (d)
9	(a) (b) (c) (d)	39	(a) (b) (c) (d)	69	(a) (b) (c) (d)	99	(a) (b) (c) (d)
10	(a) (b) (c) (d)	40	(a) (b) (c) (d)	70	(a) (b) (c) (d)	100	(a) (b) (c) (d)
11	(a) (b) (c) (d)	41	(a) (b) (c) (d)	71	(a) (b) (c) (d)	101	(a) (b) (c) (d)
12	(a) (b) (c) (d)	42	(a) (b) (c) (d)	72	(a) (b) (c) (d)	102	(a) (b) (c) (d)
13	(a) (b) (c) (d)	43	(a) (b) (c) (d)	73	(a) (b) (c) (d)	103	(a) (b) (c) (d)
14	(a) (b) (c) (d)	44	(a) (b) (c) (d)	74	(a) (b) (c) (d)	104	(a) (b) (c) (d)
15	(a) (b) (c) (d)	45	(a) (b) (c) (d)	75	(a) (b) (c) (d)	105	(a) (b) (c) (d)
16	(a) (b) (c) (d)	46	(a) (b) (c) (d)	76	(a) (b) (c) (d)	106	(a) (b) (c) (d)
17	(a) (b) (c) (d)	47	(a) (b) (c) (d)	77	(a) (b) (c) (d)	107	(a) (b) (c) (d)
18	(a) (b) (c) (d)	48	(a) (b) (c) (d)	78	(a) (b) (c) (d)	108	(a) (b) (c) (d)
19	(a) (b) (c) (d)	49	(a) (b) (c) (d)	79	(a) (b) (c) (d)	109	(a) (b) (c) (d)
20	(a) (b) (c) (d)	50	(a) (b) (c) (d)	80	(a) (b) (c) (d)	110	(a) (b) (c) (d)
21	(a) (b) (c) (d)	51	(a) (b) (c) (d)	81	(a) (b) (c) (d)	111	(a) (b) (c) (d)
22	(a) (b) (c) (d)	52	(a) (b) (c) (d)	82	(a) (b) (c) (d)	112	(a) (b) (c) (d)
23	(a) (b) (c) (d)	53	(a) (b) (c) (d)	83	(a) (b) (c) (d)	113	(a) (b) (c) (d)
24	(a) (b) (c) (d)	54	(a) (b) (c) (d)	84	(a) (b) (c) (d)	114	(a) (b) (c) (d)
25	(a) (b) (c) (d)	55	(a) (b) (c) (d)	85	(a) (b) (c) (d)	115	(a) (b) (c) (d)
26	(a) (b) (c) (d)	56	(a) (b) (c) (d)	86	(a) (b) (c) (d)	116	(a) (b) (c) (d)
27	(a) (b) (c) (d)	57	(a) (b) (c) (d)	87	(a) (b) (c) (d)	117	(a) (b) (c) (d)
28	(a) (b) (c) (d)	58	(a) (b) (c) (d)	88	(a) (b) (c) (d)	118	(a) (b) (c) (d)
29	(a) (b) (c) (d)	59	(a) (b) (c) (d)	89	(a) (b) (c) (d)	119	(a) (b) (c) (d)
30	(a) (b) (c) (d)	60	(a) (b) (c) (d)	90	(a) (b) (c) (d)	120	(a) (b) (c) (d)

Calculate Your Score

Correct (✓)	
Incorrect (✓)	
Unattempted	
Total Score	
Accuracy (%)	

Reasons for Incorrect Answers?

1. Lack of Knowledge/Existing Source Insufficient	
2. Lack of Multiple Revision	
3. Common Sense Mistakes	

Note :

1. Calculate total score as correct answers carry 2 marks each 1/3rd marks will deducted for **Incorrect** Answers.
2. Calculate Accuracy (%) by dividing the number of correct answers to the total number of attempted questions.

Past Learning

1. With reference to the cultural history of India, consider the following statements : **(2018)**

1. Most of the Tyagaraja Kritis are devotional songs in praise of Lord Krishna.
2. Tyagaraja created several new rages.
3. Annamacharya and Tyagaraja are contemporaries.
4. Annamacharya kirtanas are devotional songs in praise of Lord Venkateshwara.

Which of the statements given above are correct?

(a) 1 and 3 only
(b) 2 and 4 only
(c) 1, 2 and 3
(d) 2, 3 and 4

2. A community of people called Manganiyars is well-known for their **(2014)**

(a) martial arts in North-East India
(b) musical tradition in North-West India
(c) classical vocal music in South India
(d) pietra dura tradition in Central India

3. With reference to Dhrupad, one of the major traditions of India that has been kept alive for centuries, which of the following statements is correct? **(2012)**

1. Dhrupad originated and developed in the Rajput kingdoms during the Mughal period.
2. Dhrupad is primarily a devotional and spiritual music.
3. Dhrupad Alap uses Sanskrit syllables from mantras.

Select the correct answer using the codes given below.

(a) 1 and 2 (b) 2 and 3
(c) 1, 2 and 3 (d) None of these

4. The brothers Umakant and Ramakant Gundecha are **(2009)**

(a) Dhrupad vocalists
(b) Kathak dancers
(c) Sarod maestros
(d) Tabla players

5. Match List I with List II and select the correct answer using the codes given below the lists. **(2009)**

List I (Famous Persons)		List II (Well-Known as)	
A.	Amrita Shergil	1.	Dancer
B.	Bhimsen Joshi	2.	Painter
C.	Rukmini Devi Arundale	3.	Poet
D.	Suryakant Tripathi 'Nirala'	4.	Singer

Codes

	A	B	C	D
(a)	2	1	4	3
(b)	2	4	1	3
(c)	3	1	4	2
(d)	3	4	1	2

6. Consider the following statements. **(2003)**

1. Kitab-i-Nauras, a collection of songs in praise of Hindu deities and Muslim saints, was written by Ibrahim Adil Shah II.
2. Amir Khusrau was the originator in India of the early from of the musical style known as Qawali.

Which of these statements is/are correct?

(a) Only 1 (b) Only 2
(c) Both 1 and 2 (d) Neither 1 nor 2

7. Match List I with List II and select the correct answer using the codes given below the lists. **(2001)**

List I		List II	
A.	Kalamandalam Kshemavaty	1.	Kathakali
B.	Kottakkal Sivaraman	2.	Manipuri
C.	Lakshmi Viswanathan	3.	Mohiniyattam
D.	N Madhabi Devi	4.	Bharatanatyam

Codes

	A	B	C	D
(a)	1	3	2	4
(b)	1	3	4	2
(c)	3	1	4	2
(d)	3	1	2	4

Detailed Solutions

Assessment Round

1. *(b)* Only two

- **Statement 1 is correct:** Gandharva Veda is an Upaveda of the Samaveda. The Samaveda is a collection of sung rather than recited hymns, making it closely **associated with music and chant**. Gandharva Veda is a text that provides knowledge about **musical scales**, the **organisation of notes**, and the theory behind melodic compositions.
- **Statement 2 is incorrect:** Brihaddesi is a seminal work in **Sanskrit, not Tamil, written by the musicologist Matanga**. The text dates back to around the 6th to 9th centuries CE and is considered one of the most important early works that discuss the concepts of '**Raga**' and '**Shruti.**' Brihaddesi isn't specifically focused on the Chola period. It is more of a **pan-Indian treatise** on music, laying down theories that influenced both **Hindustani and Carnatic music traditions.**
- **Statement 3 is correct:** Sangita Ratnakara, written by **Sarngadeva in the 13th century**, is one of the most comprehensive and revered texts in Indian classical music. It is referred to as the '**Sangita Samhita**' and is considered as the 'ocean of music and dance.'

Thus, option (b) is the correct answer.

2. *(a)* Sangita Makaranda

- The ancient text referred to here is the **Sangita Makaranda**. Authored by the **sage Narada**, this work is one of the foundational texts of **Indian classical music**. It offers a unique categorisation of ragas into **male (Purusha), female (Stri), and neuter (Napunsaka)**. This categorisation is based on the emotional and aesthetic qualities of the ragas, linking them to specific times of the day, seasons, and even gender-based characteristics.
- It is a key text that explores the **emotional depth and expressiveness of ragas**. The text goes beyond the technical aspects of music, delving into how ragas evoke different emotions (Rasas) in the listener. Sangita Makaranda has had a lasting impact on **both Hindustani and Carnatic music traditions.**

Thus, option is (a) the correct answer.

3. *(d)* 1, 2 and 3

- **Statement 1 is correct:** The Natyashastra is one of the oldest texts in Sanskrit on performing arts, including **music, dance, and drama**. Written between 200 BCE and 200 CE, the Natyashastra lays the foundation for the theory of music in India. It discusses various aspects of musical theory, including notes (Swaras), scales (Murchanas), and modes (Jatis).
- **Statement 2 is correct:** The Natyashastra is a multi-faceted work that covers a wide range of topics related to the performing arts. It describes different types of musical instruments, including **string (Tata), wind (Sushira), percussion (Avanaddha) and solid (Ghana) instruments.** The text also categorises **Swaras (musical notes) and Jatis (basic melodic frameworks)** and provides guidelines for composing music.
- **Statement 3 is correct:** Bharat Muni is traditionally credited with **composing the Natyashastra.** Although the exact dates of his life are uncertain, his work has been foundational for the Indian classical arts.

Thus, option (d) is the correct answer.

4. *(a)* 1 and 2 only

- **Statement 1 is incorrect:** The raga Kharaharapriya, associated with Carnatic music, is a relatively modern concept compared to the ancient Vedic hymns. While the Sama Veda is the source of the musical tradition in India, it focuses more on chanting specific hymns (Sama) rather than the structured raga system that developed much later.
- **Statement 2 is incorrect:** The Sama Veda is primarily a collection of melodies (Sama)

used in ritualistic chanting, rather than a text that discusses dance and music collectively. While the Vedic hymns have a musical quality, the systematic study of music and dance as interconnected disciplines emerged much later in texts like the Natyashastra.

- **Statement 3 is correct:** The Gandharva Veda, an Upaveda of the Sama Veda, is considered to be a treatise on the science of music, particularly related to the ritualistic chanting of the Vedas. It lays the foundation for understanding the musical aspects of the Vedas, including the use of Swaras (notes) in chanting.

Thus, option (a) is the correct answer.

5. *(b)* Only two

- **Statement 1 is correct:** Sangita Sudhakara was authored by Someshwara, a king of the Chalukya dynasty, around the 13th century. This text is notable for its detailed discussions on **the theory of music, covering various aspects like rhythm (Tala), melody (Raga),** and different musical forms. It reflects the rich musical heritage of the Chalukya period, providing insights into both **Hindustani and Carnatic traditions.**
- **Statement 2 is incorrect:** Gita Govinda, composed by the 12th-century poet Jayadeva, is a devotional work dedicated to **the love between Krishna and Radha.** The text is structured as a sequence of lyrical verses and songs that convey the emotional and devotional aspects of their relationship. Although it is set to music and uses specific ragas and talas, Gita Govinda is not a technical treatise on music. Instead, it is more focused on the expression of **bhakti (devotion) through poetry and music,** rather than providing a systematic analysis of musical elements.
- **Statement 3 is correct:** Sangraha Choodamani is an important text in the Carnatic music tradition, **attributed to Govindacharya.** It is one of the earliest works to detail the classification of ragas in the Carnatic music system, particularly through the use of the **Melakarta (parent raga)** scheme. This text is crucial for understanding the structure and organisation of ragas in Carnatic music and is still referenced by musicologists and performers today.

Thus, option (b) is the correct answer.

6. *(a)* Only one

- **Statement 1 is incorrect:** A Swara is a musical note that is **part of the octave.** There are seven basic Swaras in Indian classical music: Sa, Re, Ga, Ma, Pa, Dha, and Ni. Each Swara is a distinct pitch, but it is **not the smallest detectable pitch;** that would be the Shruti.
- **Statement 2 is incorrect:** Shruti refers to the **smallest pitch intervals** that can be detected by the **human ear,** not the arrangement of Swaras. The concept of Shruti is fundamental in Indian music, where it is believed that there are **22 Shrutis in an octave.** These form the microtonal framework within which the Swaras are defined.
- The arrangement of Swaras in sequences is better described by the terms Raga or Jati, rather than Shruti.
- **Statement 3 is correct:** Tala is a concept that refers to the **rhythmic aspect** of Indian classical music. It is a **repeating cycle of beats** that sets the timing and structure for a musical performance. The cycle can vary in length, from simple cycles like Dadra (6 beats) to more complex ones like Jhaptal (10 beats) or Teental (16 beats).

Thus, option (a) is the correct answer.

7. *(a)* 1-A, 2-B, 3-C, 4-D

- (1-A): **Raga Bhairav** is traditionally associated with **peace and tranquility.** It is a morning raga and is known for its **calm and meditative mood,** often invoking a sense of devotion and solemnity. This raga is considered auspicious and is commonly used in the performance of devotional and classical compositions.
- (2-B): **Raga Deepak** is linked with the **element of fire** and is known for its **intense and energetic mood.** While it is more traditionally associated with bringing heat or light, it also embodies the qualities of **courage and valour.** It is a raga that invokes strong emotions, often used in compositions that require a bold expression.

- **(3-C): Raga Shree** is associated with the late afternoon and is linked with **feelings of solemnity and devotion**, invoking a sense of **reverence and satisfaction.** It is not typically associated with gladness but rather with a more serious, contemplative mood.
- **(4-D): Raga Malkaus** is known for its **deep, serious, and somewhat melancholic mood**, often evoking feelings of **bravery and valour.** It is a midnight raga and is associated with the heroic and courageous aspects of human emotion, making it a powerful raga for depicting bravery.

Thus, option (a) is the correct answer.

8. *(b)* 2 and 3 only

- **Statement 1 is incorrect**: An Audava Raga is a pentatonic raga, meaning it consists of **five notes (Swaras)**. However, the statement incorrectly mentions 'containing five ragas'. Audava Ragas are defined by their structure, using only five notes in ascending and descending scales, making them simpler in comparison to heptatonic or hexatonic ragas.
- **Statement 2 is correct**: A Sampurna Raga **uses all seven notes (Swaras)** of the scale in both ascending (Arohana) and descending (Avarohana) orders. These ragas are complete in terms of their melodic range and are some of the most versatile ragas in Indian classical music.
- **Statement 3 is correct**: Jatis are fundamental to the structure of a Raga, as they determine the number of notes used and their arrangement. The three main types of Jatis are **Audava (5 notes), Shadava (6 notes) and Sampurna (7 notes)**, which define the Raga's form and melodic characteristics.

Thus, option (b) is the correct answer.

9. *(a)* 1 only

- **Statement 1 is correct**: Ghan Vadya refers to solid instruments that **produce sound when the entire body of the instrument vibrates.** Examples include instruments like cymbals (Manjira) and gongs, where the entire material vibrates to create sound. These are typically percussion instruments that **do not require a membrane or strings** to produce sound.
- **Statement 2 is incorrect**: Sushir Vadya refers to wind instruments that produce sound **when air is blown through them**. The vibration is created by the **flow of air rather than by stretched strings.** Examples include the **flute (Bansuri) and Shehnai**, where the player's breath is crucial for producing sound.
- **Statement 3 is incorrect**: Tat Vadya refers to string instruments where sound is produced by the **vibration of stretched strings.** Instruments like the **sitar, veena and guitar** fall under this category. The sound is generated by plucking, striking, or bowing the strings, not by the flow of wind.

Thus, option (a) is the correct answer.

10. *(a)* 1 only

- **Statement 1 is correct**: Tala refers to the rhythmic cycle that underpins a musical performance. It is a framework within which **rhythm and tempo are organised.** Laya, on the other hand, refers to the **tempo or speed of the music.** Laya is the concept that describes the repetitive and **cyclical nature** of rhythm in music, which is precisely what Tala governs.
- **Statement 2 is incorrect**: Shruti refers to the **smallest audible pitch** difference that the human ear can detect, which forms the basis for the Swaras in Indian music. The arrangement of Swaras in sequences, however, **is known as Raga.**
- **Statement 3 is incorrect**: Tala is not related to pitch; it is entirely concerned with rhythm. The smallest integral part of pitch would be more accurately **described by Shruti**, which divides the **octave into microtones.**

Thus, option (a) is the correct answer.

11. *(d)* Dhrupad

- Dhrupad is one of the oldest forms of Indian classical music, and it flourished under the patronage of Mughal Emperor Akbar, who was a great supporter of the arts. Raja Man Singh Tomar of Gwalior is also historically significant in promoting Dhrupad during his reign, establishing Gwalior as a center for this vocal style. It is a classical form that emphasises individual performance.

- Dhrupad is the oldest surviving form of Indian classical music, with its origins traced back to the Vedic chants. It is known for its solemn and meditative nature, typically performed by a solo singer who explores the nuances of ragas in great depth.

Thus, option (d) is the correct answer.

12. *(d)* 1, 2 and 3

- **Statement 1 is correct**: Thumri is a light classical vocal form that is highly expressive and emotional. It is often associated with **themes of love, longing, and devotion,** making it versatile enough to be romantic as well as devotional. The lyrics of Thumri typically revolve around the playful and tender aspects of the relationship between **Radha and Krishna**, but they can also explore other romantic or devotional themes.
- **Statement 2 is correct**: Thumri is performed towards the **end of a Khayal concert as a lighter**, more expressive form that contrasts with the more serious and structured Khayal. Its lyrical and emotive content makes it an ideal conclusion to a concert, leaving the audience.
- **Statement 3 is correct**: Thumri is traditionally sung in **Braj Bhasha, a dialect of Hindi** that is associated with the region of Braj, the land of Krishna. Braj Bhasha's lyrical richness and rhythmic beauty make it perfectly suited for the emotive and expressive qualities of Thumri.

Thus, option (d) is the correct answer.

13. *(b)* Khayal

- **Amir Khusrau, a 13th-century Sufi musician,** poet and scholar, is credited with the creation of Khayal. He was a significant figure in the **Delhi Sultanate's court** and played a crucial role in the development of Indian classical music. **Khusrau's innovations** laid the groundwork for Khayal, which later became one of the most popular forms of classical vocal music in North India.
- **Khayal evolved out of Qawwali** which is a devotional form of music that is associated with the Sufi tradition and is known for its powerful and emotive style. Khayal is known for its flexibility and its two-part structure, where the **Asthayi serves** as the main thematic line, and the **Antara** explores the higher octave and further elaborates the raga.

Thus, option (b) is the correct answer.

14. *(c)* Both 1 and 2

- **Statement 1 is correct**: Tarana is a form where **meaningless syllables** are sung at a **fast tempo**, to showcase the singer's **command of rhythm and speed.** It is a vibrant and rhythmic form of classical music that focuses more on the musicality of the syllables rather than lyrical content.
- Tappa is a semi-classical form that is known for its **intricate and rapid-fire melodic phrases.** Originating from the folk songs of **camel riders in Punjab**, Tappa compositions are marked by their **quick tempo, crisp enunciation** and the emotional intensity of the lyrics, which are often about love or longing.
- **Statement 2 is correct: Amir Khusrau** is credited with **inventing Tarana**, a style that he developed to include rhythmic syllables as a form of musical expression. Tappa, on the other hand, is deeply rooted in the **folk traditions of Punjab** and was popularised as a classical form by musicians who adapted these folk melodies into more structured compositions.

Thus, option (c) is the correct answer.

15. *(b)* Only two

- **Statement 1 is correct**: In Carnatic music, the lyrics are composed **with deep philosophical, devotional or emotional content.** These lyrics, typically written in classical languages like **Telugu, Tamil, or Sanskrit**, are an essential aspect of the composition, contributing to the overall spiritual and aesthetic experience. The focus on lyrical quality ensures that the **words convey profound meanings.** The lyrics are meant to **invoke a deep sense of devotion** (Bhakti) and are often dedicated to deities, making them central to the genre.
- **Statement 2 is correct**: Carnatic music is highly structured and adheres closely to predefined **compositions (Kritis)**. Each Kriti is set to a specific raga (melodic framework)

and tala (rhythmic cycle), with **limited scope for improvisation** compared to Hindustani music. The improvisation that does occur is typically confined to certain sections of a performance, such as **Alapana** (a slow, improvisational exploration of the raga) or **Kalpana Swaras** (improvised swara sequences).

- **Statement 3 is incorrect:** In Carnatic music, the Charana is not the first part of a formal composition. Instead, the **Pallavi is the first part**, followed by the Anupallavi and then the Charana.

Thus, option (b) is the correct answer.

16. *(b)* Only two

- **Statement 1 is correct:** Tyagaraja, one of the most revered composers in Carnatic music, is known for his **devotion to Lord Rama**. The **Panchratna Kritis**, which means "five gems," are five of his most famous compositions, each set in a different raga. They have performed annually at the Tyagaraja Aradhana, a festival held in his honour, and are cherished for their **melodic beauty and spiritual depth.**
- **Statement 2 is incorrect:** Muthuswami Dikshitar, another member of the Carnatic music trinity, composed his kritis **primarily in Sanskrit**. His compositions are known for their scholarly approach, combining deep musical knowledge with rich lyrical content that often includes references to Hindu mythology, temples, and deities.
- **Statement 3 is correct:** Syama Sastri is known for his contributions to the genre of Svarajati, which are considered precursors to the more elaborate Varnams. His Svarajatis are known for their depth of emotion and are still widely performed today. These compositions typically focus on the worship of the goddess Kamakshi, reflecting Syama Sastri's deep devotion and his role in the development of the Bhakti movement within Carnatic music.

Thus, option (b) **is the correct answer.**

17. *(b)* Purandara Dasa

- Purandara Dasa is revered as the '**Sangeeta Pitamaha**' or Father of Carnatic Music for his contributions to the pedagogy and structure of the musical tradition. He developed the foundational exercises (**Sarali Varisai, Janta Varisai, etc.**) that are still used today to train students in the basics of Carnatic music.
- His compositions, primarily in Kannada, are devotional songs that continue to be performed with great reverence.
- He was a prominent **bhakti saint during the Vijayanagara Empire**. The Bhakti movement emphasised personal devotion to a deity and was characterised by the compositions of devotional songs (bhajans and kirtans) in regional languages.
- By codifying the system, he ensured that the musical tradition could be taught and preserved for future generations. The **recognition of 84 ragas** shows a deep understanding and **classification of the melodic structures** in South Indian classical music.

Thus, option (b) is the correct answer.

18. *(c)* Both 1 and 2

- **Statement 1 is correct:** Hindustani music, which is predominant in North India, is characterised by the existence of various Gharanas, or schools of music. Each Gharana has its **unique style, technique and interpretation of ragas,** passed down through generations of musicians. Gharanas like **Gwalior, Jaipur-Atrauli and Kirana** have played a significant role in shaping the Hindustani classical tradition.
- In contrast, Carnatic music, which is predominant in South India, **does not have a Gharana** system. Instead, Carnatic music emphasises a more standardised approach, with a focus on compositions (Kritis) by great composers, making the style more uniform across practitioners.
- **Statement 2 is correct:** Hindustani music often emphasises emotional expression, with a focus on the **mood (Rasa) of the raga**. The performances are highly improvisational, allowing the musician to explore the emotional depth of the raga through **Alap, Bandish and Tans.**

- In contrast, Carnatic music, while also emotional, places a stronger emphasis on the philosophical and devotional aspects. The compositions in Carnatic music are often deeply rooted in spirituality and convey philosophical ideas through their lyrics.

Thus, option (c) is the correct answer.

19. *(c)* Both 1 and 2

- **Statement 1 is correct:** Hindustani music is known for its improvisational freedom. The structure of a raga performance in Hindustani music typically includes an Alap (a slow, improvisational introduction) followed by the Bandish (a fixed composition) and Tans (fast-paced improvisational passages).
- This format allows the musician to explore the raga extensively, with significant room for personal expression and creativity.
- **Statement 2 is correct:** Carnatic music places a strong emphasis on **pre-composed pieces known as Kritis**, composed by great composers such as **Tyagaraja, Muthuswami Dikshitar and Syama Sastri.** These compositions are performed with a **high degree of fidelity** to the original structure, which includes specific ragas, talas, and lyrical content.

While there is room for improvisation in sections like **Alapana** (melodic improvisation), **Niraval** (improvisation of the melody of a line of a Kriti), and **Kalpana Swaras** (improvisation of notes), the scope is generally more limited compared to Hindustani music.

Thus, option (c) is the correct answer.

20. *(b)* Only two

- **Statement 1 is correct:** Qawwali is a form of devotional music that originated within the **Sufi tradition.** Amir Khusrau, a 13th-century poet and musician, is credited with **popularising Qawwali.** It is characterised by its **energetic rhythms, repetitive choruses,** and **spiritual lyrics,** designed to induce a state of religious ecstasy.
- **Statement 2 is correct:** Rabindra Sangeet, the music composed by Rabindranath Tagore, blends elements of classical ragas with the simplicity and **expressiveness of Bengali folk music.** Tagore's compositions cover a wide range of emotions and themes, from devotion and patriotism to love and nature.
- **Statement 3 is incorrect:** Ghazals are a poetic form that originated in Arabic literature and were later adopted in Persian and Urdu traditions. They became popular in India during the Mughal period, but they were not introduced by **Chaitanya Mahaprabhu.**
- Chaitanya Mahaprabhu was a 15th-century saint and the proponent of the Gaudiya Vaishnavism tradition, known for his devotional songs **(Kirtans)** and emphasis on Bhakti (devotion), not for Ghazals.

Thus, option (b) is the correct answer.

21. *(a)* 1 only

- **Statement 1 is correct:** Gana Sangeet refers to songs that are typically sung in groups or choirs and are associated with **themes of patriotism and social reform.** These songs gained popularity during the Indian independence movement, where they were used to **inspire collective action and solidarity.** The lyrics emphasise themes of unity, resistance and national pride.
- **Statement 2 is incorrect:** Gana Sangeet is not primarily composed of love songs. While it may occasionally include themes of love, its primary focus is on patriotism, social issues, and collective action.
- **Statement 3 is incorrect:** Gana Sangeet was not started by Mirza Ghalib. Mirza Ghalib was a 19th-century Urdu and Persian poet, known for his Ghazals, which are lyrical and often focus on themes of love, loss, and existential contemplation.

Thus, option (a) is the correct answer.

22. *(b)* Only two

- **Statement 1 is correct:** The Kirana Gharana, one of the most prominent Gharanas in Hindustani classical music, is known for its emphasis on the **emotional expression of ragas.** Founded by **Ustad Abdul Karim Khan,** the Kirana Gharana places great importance on slow, sustained notes and intricate voice modulations to convey the mood (Rasa) of the raga.

- **Statement 2 is correct:** The Gwalior Gharana is one of the oldest and most influential Gharanas in Hindustani classical music, particularly known for its **Khayal singing.** It emphasises clarity of pronunciation, a steady tempo, and a structured approach to raga development.
- **Statement 3 is incorrect:** While the Jaipur-Atrauli Gharana, founded by Alladiya Khan, is known for its **intricate and complex raga renditions,** it is not primarily focused on **rhythm.** Instead, this Gharana is celebrated for its elaborate and precise treatment of rare and complex ragas, often involving intricate note patterns and long, sustained phrases. The emphasis is on the purity and complexity of ragas, rather than on rhythmic aspects.

Thus, option (b) is the correct answer.

23. *(b)* Only two

- **Statement 1 is incorrect:** Pandavani is a traditional form of storytelling that involves the singing of **tales from the Mahabharata, particularly focusing on the exploits of the Pandava brothers.** The performer, often accompanied by minimal instruments like the tambura, narrates the story through song and dramatic gestures, bringing the characters and events to life.
- **Statement 2 is correct:** In Pandavani performances the lead singer, who is **usually seated, uses symbolic gestures, facial expressions, and vocal modulations** to portray different characters and emotions. The tambura (a string instrument) is often used as a prop to symbolise various objects, such as a bow, a mace, or a chariot, adding a dramatic element to the storytelling.
- **Statement 3 is correct:** Pandavani is a folk music tradition that is deeply rooted in the culture of Chhattisgarh. It is an important part of the region's oral storytelling tradition and is performed during various cultural and religious festivals.

Thus, option (b) is the correct answer.

24. *(a)* 1-D, 2-B, 3-A, 4-C

- **(1-D): Pankhida** is a traditional folk song from **Rajasthan.** It is typically sung by peasants while working in the fields. The word 'Pankhida' literally means 'lover,' and the songs often express longing and love. The music is usually accompanied by simple instruments like the **algoza (a double flute) and manjira (small cymbals),** adding to its rustic charm.
- **(2-B): Mando** is a classical form of **Goa folk music** that blends the influences of Indian and Western traditions, especially **Portuguese.** It is known for its slow and melodious tunes that often deal with themes of **love, tragedy and social issues.** The lyrics are typically in **Konkani,** the local language of Goa.
- **(3-A): Hori** is a traditional folk song associated with the festival of **Holi in Uttar Pradesh.** The songs are characterised by their playful and celebratory nature, often involving themes of love and the playful relationship between **Krishna and Radha.**
- **(4-C): Chhakri** is traditional folk music in **Kashmir.** It is a group song, usually performed by **both men and women** and is characterised by its simple yet melodious tunes. The lyrics deal with themes of **love, nature and the beauty of the Kashmiri landscape.** Chhakri is typically accompanied by instruments like the rabab, sarangi and noot.

Thus, option (a) is the correct answer.

25. *(b)* It is sung by peasants in Rajasthan while working in the fields.

- **Statement (a) is correct:** Rasiya Geet is closely associated with the **region of Braj,** which is known as the land of Lord Krishna. These songs often depict the playful and romantic episodes of Krishna's life, particularly his interactions with the **Gopis.**
- **Statement (b) is incorrect:** Rasiya Geet is not typically associated with the peasants of Rajasthan. Instead, it is a folk music tradition of Mathura Vrindavan, which is located in the present-day state of Uttar Pradesh.
- **Statement (c) is correct:** Rasiya Geet is woven into the daily life and culture of the people in Braj. These songs are sung during various **occasions, such as festivals, weddings** and other communal gatherings, reflecting

the deep connection between the music and the cultural practices of the region.

- **Statement (d) is correct:** While Rasiya Geet is most prominently associated with the Holi festival, it is not confined to any single festival. The songs are performed on various occasions throughout the year, making them a versatile and integral part of the Braj folk tradition.

Thus, option (b) is the correct answer.

26. *(a)* Laman

- Laman is a traditional form of folk singing in the **Kullu Valley, Himachal Pradesh,** where groups sing in response to each other from distant hilltops. The unique geographic and cultural context of the region gives rise to this fascinating and interactive musical form, which serves both as entertainment and a means of social interaction.
- These **participants rarely see each other's faces during the singing, this practice** is common in regions with challenging terrain, where the natural environment influences the way cultural practices develop, including music and dance.

Thus, option (a) is the correct answer.

27. *(b)* Kajri

- Kajri is a traditional folk song of Uttar Pradesh, sung by **women during the monsoon season.** The song's lyrics often express longing for the beloved, with the onset of rains symbolising the yearning for reunion.
- The practice of singing Kajri all night in a **semi-circle is a cherished cultural tradition,** reflecting the deep connection between nature, agriculture, and human emotions in rural Indian life.

Thus, option (b) is the correct answer.

28. *(b)* Only two

- **Statement 1 is correct:** Shakunakhar songs are sung during religious ceremonies of baby shower, childbirth, Chhati (a ritual done on the sixth day from the birth of a child) Ganesh pooja, etc.
- **Statement 2 is incorrect:** Shakunakhar songs are sung **only by women, without any instrumental accompaniment.**
- **Statement 3 is correct:** Shakunakhar is a traditional folk music style from the Kumaon region, which is known for its distinct cultural practices and musical forms.

Thus, option (b) is the correct answer.

29. *(b)* Only two

- **Statement 1 is correct:** Alha is a traditional ballad that recounts the heroic deeds of Alha and his brother Udal, who were legendary warriors known for their bravery and loyalty. They were children of **Dasraj,** a commander in the army of **Chandel king Parmal.** The ballads are usually sung in a powerful and dramatic style, evoking the valor and martial spirit of the warriors.
- **Statement 2 is correct:** Alha is one of the most popular forms of **folk music in Bundelkhand,** a region that spans parts of Uttar Pradesh and Madhya Pradesh.
- **Statement 3 is incorrect :** While Alha can be sung on various occasions, it is not specifically associated with the festival of Holi. The ballads are more often performed during **other cultural and religious gatherings,** and their primary focus is on recounting historical and heroic tales rather than being tied to a particular festival like Holi.

Thus, option (b) is the correct answer.

30. *(a)* 1-A, 2-B, 3-C, 4-D

- **(1-A): Powada** is a traditional form of **Marathi ballad** that narrates the heroic deeds of warriors and historical figures. It is known for its **powerful and vigorous style.** Powada performances are accompanied by traditional instruments like the **dholki and tasha.**
- **(2-B): Teej Songs** are traditional folk songs sung by **women in Rajasthan** and **Uttar Pradesh** during the Teej festival. This festival is celebrated in the monsoon season and is dedicated to the **goddess Parvati.** The songs are characterised by their **joyful and festive mood,** often expressing themes of love, devotion and the monsoon season.
- **(3-C): Tappa** is a semi-classical vocal form that originated from the folk songs of **camel riders in Punjab.** It is known for its rapid tempo and intricate melodic patterns, making it a challenging form for singers.

- **(4-D): Burrakatha** is a traditional folk art form from **Andhra Pradesh** that combines storytelling, music, and dramatisation. It involves a lead performer (**the storyteller**) who narrates the story while playing a **tambura** and two assistants who provide **rhythmic support and dialogue.**

Thus, option (a) is the correct answer.

31. *(a)* 1-C, 2-A, 3-D, 4-B

- **(1-C): Bhakha** is a traditional folk music form from the **Jammu and Kashmir region.** It is sung during **religious and social ceremonies,** reflecting the cultural and spiritual heritage of the region. The songs are typically performed in **Dogri or other local languages** and are accompanied by instruments like the dhol and harmonium.
- (2-A): Daskathia is a unique form of folk storytelling from **Odisha**, involving **two performers** who narrate mythological and religious stories. The performance is characterised by the use of rhythmic clapping (known as 'kathia') and chanting, creating a captivating and rhythmic narrative experience.
- (3-D): **Sana Lamok** is a traditional folk music form from **Manipur**. It is associated with the rituals and cultural practices of the Manipuri people, often performed during religious and ceremonial occasions.
- (4-B): **Saikuti Zai** is a traditional **Mizo folk music** form, performed during social and cultural gatherings in Mizoram. The songs are often reflective of the Mizo community's history, struggles, and social values. The music is typically accompanied by traditional instruments like the drum and bamboo flute.

Thus, option (a) is the correct answer.

32. *(b)* Only two

- **Statement 1 is correct:** Basant Geet is traditionally sung in the **Garhwal region** during the festival of **Basant Panchmi**, which marks the arrival of spring.
- **Statement 2 is correct:** Basant Geet is closely associated with the **spring season**, a time of renewal and growth in the Garhwal region. The songs are an expression of gratitude and celebration for the new life that the season brings, often focusing on the vibrant colours and blooming flowers that characterise spring.
- **Statement 3 is incorrect:** While Basant Geet is an important part of the spring festival, it is **not exclusively performed by men**, nor is it specifically tied to the activity of making floor designs with rice flour. The songs are generally performed by both men and women in a communal setting, celebrating the season together.

Thus, option (b) is the correct answer.

33. *(d)* Neither 1 nor 2

- **Statement 1 is correct:** Chai Hia songs are traditional folk songs performed during the **Chapchar Kut festival**, which is a spring festival celebrated in **Mizoram**. These songs are joyful and celebratory, marking the **end of the clearing of the jhum fields.** On the other hand, Bhuta songs are **ritualistic songs from Kerala**, performed during ceremonies to appease spirits and **ward off evil**. These songs are part of the Bhuta worship tradition, which is unique to the **Tulu-speaking people** of Karnataka and Kerala.
- **Statement 2 is correct:** Chai Hia songs are typically performed **by both men and women**, reflecting the communal nature of the festival and the inclusive spirit of the celebrations. Bhuta songs, on the other hand, are primarily **performed by men**, often by specific groups or communities that are involved in the ritualistic traditions of Bhuta worship. The performances are intense and involve complex rituals, which are typically carried out by men.

Thus, option (d) is the correct answer.

34. *(d)* Neither 1 nor 2

- **Statement 1 is correct:** Ja-jin-ja and Nyioga are both traditional songs from **Arunachal Pradesh**, associated with marriage ceremonies. Ja-jin-ja is typically sung **during the actual marriage ceremony**, reflecting the joy and sacredness of the occasion. Nyioga, on the other hand, is sung **after the marriage ceremony**, often during the farewell of the couple, symbolising the completion of the rituals and the beginning of the couple's new life together.

- **Statement 2 is correct:** Ja-jin-ja songs are often performed as part of the welcoming rituals for the bride, celebrating her arrival and the union of the families. Nyioga songs, conversely, are sung **during the farewell,** marking the departure of the couple and wishing them well in their new life. These songs are deeply rooted in the cultural practices of the tribes in Arunachal Pradesh.

Thus, option (d) is the correct answer.

35. *(c)* Both 1 and 2

- **Statement 1 is correct:** Zikir is a form of devotional music that embodies the **teachings of Islam,** particularly those related to the **Sufi tradition.** It is performed in Assam by Muslim communities and focuses on spiritual themes and moral teachings.
- Borgeet, on the other hand, is a set of devotional songs composed by the **Assamese saint Srimanta Sankardeva,** associated with the **Ekasarana Dharma** (the Vaishnavite tradition in Assam). Borgeets are sung in praise of **Lord Krishna** and are an integral part of the Assamese Vaishnavite culture.
- **Statement 2 is correct:** Zikir is typically performed in groups, with a leader singing the verses and the group responding in a chorus, creating a communal and participatory form of worship. Borgeet, while it can be **performed in groups, is also rendered as a solo performance,** where the singer explores the devotional and emotional depths of the composition, accompanied by traditional instruments like the **dhol (drum) and taal (cymbals).**

Thus, option (c) is the correct answer.

36. *(a)* 1 only

- **Statement 1 is correct:** Dollu Kunitha is a popular **drum dance from Karnataka,** named after the 'dollu,' **a large drum** used in the performance. The dance is primarily performed by the **Kuruba community** and is known for its vigorous and energetic movements. The dancers, typically male, carry the large drums and beat them rhythmically while performing complex dance sequences.
- **Statement 2 is incorrect:** Dollu Kunitha **is not a solo dance form;** it is performed by a group of drummers who synchronise their movements and drum beats to create a powerful and dynamic performance. The dance is marked by its **collective energy and coordination** among the performers, making it a quintessential group performance.

Thus, option (a) is the correct answer.

Past Learning (Answers)

1 (b)	**2** (b)	**3** (b)	**4** (a)	**5** (b)	**6** (c)	**7** (c)

CHAPTER 10 Foreign Travelers

Assessment Round

1. Arrange the following travelers in the correct chronological order of their visits to India:

1. Fa-Hien
2. Megasthenes
3. Ibn Battuta
4. Al-Biruni

Choose the correct answer from the codes given below:

(a) 1-2-3-4 (b) 2-1-4-3
(c) 1-3-2-4 (d) 3-2-1-4

2. Arrange the following travelers by the dynasty they visited during their time in India:

1. Marco Polo 2. Hiuen Tsang
3. Al-Sulaiman 4. Al-Masudi

Choose the correct order according to the dynasties:

(a) 3-2-4-1 (b) 4-3-1-2
(c) 2-3-4-1 (d) 1-3-2-4

3. Consider the following statements about Jean Antoine Dubois:

1. He was a French Catholic missionary who travelled to North India.
2. Locals called him Dodda Swami.
3. He wrote the book Hindu Manners, Customs and Ceremonies.

How many of the above statements is/are correct?

(a) Only one (b) Only two
(c) All three (d) None

4. Consider the following statements regarding Jean Baptiste Tavernier:

Statement I: Jean Baptiste Tavernier was a French diamond merchant who visited India multiple times during the reigns of Shah Jahan and Aurangzeb.

Statement II: He discovered and purchased the Blue Diamond, which was sold to Louis XIV of France.

Which one of the following is correct in respect of the above statements?

(a) Both Statement I and Statement II are correct, and Statement II is the correct explanation for Statement I
(b) Both Statement I and Statement II are correct, and Statement II is not the correct explanation for Statement I
(c) Statement I is correct, but Statement II is incorrect
(d) Statement I is incorrect, but Statement II is correct

5. Consider the following travelers:

1. Francois Bernier
2. Niccolao Manucci
3. Peter Mundy
4. Jean de Thevenot

How many of the above travelers visited India during the reign of Shah Jahan?

(a) Only one
(b) Only two
(c) Only three
(d) All four

6. With reference to Sir Thomas Roe, consider the following statements:

1. Sir Thomas Roe was an English diplomat who visited India during the reign of Akbar.
2. He was a member of the House of Commons.
3. He received permission to set up an English factory at Surat.

Which of the given above statements is/are incorrect?

(a) 2 and 3 only (b) 2 only
(c) 1 only (d) 1, 2 and 3

7. Which of the following books were written by travelers who visited India during the Mughal period?

1. Travels in India by Jean Baptiste Tavernier
2. Storia do Mogor by Niccolao Manucci
3. A Voyage to East India by Sir Thomas Roe
4. Hindu Manners, Customs and Ceremonies by Jean Antoine Dubois

Select the correct answer from the codes given below:

(a) 1 and 3 only (b) 1, 2 and 3 only
(c) 1, 2, 3 and 4 (d) 2 and 4 only

8. Consider the following travelers who documented the social and economic conditions in India:

1. Francois Pelsaert
2. Francis Bernier
3. John Fryer
4. Pietra della Valle
5. Peter Mundy

Which of the above travelers provided accounts of the Mughal Empire's economic conditions?

(a) 1 and 3 only (b) 1, 2 and 3 only
(c) 1, 2, 4 and 5 only (d) 1, 2, 3, 4 and 5

9. Which of the following travelers observed the economic conditions and the lives of common people during their travels in India?

1. Francisco Pelsaert - wrote about the scarcity of food among peasants.
2. Jean de Thevenot - documented the trading practices in Cambay.
3. Jean Baptiste Tavernier - focused primarily on the diamond trade.

Select the correct answer using the codes given below:

(a) 1, 2 and 3
(b) 2 only
(c) 1 and 3 only
(d) 2 and 3 only

10. Which of the following statements best describes Peter Mundy?

(a) Italian doctor who became a Siddha practitioner
(b) French philosopher who wrote about Mughal workshops
(c) British travelers who documented the famine in Gujarat
(d) Dutch travelers who wrote about peasant conditions

11. Arrange the following travelers in the correct chronological order of their visits to India:

1. Sir Thomas Roe
2. Francisco Pelsaert
3. Jean Antoine Dubois
4. Niccolao Manucci

Choose the right answer from the codes given below:

(a) 1-2-4-3
(b) 1-4-2-3
(c) 3-1-2-4
(d) 1-3-4-2

12. Identify the travelers based on the following statements:

1. He was an Italian travelers who reached Surat.
2. He analysed the Sati practice and religious tolerance among Indians.
3. He was associated with the Nayaka of Keladi.

Choose the correct answer from the codes given below:

(a) Gemelli Careri
(b) Jean Baptiste Tavernier
(c) Jean de Thevenot
(d) Pietro della Valle

13. Consider the following statements regarding Edward Terry:

Statement I: Edward Terry accompanied Sir Thomas Roe as a priest and teacher.

Statement II: Edward Terry wrote about the coinage of India during Jahangir's reign.

Which one of the following is correct in respect of the above statements?

(a) Both Statements I and II are correct and Statement II is the correct reason for Statement I.

(b) Both Statements I and II are correct and Statement II is not the correct reason for Statement I.

(c) Statement I is correct, but Statement II is not correct.

(d) Statement I is not correct, but Statement II is correct.

14. According to the writings of Domingo Paes, the people in the Vijayanagara Empire were known for their expertise in which of the following areas?

1. Advanced irrigation technology
2. Multi-cultural cropping
3. Temple architecture
4. Astrology

Select the correct answer using the codes given below:

(a) 1, 2 and 3 only
(b) 2, 3 and 4 only
(c) 1, 3 and 4 only
(d) 1, 2, 3 and 4

15. According to the observations of Abdur Razzak, the court of the Vijayanagara Empire was known for which of the following activities?

1. Ocean trade
2. Ayurveda
3. Fortified settlements
4. Social gatherings

Select the correct answer using the codes given below:

(a) 1, 3 and 4 only
(b) 2 and 3 only
(c) 1, 2 and 3 only
(d) 1, 2, 3 and 4

16. The travelers Caesar Fredrick who visited the Vijayanagara Empire, made certain observations about the societal conditions. In this context, which of the following statements is/are correct?

1. The empire had well-organised social structures before the Battle of Talikota.
2. Merchants were heavily taxed at barrier stations.
3. The society was largely immune to external invasions due to its military strength.

Select the correct answer using the codes given below:

(a) 1 only
(b) 2 and 3 only
(c) 1 and 2 only
(d) 2 only

17. During his travels in the Mughal Empire, William Hawkins observed several aspects of Indian culture and administration. In this context, which of the following statements is/are correct?

1. English traders were welcomed with open arms and given priority over local merchants.
2. There were structured judicial systems involving local laws and customs.
3. The Mughal court practiced religious tolerance under Emperor Jahangir.

Select the correct answer using the codes given below.

(a) 1 only
(b) 2 and 3 only
(c) 1 and 3 only
(d) 2 only

18. In the accounts of Jean Hughen Van Linschotten during the Mughal era, which of the following practices were documented?

1. The use of advanced maritime navigation techniques.
2. Taxation of goods at city borders and trade routes.
3. Strict enforcement of religious conformity by the state.

Select the correct answer using the codes given below :

(a) 1 and 2 only (b) 2 only
(c) 3 only (d) 1, 2 and 3

19. Which foreign travelers, known for his work as a Portuguese priest during the Mughal Empire, documented the wealth and grandeur of the Mughal court, including references to precious stones and Akbar's opulent lifestyle and became teacher Murad?

(a) William Finch
(b) Antonio Monserrate
(c) Ludovico De Varthema
(d) John Huyghen van Linschoten

20. Abdur Razzak, the travelers to Vijayanagara, had referred to the presence of several flower merchants in Vijayanagara and noted a particular flower that seemed as necessary as food to the people of that part. Which variety of flowers was being referred to by Abdur Razzak?

(a) Jasmine
(b) Lotus
(c) Hibiscus
(d) Rose

Past Learning

1. According to Portuguese writer Nuniz, the women in the Vijayanagara Empire were experts in which the following areas? **(2021)**

(1) Wrestling
(2) Astrology
(3) Accounting
(4) Soothsaying

Select the correct answer using the codes given below :

(a) 1, 2 and 3 only (b) 1, 3 and 4 only
(c) 2 and 4 only (d) 1, 2, 3 and 4

2. Which one of the following foreign travelers elaborately discussed about diamonds and diamond mines of India? **(2018)**

(a) Francois Bernier
(b) Jean-Baptiste Tavernier
(c) Jean de Thevenot
(d) Abbe Barthelemy Carre

3. The Chinese travelers Yuan Chwang (Hiuen Tsang) who visited India recorded the general conditions and culture of India at that time. In this context, which of the following statements is/are correct? **(2013)**

1. The roads and river-routes were completely immune from robbery.
2. As regards punishment for offences, ordeals by fire, water and poison were the instruments for determining the innocence or guilt of a person.
3. The tradesmen had to pay duties at ferries and barrier stations.

Select the correct answer using the codes given below :

(a) 1 only
(b) 2 and 3 only
(c) 1 and 3 only
(d) 1, 2 and 3

OMR SHEET

Assessment Round

1	a	b	c	d	31	a	b	c	d	61	a	b	c	d	91	a	b	c	d
2	a	b	c	d	32	a	b	c	d	62	a	b	c	d	92	a	b	c	d
3	a	b	c	d	33	a	b	c	d	63	a	b	c	d	93	a	b	c	d
4	a	b	c	d	34	a	b	c	d	64	a	b	c	d	94	a	b	c	d
5	a	b	c	d	35	a	b	c	d	65	a	b	c	d	95	a	b	c	d
6	a	b	c	d	36	a	b	c	d	66	a	b	c	d	96	a	b	c	d
7	a	b	c	d	37	a	b	c	d	67	a	b	c	d	97	a	b	c	d
8	a	b	c	d	38	a	b	c	d	68	a	b	c	d	98	a	b	c	d
9	a	b	c	d	39	a	b	c	d	69	a	b	c	d	99	a	b	c	d
10	a	b	c	d	40	a	b	c	d	70	a	b	c	d	100	a	b	c	d
11	a	b	c	d	41	a	b	c	d	71	a	b	c	d	101	a	b	c	d
12	a	b	c	d	42	a	b	c	d	72	a	b	c	d	102	a	b	c	d
13	a	b	c	d	43	a	b	c	d	73	a	b	c	d	103	a	b	c	d
14	a	b	c	d	44	a	b	c	d	74	a	b	c	d	104	a	b	c	d
15	a	b	c	d	45	a	b	c	d	75	a	b	c	d	105	a	b	c	d
16	a	b	c	d	46	a	b	c	d	76	a	b	c	d	106	a	b	c	d
17	a	b	c	d	47	a	b	c	d	77	a	b	c	d	107	a	b	c	d
18	a	b	c	d	48	a	b	c	d	78	a	b	c	d	108	a	b	c	d
19	a	b	c	d	49	a	b	c	d	79	a	b	c	d	109	a	b	c	d
20	a	b	c	d	50	a	b	c	d	80	a	b	c	d	110	a	b	c	d
21	a	b	c	d	51	a	b	c	d	81	a	b	c	d	111	a	b	c	d
22	a	b	c	d	52	a	b	c	d	82	a	b	c	d	112	a	b	c	d
23	a	b	c	d	53	a	b	c	d	83	a	b	c	d	113	a	b	c	d
24	a	b	c	d	54	a	b	c	d	84	a	b	c	d	114	a	b	c	d
25	a	b	c	d	55	a	b	c	d	85	a	b	c	d	115	a	b	c	d
26	a	b	c	d	56	a	b	c	d	86	a	b	c	d	116	a	b	c	d
27	a	b	c	d	57	a	b	c	d	87	a	b	c	d	117	a	b	c	d
28	a	b	c	d	58	a	b	c	d	88	a	b	c	d	118	a	b	c	d
29	a	b	c	d	59	a	b	c	d	89	a	b	c	d	119	a	b	c	d
30	a	b	c	d	60	a	b	c	d	90	a	b	c	d	120	a	b	c	d

Calculate Your Score

Correct (✓)	
Incorrect (✓)	
Unattempted	
Total Score	
Accuracy (%)	

Reasons for Incorrect Answers?

1. Lack of Knowledge/Existing Source Insufficient	
2. Lack of Multiple Revision	
3. Common Sense Mistakes	

Note :

1. Calculate total score as correct answers carry 2 marks each 1/3rd marks will deducted for **Incorrect** Answers.
2. Calculate Accuracy (%) by dividing the number of correct answers to the total number of attempted questions.

Detailed Solutions

Assessment Round

1. *(b)* 2-1-4-3

- **Megasthenes (302-296 BCE** was the ambassador of Seleucus Nicator to the court of Chandragupta Maurya. He was known for his book **Indica**, which provides a detailed account of the Mauryan empire. He also observed Pataliputra, the capital of the Mauryan empire, as a well-fortified and advanced city.
- **Fa-Hien (399 CE-414 CE) was a Chinese** Buddhist monk who travelled to India during the Gupta period. His travelogue **Fo-Kuo-Ki** (A Record of Buddhist Kingdoms) provides insights into Indian society, Buddhism and the monasteries of the time. Fa-Hien documented the administration of law and justice during the Gupta period, mentioning how moral principles were emphasised over harsh punishments.
- **Al-Biruni** (1024 CE-1030 CE) was an Iranian scholar who travelled to India with Mahmud Ghazni. Often called the **Father of Indology**, Al-Biruni's work **Kitab al-Hind** is a comprehensive study of India.
- **Ibn Battuta** (1333 CE-1347 CE) was a Moroccan travelers who visited India during the reign of Muhammad bin Tughlaq. His travels were recorded in **Rihla**, providing a vivid picture of the medieval world, including India's political landscape, the lavish lifestyle of Sultan Muhammad bin Tughlaq and the thriving trade routes.

Thus, option (b) is the correct answer.

2. *(c)* 2-3-4-1

- **Hiuen Tsang** (c. 630-645 CE) visited during the **Pushyabhuti Dynasty** under Harshavardhan. He documented his travels in **Si-Yu-Ki**, highlighting the educational centers like **Nalanda** and the Buddhist culture prevalent in India at the time.
- **Al-Sulaiman** (850 CE) visited during the **Rashtrakuta and Pala Dynasties.** He was a Persian merchant, known for his work **Silsila-ut-Tawarikh,** where he provided observations on India's political and economic conditions.
- **Al-Masudi** (915 CE) visited during **Gurjara-Pratihara Dynasty.** He was known for his work **Muruj ul-Zehab** (The Meadows of Gold), he offered insights into the economic prosperity and geographic understanding of India during his time.
- **Marco Polo** (1292 CE-1294 CE) visited during the **Pandya** and **Kakatiya Dynasties.** His books, including **The Travels of Marco Polo**, described India's exotic goods, particularly its spices and pearls and the rich cultural tapestry he encountered.

Thus, option (c) is the correct answer.

3. *(b)* Only two

- **Statement 1 is incorrect:** Jean Antoine Dubois was a **French Catholic missionary** who traveled to **South India,** not North India. He spent significant time studying and integrating into South Indian society, particularly in the **Tamil region**, where he observed local customs and practices.
- **Statement 2 is correct:** Locals called him **Dodda Swami,** which translates to **Tall Swami** in Kannada. This nickname reflects the respect and familiarity the local population had with him.
- **Statement 3 is correct :** Jean Antoine Dubois is best known for his book **Hindu Manners, Customs and Ceremonies.** This work provides a detailed account of the social and religious practices of Hindus in South India during the late 18th and early 19th centuries.
- **Thus, option (b) is the correct answer.**

4. *(b)* Both Statement I and Statement II are correct and Statement II is not the correct explanation for Statement I.

- **Statement I is correct:** Jean Baptiste Tavernier was a renowned **French travelers and diamond merchant** who visited India **six times during the reigns of Mughal emperors**

Shah Jahan and Aurangzeb. His travels focused on acquiring and trading precious stones, particularly diamonds, which were abundant in India.

- **Statement II is also correct:** Tavernier is famously associated with discovering the **Blue Diamond**, known today as the **Hope Diamond.** He acquired this stone during his travels in India and later sold it to **King Louis XIV of France.**
- However, Statement II is not the direct explanation for Statement I. While Tavernier's discovery of the Tavernier Blue diamond is a significant achievement, it does not directly explain his multiple visits to India.

Thus, option (b) is the correct answer.

5. *(b)* Only two

- **Statement 1 is incorrect: Francois Bernier** did not visit India during Shah Jahan's reign but during **Aurangzeb's rule.** Bernier arrived in India in **1658**, the same year Aurangzeb became emperor.
- **Statement 2 is correct: Niccolao Manucci** visited India during the later part of **Shah Jahan's reign and continued his stay through Aurangzeb's era.** As a young Italian adventurer, he served various Mughal nobles and documented his experiences in his work **Storia do Mogor**, offering valuable insights into Mughal court life and politics.
- **Statement 3 is correct: Peter Mundy** visited India during the reign of **Shah Jahan.** His travels from 1630 to 1634 allowed him to observe the Mughal Empire at its height under Shah Jahan's rule.
- **Statement 4 is incorrect: Jean de Thevenot** visited India after **Shah Jahan's rule**, arriving in 1666, **during Aurangzeb's reign.** Thevenot's writings focus on the social and commercial practices in India, which were evolving under Aurangzeb's conservative policies.

Thus, option (b) is the correct answer.

6. *(c)* 1 only

- **Statement 1 is incorrect: Sir Thomas Roe was an English diplomat** who visited India during the reign of **Jahangir, not Akbar.** He arrived in 1615 as an ambassador of **King James I of England** and sought to secure trading rights for the English East India Company at the Mughal court.
- **Statement 2 is correct:** Sir Thomas Roe was indeed a member of the **House of Commons.** His background as a **parliamentarian and diplomat** gave him the skills and credentials necessary to represent English interests at the Mughal court.
- **Statement 3 is correct:** During his mission, Roe successfully negotiated the establishment of an **English factory in Surat.** It marked the beginning of English commercial presence in India, laying the groundwork for future expansion and influence.

Thus, option (c) is the correct answer.

7. *(b)* 1, 2 and 3 only

- **Statement 1 is correct: Jean Baptiste Tavernier's travels in India** are based on his extensive journeys during the Mughal period, particularly under the reigns of Shah Jahan and Aurangzeb. His observations and detailed descriptions of the **diamond trade and Mughal society** provide invaluable historical insights into the period.
- **Statement 2 is correct: Niccolao Manucci's Storia do Mogor** is a comprehensive account of Manucci's experiences in India, where he served in various capacities within the Mughal court. His writings offer a unique perspective on the **political and cultural landscape of Mughal India.**
- **Statement 3 is correct: 'A Voyage to East India'** documents **Sir Thomas Roe**'s diplomatic mission to Jahangir's court. Roe's narratives provide critical insights into the political dynamics and trade negotiations of the Mughal period, reflecting his efforts to secure **trading privileges for England.**
- **Statement 4 is incorrect:** Jean Antoine Dubois's **Hindu Manners, Customs and Ceremonies** are not related to the Mughal period. Instead, it is an ethnographic study of South Indian customs and practices, conducted during the **early 19th century** under British colonial influence.

Thus, option (b) is the correct answer.

8. *(c)* 1, 2, 4 and 5 only

- **Francois Pelsaert** wrote extensively about the **economic conditions in the Mughal Empire,** particularly focusing on the **dire situation of the peasants.** He documented how the **oppressive tax system** and **poor agricultural conditions** led to widespread poverty, providing insights into the economic challenges faced by common people.
- **Francis Bernier**: As a French physician and philosopher, Bernier offered a detailed account of the economic and social conditions under **Aurangzeb's reign.** He analyzed the inefficiencies in the Mughal administration and the **negative impact of excessive land ownership** by nobility on the empire's economy.
- **John Fryer's** accounts were more focused on the **commercial and urban aspects** of Indian cities like **Surat and Bombay rather than the broader economic conditions of the Mughal Empire.**
- **Pietra della Valle**: An Italian travelers who explored various regions in India, **Della Valle** commented on religious tolerance and economic activities, including trade practices and local markets. His observations provide a valuable perspective on the economic landscape during the Mughal period.
- **Peter Mundy**: A British merchant, Mundy wrote about the **economic conditions of India during his travels in the early 17th century.** He documented the impact of famines and the role of trade communities, such as the **Banjaras,** in the economy.

Thus, option (c) **is the correct answer.**

9. *(a)* 1, 2 and 3

- **Francisco Pelsaert's** accounts highlight the **oppressive tax regime and the resulting food scarcity,** making him a key source for understanding rural economic conditions during that period.
- **Jean de Thevenot** provided insights into the commercial activities in places **like Cambay, documenting trading practices** and the roles of merchants in the economy. His observations contribute to understanding the economic infrastructure and its influence on regional prosperity.
- **Jean Baptiste Tavernier**: While Tavernier's primary focus was on the **diamond trade,** his travels provided broader insights into the Mughal economy. His documentation of the diamond industry reflects the **wealth and economic power** of the empire, offering a glimpse into its economic dynamics.

Thus, option (a) **is the correct answer.**

10. *(c)* British travelers who documented the famine in Gujarat

Peter Mundy was a British travelers who extensively documented the socio-economic conditions of the regions he visited. He provided valuable insights into the famine in Gujarat and the living standards of the Mughal Empire's populace, highlighting the plight of common people during difficult times.

Thus, option (c) **is the correct answer.**

11. *(a)* 1-2-4-3

- **Sir Thomas Roe** arrived in **India in 1615 during Jahangir's reign.** His diplomatic mission set the stage for the establishment of English trade and influence in India, marking the beginning of formal English-Mughal relations.
- **Francisco Pelsaert** visited India around 1620-1627. His accounts of the economic conditions, particularly in Agra and its surroundings, are vital historical sources for understanding the Mughal Empire under Jahangir and Shah Jahan.
- **Niccolao Manucci** arrived in India in 1656 and remained active through the reign of Aurangzeb.
- **Jean Antoine Dubois** visited India much later, in the late 18th century. His work focused on South Indian society and customs, distinct from the earlier travelers' accounts of the Mughal Empire.

Thus, option (a) **is the correct answer.**

12. *(d)* Pietro della Valle

- **Pietro della Valle, an Italian travelers,** indeed reached Surat, a key port city during his travels in India. His journey was part of his larger expedition across the Middle East and

India. He documented various Indian customs and social practices, including **the Sati ritual, highlighting the complex religious and cultural landscape of India.**

- Pietro della Valle was connected with the **Nayaka of Keladi**, which underscores his interactions with regional powers and his interest in the political dynamics of India. This association provided him with a unique perspective on **local governance and cultural practices.**

Thus, option (d) is the correct answer.

13. *(b)* Both Statements I and II are correct and Statement II is not the correct reason for Statement I.

- **Statement 1 is correct: Edward Terry** was indeed a priest who accompanied **Sir Thomas Roe** on his diplomatic mission to the Mughal court of Jahangir. As Roe's chaplain, Terry provided spiritual guidance and support during their time at the court.
- **Statement 2 is correct:** Terry wrote about various aspects of the Mughal Empire, including its economic practices, where he described the **coinage systems** and economic conditions under **Jahangir's rule.**
- Reasoning: Terry's writings on coinage stem from his broader observations as a travelers, not because he was accompanying Roe specifically for economic analysis.

Thus, option (b) is the correct answer.

14. *(a)* 1, 2 and 3 only

- Domingo Paes highlighted the **advanced irrigation systems** in the **Vijayanagara Empire**, reflecting their engineering prowess and agricultural efficiency. The empire was known for its **multicultural agricultural practices**, as noted by Paes, which supported a variety of crops due to its advanced irrigation.
- **Paes** gave detailed accounts of the architectural **grandeur of temples**, indicating the **artistic and engineering skills** of the Vijayanagara people. Although Paes never mentioned that astrology was a respected field in Indian culture.

Thus, option (a) is the correct answer.

15. *(a)* 1, 3 and 4 only

- Abdur Razzak, a Persian travelers, documented the thriving ocean trade of the Vijayanagara Empire, emphasising its role as a significant trading hub. He did **not explicitly mention Ayurveda in his accounts,** astrology was part of the cultural practices but not specifically noted as expertise.
- He observed the strong defensive architecture of the empire, including its well-planned forts and city defences. According to him, the **Royal Court** was known for its **vibrant social life**, with various events and **social gatherings** that showcased its cultural richness.

Thus, option (a) is the correct answer.

16. *(c)* 1 and 2 only

- **Statement 1 is correct: Caesar Fredrick** documented the aftermath of the **Battle of Talikota** (1565 CE), which led to the downfall of the Vijayanagara Empire. The once well-organised social and political structures crumbled, resulting in chaos and economic decline.
- **Statement 2 is correct:** Fredrick noted that **merchants faced substantial taxes** at barrier stations and checkpoints, reflecting the complex trade networks within the **Vijayanagara Empire :** These taxes were part of a structured economic system intended to generate revenue for the empire.
- **Statement 3 is incorrect:** Although the Vijayanagara Empire had formidable military capabilities, it was not immune to invasions, as evidenced by its **defeat at Talikota.** The alliance of Deccan Sultanates successfully breached Vijayanagara's defences, marking a significant shift in South Indian power dynamics.

Thus, option (c) is the correct answer.

17. *(b)* 2 and 3 only

- **Statement 1 is incorrect: William Hawkins** was an English ambassador who arrived at Jahangir's court to negotiate trade privileges for the British East India Company. While he was granted a **mansab and trading rights, English traders were not prioritised over local merchants.** Hawkins faced significant competition from established **Portuguese traders** and local merchants who had deep-rooted ties within the **empire's economy.**

- **Statement 2 is correct:** Hawkins observed the structured judicial systems that incorporated a blend of local laws and Mughal administrative practices. This judicial framework ensured justice and order across the empire, drawing from **traditional customs and Islamic law.**
- **Statement 3 is correct:** Emperor Jahangir's reign is noted for its **relative religious tolerance**, which was a continuation of **Akbar's policies**. Hawkins documented Jahangir's inclusive approach, where people of different faiths coexisted peacefully under the empire's rule.

Thus, option (b) is the correct answer.

18. *(a)* 1 and 2 only

- **Statement 1 is correct:** Jean Hughen Van Linschotten, a Dutch travelers and merchant, documented the advanced **maritime navigation techniques** used by Indian seafarers, along the Malabar Coast. His writings provide detailed insights into the sophisticated knowledge of navigation and shipbuilding, which allowed Indian traders to conduct extensive trade across the Indian Ocean.
- **Statement 2 is correct:** Linschotten noted the **taxation of goods at city borders and trade routes**, reflecting the Mughal Empire's structured economic system. These taxes were collected at various **checkpoints**. This system not only supported the empire's economy but also demonstrated its administrative control over commerce, providing security and infrastructure that facilitated trade.
- **Statement 3 is incorrect:** While religion played a crucial role in Mughal society, **strict state-enforced religious conformity was not** prevalent during Linschotten's observations. The Mughal rulers, particularly under Akbar and Jahangir, practiced a degree of religious tolerance, allowing various communities to practice their faiths freely.

Thus, option (a) is the correct answer.

19. *(b)* Antonio Monserrate

- **Antonio Monserrate was a Portuguese Jesuit priest** who travelled to the Mughal Empire during the reign of Emperor Akbar in 1579. He was part of the first Jesuit mission to the Mughal court, which aimed to promote Christianity and build relations with the Mughal rulers. Monserrate became the **tutor to Murad, Akbar's second son**, reflecting the Mughal emperor's interest in European knowledge and education.
- Monserrate documented his experiences in the Mughal Empire in his book, The **Commentary of Father Monserrate.** His writings provide a detailed account of the **Mughal court's opulence**, highlighting the use of precious stones and jewels, including diamonds, in the emperor's attire and decorations.

Hence, option (b) is the correct answer.

20. *(a)* Jasmine

- **Abdur Razzak, a Persian diplomat** and travelers, visited the Vijayanagara Empire in the 15th century and in his writings, he specifically mentioned the vibrant and bustling flower markets in Vijayanagara. He noted that **jasmine flowers** were not just popular but were considered essential by the local population, almost as necessary as food.
- These flowers were widely used for **religious ceremonies, decorations and personal adornment.** The fragrance and beauty of jasmine made it highly valued in the daily lives of the people in the Vijayanagara Empire.

Thus, option (a) is the correct answer.

Past Learning (Answers)

1 (d) **2** (b) **3** (b)

CHAPTER 11 Science and Technology

Assessment Round

Topic 1 : Ancient India

1. With reference to the Stone Age, consider the following statements:

1. The first evidence of metallurgy in the Stone Age is found at Mehrgarh.
2. Neolithic people had knowledge of dentistry, as evidenced by drilled teeth found in Mehrgarh.
3. The invention of the wheel occurred during the Neolithic Age.

Which of the statements given above is/are correct?

(a) 2 only
(b) 1 and 2 only
(c) 2 and 3 only
(d) 1, 2 and 3

2. With reference to the Indus Valley Civilisation, consider the following statements:

1. The people of the Indus Valley knew the technique of keyhole skull surgery.
2. They obtained copper from the Aravali Hills and made bronze using tin and copper.
3. The Bronze Dancing Girl statue was discovered in Harappa.

How many of the statements given above is/are correct?

(a) Only one
(b) Only two
(c) All three
(d) None

3. With reference to ancient Indian medical sciences, consider the following statements:

1. The Ashwini Kumars were considered practitioners of medicine and were given divine status.
2. The Atharvaveda is the first text to mention diseases, cures and magical charms.
3. The emergence of Ayurveda began with the appendix of the Atharvaveda.
4. Takshashila and Varanasi emerged as centers for learning medical sciences.
5. Gayayurveda and Ashvayurveda are specific branches of Ayurveda dealing with bovine species and horses, respectively.

How many of the statements given above are correct?

(a) Only three
(b) Only four
(c) All five
(d) None

4. Consider the following sulvasutras:

1. Baudhayana Sulvasutra
2. Manava Sulvasutra
3. Apastamba Sulvasutra
4. Katyayana Sulvasutra

Which of the above are recognised as the four great sulvasutras?

(a) 1 and 3 only
(b) 1, 2 and 3 only
(c) 2, 3 and 4 only
(d) 1, 2, 3 and 4

5. Consider the following texts:

1. Mundaka Upanishad
2. Chandogya Upanishad
3. Baudhayana Sulvasutra
4. Apastamba Sulvasutra

Which of the above texts discuss concepts related to geometry and the Pythagorean Theorem?

(a) 1 and 2 only (b) 3 and 4 only
(c) 2, 3 and 4 only (d) 1, 2, 3 and 4

6. With reference to ancient Indian astronomy, consider the following statements:

1. The Taittiriya Brahmana mentions early references to the sun, moon and seasons.
2. Indian astronomers during this period knew about Jupiter, Mars and Venus.
3. Vedic literature discusses the concept of heliocentric theory.

How many of the statements given above is/are correct?

(a) Only one (b) Only two
(c) All three (d) None

7. Which of the following statements about ancient Indian concepts of physics and chemistry is incorrect?

(a) The five elements (Panchabhutas) were identified with the human senses of perception.
(b) The concept of 'Parmanu' or the smallest particle was introduced by Kanada.
(c) Rasasiddha and Rasa Tantra were texts focused on the science of liquids.
(d) Vedic literature makes no mention of gases such as copper or bronze.

8. Consider the following concepts discussed in the Sthananga Sutra:

1. Parikrama (fundamental operations)
2. Vyavahara (determination)
3. Rajju (geometry)
4. Vikalpa (permutation and combination)

Which of the above concepts relates to ancient Indian mathematics?

(a) 1 and 3 only (b) 1, 2 and 4 only
(c) 1, 2, 3 and 4 (d) 2, 3 and 4 only

9. Identify the text based on the following descriptions:

1. Written by Charak during the reign of Kanishka.
2. It deals with digestion, metabolism and the immune system.
3. It emphasises the importance of the balance of three doshas: bile, phlegm and wind.

Choose the correct answer from the options given below :

(a) Sushruta Samhita
(b) Charak Samhita
(c) Ashtanga Hridaya Samhita
(d) Vagbhata Samhita

10. Identify the text based on the following descriptions:

1. Known as the first comprehensive text on surgery and obstetrics.
2. Associated with the Banaras School of Medical Sciences.
3. It deals with rhinoplasty and cataract surgery.

Choose the correct answer from the options given below :

(a) Charak Samhita
(b) Sushruta Samhita
(c) Ashtanga Hridaya Samhita
(d) Vagbhata Samhita

11. Which of the following statements about the sections of Aryabhatiyam is incorrect?

(a) Gitikapada deals with large numbers and units of time.
(b) Golapada explains the Earth's shape and the cause of day and night.
(c) Kalakriyapada deals with the motion of planets and their positions.
(d) Gonitapada explains the concept of astrology and horoscopes.

12. Consider the following works associated with Varahamihira:

1. Brihatsamhita 2. Panchasiddhantika
3. Laghu Jataka

Which of the above are recognised as major works by Varahamihira?

(a) 1 and 2 only (b) 1 and 3 only
(c) 2 and 3 only (d) 1, 2 and 3

13. Which of the following statements about ancient Indian metallurgy is incorrect?

(a) The Mehrauli iron pillar is known for its rust-free composition.

(b) Varahamihira's work includes explanations of the carburization process.

(c) The Sultan Ganj Buddha was cast using the lost wax technique.

(d) The construction of the iron pillar is attributed to the Gupta dynasty.

14. With reference to ancient Indian medical sciences, consider the following statements:

1. Vagbhata wrote the Ashtangasamgraha and Ashtangahridayasamhita.
2. Hastayurveda, the science of elephants, was written by Palakapya.
3. The Rasachikitsa text by Nagarjuna focuses on mineral medicines.

How many of the statements given above are correct?

(a) Only two (b) Only three
(c) All three (d) None

15. With reference to ancient Indian mathematics and metallurgy, consider the following statements:

1. Brahmagupta's work introduced the concept of zero and negative numbers.
2. Nagarjuna developed new techniques for whitening copper.
3. Bhaskara I's work focused on the concepts of sine and cosine.

How many of the statements given above is/are correct?

(a) Only one (b) Only two
(c) All three (d) None

Topic 2 : Medieval India

16. With reference to ancient Indian mathematics, consider the following statements:

1. Mahaviracharya authored the Ganit Sara Sangraha, a comprehensive text on mathematics.
2. Sridhar wrote Ganitsar, contributing significantly to ancient Indian mathematical knowledge.
3. Bhaskara II wrote the Siddhant Shiromani, which includes four sections covering various mathematical disciplines.
4. Aryabhata II authored the Aryasiddhanta, which dealt with both astronomy and mathematics.

How many of the statements given above are incorrect?

(a) Only two
(b) Only three
(c) All four
(d) None

17. Consider the following scholars and their contributions:

1. Charaka wrote Charaka Samhita, an important medical text.
2. Madhava-kara authored Rugvinishchaya, which focuses on diagnosis and pathology.
3. Nagarjuna wrote Rasaratnakar, guided by the idea of the elixir of life.
4. The Arabic translation of Sushruta Samhita is known as Kitab Shah Shun al-Hindi.

How many of the statemetns given above is/are correctly matched?

(a) Only one
(b) Only two
(c) Only three
(d) All four

18. Consider the following sections of Bhaskara II's Siddhant Shiromani:

1. Lilavati (Algebra)
2. Bijaganit (Arithmetic)
3. Grahaganita (Astronomy)
4. Goladhyaya (Geometry)

How many of the sections given above is/are correctly matched?

(a) Only one
(b) Only two
(c) Only three
(d) All four

19. With reference to medieval Indian mathematics and astronomy, consider the following statements:

1. Narayan Pandit authored Ganit Kaumudi and Bijaganitavatamsa.
2. Nilkanth Somyaji wrote the Tantrasamgraha, which is primarily an astronomical book.
3. Dalail-i-Firozshahi is a translation of Indian texts into Persian under Firoz Shah Tughlaq.

How many of the statements given above is/are correct?

(a) Only one (b) Only two
(c) All three (d) None

20. Arrange the following new technologies introduced during the Delhi Sultanate period in chronological order:

1. Paper-making
2. Introduction of the Persian wheel for irrigation
3. Charkha
4. Introduction of iron stirrups

Choose the correct sequence from the codes given below:

(a) 1 - 4 - 3 - 2
(b) 4 - 1 - 3 - 2
(c) 1 - 3 - 4 - 2
(d) 3 - 4 - 1 - 2

21. With reference to Mughal-era technological advancements, consider the following statements:

1. The draw loom was introduced in the 17th century CE, facilitating the weaving of complex textiles.
2. Glass crafts, particularly mirrors and spectacles, became significant in the 18th century CE.
3. The shipbuilding industry during the Mughal period saw the introduction of iron nails and clamps.

How many of the statements given above is/are correct?

(a) Only one (b) Only two
(c) All three (d) None

Past Learning

1. With reference to the history of India, the terms 'kulyavapa' and 'dronavapa' denote **(2020)**

(a) measurement of land
(b) coins of different monetary value
(c) classification of urban land
(d) religious rituals

2. Consider the following: **(2015)**

The arrival of Babur into India led to the

1. introduction of gunpowder in the subcontinent
2. introduction of the arch and dome in the region's architecture
3. establishment of the Timurid dynasty in the region

Select the correct answer using the codes given below:

(a) 1 and 2 only (b) 3 only
(c) 1 and 3 only (d) 1, 2 and 3

3. With reference to the scientific progress of ancient India, which of the statements given below are correct? **(2012)**

1. Different kinds of specialised surgical instruments were in common use by the 1st century AD.
2. Transplant of internal organs in the human body had begun by the beginning of the 3rd century AD.
3. The concept of the sine of an angle was known in the 5th century AD.
4. The concept of cyclic quadrilaterals was known in 7th century AD.

Select the correct answer using the codes given below:

(a) 1 and 2 only
(b) 3 and 4 only
(c) 1, 3 and 4 only
(d) 1, 2, 3 and 4

OMR SHEET

Assessment Round

1	a	b	c	d	31	a	b	c	d	61	a	b	c	d	91	a	b	c	d
2	a	b	c	d	32	a	b	c	d	62	a	b	c	d	92	a	b	c	d
3	a	b	c	d	33	a	b	c	d	63	a	b	c	d	93	a	b	c	d
4	a	b	c	d	34	a	b	c	d	64	a	b	c	d	94	a	b	c	d
5	a	b	c	d	35	a	b	c	d	65	a	b	c	d	95	a	b	c	d
6	a	b	c	d	36	a	b	c	d	66	a	b	c	d	96	a	b	c	d
7	a	b	c	d	37	a	b	c	d	67	a	b	c	d	97	a	b	c	d
8	a	b	c	d	38	a	b	c	d	68	a	b	c	d	98	a	b	c	d
9	a	b	c	d	39	a	b	c	d	69	a	b	c	d	99	a	b	c	d
10	a	b	c	d	40	a	b	c	d	70	a	b	c	d	100	a	b	c	d
11	a	b	c	d	41	a	b	c	d	71	a	b	c	d	101	a	b	c	d
12	a	b	c	d	42	a	b	c	d	72	a	b	c	d	102	a	b	c	d
13	a	b	c	d	43	a	b	c	d	73	a	b	c	d	103	a	b	c	d
14	a	b	c	d	44	a	b	c	d	74	a	b	c	d	104	a	b	c	d
15	a	b	c	d	45	a	b	c	d	75	a	b	c	d	105	a	b	c	d
16	a	b	c	d	46	a	b	c	d	76	a	b	c	d	106	a	b	c	d
17	a	b	c	d	47	a	b	c	d	77	a	b	c	d	107	a	b	c	d
18	a	b	c	d	48	a	b	c	d	78	a	b	c	d	108	a	b	c	d
19	a	b	c	d	49	a	b	c	d	79	a	b	c	d	109	a	b	c	d
20	a	b	c	d	50	a	b	c	d	80	a	b	c	d	110	a	b	c	d
21	a	b	c	d	51	a	b	c	d	81	a	b	c	d	111	a	b	c	d
22	a	b	c	d	52	a	b	c	d	82	a	b	c	d	112	a	b	c	d
23	a	b	c	d	53	a	b	c	d	83	a	b	c	d	113	a	b	c	d
24	a	b	c	d	54	a	b	c	d	84	a	b	c	d	114	a	b	c	d
25	a	b	c	d	55	a	b	c	d	85	a	b	c	d	115	a	b	c	d
26	a	b	c	d	56	a	b	c	d	86	a	b	c	d	116	a	b	c	d
27	a	b	c	d	57	a	b	c	d	87	a	b	c	d	117	a	b	c	d
28	a	b	c	d	58	a	b	c	d	88	a	b	c	d	118	a	b	c	d
29	a	b	c	d	59	a	b	c	d	89	a	b	c	d	119	a	b	c	d
30	a	b	c	d	60	a	b	c	d	90	a	b	c	d	120	a	b	c	d

Calculate Your Score

Correct (✓)	
Incorrect (✓)	
Unattempted	
Total Score	
Accuracy (%)	

Reasons for Incorrect Answers?

1. Lack of Knowledge/Existing Source Insufficient	
2. Lack of Multiple Revision	
3. Common Sense Mistakes	

Note :

1. Calculate total score as correct answers carry 2 marks each 1/3rd marks will deducted for **Incorrect** Answers.
2. Calculate Accuracy (%) by dividing the number of correct answers to the total number of attempted questions.

Detailed Solutions

Assessment Round

1. *(d)* 1, 2 and 3

- **Statement 1 is correct:** The site of **Mehrgarh,** located in present-day Pakistan, is one of the earliest sites to show evidence of copper metallurgy. While this evidence dates back to around 6000 BCE, it is part of the Chalcolithic Age (Copper Age), which directly followed the Neolithic period.
- **Statement 2 is correct:** Archaeologists discovered evidence of ancient **dentistry at Mehrgarh,** where Neolithic people used stone drills to bore holes in molar teeth. These findings are dated to around 7000-5500 BCE, indicating that the people of this era had developed a surprisingly advanced understanding of dental care for their time.
- **Statement 3 is correct:** The **invention of the wheel** is typically associated with the late Neolithic period, around **3500 BCE.** The earliest wheels were likely used for pottery and later adapted for use in carts and transportation. This innovation marks a significant technological advancement in human history.

Thus, option (d) is the correct answer.

2. *(b)* Only two

- **Statement 1 is correct:** There is evidence from sites like **Lothal** and **Kalibangan** that the Indus Valley people performed trepanation, a form of keyhole skull surgery. This was likely done to treat head injuries or medical conditions, indicating advanced surgical practices for the time.
- **Statement 2 is correct:** The **Indus Valley Civilisation** sourced copper from the Aravali Hills and combined it with tin to produce bronze, an alloy that was widely used for making tools, weapons and ornaments.
- **Statement 3 is incorrect:** The famous Bronze Dancing Girl statue, which is one of the most iconic artifacts of the Indus Valley Civilisation, was discovered in Mohenjo-daro, not Harappa.

Thus, option (b) is the correct answer.

3. *(c)* All five

- **Statement 1 is correct:** The **Ashwini Kumars** are regarded as the **twin deities of medicine** in Vedic literature. They are frequently mentioned in the Rigveda, where they are depicted as **divine physicians** with the power to heal and perform miraculous medical feats.
- **Statement 2 is correct:** The **Atharvaveda,** one of the four Vedas, is known for its extensive references to various diseases, their cures and **magical charms** used in healing.
- **Statement 3 is correct: Ayurveda,** which means the **science of life** is traditionally attributed to the Atharvaveda. It contains detailed descriptions of medicinal herbs and treatments, forming the foundation for the later development of Ayurveda as a comprehensive system of medicine.
- **Statement 4 is correct: Takshashila (modern-day Taxila) and Varanasi (Benares)** were among the most prominent centers for learning and scholarship in ancient India. These cities attracted students from across the region and were renowned for their medical schools, where Ayurveda was taught alongside other sciences.
- **Statement 5 is correct: Gayayurveda and Ashvayurveda** are specialised branches of **Ayurveda** that focus on the treatment of **bovine species** (cattle) and **horses,** respectively. These texts provide detailed guidelines on the care, treatment and management of these animals, reflecting the importance of veterinary science in ancient India.

Thus, option (c) is the correct answer.

4. *(d)* 1, 2, 3 and 4

- **Option 1 is correct:** The **Baudhayana Sulvasutra** is one of the earliest and most significant sulvasutras, focusing on geometric principles necessary for constructing altars and other religious structures. It also contains the earliest known statement of the **Pythagorean Theorem.**

- **Option 2 is correct:** The **Manava Sulvasutra** is another important text in the sulvasutra tradition, offering insights into the **mathematical and geometric techniques** used in Vedic rituals. It is attributed to the Manava school of thought.
- **Option 3 is correct:** The **Apastamba Sulvasutra** is a key text that further elaborates on the geometric principles found in earlier sulvasutras. It is associated with the Apastamba school of thought, known for its contributions to Indian mathematics.
- **Option 4 is correct:** The **Katyayana Sulvasutra** is the fourth major text in the Sulvasutra tradition. It is known for its detailed treatment of **geometry**, particularly in the context of constructing ritual altars.

Thus, option (d) is the correct answer.

5. *(b)* 3 and 4 only

- **Option 1 is incorrect:** The **Mundaka Upanishad** is a philosophical text that discusses the nature of knowledge and the difference between higher and lower forms of wisdom. It does not deal with geometry or mathematical concepts.
- **Option 2 is incorrect:** The **Chandogya Upanishad** is primarily a philosophical and theological text that explores the nature of the universe, the self and the ultimate reality (Brahman). It does not cover geometry or the Pythagorean Theorem.
- **Option 3 is correct:** The **Baudhayana Sulvasutra** contains one of the earliest references to the Pythagorean Theorem, demonstrating the ancient Indian understanding of geometric principles necessary for constructing altars.
- **Option 4 is correct:** The **Apastamba Sulvasutra** also discusses geometric principles, including the Pythagorean Theorem, as part of the guidelines for constructing Vedic altars.

Thus, option (b) is the correct answer.

6. *(b)* Only two

- **Statement 1 is correct:** The **Taittiriya Brahmana**, a key text of the **Krishna Yajurveda**, contains references to the Sun (Surya), the Moon (Chandra) and various seasonal changes. This indicates an early understanding of the importance of celestial bodies in agricultural and religious practices.
- **Statement 2 is correct:** Indian astronomers of the Vedic period had a profound understanding of the night sky. They identified and named various planets, including **Jupiter (Brihaspati), Mars (Angaraka) and Venus (Shukra)** and their movements were observed for both religious and practical purposes.
- **Statement 3 is incorrect:** Vedic literature **does not** discuss the concept of heliocentric theory (the idea that the Sun is at the center of the solar system). This theory was proposed much later by astronomers like **Copernicus in the West.** Instead, ancient Indian astronomy largely adhered to a geocentric view, where the Earth was considered the center of the universe.

Thus, option (b) is the correct answer.

7. *(d)* Vedic literature makes no mention of gases such as copper or bronze.

- **Option (a) is correct:** The **Panchabhutas**, or **five elements (earth, water, fire, air and ether)**, were indeed associated with the human senses of perception-smell (earth), taste (water), sight (fire), touch (air) and sound (ether). This concept is fundamental to both Vedic philosophy and Ayurveda.
- **Option (b) is correct:** The concept of **'Parmanu'** which refers to the smallest indivisible particle of matter, was introduced by the sage Kanada, the founder of the Vaisheshika school of philosophy.
- **Option (c) is correct: Rasasiddha** and **Rasa Tzantra** were ancient Indian texts focused on the science of alchemy and liquids, particularly the transformation of base metals into gold and the preparation of medicinal substances.
- **Option (d) is incorrect: Vedic literature** does mention metals like **copper and bronze,** especially in the context of tools, weapons and rituals.

Thus, option (d) is the correct answer.

8. *(c)* 1, 2, 3 and 4

8. *(c)* 1, 2, 3 and 4

- **Option 1 is correct: Parikrama** refers to the **basic mathematical operations**, which are fundamental in any mathematical system. In the context of ancient Indian mathematics, this would include addition, subtraction, multiplication and division.
- **Option 2 is correct: Vyavahara** involves the **application of mathematical operations** to solve practical problems, a key aspect of ancient Indian mathematical texts.
- **Option 3 is correct: Rajju** refers to the **geometric principles used in Vedic rituals,** particularly for the construction of altars. Geometry was a crucial part of Vedic mathematics, as reflected in the sulvasutras.
- **Option 4 is correct:** Vikalpa refers to **combinatorial mathematics**, which deals with the different ways objects can be arranged or combined. This concept is essential in the study of permutations and combinations in mathematics.

Thus, option (c) is the correct answer.

9. *(b)* Charak Samhita

The **Charak Samhita** is a foundational text of **Ayurveda**, written by **Charak** during the reign of the Kushan emperor **Kanishka** (around the 2nd century CE). It provides detailed descriptions of the human body's functioning, with a particular focus on digestion, metabolism and the immune system. The text also introduces the concept of the three doshas-**Vata** (wind), **Pitta** (bile) and **Kapha** (phlegm)-which are central to Ayurvedic diagnosis and treatment.

Thus, option (b) is the correct answer.

10. *(b)* Sushruta Samhita

The **Sushruta Samhita** is the earliest and most comprehensive **text on surgery and obstetrics in** ancient India. Written by Sushruta, who is often referred to as the **father of surgery** this text is associated with the Banaras (Varanasi) School of Medical Sciences. It provides detailed instructions on various surgical procedures, including rhinoplasty (reconstruction of the nose) and cataract surgery, as well as the ethical and practical aspects of medical practice.

Thus, option (b) is the correct answer.

11. *(d)* Gonitapada explains the concept of astrology and horoscopes.

- **Option 1 is correct: Gitikapada** is the first section of **Aryabhatiyam**, a text composed by Aryabhata, that primarily deals with metrical structures and large units of time. Aryabhata introduces the concept of 'Kalpa' (a large cosmic cycle of time) and its subdivisions, explaining the duration of the universe in terms of Yugas (ages) and Mahayugas.
- **Option (b) is correct:** The **Golapada** section of Aryabhatiya focuses on **spherical** astronomy, which includes discussions on the Earth's shape, the horizon, celestial spheres and the causes of day and night.
- **Option (c) is correct: Kalakriyapada**, another section of Aryabhatiya, deals with the **measurement of time (Kala), planetary motions and eclipses.** Aryabhata's understanding of the relative motion of planets, including their elliptical orbits, was remarkably advanced.
- **Option (d) is incorrect: Gonitapada** is the section of Aryabhatiyam that deals with **arithmetic and geometry**, not astrology or horoscopes. It includes a range of mathematical topics such as basic arithmetic operations, algebraic identities, geometric calculations and the famous approximation of π (Pi) to 3.1416.

Thus, option (d) is the correct answer.

12. *(d)* 1, 2 and 3

- **Option 1 is correct:** The **Brihatsamhita,** written by **Varahamihira**, is an encyclopedic text on a wide range of subjects, including astronomy, astrology, architecture, agriculture and gemology. It is one of the most comprehensive ancient Indian texts, often referred to as the 'Great Compilation' due to its extensive coverage.
- **Option 2 is correct:** The **Panchasiddhantika** is another major work of Varahamihira, focusing on **astronomy**. It is a critical compilation of five earlier astronomical treatises: the Surya Siddhanta, the Paitamaha Siddhanta, the Paulisa Siddhanta, the Romaka Siddhanta and the Vasishtha Siddhanta.

- **Option 3 is correct:** The **Laghu Jataka** is one of the key texts on **astrology** attributed to Varahamihira. It focuses on horoscopic astrology, providing methods for casting horoscopes, interpreting planetary positions and predicting life events based on astrological charts.

Thus, option (d) is the correct answer.

13. *(b)* Varahamihira's work includes explanations of the carburization process.

- **Option (a) is correct:** The Mehrauli iron pillar, located in Delhi, is one of the most famous examples of ancient Indian metallurgy. Erected during the **reign of Chandragupta II in the Gupta period**, this pillar is remarkable for its rust-resistant composition, which has withstood corrosion for over 1,600 years. The pillar stands about 7 **meters tall and weighs more than 6 tons.**
- **Option (b) is incorrect:** While Varahamihira made significant contributions to astronomy, astrology and natural sciences, his works do not include the carburisation process, which is a method used in metallurgy to harden iron by infusing it with carbon.
- **Option (c) is correct:** The Sultan Ganj Buddha, a large bronze statue from the Gupta period, was indeed created using the **lost wax casting technique, also known** as **cire perdue.** This method involves creating a wax model of the sculpture, which is then encased in a clay mold. Once the mold is heated, the wax melts away, leaving a hollow space that is filled with molten metal to create the final statue.
- **Option (d) is correct:** The construction of the Mehrauli iron pillar is attributed to the Gupta dynasty, specifically during the reign of Chandragupta II. The pillar was originally erected in Udayagiri, near modern-day Bhopal and later moved to Delhi by one of the later rulers. The Gupta dynasty is renowned for its advancements in metallurgy, as well as its contributions to art, literature and science.

Thus, option (b) is the correct answer.

14. *(c)* All three

- **Statement 1 is correct: Vagbhata** was one of the most influential figures in ancient Indian **medicine.** He authored two major texts: the **Ashtangasamgraha** and the **Ashtangahridayasamhita.** These texts are comprehensive treatises on Ayurveda, covering topics such as diagnosis, treatment, surgery and the management of various diseases.
- **Statement 2 is correct: Hastayurveda,** attributed to the sage **Palakapya,** is a specialised branch of Ayurveda that deals with the **health and management of elephants.** In ancient India, elephants were not only revered animals but also played a crucial role in warfare and ceremonial activities.
- **Statement 3 is correct:** The **Rasachikitsa** is a text attributed to **Nagarjuna,** an alchemist and philosopher who made significant contributions to ancient Indian chemistry and medicine. Rasachikitsa focuses on the use of minerals and metals in medicine, **particularly mercury and its compounds.**

Thus, option (c) is the correct answer.

15. *(b)* Only two

- **Statement 1 is correct: Brahmagupta,** one of the most celebrated mathematicians of ancient India, wrote Brahmasphutasiddhanta famous for its **treatment of zero** as a number, as well as its introduction of rules for arithmetic operations involving zero. He is also credited with the earliest known use of negative numbers.
- **Statement 2 is correct: Nagarjuna,** known for his work in **alchemy and medicine,** is also credited with developing techniques for refining and whitening metals, particularly copper. The process of whitening copper involved the application of certain chemicals and heat treatment to give the metal a silver-like appearance.
- **Statement 3 is incorrect: Bhaskara I**'s work did include discussions on astronomical calculations, but the development of sine and cosine as mathematical functions was more thoroughly explored by **Bhaskara II** in his work **Siddhant Shiromani.**

Thus, option (b) is the correct answer.

16. *(d)* None

- **Statement 1 is correct: Mahaviracharya,** also known as Mahavira, was an important mathematician of the 9th century CE. His work, **Ganit Sara Sangraha** is a significant mathematical text that covers a wide range of topics, including arithmetic, geometry and combinatorics.
- **Statement 2 is correct: Sridhar,** another key figure in ancient Indian mathematics, authored the text **'Ganitsar,'** which focused on arithmetic and algebra. Sridhar is credited with developing algorithms for solving quadratic and cubic equations, as well as for computing square and cube roots.
- **Statement 3 is correct: Bhaskara II,** often referred to as **Bhaskaracharya,** was one of the most brilliant mathematicians and astronomers of medieval India. His work **Siddhanta Shiromani** is divided into four sections: **Lilavati** (dealing with arithmetic), **Bijaganita** (algebra), **Grahaganita** (astronomy) and **Goladhyaya** (spherical trigonometry).
- **Statement 4 is correct: Aryabhata II,** another prominent figure in Indian astronomy and mathematics, wrote the Aryasiddhanta, which is a significant text dealing with both these disciplines.

Thus, option (d) is the correct answer.

17. *(d)* All four

- **Statement 1 is correct** Charaka is credited with the authorship of **Charaka Samhita** a medical text that contributes to the vast body of Ayurvedic literature dealing with various aspects of medicine, including the diagnosis and treatment of diseases, the preparation of medicinal formulations and possibly surgical procedures.
- **Statement 2 is correct: Madhava-kara,** also known as **Madhava,** was a significant figure in the development of medical diagnostics in ancient India. His work **Rugvinishchaya** is focused on the **diagnosis** (Nidana) **and pathology** (Samprapti) of diseases.
- **Statement 3 is correct: Nagarjuna,** often referred to as the **father of Indian alchemy** authored **Rasaratnakar,** which is a treatise on alchemy and the use of metals and minerals in medicine. The text is guided by the idea of the elixir of life, a substance believed to grant immortality or rejuvenation.
- **Statement 4 is correct:** The Sushruta Samhita, one of the foundational texts of Ayurveda, was translated into Arab scholars as 'Kitab Shah Shun al-Hindi'. during the Islamic Golden Age.

Thus, option (d) is the correct answer

18. *(b)* Only two

- **Option 1 is incorrect:** The **Lilavati** section of **Bhaskara II's Siddhanta Shiromani actually** deals with arithmetic, not algebra. The name Lilavati is often associated with a story in which Bhaskara named this section after his daughter and it covers topics such as arithmetic operations, number theory and practical problems.
- **Option 2 is incorrect:** The **Bijaganit** section is correctly associated with **algebra,** not arithmetic. This section delves into solving equations, algebraic identities and various other algebraic techniques.
- **Option 3 is correct:** The **Grahaganita** section focuses on the mathematical aspects of including the calculation of planetary positions, eclipses and other celestial phenomena.
- **Option 4 is correct:** The **Goladhyaya** section of **Bhaskara II's Siddhanta Shiromani** focuses on **spherical geometry and trigonometry,** which are essential for understanding celestial mechanics. This section includes discussions on the spherical shape of the Earth, the calculation of great circles (such as the equator) and various trigonometric functions.

Thus, option (b) is the correct answer.

19. *(c)* All three

- **Statement 1 is correct: Narayan Pandit** was a significant mathematician in medieval India, known for his works **Ganit Kaumudi** and **Bijaganitavatamsa.** Ganit Kaumudi is a treatise that covers a broad range of mathematical topics, including arithmetic, algebra and combinatorics.

- **Statement 2 is correct: Nilkanth Somyaji**, a scholar from Kerala, authored **Tantrasamgraha**, a significant text in the field of astronomy. This work deals with various astronomical calculations, including the determination of planetary positions and eclipses.
- **Statement 3 is correct: Dalail-i-Firozshahi** is indeed a Persian translation of Indian texts, commissioned by **Sultan Firoz Shah Tughlaq**. The translation of scientific and literary works into Persian during the Delhi Sultanate and Mughal periods was part of a broader effort to integrate and preserve knowledge from various cultures.

Thus, option (c) is the correct answer.

20. *(b)* 4 - 1 - 3 - 2

- The **introduction of iron stirrups** was Introduced to India during the **12th century**, primarily through the Turks. It was a crucial innovation in military technology allowing greater stability for riders on horseback, which in turn made cavalry units more effective in battle. This innovation played a significant role in the success of the Delhi Sultanate's military campaigns.
- **Paper-making technology** was introduced to India during the **13th century**, primarily through contacts with the Islamic world. The introduction of paper significantly influenced administrative practices, record-keeping and literary production, as it replaced the use of more cumbersome materials like palm leaves.
- The **Charkha**, or spinning wheel, was introduced in the **14th century**. It revolutionised textile production in India, making the process of spinning yarn much faster and more efficient.
- The **Persian wheel**, also known as the **saqiya** was introduced in the **15th century** and had a profound impact on agriculture in India. This technology allowed for more efficient irrigation of fields, which in turn boosted agricultural productivity.

Thus, option (b) is the correct answer.

21. *(c)* All three

- **Statement 1 is correct**: The **draw loom**, introduced in the **17th century CE**, was an important technological advancement in the Mughal textile industry. It allowed weavers to produce intricate patterns in fabrics, particularly in silk and brocade textiles, which were highly valued in both domestic and international markets.
- **Statement 2 is correct: Glass crafts**, including the production of mirrors and spectacles, became more prominent during the **18th century CE** in India. These items were both functional and decorative, with mirrors being used in architecture (e.g., in palaces like the Sheesh Mahal) and spectacles becoming more widely available for correcting vision.
- **Statement 3 is correct**: The **shipbuilding industry** in Mughal India was advanced, with the introduction of **iron nails, clamps and other metal fastenings** being a significant development. These innovations made ships stronger and more durable, which was essential for the empire's trade and military activities.

Thus, option (c) is the correct answer.

Past Learning (Answers)

1 (a) **2** (b) **3** (c)

CHAPTER

12 Education System

Assessment Round

1. Consider the following statements:

Statement I: The medium of instruction in the Brahmanical education system involved three steps: Shravana, Manana, and Nididhyasana.

Statement II: In the Buddhist education system, the medium of instruction was Sanskrit and steps were similar to those followed by the Brahmanical system.

Which one of the following is correct in respect of the above statements?

(a) Both Statement I and Statement II are correct and Statement II is the correct explanation for Statement I.

(b) Both Statement I and Statement II are correct and Statement II is not the correct explanation for Statement I.

(c) Statement I is correct but Statement II is incorrect.

(d) Statement I is incorrect but Statement II is correct.

2. Consider the following statements about Taxila University:

1. It was built in the 6th century BCE on the banks of the Indus River.
2. The Huns destroyed it in the 7th century BCE.
3. Panini, an important teacher at Taxila University, was from the 5th century BCE.

How many of the above statements is/are correct?

(a) Only one (b) Only two
(c) All three (d) None

3. Consider the following statements about Nalanda University:

1. It was founded by Kumaragupta I in the 5th century AD.
2. Ratnasagar, Ratnadadhi, and Ratnaranjaka were the three main buildings associated with it.
3. Alexander Cunningham identified it in 1861-62 CE.

How many of the above statements is/are correct?

(a) Only one (b) Only two
(c) All three (d) None

4. Identify the historical site based on the following statements:

1. It is presently located in Bihar Sharif.
2. It was made by Gopala I in the 8th century CE.
3. It was destroyed by the Khiljis in the 12th century CE.
4. The ancient Buddhist scholar Atisha Dipankara Srijana studied here.

Choose the correct answer from the codes given below:

(a) Nalanda University
(b) Vikramashila University
(c) Odantapuri Mahavihara
(d) Somapura Mahavihara

5. With reference to the 'Educational Systems of Ancient India', consider the following statements:

1. Jain educational centers were known as Jinalayas and Basadis.
2. Brahminical education institutions included Gurukuls, Ghatikas, Agraharas, Mathas, and Brahmapuris.
3. The Buddhist education system had a significant varna bias, similar to the Brahminical system.

Which of the given above statements(s) is/are correct?

(a) 1 and 2 only
(b) 2 only
(c) 3 only
(d) 1, 2 and 3

6. Consider the following pairs:

	Place	Historical Significance
1.	Nadia	The confluence of the Ganga and Jalangi rivers
2.	Ujjain	Varahamihira and Brahmagupta were scholars here
3.	Kanchipuram	Associated with the Dvaita school of thought
4.	Sharda Peeth	Ibn-Battuta recorded this place for the first time

How many pairs given above is/are correctly matched?

(a) Only one pair
(b) Only two pairs
(c) Only three pairs
(d) All four pairs

7. Which of the following correctly describes the ceremonies mentioned in Buddhist monastic traditions?

(a) Pabbajja refers to the ordination ceremony for higher monks, while Upasampada is for novice monks.
(b) Pabbajja is the lower ordination ceremony for entering novice rank, whereas Upasampada is the higher ordination to become a full monk.
(c) Pabbajja is a ceremony for laypeople, and Upasampada is a ceremony for all Buddhist followers.
(d) Pabbajja and Upasampada are both ceremonies for ordaining Buddhist nuns only.

8. Consider the following pairs:

	Institution	Significance
1.	Vikramshila Mahavihara	Flourished under the Rashtrakutas in Karnataka.
2.	Jagaddala Mahavihara	Founded by Dharmapala in the 8th century AD, located in present-day Bihar.
3.	Manyakheta	Built by Ramapala in the 11th century AD, emphasised Vajrayana Buddhism, located in modern-day Bangladesh.

Which of the pairs given above are correctly matched?

(a) 1 and 3 only
(b) 2 and 3 only
(c) 1 and 2 only
(d) None

9. Which of the following correctly describes the traditional Islamic education system:

(a) Maktab refers to higher education institutions, while Madrasa provides primary education, and Khanqah focuses on secular learning.
(b) Maktab is for primary education, Madrasa offers higher education, and Khanqah is a center for Sufi learning.
(c) Maktab and Madrasa are both institutions for Sufi learning, while Khanqah is for primary education.
(d) Maktab is a place for Sufi learning, Madrasa is for higher education, and Khanqah provides primary education.

OMR SHEET

Assessment Round

1	(a) (b) (c) (d)	31	(a) (b) (c) (d)	61	(a) (b) (c) (d)	91	(a) (b) (c) (d)
2	(a) (b) (c) (d)	32	(a) (b) (c) (d)	62	(a) (b) (c) (d)	92	(a) (b) (c) (d)
3	(a) (b) (c) (d)	33	(a) (b) (c) (d)	63	(a) (b) (c) (d)	93	(a) (b) (c) (d)
4	(a) (b) (c) (d)	34	(a) (b) (c) (d)	64	(a) (b) (c) (d)	94	(a) (b) (c) (d)
5	(a) (b) (c) (d)	35	(a) (b) (c) (d)	65	(a) (b) (c) (d)	95	(a) (b) (c) (d)
6	(a) (b) (c) (d)	36	(a) (b) (c) (d)	66	(a) (b) (c) (d)	96	(a) (b) (c) (d)
7	(a) (b) (c) (d)	37	(a) (b) (c) (d)	67	(a) (b) (c) (d)	97	(a) (b) (c) (d)
8	(a) (b) (c) (d)	38	(a) (b) (c) (d)	68	(a) (b) (c) (d)	98	(a) (b) (c) (d)
9	(a) (b) (c) (d)	39	(a) (b) (c) (d)	69	(a) (b) (c) (d)	99	(a) (b) (c) (d)
10	(a) (b) (c) (d)	40	(a) (b) (c) (d)	70	(a) (b) (c) (d)	100	(a) (b) (c) (d)
11	(a) (b) (c) (d)	41	(a) (b) (c) (d)	71	(a) (b) (c) (d)	101	(a) (b) (c) (d)
12	(a) (b) (c) (d)	42	(a) (b) (c) (d)	72	(a) (b) (c) (d)	102	(a) (b) (c) (d)
13	(a) (b) (c) (d)	43	(a) (b) (c) (d)	73	(a) (b) (c) (d)	103	(a) (b) (c) (d)
14	(a) (b) (c) (d)	44	(a) (b) (c) (d)	74	(a) (b) (c) (d)	104	(a) (b) (c) (d)
15	(a) (b) (c) (d)	45	(a) (b) (c) (d)	75	(a) (b) (c) (d)	105	(a) (b) (c) (d)
16	(a) (b) (c) (d)	46	(a) (b) (c) (d)	76	(a) (b) (c) (d)	106	(a) (b) (c) (d)
17	(a) (b) (c) (d)	47	(a) (b) (c) (d)	77	(a) (b) (c) (d)	107	(a) (b) (c) (d)
18	(a) (b) (c) (d)	48	(a) (b) (c) (d)	78	(a) (b) (c) (d)	108	(a) (b) (c) (d)
19	(a) (b) (c) (d)	49	(a) (b) (c) (d)	79	(a) (b) (c) (d)	109	(a) (b) (c) (d)
20	(a) (b) (c) (d)	50	(a) (b) (c) (d)	80	(a) (b) (c) (d)	110	(a) (b) (c) (d)
21	(a) (b) (c) (d)	51	(a) (b) (c) (d)	81	(a) (b) (c) (d)	111	(a) (b) (c) (d)
22	(a) (b) (c) (d)	52	(a) (b) (c) (d)	82	(a) (b) (c) (d)	112	(a) (b) (c) (d)
23	(a) (b) (c) (d)	53	(a) (b) (c) (d)	83	(a) (b) (c) (d)	113	(a) (b) (c) (d)
24	(a) (b) (c) (d)	54	(a) (b) (c) (d)	84	(a) (b) (c) (d)	114	(a) (b) (c) (d)
25	(a) (b) (c) (d)	55	(a) (b) (c) (d)	85	(a) (b) (c) (d)	115	(a) (b) (c) (d)
26	(a) (b) (c) (d)	56	(a) (b) (c) (d)	86	(a) (b) (c) (d)	116	(a) (b) (c) (d)
27	(a) (b) (c) (d)	57	(a) (b) (c) (d)	87	(a) (b) (c) (d)	117	(a) (b) (c) (d)
28	(a) (b) (c) (d)	58	(a) (b) (c) (d)	88	(a) (b) (c) (d)	118	(a) (b) (c) (d)
29	(a) (b) (c) (d)	59	(a) (b) (c) (d)	89	(a) (b) (c) (d)	119	(a) (b) (c) (d)
30	(a) (b) (c) (d)	60	(a) (b) (c) (d)	90	(a) (b) (c) (d)	120	(a) (b) (c) (d)

Calculate Your Score

Correct (✓)	
Incorrect (✓)	
Unattempted	
Total Score	
Accuracy (%)	

Reasons for Incorrect Answers?

1. Lack of Knowledge/Existing Source Insufficient	
2. Lack of Multiple Revision	
3. Common Sense Mistakes	

Note :

1. Calculate total score as correct answers carry 2 marks each 1/3rd marks will deducted for **Incorrect** Answers.
2. Calculate Accuracy (%) by dividing the number of correct answers to the total number of attempted questions.

Past Learning

1. In which one of the following regions was Dhanyakataka, which flourished as a prominent Buddhist centre under the Mahasanghikas, located? **(2023)**

(a) Andhra
(b) Gandhara
(c) Kalinga
(d) Magadha

2. With reference to the cultural history of India, the memorising of chronicles, dynastic histories and epic tales was the profession of who of the following? **(2017)**

(a) Shramana
(b) Parivrajaka
(c) Agrahaarika
(d) Maagadha

3. In the context of the history of India, consider the following pairs: **(2017)**

	Term	Description
1.	Eripatti	Land, revenue from which was set apart for the maintenance of the village tank
2.	Taniyurs	Villages donated to a single Brahmin or a group of Brahmins
3.	Ghatikas	Colleges generally attached to the temples

Which of the pairs given above is/are correctly matched?

(a) 1 and 2
(b) 3 only
(c) 2 and 3
(d) 1 and 3

Detailed Solutions

Assessment Round

1. *(c)* Statement I is correct but Statement II is incorrect

- **Statement I is correct:** The Brahmanical education system used Sanskrit as the medium of instruction with a structured approach involving **Shravana (Listening), Manana (Internalisation), and Nididhyasana (Meditation)**. This method emphasized deep comprehension and contemplation of the teachings.
- **Statement II is incorrect:** The Buddhist education system used Pali as the medium of instruction and followed three different steps: Discipline, Meditation, and Wisdom. These steps focused on ethical conduct, mental training, and gaining insight, distinct from the Brahmanical method.

Thus, option (c) is the correct answer.

2. *(b)* Only two

- **Statement 1 is correct:** Taxila University was built in the **6th century** BCE on the banks of the Indus River. It offered studies in various subjects such as the Vedas, law, medicine, archery, hunting, military science, and astronomy
- **Statement 2 is incorrect:** The Huns destroyed it in the **5th century BCE.**
- **Statement 3 is correct:** The university was a prominent centre of learning, attracting notable teachers like **Panini in the 5th century** BCE, Chanakya/Kautilya, and Kumaralata (a Sautrantika scholar). It also educated prominent students including **Pasenadi**, the king of Kosala and an **Upasaka** of Buddhism, **Jivaka**, the personal doctor of Buddha and **Bimbisara, Charaka**, the father of medicine, **Chandragupta Maurya**, Atreya, Thus and **Agnivesha.**

Thus, option (b) is the correct answer.

3. *(c)* All three

- **Statement 1 is correct:** Nalanda University was founded by **Kumaragupta** I of the Gupta dynasty in the 5th century CE and is located in present-day Nalanda, Bihar, India.
- **Statement 2 is correct:** The university was also known as Dharm Gunj, or the Mountain of Truth, and featured three main buildings: **Ratnasagar, Ratnadadhi, and Ratnarajaka.** The university was destroyed by Bakhtiyar Khilji in the 12th century CE.
- **Statement 3 is correct: Alexander Cunningham** identified the site in 1861-62 CE. The ruins of Nalanda were recognised as a UNESCO World Heritage site in January 2009.

Thus option (c) is the correct answer.

4. *(c)* Odantapuri Mahavihara

- **Odantapuri Mahavihara**, also known as Odantapura or Uddandapura, is an ancient Buddhist monastery located in present-day **Bihar Sharif, Bihar**, India. It was established by Gopala I, the first ruler of the **Pala Dynasty**, in the 8th century CE.
- Odantapuri played a significant role in the spread of Buddhism and was a prominent center of learning, attracting scholars and students from various regions. Notable figures such as **Atisha Dipankara Srijana**, an influential Buddhist scholar, studied here. The monastery housed around **12,000 monks at its peak** and had a vast library containing numerous Brahmanical and Buddhist texts.
- The invading forces led by **Muhammad bin Bakhtiyar Khilji** sacked the monastery, burning its library and causing the surviving monks to flee to regions like Nepal and Tibet.

Thus, option (c) is the correct answer.

5. *(a)* 1 and 2 only

- **Statement 1 is correct:** Jain educational centers are indeed referred to as **Jinalayas** and **Basadis. Jinalayas** were **places of worship and learning**, reflecting the Jain community's emphasis on non-violence, truth and asceticism.

- **Basadis** served as **educational hubs** where Jain monks and scholars would impart teachings from Jain canonical texts, such as the **Agamas.**
- **Statement 2 is correct:** Brahminical education was structured around various types of institutions which include **Gurukuls, Ghatikas, Agraharas, Mathas, and Brahmapuris,** each serving specific purposes:
- **Gurukuls:** These were the traditional schools where students lived with their teachers (gurus) and learned subjects like the Vedas, Upanishads, and other aspects of Hindu philosophy and sciences.
- **Ghatikas:** They were attached to temples, where higher education in philosophy and logic was imparted. Ghatikas attracted scholars from different **regions, enhancing the exchange of ideas.**
- **Agraharas:** These were villages granted to Brahmins, often with schools attached, promoting the study of sacred texts and rituals. Agraharas helped maintain religious practices and scholarly traditions within Brahmin communities.
- **Mathas:** These were monastic institutions that served as centers of learning, particularly for the study of Vedanta and other philosophical systems.
- **Brahmapuris:** These were urban centers that housed Brahmin scholars and served as hubs for intellectual and cultural activities.
- **Statement 3 is incorrect:** The Buddhist education system was characterised by **its inclusivity and lack of varna bias,** distinguishing it from the Brahminical system, which restricted education to the upper three varnas (Brahmins, Kshatriyas, and Vaishyas). Buddhist monastic institutions, known as **Viharas or Mahaviharas,** were open to individuals from **all social backgrounds,** including those from lower castes.

Thus, option (a) is the correct answer.

6. *(b)* Only two pairs

- **Pair 1 is correct:** Nadia, also known as Nabadwip, is indeed located at the confluence of the **Ganga and Jalangi** rivers in West Bengal. **Raghunath Shiromani,** a notable logician and scholar of the **Navya Nyaya** (New Logic) school, established a school of logic here in the 15th century CE. It was often referred to as the **Oxford of Bengal** due to its scholarly activities.
- **Pair 2 is correct:** Ujjain was a prominent center of learning and astronomy in ancient India. It was home to great scholars such as **Varahamihira and Brahmagupta,** Varahamihira was known for his encyclopedic work, **Brihat Samhita,** while Brahmagupta wrote influential texts like **Brahmasphutasiddhanta,** which laid foundational principles in mathematics.
- **Pair 3 is incorrect:** Kanchipuram, located in **Tamil Nadu,** was known as a major center of learning and culture, particularly under the Pallava dynasty. It was famous for its **Ghatikasthanam,** an important educational institution that attracted scholars from all over India. However, it was not specifically associated with the **Dvaita school of thought,** which is linked to the philosopher **Madhavacharya** and centered in regions like **Udupi.**
- **Pair 4 is incorrect:** Sharda Peeth is identified as a temple university situated in the region of modern-day **Pakistan-occupied Kashmir.** It was built on the banks of the **Neelam River** and played a pivotal role in the development of the Sharda script, which was used for Sanskrit and Kashmiri languages. **Al-Biruni, the Persian scholar,** documented Sharda Peeth in his travel accounts.

Thus, option (b) is the correct answer

7. *(b)* Pabbajja is the lower ordination ceremony for entering novice rank, whereas Upasampada is the higher ordination to become a full monk.

- Pabbajja is a Pali term meaning going forth and refers to the ceremony marking the **entrance into the monastic life as a novice,** or samanera for males and samaneri for females. During Pabbajja, candidates shave their heads, don monastic robes, and formally take refuge in the Buddha, Dharma (the teachings), and Sangha (the monastic community).

- Upasampada is a Pali term meaning **approaching or receiving** and refers to the **higher ordination ceremony** for becoming a fully ordained **monk (bhikkhu) or nun (Bhikkhuni)**. Upasampada allows individuals to fully participate in the monastic community, including taking on teaching roles, officiating ceremonies, and participating in the communal decision-making process.

Thus, option (b) is the correct answer.

8. *(d)* None

- **Pair 1 is not correctly matched: Vikramshila Mahavihara** was founded by **Dharmapala in the 8th** century AD and is located in Bhagalpur, Bihar. The focus was on Vajrayana Buddhism and studies in various disciplines such as Vedic sciences, astronomy, law, grammar, and philosophy.
- **Pair 2 is not correctly matched**: Jagaddala **Mahavihara** was built by Ramapala of the Pala dynasty in the 11th century AD and is located in present-day Bangladesh. It emphasised Vajrayana Buddhism, and Vidyakara compiled the Subhasitaratnakosa here.
- **Pair 3 is not correctly matched: Manyakheta** flourished under the **Rashtrakutas in Karnataka** and was a significant center of learning, particularly known as a **Matha** of the **Dvaita school of thought**. It was also a hub for scholars of Jainism, Buddhism, and Hinduism.

Thus, option (d) is the correct answer.

9. *(b)* Maktab is for primary education, Madrasa offers higher education, and Khanqah is a center for Sufi learning.

- **Maktab**: Traditionally, a Maktab is a place where children receive **primary education.** It serves as the foundation of the Islamic education system, teaching basic reading, writing, and religious studies, including Quranic education.
- **A Madrasa** is an institution **for higher education** where students engage in more advanced studies of the Quran, Hadith, Islamic law, theology, and other subjects. It is often equivalent to a university in the Islamic educational context.
- **Khanqah**: Khanqah refers to a **Sufi lodge or retreat** where followers engage in spiritual learning and practice under the guidance of a Sufi master. It is a place dedicated to the practice of Sufism, focusing on spiritual development, meditation, and communal prayers.

Thus, option (b) is the correct answer.

Past Learning (Answers)

1 (a) **2** (d) **3** (d)

CHAPTER 13

UNESCO World Heritage Sites

Assessment Round

Topic 1 : UNESCO World Heritage Sites

1. With reference to UNESCO World Heritage Sites, consider the following statements:

1. As of October 2023, India has 42 UNESCO World Heritage Sites.
2. The first-ever UNESCO World Heritage site listed in India was Ajanta Caves.
3. UNESCO is headquartered in Paris and has 195 member states.

How many of the statements given above is/are correct?

(a) Only one
(b) Only two
(c) All three
(d) None

2. About the Archaeological Survey of India (ASI), consider the following statements:

1. ASI is the nodal organisation for archaeological research and the preservation of heritage in India.
2. It was established in 1861 by Alexander Cunningham, who is also considered the father of Indian Archaeology.
3. ASI is responsible for maintaining all of India's natural UNESCO World Heritage Sites.

How many of the statements given above is/are correct?

(a) Only one (b) Only two
(c) All three (d) None

3. Consider the following statements about the first UNESCO World Heritage Site:

1. The first-ever site listed under UNESCO was the Galapagos Islands in Ecuador.
2. In India, the first site listed in 1983 was the Taj Mahal.

Which of the statements given above is/are correct?

(a) 1 only (b) 2 only
(c) Both 1 and 2 (d) Neither 1 nor 2

4. With reference to the Taj Mahal, consider the following statements:

1. The Taj Mahal is a mausoleum of red sandstone built by Shah Jahan in memory of his wife Mumtaz Mahal.
2. It is famous for its symmetry, Quranic inscriptions, and pietra dura style of ornamentation.
3. The Taj Mahal was declared a centrally protected monument of national importance in December 1920.

Which of the statements given above is/are correct?

(a) 1 only (b) 2 and 3 only
(c) 1 and 3 only (d) 1, 2 and 3

5. Regarding the Konark Sun Temple, consider the following statements:

1. The Konark Sun Temple, also known as the White Pagoda, was built in the 13th century CE by King Narsinghadeva I of the Eastern Ganga dynasty.
2. The temple is dedicated to the Sun God and is famous for its chariot-shaped structure with 12 pairs of intricately carved stone wheels and seven horses symbolising the days of the week.
3. The temple was designed by the chief architect, Bishu Maharana.

Which of the statements given above are correct?

(a) 1 and 2 only
(b) 2 and 3 only
(c) 1 and 3 only
(d) 1, 2 and 3

6. Consider the following pairs.

1. Group of Monuments at Hampi	Located in the Tungabhadra river basin, was the capital of the Chola Empire.
2. Fatehpur Sikri	Built by Mughal Emperor Akbar, known as the 'City of Victory.'
3. Churches and Convents of Goa	Built during the 16th and 18th centuries CE by the Portuguese.

How many pairs given above is/are incorrectly matched?

(a) Only one (b) Only two
(c) All three (d) None

7. About the Mountain Railways of India, consider the following statements:

1. The Darjeeling Himalayan Railways, Nilgiri Mountain Railways, and Kalka Shimla Railways are collectively known as the Mountain Railways of India.
2. These railways are recognised by UNESCO as World Heritage Sites.
3. The Nilgiri Mountain Railways was the first to be recognised, followed by the Darjeeling and Kalka Shimla Railways.

Which of the statements given above are correct?

(a) 1 and 2 only
(b) 2 and 3 only
(c) 1 and 3 only
(d) 1, 2 and 3

8. With reference to the Mountain Railways of India, consider the following pairs:

1. Darjeeling Himalayan Railways	Opened in 1881 between Siliguri and Darjeeling.
2. Nilgiri Mountain Railways	Opened in 1908, runs between Mettupalayam and Udhagamandalam.
3. Kalka Shimla Railways	Built in the mid-19th century, recognised as a World Heritage Site in 2008.

How many pairs given above is/are correctly matched?

(a) Only one (b) Only two
(c) All three (d) None

9. Match the following important railway routes with their respective locations:

1. Darjeeling Himalayan Railways	A. West Bengal
2. Nilgiri Mountain Railways	B. Tamil Nadu
3. Kalka Shimla Railways	C. Himachal Pradesh
4. Mahabodhi Express	D. Bihar

Choose the correct option from the below:

(a) 1-A, 2-B, 3-C, 4-D
(b) 1-C, 2-A, 3-B, 4-D
(c) 1-A, 2-C, 3-B, 4-D
(d) 1-D, 2-C, 3-B, 4-A

10. Which of the following statements about the Hill Forts of Rajasthan is incorrect?

(a) There are six forts included in the list.
(b) Chittor Fort is located in Jodhpur.
(c) Amer Fort is in Jaipur.
(d) Ranthambore Fort is in Sawai Madhopur.

11. Arrange the following events related to World Heritage Sites in chronological order:
1. Discovery of Dholavira
2. Construction of Rani-Ki-Vav
3. Founding of Jaipur City
4. Inclusion of Mahabodhi Temple in UNESCO World Heritage List

Choose the correct option from the codes given below:
(a) 2 - 3 - 4 - 1
(b) 2 - 3 - 1 - 4
(c) 3 - 2 - 4 - 1
(d) 1 - 2 - 3 - 4

12. Identify the UNESCO World Heritage Site based on the following statements:
1. It is one of the earliest Buddhist temples, made entirely of brick by Emperor Ashoka.
2. The complex includes the Bodhi Tree, Vajrasana (Diamond Throne), and a grand temple that is 50 meters high.

Select the correct from the options given below.
(a) Mahabodhi Temple Complex
(b) Ajanta Caves
(c) Sanchi Stupa
(d) Nalanda Mahavihara

13. Consider the following forts:

1. Chittor Fort	2. Kumbhalgarh Fort
3. Amer Fort	4. Jaisalmer Fort
5. Gagron Fort	6. Ranthambore Fort

Which of the above forts are part of the Hill Forts of Rajasthan UNESCO World Heritage Site?
(a) 1, 2, 3, 4, 5 and 6
(b) 1, 2, 3 and 4 only
(c) 1, 2, 4, 5 and 6 only
(d) 1, 2, 3 and 5 only

14. Identify the UNESCO World Heritage Site based on the following statements:
1. This walled city was established on the eastern bank of the Sabarmati River in the 15th century CE.
2. It is known for its harmonious coexistence of architecture from various religions, including mosques, Hindu temples, and Jain temples.

Choose the correct answer from the option given below:
(a) Historic City of Ahmedabad
(b) Old Goa
(c) Jaipur City
(d) Fatehpur Sikri

15. Identify the UNESCO World Heritage Site based on the following statements:
1. It was constructed during the reign of the Kakatiya dynasty and is dedicated to Lord Shiva.
2. This temple is known for its unique architectural feature called the sandbox technique, which helps it withstand earthquakes.

Choose the correct answer from the options given below:
(a) Brihadeshwara Temple
(b) Kakatiya Rudreshwara (Ramappa) Temple
(c) Pattadakal Temples
(d) Mahabalipuram Temples

16. With reference to the Kaziranga National Park, consider the following statements:
1. It was declared a national park in 1974 and is also a tiger reserve.
2. It has the world's largest population of one-horned rhinoceroses.
3. The Diphu River passes through the park.

How many of the statements given above is/are correct?
(a) Only one (b) Only two
(c) All three (d) None

17. With reference to the Sundarbans National Park, consider the following statements:
1. It has the world's largest patch of mangrove forests, shared by India and Bangladesh.
2. It is a tiger reserve and a biosphere reserve included in UNESCO's MAB programme.
3. The River Manas passes through it.

Which of the statements given above is/are correct?
(a) 1 and 2 only
(b) 2 only
(c) 1 and 3 only
(d) 2 and 3 only

18. Consider the following statements about the Western Ghats and the Eastern Ghats:

1. The Western Ghats are older than the Himalayas.
2. The Eastern Ghats have more biodiversity than the Western Ghats.
3. Western Ghats were recognised as a world heritage site earlier than Eastern Ghats.

Which of the statements given above is/are incorrect?

(a) 1 only (b) 2 and 3 only
(c) 1 and 3 only (d) 1, 2 and 3

19. Regarding the Great Himalayan National Park, consider the following statements:

1. It is located in the Kullu district of Himachal Pradesh.
2. It has 25 different types of forests within it.
3. It is a UNESCO World Heritage Site recognised in 2019 for its unique biodiversity.

Which of the statements given above are correct?

(a) 1 and 2 only (b) 2 and 3 only
(c) 1 and 3 only (d) 1, 2 and 3

20. Arrange the following UNESCO-recognised heritage sites in India in the order they were declared World Heritage Sites:

1. Kaziranga National Park
2. Manas Wildlife Sanctuary
3. Sundarbans National Park
4. Western Ghats

Choose the correct sequence from the options given below:

(a) 1 - 2 - 3 - 4 (b) 1 - 3 - 2 - 4
(c) 2 - 1 - 3 - 4 (d) 3 - 1 - 2 - 4

21. Identify the UNESCO World Heritage Site based on the following statements:

1. It is recognised for its biodiversity and is part of a biosphere reserve.
2. It is located along the Brahmaputra River and is a key habitat for species like the one-horned rhinoceros and tigers.

Choose the correct answer from the options below

(a) Kaziranga National Park
(b) Manas Wildlife Sanctuary
(c) Sundarbans National Park
(d) Nanda Devi and Valley of Flowers National Park

22. Arrange the following UNESCO World Heritage Sites in the order they were inscribed:

1. Group of Monuments at Pattadakal
2. Qutub Minar and Its Monuments
3. Santiniketan
4. Humayun's Tomb

Choose the correct chronological order from the codes given below.

(a) 1 - 2 - 3 - 4 (b) 1 - 4 - 2 - 3
(c) 2 - 4 - 3 - 1 (d) 1 - 3 - 4 - 2

23. Match the following UNESCO World Heritage Sites with their respective states:

Site	States
1. Ajanta Caves	A. Aurangabad
2. Group of Monuments at Mahabalipuram	B. Tamil Nadu
3. Elephanta Caves	C. Madhya Pradesh
4. Khajuraho Group of Monuments	D. Maharashtra

Choose the correct option from the below:

(a) 1-A, 2-B, 3-D, 4-C
(b) 1-A, 2-C, 3-B, 4-D
(c) 1-B, 2-A, 3-C, 4-D
(d) 1-C, 2-A, 3-B, 4-A

24. Match the following UNESCO World Heritage Sites with their years of inscription:

Site	Year
1. Taj Mahal	A. 1983
2. Great Living Chola Temples	B. 1987
3. Chandigarh Capitol Complex	C. 2016
4. Dholavira	D. 2021

Choose the correct option from the codes below:

(a) 1-A, 2-B, 3-C, 4-D
(b) 1-B, 2-C, 3-A, 4-D
(c) 1-A, 2-C, 3-B, 4-D
(d) 1-C, 2-B, 3-A, 4-D

25. With reference to Dholavira, consider the following statements:

1. Dholavira is the fifth largest metropolis of the Indus Valley civilisation discovered in 1968 by archaeologist Jagat Pati Joshi.
2. It is located on the Khadir bet island of the Rann of Kutch, and the Tropic of Cancer passes through it.
3. Dholavira was known for its elaborate system of town planning, water harvesting, and management by building dams.

How many of the statements given above is/are correct?

(a) Only one (b) Only two
(c) All three (d) None

26. Identify the UNESCO World Heritage Site based on the following statements:

1. This site, established in 1862 by Debendranath Tagore, is located in the Birbhum district of West Bengal.
2. It was later developed into a school by Rabindranath Tagore in 1901, following the Brahmacharya Ashram model, and eventually became known as Visva Bharati University.
3. The name of this site means 'abode of peace.'

Choose the correct option/site from the below:

(a) Nalanda Mahavihara
(b) Santiniketan
(c) Kalakshetra
(d) Nalanda University

Topic 2 : UNESCO Intangible Cultural Heritage

27. With reference to Intangible Cultural Heritage, consider the following statements:

1. Intangible cultural heritage is exclusively traditional and no longer practiced.
2. The concept of intangible cultural heritage includes both living traditions and modern cultural practices.
3. The Intangible Cultural Heritage list is published by the International Committee for the Conservation of Cultural Monuments.

How many of the statements given above is/are correct?

(a) Only one (b) Only two
(c) All three (d) None

28. Match the following Intangible Cultural Heritage elements with their respective states:

List I		List II
1. Kalbelia Folk Dance	A.	Rajasthan
2. Kumbh Mela (Ujjain)	B.	Madhya Pradesh
3. Sankirtana	C.	Ladakh
4. Buddhist Chanting	D.	Manipur

Choose the correct option from the codes given below:

(a) 1-A, 2-B, 3-D, 4-C
(b) 1-A, 2-B, 3-D, 4-C
(c) 1-B, 2-A, 3-C, 4-D
(d) 1-C, 2-A, 3-B, 4-D

29. Regarding Intangible Cultural Heritage, which of the following aspects apply to the inscriptions on the UNESCO list?

1. The inscription process is community-driven.
2. Intangible cultural heritage must be historically documented for inclusion.
3. The list was established in 2008.

Select the correct answer using the codes given below:

(a) 1, 2 and 3 (b) 1 only
(c) 1 and 3 only (d) 2 and 3 only

30. With reference to the Ramlila, consider the following statements:

1. Ramlila is performed exclusively in the regions of Northern India.
2. It was inscribed on the UNESCO Representative List of the Intangible Cultural Heritage of Humanity in 2008.
3. Ramlila performances are strictly religious and do not include any theatrical elements.

How many of the statements given above is/are correct?

(a) Only one (b) Only two
(c) All three (d) None

31. How do you distinguish between Kutiyattam and Mudiyettu performances?

1. Kutiyattam is a theatrical performance, whereas Mudiyettu is primarily a ritual dance-drama.
2. Kutiyattam is performed inside temples, while Mudiyettu is performed in open spaces.

Which of the statements given above is/are correct?

(a) 1 only (b) 2 only
(c) Both 1 and 2 (d) Neither 1 nor 2

32. Identify the Intangible Cultural Heritage element based on the following statements:

1. It is a ritual theatre and dance-drama inscribed in 2010.
2. It depicts the story of Goddess Kali and the demon Darika.
3. It is performed annually in temples during the Bhagavati Kavu festival.

Select the correct answer from the options given below :

(a) Ramman (b) Kutiyattam
(c) Mudiyettu (d) Sankirtana

33. With reference to the Sattriya dance, consider the following statements:

1. It was inscribed in the UNESCO Representative List of the Intangible Cultural Heritage of Humanity in 2013.
2. Sattriya is a ritual dance of Vaishnavism performed in monasteries.
3. It is traditionally performed only by male monks.

How many of the statements given above is/are not correct?

(a) Only one (b) Only two
(c) All three (d) None

34. With reference to Durga Puja of Kolkata, consider the following statements:

1. Durga Puja was the first festival from Asia to be included in the UNESCO Intangible Heritage list.
2. It is a nine-day festival culminating on the day of Dashami.
3. Beautifully designed clay models of Goddess Durga are made from clay pulled from the Ganga River.

How many of the statements given above is/are correct?

(a) Only one (b) Only two
(c) All three (d) None

35. Which of the following statements about Nawrouz is incorrect?

(a) Nawrouz is celebrated on 21st March, marking the beginning of spring and the day of the equinox.
(b) It was inscribed in the UNESCO list in 2016.
(c) Nawrouz is exclusively celebrated by the Parsi community in India.
(d) It is also known as Jamshed Nawrouz in India.

36. With reference to Yoga, consider the following statements:

1. Yoga was inscribed in the UNESCO Representative List of the Intangible Cultural Heritage of Humanity in 2016.
2. International Yoga Day is celebrated on 21st June every year.
3. Yoga is solely based on physical exercises and does not include any spiritual or mental practices.

How many of the statements given above is/are correct?

(a) Only one (b) Only two
(c) All three (d) None

37. Identify the cultural element based on the following statements:

1. It includes folk songs and dances performed by the Kalbelia community of Rajasthan.
2. The Kalbelia tribe was historically a snake-handler community.
3. The dance involves swirling, graceful movements performed exclusively by women.

Choose the correct option from the below:

(a) Chhau dance (b) Kalbelia dance
(c) Mudiyettu (d) Sankirtana

38. Arrange the following cultural elements according to the year they were inscribed in the UNESCO Representative List of the Intangible Cultural Heritage of Humanity:

1. Nawrouz
2. Kumbh Mela
3. Durga Puja of Kolkata
4. Yoga
5. Kalbelia Dance

Choose the correct chronological order from the codes given below:
(a) 5 - 1 - 4 - 2 - 3
(b) 1 - 5 - 4 - 3 - 2
(c) 3 - 2 - 5 - 1 - 4
(d) 4 - 5 - 2 - 1 - 3

Topic 3 : UNESCO Creative Cities Network

39. With reference to the UNESCO Creative Cities Network (UCCN), consider the following statements:

1. The UCCN was created in 2004 to promote cooperation among cities that identify creativity as a strategic factor for sustainable urban development.
2. The Creative Cities tag is awarded by UNESCO on World Heritage Day.
3. There are more than 350 creative cities worldwide, representing seven fields including Crafts and Folk Art, Design, and Media Arts.

How many of the statements given above is/are correct?
(a) Only one (b) Only two
(c) All three (d) None

40. Match the following UNESCO Creative Cities in India with their respective fields of recognition:

List I	List II
1. Hyderabad	A. Crafts and Folk Art
2. Srinagar	B. Film
3. Gwalior	C. Gastronomy
4. Mumbai	D. Music

Choose the correct option from the codes given below:
(a) 1-C, 2-A, 3-D, 4-B
(b) 1-D, 2-C, 3-A, 4-B
(c) 1-A, 2-D, 3-B, 4-C
(d) 1-C, 2-B, 3-D, 4-A

41. Arrange the following Indian cities according to the year they were designated as UNESCO Creative Cities:

1. Varanasi
2. Chennai
3. Jaipur
4. Kozhikode

Choose the correct chronological order from the codes given below:
(a) 3 - 1 - 2 - 4 (b) 1 - 3 - 2 - 4
(c) 4 - 2 - 1 - 3 (d) 2 - 4 - 1 - 3

OMR SHEET

Assessment Round

1	a	b	c	d	31	a	b	c	d	61	a	b	c	d	91	a	b	c	d
2	a	b	c	d	32	a	b	c	d	62	a	b	c	d	92	a	b	c	d
3	a	b	c	d	33	a	b	c	d	63	a	b	c	d	93	a	b	c	d
4	a	b	c	d	34	a	b	c	d	64	a	b	c	d	94	a	b	c	d
5	a	b	c	d	35	a	b	c	d	65	a	b	c	d	95	a	b	c	d
6	a	b	c	d	36	a	b	c	d	66	a	b	c	d	96	a	b	c	d
7	a	b	c	d	37	a	b	c	d	67	a	b	c	d	97	a	b	c	d
8	a	b	c	d	38	a	b	c	d	68	a	b	c	d	98	a	b	c	d
9	a	b	c	d	39	a	b	c	d	69	a	b	c	d	99	a	b	c	d
10	a	b	c	d	40	a	b	c	d	70	a	b	c	d	100	a	b	c	d
11	a	b	c	d	41	a	b	c	d	71	a	b	c	d	101	a	b	c	d
12	a	b	c	d	42	a	b	c	d	72	a	b	c	d	102	a	b	c	d
13	a	b	c	d	43	a	b	c	d	73	a	b	c	d	103	a	b	c	d
14	a	b	c	d	44	a	b	c	d	74	a	b	c	d	104	a	b	c	d
15	a	b	c	d	45	a	b	c	d	75	a	b	c	d	105	a	b	c	d
16	a	b	c	d	46	a	b	c	d	76	a	b	c	d	106	a	b	c	d
17	a	b	c	d	47	a	b	c	d	77	a	b	c	d	107	a	b	c	d
18	a	b	c	d	48	a	b	c	d	78	a	b	c	d	108	a	b	c	d
19	a	b	c	d	49	a	b	c	d	79	a	b	c	d	109	a	b	c	d
20	a	b	c	d	50	a	b	c	d	80	a	b	c	d	110	a	b	c	d
21	a	b	c	d	51	a	b	c	d	81	a	b	c	d	111	a	b	c	d
22	a	b	c	d	52	a	b	c	d	82	a	b	c	d	112	a	b	c	d
23	a	b	c	d	53	a	b	c	d	83	a	b	c	d	113	a	b	c	d
24	a	b	c	d	54	a	b	c	d	84	a	b	c	d	114	a	b	c	d
25	a	b	c	d	55	a	b	c	d	85	a	b	c	d	115	a	b	c	d
26	a	b	c	d	56	a	b	c	d	86	a	b	c	d	116	a	b	c	d
27	a	b	c	d	57	a	b	c	d	87	a	b	c	d	117	a	b	c	d
28	a	b	c	d	58	a	b	c	d	88	a	b	c	d	118	a	b	c	d
29	a	b	c	d	59	a	b	c	d	89	a	b	c	d	119	a	b	c	d
30	a	b	c	d	60	a	b	c	d	90	a	b	c	d	120	a	b	c	d

Calculate Your Score

Correct (✓)	
Incorrect (✓)	
Unattempted	
Total Score	
Accuracy (%)	

Reasons for Incorrect Answers?

1. Lack of Knowledge/Existing Source Insufficient	
2. Lack of Multiple Revision	
3. Common Sense Mistakes	

Note :

1. Calculate total score as correct answers carry 2 marks each 1/3rd marks will deducted for **Incorrect** Answers.
2. Calculate Accuracy (%) by dividing the number of correct answers to the total number of attempted questions.

Past Learning

1. Which one of the following ancient towns is well-known for its elaborate system of water harvesting and management by building a series of dams and channelising water into connected reservoirs? **(2021)**

(a) Dholavira
(b) Kalibangan
(c) Rakhigarhi
(d) Ropar

2. Which one of the following statements is correct? **(2021)**

(a) Ajanta Caves lie in the gorge of Waghora River.
(b) Sanchi Stupa lies in the gorge of Chambal River.
(c) Pandu-lena Cave Shrines lie in the gorge of Narmada River.
(d) Amaravati Stupa lies in the gorge of Godavari River.

3. Building 'Kalyaana Mandapas' was a notable feature in the temple construction in the kingdom of **(2019)**

(a) Chalukya
(b) Chandela
(c) Rashtrakuta
(d) Vijayanagara

4. With reference to the cultural history of India, consider the following statements: **(2018)**

1. White marble was used in making Buland Darwaza and Khankah at Fatehpur Sikri.
2. Red Sandstone and marble were used in making Bara Imambara and Rumi Darwaza in Lucknow.

Which of the statements given above is/are correct?

(a) 1 only (b) 2 only
(c) Both 1 and 2 (d) Neither 1 nor 2

5. With reference to Manipuri Sankirtana, consider the following statements: **(2017)**

1. It is a song and dance performance.
2. Cymbals are the only musical instruments used in the performance.
3. It is performed to narrate the life and deeds of Lord Krishna.

Which of the statements given above is/are correct?

(a) 1, 2 and 3 (b) 1 and 3 only
(c) 2 and 3 only (d) 1 only

6. What is/are common to the two historical places known as Ajanta and Mahabalipuram? **(2016)**

1. Both were built in the same period.
2. Both belong to the same religious denomination.
3. Both have rock-cut monuments.

Select the correct answer using the codes given below.

(a) 1 and 2 only
(b) 3 only
(c) 1 and 3 only
(d) None of the statements given above is correct

7. Consider the following sites /monuments. **(2005)**

1. Champaner-Pavagadh Archaeological Park
2. Chhatrapati Shivaji Railway Station, Mumbai
3. Mamallapuram
4. Sun Temple (Konark Temple)

Which of the above are included in the World Heritage List of UNESCO?

(a) 1, 2 and 3
(b) 1, 3 and 4
(c) 2 and 4
(d) All of the above

Detailed Solutions

Assessment Round

1. *(c)* All three

- **Statement 1 is correct**: India indeed had 42 UNESCO World Heritage Sites as of October 2023. This includes a diverse range of cultural, natural, and mixed heritage sites, reflecting the country's rich history and biodiversity. The list keeps expanding as more sites are inscribed.
- **Statement 2 is correct**: The **Ajanta Caves, along with the Ellora Caves, Taj Mahal, and Agra Fort**, were among the first sites from India to be inscribed on the UNESCO World Heritage list in 1983. The Ajanta Caves are famous for their ancient Buddhist rock-cut caves with exquisite murals and sculptures.
- **Statement 3 is correct**: UNESCO (United Nations Educational, Scientific and Cultural Organisation) is indeed headquartered in Paris, France. It has **195 member states** as part of its global initiative to promote peace and security through international collaboration in education, science, culture, and communication.

Thus, option (c) is the correct answer.

2. *(b)* Only two

- **Statement 1 is correct**: The **Archaeological Survey of India (ASI)** is the premier organisation responsible for archaeological research, conservation of cultural monuments, and preservation of heritage sites across India.
- **Statement 2 is correct**: **Alexander Cunningham**, often referred to as the '**Father of Indian Archaeology**' established the ASI in 1861. His work laid the foundation for systematic archaeological studies in India, and he is credited with the discovery and documentation of many significant ancient sites.
- **Statement 3 is incorrect**: While ASI is responsible for many of India's cultural heritage sites, the maintenance of natural World Heritage Sites is generally overseen by the Ministry of Environment, Forest and Climate Change, or other specialised agencies.

Thus, option (b) is the correct answer.

3. *(a)* 1 only

- **Statement 1 is correct**: The **Galapagos Islands in Ecuador** were indeed among the first sites listed under the UNESCO World Heritage program in 1978. The islands are known for their unique biodiversity and were a key location for Charles Darwin's theory of evolution.
- **Statement 2 is incorrect**: The Taj Mahal was indeed listed as a **UNESCO World Heritage Site in 1983**, but it was not the first. It was part of the initial batch of four sites from India, which included the **Ajanta Caves, Ellora Caves, and Agra Fort**.

Thus, option (a) is the correct answer.

4. *(b)* 2 and 3 only

- **Statement 1 is incorrect**: The Taj Mahal is built of **white marble**, not red sandstone. **Shah Jahan** commissioned this stunning mausoleum in memory of his beloved wife **Mumtaz Mahal**. It is one of the most iconic structures in the world and is renowned for its beauty and symmetry.
- **Statement 2 is correct**: The Taj Mahal is celebrated for its **architectural symmetry, intricate Quranic inscriptions in calligraphy**, and the **pietra dura inlay technique**, where precious and semi-precious stones are inlaid into the white marble to create stunning floral and geometric patterns.
- **Statement 3 is correct**: The Taj Mahal was declared a centrally protected monument of national importance by the **British Indian Government in December 1920**, recognising its significance as a cultural and historical landmark.

Thus, option (b) is the correct answer.

5. *(b)* 2 and 3 only

- **Statement 1 is incorrect:** The Konark Sun Temple is indeed a 13th-century CE structure, built by King **Narsinghadeva I** of the Eastern Ganga dynasty. However, it is known as the **'Black Pagoda'** due to the dark colour of its structure, not the 'White Pagoda.'
- **Statement 2 is correct:** The Konark Sun Temple is dedicated to Surya, the Sun God, and is one of the most magnificent temples in India. The temple is designed as a colossal chariot, with 12 pairs of wheels representing the 12 months of the year and seven horses representing the days of the week.
- **Statement 3 is correct:** Bishu Maharana is traditionally credited as the chief architect of the Konark Sun Temple. According to legend, it took 12 years and the combined efforts of 1,200 artisans to complete the temple.

Thus, option (b) is the correct answer.

6. *(a)* Only one

- **Pair 1 is incorrectly matched:** The Group of Monuments at Hampi is indeed located in the **Tungabhadra River basin**, but it was the capital of the **Vijayanagara Empire**, not the Chola Empire. The Chola Empire was centered in Tamil Nadu, while the Vijayanagara Empire's capital was Hampi. It became a UNESCO World Heritage Site in 1986.
- **Pair 2 is correctly matched:** Fatehpur Sikri was inscribed as a **UNESCO World Heritage Site in 1986.** Akbar built this city in the late 16th century as a new capital for the Mughal Empire, reflecting a unique blend of Indian, Persian, and Islamic architecture. Fatehpur Sikri is known as the 'City of Victory' because it was named after Akbar's victorious campaign in Gujarat in 1573.
- **Pair 3 is correctly matched:** The Churches and Convents of Goa were designated **as a UNESCO World Heritage Site in 1986.** These monuments were built by the Portuguese during their rule in India during the 16th and 16th centuries CE and are a fine example of the **Baroque architectural** style. The Basilica of Bom Jesus, which houses the **relics of St. Francis Xavier,** is among the most famous structures in this group, highlighting the spread of Christianity in Asia during the colonial period.

Thus, option (a) is the correct answer.

7. *(a)* 1 and 2 only

- **Statement 1 is correct:** These three railways are collectively recognised as the Mountain Railways of India, a UNESCO World Heritage Site. They are celebrated for their engineering marvels and the challenges they overcame due to the mountainous terrain.
- **Statement 2 is correct:** The Darjeeling Himalayan Railway was the first to be included in 1999, followed by the Nilgiri Mountain Railway in 2005, and the Kalka Shimla Railway in 2008.
- **Statement 3 is incorrect:** The Darjeeling Himalayan Railway was the first to be recognised as a UNESCO World Heritage Site in 1999. The Nilgiri Mountain Railway was recognised later in 2005, followed by the Kalka Shimla Railway in 2008.

Thus, option (a) is the correct answer.

8. *(b)* Only two

- **Statement 1 is correct:** The Darjeeling Himalayan Railway, also known as the 'Toy Train,' opened in **1881 and runs between New Jalpaiguri/Siliguri and Darjeeling,** offering a scenic journey through the Himalayan foothills. It was recognised as a UNESCO World Heritage Site in 1999, becoming the first railway of its kind to receive such an honour due to its outstanding universal value.
- **Statement 2 is correct:** The Nilgiri Mountain Railway was completed in **1908 and runs between Mettupalayam and Udhagamandalam (Ooty),** traversing the steep slopes of the Nilgiri Hills. It was recognised by UNESCO in 2005, and it is particularly noted for its rack-and-pinion rail system, which is necessary to navigate the steep gradients of the Nilgiri Hills.
- **Statement 3 is incorrect:** The Kalka Shimla Railway was **built between 1898 and 1903, not in the mid-19th century.** It was

recognised as a **UNESCO World Heritage Site in 2008** as part of the Mountain Railways of India group. The line is famous for its narrow gauge and the numerous tunnels and bridges it crosses as it winds through the Shivalik Hills.

Thus, option (b) is the correct answer.

9. *(a)* 1-A, 2-B, 3-C, 4-D

- **Darjeeling Himalayan Railways:** The Darjeeling Himalayan Railway, also known as the '**Toy Train,' is located in West Bengal.** It was the first of the Mountain Railways of India to be recognised as a **UNESCO World Heritage Site in 1999.** The railway runs between New Jalpaiguri and Darjeeling, offering scenic views of the Himalayan foothills.
- **Nilgiri Mountain Railways:** The Nilgiri Mountain Railway is located in Tamil Nadu and was recognised as a **UNESCO World Heritage Site in 2005.** This railway is famous for its unique rack and pinion system, which helps the train navigate the steep gradients of the **Nilgiri Hills, running between Mettupalayam and Udhagamandalam (Ooty).**
- **Kalka Shimla Railways:** The Kalka Shimla Railway is situated in Himachal Pradesh and was recognised as a **UNESCO World Heritage Site in 2008.** This railway is renowned for its narrow-gauge track and the numerous tunnels and bridges that traverse the hilly terrain from **Kalka to Shimla.**
- **Mahabodhi Express:** The Mahabodhi Express is a train that runs between **New Delhi and Gaya, Bihar.** Gaya is close to Bodh Gaya, the site where **Siddhartha Gautama** attained enlightenment and became the Buddha. This train connects important Buddhist pilgrimage sites and is named after the Mahabodhi Temple in Bodh Gaya.

Thus, option (a) is the correct answer.

10. *(b)* Chittor Fort is located in Jodhpur.

- **Statement (a) is correct:** The Hill Forts of Rajasthan, inscribed as a UNESCO World Heritage Site in 2013, include six forts: **Chittor Fort, Kumbhalgarh Fort, Ranthambore Fort, Amer Fort, Gagron Fort, and Jaisalmer Fort.** These forts are renowned for their **Rajput military architecture** and strategic locations in the **Aravalli Range** and **Thar Desert.**
- **Statement (b) is incorrect:** Chittor Fort is not located in Jodhpur instead it is located in **Chittorgarh, Rajasthan.** It is one of the largest forts in India and has a rich history associated with battles and the valor of Rajput kings and queens, particularly **Rana Kumbha and Rani Padmini.**
- **Statement (c) is correct:** Amer Fort is located in **Jaipur, Rajasthan.** It is known for its artistic style that blends both **Rajput and Mughal architecture.** The fort is famous for its beautiful palaces, courtyards, and the **Sheesh Mahal.**
- **Statement 4 is correct:** Ranthambore Fort is located in **Sawai Madhopur, Rajasthan.** It is situated within the **Ranthambore National Park,** a famous tiger reserve. The fort was historically significant as a stronghold of the **Chauhan dynasty** and later became part of the Mughal Empire.

Thus, option (b) is the correct answer.

11. *(b)* 2 - 3 - 1 - 4

- The correct chronological order is:
- **Construction of Rani-Ki-Vav (11th century CE):** Rani-Ki-Vav, the Queen's Stepwell, was constructed in the 11th century CE in Patan, Gujarat, by Queen Udayamati in memory of her husband, King Bhimdev I. It was inscribed as a UNESCO World Heritage Site in 2014.
- **Founding of Jaipur City (1727 CE):** Jaipur was founded by Maharaja Sawai Jai Singh II in 1727 CE. Known as the Pink City, Jaipur was included in the UNESCO World Heritage list in 2019.
- **Discovery of Dholavira (1968 CE):** Dholavira, an archaeological site of the Indus Valley Civilisation, was discovered by J.P. Joshi in 1968. It was inscribed as a UNESCO World Heritage Site in 2021.

- **Inclusion of Mahabodhi Temple in UNESCO World Heritage List (2002)**: The Mahabodhi Temple in Bodh Gaya, Bihar, where Buddha is believed to have attained enlightenment, was inscribed as a UNESCO World Heritage Site in 2002.

Thus, option (b) is the correct answer.

12. *(a)* Mahabodhi Temple Complex

- The **Mahabodhi Temple Complex**, located in **Bodh Gaya, Bihar,** is one of the most important and sacred Buddhist pilgrimage sites in the world. It is traditionally recognised as the location where Siddhartha Gautama attained enlightenment and became the Buddha around 500 BCE.
- **Emperor Ashoka**, who played a significant role in the spread of Buddhism, visited Bodh Gaya about 250 years after the Buddha's enlightenment and is credited with constructing the original temple at this site.
- The temple complex includes the Bodhi Tree, which is considered a direct descendant of the original tree under which the Buddha meditated. The **Vajrasana**, or **Diamond Throne**, is a stone platform placed at the site of Buddha's meditation, and the temple itself is an outstanding example of Indian brickwork architecture.

Thus, option (a) is the correct answer.

13. *(a)* 1, 2, 3, 4, 5 and 6

- The Hill Forts of Rajasthan recognised as a UNESCO World Heritage Site in 2013, include six majestic forts that exemplify the Rajput military architecture and their historical significance.
- **Chittor Fort**: Located in Chittorgarh, this is the **largest fort in India** and has witnessed numerous historic battles. It was the capital of Mewar and is known for its association with legendary figures like Maharana Pratap and Queen Padmini.
- **Kumbhalgarh Fort**: Built by **Rana Kumbha** in the 15th century, this fort is renowned for its massive walls, which stretch over 36 kilometers, making it the second-longest continuous wall in the world after the Great Wall of China.
- **Amer Fort**: Located in **Jaipur**, Amer Fort is famous for its artistic elements, blending Hindu and Mughal architecture. The fort's Sheesh Mahal (Mirror Palace) and the Diwan-i-Khas are highlights of this architectural marvel.
- **Jaisalmer Fort**: Often referred to as the **Golden Fort** this fort is made of yellow sandstone and stands proudly in the middle of the Thar Desert. It is still inhabited by a population, making it one of the few **'living forts'** in the world.
- **Gagron Fort**: Located in **Jhalawar**, Gagron Fort is unique as it is both a hill and water fort, surrounded by the Ahu and Kali Sindh rivers. Its strategic location made it an important military site in the medieval period.
- **Ranthambore Fort**: Situated in **Sawai Madhopur**, this fort was a critical stronghold for the Chauhan dynasty before falling to the Delhi Sultanate. It is located within the Ranthambore National Park, a famous tiger reserve.

Thus, option (a) is the correct answer.

14. *(a)* Historic City of Ahmedabad

- The **Historic City of Ahmedabad**, founded by **Sultan Ahmad Shah in 1411 CE,** is located on the eastern bank of the **Sabarmati River in Gujarat**. The city is renowned for its well-planned layout, with a distinct grid system of streets and central squares, making it one of the first planned cities in India. It became a UNESCO World Heritage Site in 2017.
- The **Jama Masjid, built by Sultan Ahmad Shah**, is one of the most prominent mosques in the city, known for its blend of Hindu and Islamic architectural styles. The **Sidi Saiyyed** Mosque is famous for its intricate stone latticework, especially the Tree of Life window, which has become an iconic symbol of Ahmedabad. The city also boasts numerous Hindu and Jain temples, such as the Swaminarayan Temple and the Hathee Singh Jain Temple, which are renowned for their intricate carvings and beautiful domes.

Thus, option (a) is the correct answer.

15. *(b)* Kakatiya Rudreshwara (Ramappa) Temple

- The **Kakatiya Rudreshwara Temple,** commonly known as the **Ramappa Temple,** is located in the village of Palampet in Telangana. Constructed during the reign of the Kakatiya dynasty in the early 13th century (1213 CE), the temple is dedicated to Lord Shiva.
- The temple is renowned for its unique '**sandbox technique**' where the foundation of the temple is filled with a mixture of sand, clay, and other materials, making it highly resilient to earthquakes and other seismic activities.

Thus, option (b) is the correct answer.

16. *(b)* Only two

- **Statement 1 is correct: Kaziranga National Park,** located in **Assam,** is a globally significant protected area recognised for its rich biodiversity. It was declared a reserve forest in 1908 and upgraded to a national park in 1974. In 1985, it was designated as a UNESCO World Heritage Site.
- **Statement 2 is correct:** The park's success in the conservation of the Indian one-horned rhinoceros is globally recognised, and it currently supports the **largest population** of this species in the world. As of the latest census, the park hosts over 2,400 rhinoceroses, making it a critical site for the species' survival.
- **Statement 3 is incorrect:** Diphu River does not pass through Kaziranga; instead, the **Brahmaputra River** forms the northern boundary of the park, and the smaller Diphlu River, not Diphu, flows through the park.

Thus, option (b) is the correct answer.

17. *(a)* 1 and 2 only

- **Statement 1 is correct:** The Sundarbans National Park, part of the **larger Sundarbans mangrove** forest, is the world's largest tidal halophytic mangrove forest, shared between India and Bangladesh.
- **Statement 2 is correct:** It is particularly known for its Royal Bengal Tigers, which have adapted to the mangrove habitat and are known to swim between the islands. The Sundarbans is not only a tiger reserve but also recognised as a biosphere reserve under **UNESCO's Man and the Biosphere (MAB) programme.**
- **Statement 3 is incorrect:** River Manas does not pass through the Sundarbans; the area is primarily influenced by the **Ganges, Brahmaputra, and Meghna** river systems, which create the delta and the extensive network of waterways that define the Sundarbans.

Thus, option (a) is the correct answer.

18. *(b)* 2 and 3 only

- **Statement 1 is correct:** The Western Ghats, also known as the Sahyadri Range, **are older than the Himalayas,** with their formation dating back to **around 150 million years ago** during the break-up of the **supercontinent Gondwana.** This rich biodiversity is due to the diverse range of ecosystems found within the Ghats, including tropical and subtropical rainforests. They are one of the **world's eight 'hottest hotspots'** of biological diversity, home to over 7,000 species of flowering plants, 139 mammal species, 508 bird species, and 179 amphibian species.
- **Statement 2 is incorrect:** The Eastern Ghats, while geologically older, are **not as rich in biodiversity as the Western Ghats.** The Eastern Ghats are a discontinuous range of mountains running along the Eastern coast of India and **are less forested and less diverse in terms of flora and fauna** compared to the Western Ghats. The Western Ghats, due to their continuous range, diverse climate, and dense forests, support a much higher level of biodiversity.
- **Statement 3 is incorrect: Western Ghats** were recognised as a UNESCO World Heritage Site in 2012, highlighting their importance in biodiversity conservation and the rich cultural heritage of the region. The Eastern Ghats, on the other hand, **have not been recognised** as a UNESCO World Heritage Site.

Thus, option (b) is the correct answer.

19. *(a)* 1 and 2 only

- **Statement 1 is correct**: The Great Himalayan National Park (GHNP), located in the Kullu district of Himachal Pradesh, is one of India's most pristine and biologically diverse protected areas.
- **Statement 2 is correct**: GHNP supports 25 different types of forests, including oak, deodar, pine, and rhododendron forests, which provide habitats for a wide range of wildlife.
- **Statement 3 is incorrect**: The Great Himalayan National Park was inscribed as a **UNESCO World Heritage Site in 2014, not 2019**. It was recognised under the **'Outstanding Universal Value'** criteria for its exceptional biodiversity and the conservation of its unique and diverse ecosystems. The park is also part of the **UNESCO World Network of Biosphere Reserves**, highlighting its importance for biodiversity conservation on a global scale.

Thus, option (a) is the correct answer.

20. *(c)* 2 - 1 - 3 - 4

- **Manas Wildlife Sanctuary** was inscribed in **1985**, located in **Assam** and is known for its rare and endangered wildlife, including the Assam Roofed Turtle, Hispid Hare, Golden Langur, and Pygmy Hog.
- **Kaziranga National Park** was also inscribed in 1985, Kaziranga, located in Assam, is recognised for having the world's largest population of one-horned rhinoceroses.
- **Sundarbans National Park** was inscribed in 1987 and is located in the Sundarbans delta in West Bengal.
- **Western Ghats** were inscribed as a UNESCO World Heritage Site in 2012.

Thus, option (c) is the correct answer.

21. *(a)* Kaziranga National Park

- **Kaziranga National Park**, located in the floodplains of the **Brahmaputra River in Assam**, is internationally recognised for its significant role in wildlife conservation. The park was designated a UNESCO World Heritage Site in 1985 due to its exceptional natural environment and biodiversity.
- Kaziranga is particularly renowned for harbouring the world's largest population of the Indian **one-horned rhinoceros**, with more than 2,400 individuals currently inhabiting the park. Additionally, the park is a vital tiger habitat and part of **India's Project Tiger**, with one of the highest tiger densities in the world.

Thus, option (a) is the correct answer.

22. *(b)* 1 - 4 - 2 - 3

- **Group of Monuments at Pattadakal (1987)**: Located in Karnataka, was inscribed as a UNESCO World Heritage Site in 1987.
- **Humayun's Tomb (1993)**: Located in Delhi, it was inscribed as a UNESCO World Heritage Site in 1993. It is the first garden tomb on the Indian subcontinent and was a precursor to later Mughal architecture, including the Taj Mahal.
- **Qutub Minar and Its Monuments (1993)**: Also inscribed in 1993, located in Delhi and includes the Qutub Minar itself, which is the tallest brick minaret in the world.
- **Santiniketan (2023)**: Located in West Bengal, was inscribed as a UNESCO World Heritage Site in 2023. It was established by Rabindranath Tagore,

Thus, option (b) is the correct answer.

23. *(a)* 1-A, 2-B, 3-D, 4-C

- **Ajanta Caves (Maharashtra)**: The Ajanta Caves, located in Maharashtra, are a series of 30 rock-cut Buddhist cave monuments dating from the 2nd century BCE to about 480 CE.
- **Group of Monuments at Mahabalipuram (Tamil Nadu)**: Located on the Coromandel Coast in Tamil Nadu, the it was inscribed as a UNESCO World Heritage Site in 1984.
- **Elephanta Caves (Maharashtra)**: The Elephanta Caves, located on Elephanta Island near Mumbai in Maharashtra, were inscribed as a UNESCO World Heritage Site in 1987.
- **Khajuraho Group of Monuments (Madhya Pradesh)**: The Khajuraho Group of Monuments in Madhya Pradesh was inscribed as a UNESCO World Heritage Site in 1986.

Thus, option (a) is the correct answer.

24. *(a)* 1-A, 2-B, 3-C, 4-D

- **Taj Mahal (1983)**: The Taj Mahal, one of the most famous monuments in the world, was inscribed as a UNESCO World Heritage Site in 1983. Built by Emperor Shah Jahan in memory of his wife Mumtaz Mahal.
- **Great Living Chola Temples (1987)**: The Great Living Chola Temples, located in Tamil Nadu, were inscribed in 1987. These temples include the Brihadeshwara Temple in Thanjavur, the Gangaikonda Cholapuram Temple, and the Airavatesvara Temple at Darasuram.
- **Chandigarh Capitol Complex (2016)**: It waa designed by the French architect Le Corbusier, the Chandigarh Capitol Complex was inscribed as a UNESCO World Heritage Site in 2016.
- **Dholavira (2021)**: Dholavira, an archaeological site of the Harappan civilisation located in Gujarat, was inscribed as a UNESCO World Heritage Site in 2021. It is one of the most prominent sites of the ancient Indus Valley Civilisation, known for its sophisticated urban planning, including an advanced water conservation system and a well-planned city layout.

Thus, option (a) is the correct answer.

25. *(c)* All three

- **Statement 1 is correct**: Dholavira is the **fifth largest known Harappan site,** discovered in 1968 by archaeologist **Jagat Pati Joshi.** It is notable for its advanced urban planning and engineering, particularly its water conservation system. Dholavira's unique features, such as its elaborate fortifications, and the use of stone for construction, distinguish it from other Harappan sites.
- **Statement 2 is correct**: Dholavira is situated on the **Khadir bet island** in the **Rann of Kutch**, Gujarat. The site is unique for its location in a saline desert area, where the **Tropic of Cancer** passes through.
- **Statement 3 is correct**: Dholavira is renowned for its sophisticated town planning, which includes an advanced system of water harvesting and storage. The city had a well-planned layout with wide streets, a central citadel, and separate areas for different social classes. The water management system, which included large reservoirs, channels, and dams, was crucial for sustaining the city's population in the arid environment.

Thus, option (c) is the correct answer.

26. *(b)* Santiniketan

- Santiniketan, located in the **Birbhum** district of **West Bengal**, was founded by **Debendranath Tagore**, the father of Rabindranath Tagore, in 1862.
- In 1901, Rabindranath Tagore established a school there, which later evolved into Visva Bharati University in 1921.
- The name 'Santiniketan' literally translates to 'abode of peace,' reflecting the tranquil environment and the educational philosophy promoted by Tagore. Santiniketan was inscribed as a UNESCO World Heritage Site in 2023.

Thus, option (b) is the correct answer.

27. *(a)* Only one

- **Statement 1 is incorrect**: Intangible cultural heritage refers to practices, expressions, knowledge, and skills that communities, groups, and sometimes individuals recognise as part of their cultural heritage. **It is not frozen in the past but rather evolves,** demonstrating both continuity and adaptability.
- **Statement 2 is correct**: The concept of intangible cultural heritage includes **both living traditions and modern cultural practices.** UNESCO defines intangible cultural heritage as practices, representations, expressions, knowledge, and skills that communities, groups, and, in some cases, individuals recognise as part of their cultural heritage.
- **Statement 3 is incorrect**: The Intangible Cultural Heritage list is **published by the Intergovernmental Committee for the Safeguarding of the Intangible Cultural Heritage**, which is part of UNESCO (United Nations Educational, Scientific and Cultural Organisation).

Thus, option (a) is the correct answer.

28. *(a)* 1-A, 2-B, 3-D, 4-C

- The **Kalbelia** dance is a traditional dance form of the **Kalbelia tribe**, which is known for its former occupation of snake charming in **Rajasthan**. This dance is characterised by graceful and energetic movements that imitate the movements of a serpent.
- **Kumbh Mela** is one of the largest religious gatherings in the world, held every twelve years at four different locations in India: **Haridwar** (Uttarakhand), **Prayagraj** (Uttar Pradesh), **Nashik** (Maharashtra), and **Ujjain** (Madhya Pradesh).
- **Sankirtana** is a form of ritual singing, drumming, and dancing performed in the temples and other sacred spaces of **Manipur.** It is a vibrant expression of the Vaishnava faith, narrating the life and deeds of Lord Krishna.
- **Buddhist Chanting in Ladakh** is a part of the religious rituals performed by monks in monasteries. These chants, often in the Tibetan language, include mantras and prayers that are believed to invoke spiritual power and blessings.

Thus, option (a) **is the correct answer.**

29. *(c)* 1 and 3 only

- **Statement 1 is correct**: The inscription process for the UNESCO Intangible Cultural Heritage list is indeed **community-driven.** This means that the communities or groups who practice the intangible cultural heritage are actively involved in the process of nominating their cultural practices for inclusion on the UNESCO list.
- **Statement 2 is incorrect**: The requirement that Intangible Cultural Heritage must be historically documented for inclusion is not correct. While historical documentation can support a nomination, the primary criterion for inclusion is that the practice is recognised by the community as part of their cultural heritage.
- **Statement 3 is correct**: The UNESCO Intangible Cultural Heritage list was **indeed established in 2008**, following the adoption of the Convention for the Safeguarding of the Intangible Cultural Heritage in 2003.

Thus, option (c) **is the correct answer.**

30. *(a)* Only one

- **Statement 1 is incorrect: Ramlila** is not performed exclusively in the regions of Northern India. While it is most popular in the Northern states, particularly in **Uttar Pradesh**, it has also spread to other parts of India and even to Indian communities abroad.
- **Statement 2 is correct:** Ramlila was inscribed on the UNESCO Representative List of the Intangible Cultural Heritage of Humanity in **2008.** The UNESCO recognition highlights its importance as a cultural practice that has been passed down through generations and is a living tradition in many parts of India.
- **Statement 3 is incorrect**: Ramlila is indeed a religious enactment, but it is also a highly theatrical performance that involves acting, music, narration, and elaborate costumes.

Thus, option (a) **is the correct answer.**

31. *(c)* Both 1 and 2

- **Statement 1 is correct: Kutiyattam** is a classical Sanskrit **theatre** that originates **from Kerala** and is performed in temples as part of religious rituals. **Mudiyettu,** on the other hand, is a ritualistic dance-drama also from Kerala, but it is primarily a folk theatre tradition that depicts the battle between Goddess Kali and the demon Darika.
- **Statement 2 is correct: Kutiyattam** is performed **inside temple theatres** known as **Kuttampalams**, where the performances can last for several days. **Mudiyettu,** however, is performed in open spaces, usually in the temple courtyard, and is more of a communal celebration than a strictly ritualistic performance.

Thus, option (c) **is the correct answer.**

32. *(c)* Mudiyettu

- **Mudiyettu** was inscribed in the UNESCO Representative List of the Intangible Cultural Heritage of Humanity in **2010.** This inscription recognises Mudiyettu as an important cultural expression that has been preserved and transmitted through generations in Kerala.

- Mudiyettu depicts the story of **Goddess Kali and the demon Darika**. This narrative is central to the performance, which dramatises the victory of good over evil.
- Mudiyettu is performed annually in temples during the **Bhagavati Kavu festival**. The festival is dedicated to the worship of the Goddess, and the performance of Mudiyettu is seen as a way to invoke her blessings and celebrate her triumph over evil forces.

Thus, option (c) is the correct answer.

33. *(b)* Only two

- **Statement 1 is correct**: Sattriya was inscribed in the **UNESCO Representative List of the Intangible Cultural Heritage of Humanity in 2013**. This recognition highlights the importance of Sattriya as a living tradition that is an integral part of Assam's cultural heritage.
- **Statement 2 is correct**: Sattriya is a ritual dance of Vaishnavism, performed in monasteries (known as Sattras) that are dedicated to the worship of Lord Krishna.
- **Statement 3 is incorrect**. Sattriya was originally performed by monks in the Sattras, today, Sattriya is also performed by women and has moved beyond the confines of the monasteries to be performed on stage and in cultural festivals.

Thus, option (b) is the correct answer.

34. *(a)* Only one

- **Statement 1 is incorrect**. Durga Puja is an important cultural and religious festival, it was inscribed in the UNESCO list in 2021. There have been other Asian cultural elements included in the list before Durga Puja.
- **Statement 2 is incorrect**: Durga Puja is primarily celebrated over **five days (when the main worship of Durga Puja takes place)** and the festive celebration starts on the sixth day (Shashthi) when the goddess is welcomed with rituals and ends on the tenth day (Vijayadashmi) when the idols are immersed.
- **Statement 3 is correct**. Beautifully designed clay models of Goddess Durga are indeed crafted from clay that is traditionally sourced from the banks of the Ganga River. This practice holds both symbolic and practical significance, as the Ganga is considered sacred in Hinduism.

Thus, option (a) is the correct answer.

35. *(c)* Nawrouz is exclusively celebrated by the Parsi community in India.

- **Statement (a) is correct**. Nawrouz is celebrated on 21st March, marking the beginning of spring and the day of the equinox. Nawrouz, which means 'new day,' is celebrated on March 21st, aligning with the **spring equinox.**
- **Statement (b) is correct**. Nawrouz was inscribed on the UNESCO **Intangible Cultural Heritage list in 2016**, recognising its significance as a cultural practice that promotes values of peace, solidarity, and respect for nature.
- **Statement (c) is incorrect**. Nawrouz is not exclusively celebrated by the Parsi community; it is also observed by other groups, including Muslims in Central Asia, the Caucasus, the Balkans and Iran. In India, while it is most closely associated with the Parsi community.
- **Statement (d) is correct**: In India, Nawrouz is commonly known as Jamshed Navroz, especially among the Parsi community. It is named after the legendary Persian king Jamshed, who is said to have introduced the Zoroastrian calendar.

Thus, option (c) is the correct answer.

36. *(b)* Only two

- **Statement 1 is correct**. Yoga was inscribed in the UNESCO Representative List of the Intangible Cultural Heritage of Humanity in 2016. The inclusion of Yoga highlights its global significance as a practice that originated in India and has been adopted worldwide for its benefits to mental, physical, and spiritual well-being.

- **Statement 2 is correct.** International Yoga Day is celebrated annually on **21st June** a date that coincides with the summer solstice, the longest day of the year in the Northern Hemisphere.
- **Statement 3 is incorrect.** Yoga is not solely based on physical exercises; it is a comprehensive practice that encompasses mental, spiritual and physical disciplines. Yoga includes asanas (postures), pranayama (breath control), meditation and ethical principles.

Thus, option (b) is the correct answer.

37. *(b)* Kalbelia Dance

- The **Kalbelia dance** is a traditional folk dance associated with the Kalbelia community of **Rajasthan.** It is performed by women in black swirling skirts, and it is characterised by graceful and sensuous movements that mimic the movements of a snake.
- The Kalbelia tribe was indeed historically a **snake-handler community**. The men of the community used to catch snakes and trade their venom, and the dance reflects the tribe's close association with snakes.
- The dance involves swirling, graceful movements performed exclusively by women. The dancers wear traditional black skirts adorned with colourful embroidery and mirrorwork.

Thus, option (b) is the correct answer.

38. *(a)* 5 - 1 - 4 - 2 - 3

- **Kalbelia** Dance: Inscribed in **2010**, it is a traditional folk dance of the Kalbelia community of Rajasthan.
- **Nawrouz:** Inscribed in **2016**, it is a celebration of the New Year and the coming of spring, observed by various communities, including Parsis and Muslims.
- **Yoga**: Inscribed in **2016**, it is an ancient Indian practice that promotes physical, mental, and spiritual well-being. It has become a global phenomenon, celebrated through International Yoga Day on 21st June each year.
- **Kumbh Mela:** Inscribed in **2017**, it is the largest peaceful gathering in the world, held at four river-bank pilgrimage sites in India.
- **Durga Puja of Kolkata:** Inscribed in **2021**, it is a major Hindu festival celebrated in West Bengal and across India. It involves the worship of Goddess Durga and is marked by elaborate decorations, cultural performances, and processions.

Thus, option (a) is the correct answer.

39. *(b)* Only two

- **Statement 1 is correct:** The **UNESCO Creative Cities Network** (UCCN) was indeed created in 2004. The network was established to promote cooperation among cities that recognise creativity as a key factor in sustainable urban development.
- **Statement 2 is incorrect:** The Creative Cities tag is not awarded on **World Heritage Day.** Instead, the Creative Cities designation is typically announced on **World Cities Day,** which is observed on **31st October** each year. World Heritage Day, on the other hand, is observed on April 18.
- **Statement 3 is correct:** There are indeed more than **350 cities** worldwide that have been recognised as part of the UNESCO Creative Cities Network. These cities represent seven different creative fields: Crafts and Folk Art, Design, Film, Gastronomy, Literature, Media Arts, and Music.

Thus, option (b) is the correct answer.

40. *(a)* 1-C, 2-A, 3-D, 4-B

- **Hyderabad** was designated as a **UNESCO Creative City of Gastronomy in 2019.** The city's rich culinary heritage, which blends Mughlai, Persian, and local South Indian influences, earned it this recognition.
- **Srinagar** was recognised as a UNESCO Creative City in the **field of Crafts and Folk Art in 2021.** The city is renowned for its traditional crafts, including Kashmiri Pashmina shawls, carpets, and intricate woodwork.

- **Gwalior** was designated as a UNESCO Creative **City of Music in 2023**. The city has a rich musical heritage, particularly in the classical genre. It is the birthplace of the Gwalior Gharana, one of the oldest Khayal Gharanas in Hindustani classical music.
- **Mumbai** was recognised as a UNESCO **Creative City of Film in 2019**. Often referred to as the entertainment capital of India, Mumbai is home to Bollywood, the world's largest film industry by volume.

Thus, option (a) is the correct answer.

41. *(a)* 3 - 1 - 2 - 4

- **Jaipur** was designated as a UNESCO **Creative City of Crafts and Folk Art in 2015**. The city is known for its vibrant arts and crafts, including block printing, blue pottery, and jewellery making.
- **Varanasi** was designated as a UNESCO **Creative City of Music in 2015**. Known as one of the oldest continuously inhabited cities in the world, Varanasi has a deep connection with music, particularly classical music and devotional songs.
- **Chennai** was designated as a UNESCO **Creative City of Music in 2017**. The city is renowned for its rich tradition of Carnatic music, which is celebrated annually during the December Music Season.
- **Kozhikode** was designated as a UNESCO **Creative City of Literature in 2023**. Kozhikode has also been a center for the Malayalam language and literature, contributing significantly to the cultural life of Kerala.

Thus, option (a) is the correct answer.

Past Learning (Answers)

1 (a) **2** (a) **3** (d) **4** (d) **5** (b) **6** (a) **7** (d)